Procedure Checklists for

Kinn's The Medical Assistant: An Applied Learning Approach

Twelfth Edition

Procedure Checklists for

Kinn's The Medical Assistant: An Applied Learning Approach

Twelfth Edition

Deborah B. Proctor, EdD, RN
Professor and Medical Assistant Program Director
Butler County Community College
Butler, Pennsylvania

Alexandra Patricia Adams, MA, BA, RMA, CMA (AAMA)
Former Health Information Specialist Program Director
    & Administrative Medical Assisting Instructor
Ultrasound Diagnostic School (now Sanford-Brown College)
Professional Writer
Grand Prairie, Texas

3251 Riverport Lane
St. Louis, Missouri 63043

**PROCEDURE CHECKLISTS FOR
KINN'S THE MEDICAL ASSISTANT:**

ISBN: 978-1-4557-5688-9

Previous editions copyrighted 2011, 2007, 2003, 1999, 1993, 1988, 1981, 1974, 1967, 1960, 1956

ISBN: 978-1-4557-5688-9

Vice President and Publisher: Andrew Allen
Executive Content Strategist: Jennifer Janson
Content Developmental Specialist: Laurie Vordtriede
Publishing Services Manager: Julie Eddy
Senior Project Manager: Richard Barber

Printed in the United States

Last digit is the print number: 9 8 7 6 5 4 3 2

Procedure Checklists

x

Name _____ Date _____ Score _____

PROCEDURE 5-1 Recognize and Respond to Verbal Communications

MAERB/CAAHEP COMPETENCIES: IV.P.IV.11, IV.A.IV.1, IV.A.IV.2, IV.A.IV.4, IV.A.IV.5, IV.A.IV.7, IV.A.IV.8, IV.A.IV.9
ABHES COMPETENCIES: 8.f

TASK: To be able to recognize verbal communication and respond to it in a professional manner.

Equipment and Supplies
• Cards with various patient scenarios

Standards: Complete the procedure and all critical steps in _____ minutes with a minimum score of 85% within three attempts.

Scoring: Divide the points earned by the total possible points. Failure to perform a critical step, indicated by an asterisk (*), results in an unsatisfactory overall score.

Time began _____ Time ended _____ Total minutes: _____

Steps	Possible Points	Attempt 1	Attempt 2	Attempt 3
1. Choose a partner and select a scenario.	5	____	____	____
*2. Communicate the assigned message to the partner.	20	____	____	____
3. Allow the partner to respond, using active listening skills.	10	____	____	____
*4. Restate the understood message from the partner.	20	____	____	____
*5. Clarify issues that required it.	10	____	____	____
*6. Use professional wording without slang.	20	____	____	____
*7. Continue effective communication throughout the exercise.	15	____	____	____

Did the student:	Yes	No
Demonstrate sensitivity appropriate to the message being delivered?	____	____
Demonstrate empathy and impartiality when communicating with patients, family, and staff members?	____	____
Demonstrate awareness of the territorial boundaries of the person with whom he or she was communicating?	____	____
Recognize and protect personal boundaries in communication with others?	____	____
Apply active listening skills?	____	____
Demonstrate recognition of the patient's level of understanding in communications?	____	____
Communicate on the patient's level of understanding?	____	____
Analyze communications in providing appropriate responses and feedback?	____	____

1

Comments:

Points earned _____ ÷ 100 possible points = Score _____ % Score

Instructor's signature _____

2

PROCEDURE 5-2 Recognize and Respond to Nonverbal Communications

MAERB/CAAHEP COMPETENCIES: IV.P.IV.11, IV.A.IV.3, IV.A.IV.10, X.A.X.3
ABHES COMPETENCIES: 8.f

TASK: To be able to recognize nonverbal communication and respond to it in a professional manner.

Equipment and Supplies

- Cards with various statements or emotions that can be communicated nonverbally.

Standards: Complete the procedure and all critical steps in _____ minutes with a minimum score of 85% within three attempts.

Scoring: Divide the points earned by the total possible points. Failure to perform a critical step, indicated by an asterisk (*), results in an unsatisfactory overall score.

Time began _____ Time ended _____ Total minutes: _____

Steps	Possible Points	Attempt 1	Attempt 2	Attempt 3
1. Choose a partner and select a card.	5	_____	_____	_____
*2. Communicate the assigned nonverbal message to the partner.	20	_____	_____	_____
3. Allow the partner to respond, using active listening skills.	10	_____	_____	_____
*4. Restate the understood message from the partner verbally.	20	_____	_____	_____
*5. Clarify issues that require it.	10	_____	_____	_____
*6. Use professional gestures and avoiding slang when interpreting the message.	20	_____	_____	_____
*7. Continue effective communication throughout the exercise.	15	_____	_____	_____

Did the student:	Yes	No
Use appropriate body language and other nonverbal skills while communicating?	_____	_____
Demonstrate respect for individual diversity, incorporating awareness of personal bias in areas such as gender, race, religion, age, and economic status?	_____	_____
Demonstrate awareness of diversity when providing patient care and avoiding offending patients of different cultures?	_____	_____
Remain impartial and show empathy when dealing with patients?	_____	_____

Comments:

Points earned _____ ÷ 100 possible points = Score _____ % Score

Instructor's signature _____

Procedure **5-2 Recognize and Respond to Nonverbal Communications**

Name _____ Date _____ Score _____

PROCEDURE 6-1 Respond to Issues of Confidentiality

MAERB/CAAHEP COMPETENCIES: IX.P.IX.2
ABHES COMPETENCIES: 4.b, 4.g, 6.f, 11.b

TASK: To ensure that medical assistants treat all information regarding patient care as completely confidential.

Equipment and Supplies
- Copy of the Code of Ethics of the American Association of Medical Assistants
- Copy of the Medical Assistant Creed
- Copy of the Oath of Hippocrates
- Copy of the guidelines from the Health Insurance Portability and Accountability Act (HIPAA)
- Notepad and pen
- Patient's medical record

Standards: Complete the procedure and all critical steps in _____ minutes with a minimum score of 85% within three attempts.

Scoring: Divide the points earned by the total possible points. Failure to perform a critical step, indicated by an asterisk (*), results in an unsatisfactory overall score.

Time began _____ Time ended _____ Total minutes: _____

Steps	Possible Points	Attempt 1	Attempt 2	Attempt 3
1. Talk with each patient about medical care.	5	_____	_____	_____
*2. Greet patients by name and attend to their needs and questions.	20	_____	_____	_____
*3. Make sure discussions with the patient are held in a private area.	10	_____	_____	_____
*4. Use active listening and other communications skills.	20	_____	_____	_____
*5. Clarify issues that required it.	10	_____	_____	_____
*6. Reassure patients that their health information is private and confidential.	20	_____	_____	_____
*7. Explain that information cannot be kept from the physician.	10	_____	_____	_____
8. Document as required and ensure patient confidentiality.	5	_____	_____	_____

Did the student:	Yes	No
Use ethical behavior, including honesty and integrity, in performing the duties of the medical assistant's practice?	_____	_____

5

Comments:

Points earned _____ ÷ **100 possible points = Score** _____ **% Score**

Instructor's signature _____

Procedure **6-1 Respond to Issues of Confidentiality**

Name _____ Date _____ Score _____

PROCEDURE 6-2 Develop a Plan for Separating Personal and Professional Ethics

MAERB/CAAHEP COMPETENCIES: X.P.X.2
ABHES COMPETENCIES: 4.g

TASK: To determine one's ethical views before one is faced with the requirement to make an ethical decision.

Equipment and Supplies
- Pen and paper

Standards: Complete the procedure and all critical steps in _____ minutes with a minimum score of 85% within three attempts.

Scoring: Divide the points earned by the total possible points. Failure to perform a critical step, indicated by an asterisk (*), results in an unsatisfactory overall score.

Time began _____   **Time ended** _____   **Total minutes:** _____

Steps	Possible Points	Attempt 1	Attempt 2	Attempt 3
1. Study the ethical issues outlined in the chapter.	5	_____	_____	_____
*2. For each issue, make notes about personal beliefs, paying particular attention to whether you agree or disagree with the opinions of the Council on Ethical and Judicial Affairs.	10	_____	_____	_____
*3. Apply the ethical decision-making process to each issue.	20	_____	_____	_____
*4. Determine your personal stand on the issue.	20	_____	_____	_____
*5. Determine the appropriate professional stance on each issue.	20	_____	_____	_____
*6. Discuss one of the issues with a classmate, using the professional stance rather than the personal stance.	20	_____	_____	_____
*7. Interact with each classmate professionally, regardless of that individual's ethical views.	5	_____	_____	_____

Did the student:		Yes	No
Examine and consider the impact personal ethics and morals may have on the medical assistant's practice?		_____	_____

7

Comments:

Points earned _____ ÷ 100 possible points = Score _____ % Score

Instructor's signature _____

Procedure **6-2 Develop a Plan for Separating Personal and Professional Ethics**

Name _____ Date _____ Score _____

PROCEDURE 7-1 Perform Within the Scope of Practice

MAERB/CAAHEP COMPETENCIES: IX.P.IX.2, IX.A.IX.2
ABHES COMPETENCIES: 4.f.1

TASK: To perform duties within legal boundaries and within the scope of practice in the state where one is employed as a medical assistant.

Equipment and Supplies
- Computer with Internet access
- Access to text of laws and regulations affecting the scope of practice for a medical assistant

Standards: Complete the procedure and all critical steps in _____ minutes with a minimum score of 85% within three attempts.

Scoring: Divide the points earned by the total possible points. Failure to perform a critical step, indicated by an asterisk (*), results in an unsatisfactory overall score.

Time began _____   Time ended _____   Total minutes: _____

Steps	Possible Points	Attempt 1	Attempt 2	Attempt 3
1. Read the laws and regulations that apply to medical practice as assigned by the instructor.	10	_____	_____	_____
*2. Determine whether the law or regulation is applicable in your local area.	20	_____	_____	_____
*3. Read and discuss with the class one article from the Internet on relevant laws and regulations.	20	_____	_____	_____
*4. Define for the instructor the scope of practice of a medical assistant.	20	_____	_____	_____
*5. Explain the consequences of not performing within the legal scope of practice to the instructor.	20	_____	_____	_____
*6. State for the instructor three ways to stay up-to-date on applicable laws and regulations.	10	_____	_____	_____

Did the student:	**Yes**	**No**
Demonstrate an awareness of the consequences of not working within the scope of practice?	_____	_____

Comments:

Points earned _____ ÷ 100 possible points = Score _____ % Score

Instructor's signature _____

Name _____ Date _____ Score _____

PROCEDURE 7-2 Practice Within the Standard of Care for a Medical Assistant

MAERB/CAAHEP COMPETENCIES: IX.P.IX.4
ABHES COMPETENCIES: 4.f.1

TASK: To perform duties within the standard of care in the state where one is employed as a medical assistant.

Equipment and Supplies
- Computer with Internet access
- Access to text of laws and regulations affecting the standard of care for a medical assistant.

Standards: Complete the procedure and all critical steps in _____ minutes with a minimum score of 85% within three attempts.

Scoring: Divide the points earned by the total possible points. Failure to perform a critical step, indicated by an asterisk (*), results in an unsatisfactory overall score.

Time began _____   Time ended _____   Total minutes: _____

Steps	Possible Points	Attempt 1	Attempt 2	Attempt 3
1. Research the standard of care expected of a medical assistant in your state.	5	_____	_____	_____
2. With a classmate, role-play an encounter with a patient.	10	_____	_____	_____
*3. During the introduction, identify yourself as a medical assistant.	20	_____	_____	_____
4. Use reasonable care, attention, and diligence during the encounter.	20	_____	_____	_____
*5. Treat the patient carefully and professionally.	20	_____	_____	_____
6. Make accurate judgments about actions if indicated by the role-play scenario.	10	_____	_____	_____
*7. Treat the patient with a sense of equality.	10	_____	_____	_____
*8. Document the encounter with the patient as required.	5	_____	_____	_____

Comments:

Points earned _____ ÷ 100 possible points = Score _____ % Score

Instructor's signature _____

Procedure **7-2 Practice Within the Standard of Care**

Name _____ Date _____ Score _____

PROCEDURE 7-3 Incorporate the Patients' Bill of Rights into Personal Practice and Medical Office Policies

MAERB/CAAHEP COMPETENCIES: IX.P.IX.5, IX.A.IX.1

TASK: To make sure that patients' rights are honored in the daily procedures performed and policies enacted in the physician's office.

Equipment and Supplies
- Copy of the Patients' Bill of Rights
- Sample office policy and procedures manual

Standards: Complete the procedure and all critical steps in _____ minutes with a minimum score of 85% within three attempts.

Scoring: Divide the points earned by the total possible points. Failure to perform a critical step, indicated by an asterisk (*), results in an unsatisfactory overall score.

Time began _____ Time ended _____ Total minutes: _____

Steps	Possible Points	Attempt 1	Attempt 2	Attempt 3
1. Review the Patients' Bill of Rights.	10	_____	_____	_____
*2. Select a partner to play the role of a patient.	10	_____	_____	_____
*3. Briefly explain each article of the Patients' Bill of Rights to the patient.	20	_____	_____	_____
*4. Use active listening skills to address the patient's questions.	10	_____	_____	_____
*5. Ask whether the patient understands the Patients' Bill of Rights.	20	_____	_____	_____
*6. Determine whether the patient has any questions about the Patients' Bill of Rights.	20	_____	_____	_____
*7. Interact with the patient professionally.	5	_____	_____	_____
*8. Document the encounter with the patient as required.	5	_____	_____	_____

Did the student:	Yes	No
Demonstrate sensitivity to the patient's rights?	_____	_____

Comments:

Points earned _____ ÷ 100 possible points = Score _____ % Score

Instructor's signature _____

Name _____ Date _____ Score _____

PROCEDURE 7-4 Complete an Incident Report

MAERB/CAAHEP COMPETENCIES: IX.P.IX.6
ABHES COMPETENCIES: 4.a

TASK: To fill out an accurate, complete incident report that provides all legally required information.

Equipment and Supplies
- OSHA Form 301 (or other incident report form)
- Pen
- Notes taken regarding incident

Standards: Complete the procedure and all critical steps in _____ minutes with a minimum score of 85% within three attempts.

Scoring: Divide the points earned by the total possible points. Failure to perform a critical step, indicated by an asterisk (*), results in an unsatisfactory overall score.

Time began _____   Time ended _____   Total minutes: _____

Steps	Possible Points	Attempt 1	Attempt 2	Attempt 3
1. Select a partner to play the role of a patient/employee involved in an incident.	5	_____	_____	_____
*2. Interview the patient/employee about the incident.	20	_____	_____	_____
*3. Use active listening skills, asking questions to obtain a complete and accurate report.	20	_____	_____	_____
*4. Take notes as the patient/employee relates the incident.	10	_____	_____	_____
5. Read through the incident report form before entering any information.	5	_____	_____	_____
*6. Complete the incident report form without leaving any blank spaces, using professional terminology and phrasing.	20	_____	_____	_____
*7. Proofread the report for errors and omissions.	10	_____	_____	_____
*8. Review the report with the instructor.	5	_____	_____	_____
*9. Document the encounter with the patient as required.	5	_____	_____	_____

Comments:

Points earned _____ ÷ 100 possible points = Score _____ % Score

Instructor's signature _____

Procedure **7-4 Complete an Incident Report**

PROCEDURE 7-5 Apply Local, State, and Federal Legislation and Regulations Appropriate to the Medical Assisting Practice Setting

MAERB/CAAHEP COMPETENCIES: IX.P.IX.8, IX.A.IX.3
ABHES COMPETENCIES: 4.6, 4.f.1

TASK: To be aware of local, federal, and state laws and regulations that apply to the employer's facility and recognize the importance of compliance with such laws and regulations.

Equipment and Supplies
- Computer with Internet access
- Access to organizational websites that have established legislation and regulations that pertain to medical facilities
- Information about changes to and new federal and state legislation and regulations

Standards: Complete the procedure and all critical steps in _____ minutes with a minimum score of 85% within three attempts.

Scoring: Divide the points earned by the total possible points. Failure to perform a critical step, indicated by an asterisk (*), results in an unsatisfactory overall score.

Time began _____   **Time ended** _____   **Total minutes:** _____

Steps	Possible Points	Attempt 1	Attempt 2	Attempt 3
1. Review federal regulations that apply to healthcare workers.	20	_____	_____	_____
2. Review state regulations that apply to healthcare workers.	20	_____	_____	_____
*3. Prepare a report on one of the laws that affects the medical profession and practice, focusing on compliance issues.	25	_____	_____	_____
*4. Present the report to the class.	25	_____	_____	_____
5. Provide a copy of the report to the instructor.	10	_____	_____	_____

Did the student:	Yes	No
Recognize the importance of local, state, and federal legislation and regulations in the practice setting, as shown in the report given to the class?	_____	_____

Comments:

Points earned _____ ÷ 100 possible points = Score _____ % Score

Instructor's signature _____

18

Procedure **7-5 Apply Local, State, and Federal Legislation and Regulations**

Name _____ Date _____ Score _____

PROCEDURE 7-6 Report Illegal and/or Unsafe Activities and Behaviors That Affect the Health, Safety, and Welfare of Others to Proper Authorities

MAERB/CAAHEP COMPETENCIES: X.P.X.1
ABHES COMPETENCIES: 4.f

TASK: To provide a proper procedure for the medical assistant to follow when legal or ethical regulations have been breached.

Equipment and Supplies

- Contact information for regulatory and law enforcement agencies at the local, state, and federal level
- Written reports or documentation of breaches of regulations, if available

Standards: Complete the procedure and all critical steps in _____ minutes with a minimum score of 85% within three attempts.

Scoring: Divide the points earned by the total possible points. Failure to perform a critical step, indicated by an asterisk (*), results in an unsatisfactory overall score.

Time began _____ Time ended _____ Total minutes: _____

Steps	Possible Points	Attempt 1	Attempt 2	Attempt 3
1. Compile a list of all regulatory and law enforcement agencies that have jurisdiction over medical facilities in the local area.	20	_____	_____	_____
*2. Design a document describing the agencies, to be used as a reference guide in the medical facility.	25	_____	_____	_____
*3. Design a form to use when reporting illegal and/or unsafe behaviors that affect the health, safety, and welfare of others.	25	_____	_____	_____
*4. Compile a list of the types of behaviors that should be reported to authorities.	25	_____	_____	_____
*5. Provide a copy of all documents to the instructor.	5	_____	_____	_____

Comments:

Points earned _____ ÷ 100 possible points = Score _____ % Score

Instructor's signature _____

Procedure **7-6 Report Illegal and/or Unsafe Activities and Behaviors**

WORK PRODUCT 7-1

Name: _____

Complete an Incident Report

Corresponds to Procedure 7-4

MAERB/CAAHEP COMPETENCIES: IX.P.1X.5

ABHES COMPETENCIES: 4.a

OSHA's Form 301
Injury and Illness Incident Report

U.S. Department of Labor
Occupational Safety and Health Administration

Form approved OMB no. 1218-0176

This *Injury and Illness Incident Report* is one of the first forms you must fill out when a recordable work-related injury or illness has occurred. Together with the *Log of Work-Related Injuries and Illnesses* and the accompanying *Summary*, these forms help the employer and OSHA develop a picture of the extent and severity of work-related incidents.

Within 7 calendar days after you receive information that a recordable work-related injury or illness has occurred, you must fill out this form or an equivalent. Some state workers' compensation, insurance, or other reports may be acceptable substitutes. To be considered an equivalent form, any substitute must contain all the information asked for on this form.

According to Public Law 91-596 and 29 CFR 1904, OSHA's recordkeeping rule, you must keep this form on file for 5 years following the year to which it pertains.

If you need additional copies of this form, you may photocopy and use as many as you need.

Attention: This form contains information relating to employee health and must be used in a manner that protects the confidentiality of employees to the extent possible while the information is being used for occupational safety and health purposes.

Information about the employee

1) Full name

2) Street

   City _____ State _____ ZIP

3) Date of birth ___ / ___ / ___

4) Date hired ___ / ___ / ___

5) ☐ Male ☐ Female

Information about the physician or other health care professional

6) Name of physician or other health care professional

7) If treatment was given away from the worksite, where was it given?

   Facility

   Street

   City _____ State _____ ZIP

8) Was employee treated in an emergency room?
   ☐ Yes
   ☐ No

9) Was employee hospitalized overnight as an in-patient?
   ☐ Yes
   ☐ No

Information about the case

10) Case number from the *Log* _____ *(Transfer the case number from the Log after you record the case.)*

11) Date of injury or illness ___ / ___

12) Time employee began work _____ AM / PM

13) Time of event _____ AM / PM ☐ Check if time cannot be determined

14) *What was the employee doing just before the incident occurred?* Describe the activity, as well as the tools, equipment, or material the employee was using. Be specific. *Examples:* "climbing a ladder while carrying roofing materials"; "spraying chlorine from hand sprayer"; "daily computer key-entry."

15) *What happened?* Tell us how the injury occurred. *Examples:* "When ladder slipped on wet floor, worker fell 20 feet"; "Worker was sprayed with chlorine when gasket broke during replacement"; "Worker developed soreness in wrist over time."

16) *What was the injury or illness?* Tell us the part of the body that was affected and how it was affected; be more specific than "hurt," "pain," or sore." *Examples:* "strained back"; "chemical burn, hand"; "carpal tunnel syndrome."

17) *What object or substance directly harmed the employee? Examples:* "concrete floor"; "chlorine"; "radial arm saw." *If this question does not apply to the incident, leave it blank.*

18) *If the employee died, when did death occur?* Date of death ___ / ___ / ___

Completed by _____

Title _____

Phone (___) ___ - ___   Date ___ / ___ / ___

Public reporting burden for this collection of information is estimated to average 22 minutes per response, including time for reviewing instructions, searching existing data sources, gathering and maintaining the data needed, and completing and reviewing the collection of information. Persons are not required to respond to the collection of information unless it displays a current valid OMB control number. If you have any comments about this estimate or any other aspects of this data collection, including suggestions for reducing this burden, contact: US Department of Labor, OSHA Office of Statistics, Room N-3644, 200 Constitution Avenue, NW, Washington, DC 20210. Do not send the completed forms to this office.

Name _____ Date _____ Score _____

PROCEDURE 8-1 Use Office Hardware and Software to Maintain Office Systems

MAERB/CAAHEP COMPETENCIES: V.P.V.6
ABHES COMPETENCIES: 8.e.1

TASK: To use the office computer system at maximum capacity to run the various aspects of the physician's office.

Equipment and Supplies
- Computer system
- Computer software applications, loaded on the computer
- Software and instruction manuals, if needed
- Description of office computer systems
- Patient data
- Business data

Standards: Complete the procedure and all critical steps in _____ minutes with a minimum score of 85% within three attempts.

Scoring: Divide the points earned by the total possible points. Failure to perform a critical step, indicated by an asterisk (*), results in an unsatisfactory overall score.

Time began _____   Time ended _____   Total minutes: _____

Steps	Possible Points	Attempt 1	Attempt 2	Attempt 3
1. Compile a list of the ways a computer system is used in the medical office to make the practice more efficient.	5	_____	_____	_____
2. Choose one of these uses to research.	5	_____	_____	_____
*3. Research the ways the computer system can be used efficiently in the selected area.	10	_____	_____	_____
*4. Prepare a report about the system, detailing the ways the office uses it to maintain information about patients, employees, equipment, and/or supplies.	20	_____	_____	_____
*5. Prepare a class demonstration of the use of a computer office system in a medical practice.	20	_____	_____	_____
*6. Present the report and demonstration to the class.	20	_____	_____	_____
*7. Provide the instructor with a copy of the report.	20	_____	_____	_____

Comments:

Points earned _____ ÷ 100 possible points = Score _____ % Score

Instructor's signature _____

Procedure **8-1 Use Office Hardware and Software**

Name _____ Date _____ Score _____

PROCEDURE 9-1 Demonstrate Telephone Techniques

MAERB/CAAHEP COMPETENCIES: IV.P.IV.7, IV.A.IV.2
ABHES COMPETENCIES: 8.f

TASK: To answer the phone in a physician's office in a professional manner and to respond to a request for action.

Equipment and Supplies
- Telephone
- Message pad
- Pen or pencil
- Appointment book
- Computer
- Notepad

Standards: Complete the procedure and all critical steps in _____ minutes with a minimum score of 85% within three attempts.

Scoring: Divide the points earned by the total possible points. Failure to perform a critical step, indicated by an asterisk (*), results in an unsatisfactory overall score.

Time began _____ Time ended _____ Total minutes: _____

Steps	Possible Points	Attempt 1	Attempt 2	Attempt 3
*1. Answer the phone before the third ring.	5	_____	_____	_____
*2. Speak distinctly into the mouthpiece while holding it in the correct position (i.e., approximately 1 inch from the mouth).	5	_____	_____	_____
*3. Identify yourself and give the name of the office.	10	_____	_____	_____
*4. Determine the information or service the caller is requesting, taking notes, if necessary.	10	_____	_____	_____
*5. Use active listening skills.	10	_____	_____	_____
6. Screen the call, if necessary.	10	_____	_____	_____
7. Provide the caller with the requested information or service.	20	_____	_____	_____
8. If necessary, correctly transfer the call to another person.	20	_____	_____	_____
*9. Terminate the call in a pleasant manner and hang up after the caller.	10	_____	_____	_____

Comments:

Points earned _____ ÷ 100 possible points = Score _____ % Score

Instructor's signature _____

PROCEDURE 9-2 Take a Telephone Message

MAERB/CAAHEP COMPETENCIES: IV.P.IV.7, IV.A.IV.2
ABHES COMPETENCIES: 8.f

TASK: To take an accurate telephone message and follow up on the requests made by the caller.

Equipment and Supplies

- Telephone
- Computer
- Message pad
- Pen or pencil
- Notepad

Standards: Complete the procedure and all critical steps in _____ minutes with a minimum score of 85% within three attempts.

Scoring: Divide the points earned by the total possible points. Failure to perform a critical step, indicated by an asterisk (*), results in an unsatisfactory overall score.

Time began _____   Time ended _____   Total minutes: _____

Steps	Possible Points	Attempt 1	Attempt 2	Attempt 3
1. Answer the telephone correctly.	5	_____	_____	_____
2. Using a message pad or the computer system, obtain the following information from the caller, using active listening skills:				
a. The name of the person to whom the call is directed	5	_____	_____	_____
b. The name of the caller	5	_____	_____	_____
c. The caller's telephone number	5	_____	_____	_____
d. The reason for the call	5	_____	_____	_____
e. The action to be taken	5	_____	_____	_____
f. The date and time of the call	5	_____	_____	_____
g. The initials of the person taking the call	5	_____	_____	_____
*3. Repeat the information back to the caller to verify its accuracy.	20	_____	_____	_____
*4. Provide the caller with an approximate time and date the call will be returned.	10	_____	_____	_____
*5. End the call pleasantly, allowing the caller to hang up first.	20	_____	_____	_____
*6. Deliver the phone message to the appropriate person.	10	_____	_____	_____

Comments:

Points earned _____ ÷ 100 possible points = Score _____ % Score

Instructor's signature _____

Procedure **9-2 Take a Telephone Message**

Name _____ Date _____ Score _____

PROCEDURE 9-3 Call the Pharmacy with New or Refill Prescriptions

MAERB/CAAHEP COMPETENCIES: IV.P.IV.7, IV.A.IV.2
ABHES COMPETENCIES: 8.f

TASK: To call in an accurate prescription to the pharmacy for a patient in the most efficient manner.

Equipment and Supplies
- Prescription information
- Notepad
- Patient's medical record
- Telephone
- Computer and/or fax machine

Standards: Complete the procedure and all critical steps in _____ minutes with a minimum score of 85% within three attempts.

Scoring: Divide the points earned by the total possible points. Failure to perform a critical step, indicated by an asterisk (*), results in an unsatisfactory overall score.

Time began _____ Time ended _____ Total minutes: _____

Steps	Possible Points	Attempt 1	Attempt 2	Attempt 3
1. Receive the call or fax requesting a new or refill prescription from the patient or pharmacy, using appropriate telephone technique.	5	_____	_____	_____
2. Obtain the following information from the patient:				
*a. The patient's name	5	_____	_____	_____
*b. The telephone number where the patient can be reached	5	_____	_____	_____
*c. The patient's symptoms and current condition	5	_____	_____	_____
*d. The history of this condition, if applicable	5	_____	_____	_____
*e. Treatments the patient has tried	5	_____	_____	_____
*f. The pharmacy's name, phone number and fax number	5	_____	_____	_____
*3. Determine the action desired by the physician per office policy.	10	_____	_____	_____
*4. Document the request and action in the patient's medical record.	10	_____	_____	_____
*5. Call the pharmacy staff with the prescription information or fax the information back to the pharmacy.	20	_____	_____	_____
*6. Document the time and date action on the request was completed in the patient's medical record.	15	_____	_____	_____
*7. Call the patient and relate the action taken on the request.	10	_____	_____	_____

Comments:

Points earned _____ ÷ 100 possible points = Score _____ % Score

Instructor's signature _____

Procedure **9-3 Call the Pharmacy with New or Refill Prescriptions**

Name _____ Date _____ Score _____

PROCEDURE 10-1 Manage Appointment Scheduling Using Established Priorities

MAERB/CAAHEP COMPETENCIES: V.P.V.1, V.A.V.2
ABHES COMPETENCIES: 8.d

TASK: To establish the matrix of the appointment page and enter information according to office policy.

Equipment and Supplies
- Appointment book or computer
- Office procedures manual
- Information about the physician's office hours and availability
- Clerical supplies
- Calendar

Standards: Complete the procedure and all critical steps in _____ minutes with a minimum score of 85% within three attempts.

Scoring: Divide the points earned by the total possible points. Failure to perform a critical step, indicated by an asterisk (*), results in an unsatisfactory overall score.

Time began _____   Time ended _____   **Total minutes:** _____

Steps	Possible Points	Attempt 1	Attempt 2	Attempt 3
*1. Mark the times the physician will not be available to see patients to establish the matrix.	20	_____	_____	_____
2. Check the list of patients who need appointments and their chief complaints.	10	_____	_____	_____
*3. Consult guidelines to determine the time each patient will need with the physician.	15	_____	_____	_____
*4. Allot appointment times according to the patient's complaint and the facilities available.	15	_____	_____	_____
*5. Enter the patient's name and contact information in the appointment book or computer program.	20	_____	_____	_____
*6. Allow for buffer time in the morning and the afternoon for sick calls and emergencies.	20	_____	_____	_____

Comments:

Points earned _____ ÷ **100 possible points = Score** _____ **% Score**

Instructor's signature _____

Name _____ Date _____ Score _____

PROCEDURE 10-2 Schedule and Monitor Appointments

MAERB/CAAHEP COMPETENCIES: V.P.V.1
ABHES COMPETENCIES: 8.d

TASK: To manage appointments as they are cancelled, no showed, or rescheduled throughout the business day.

Equipment and Supplies
- Appointment book or computer
- Office procedure manual
- Appointment cards
- Clerical supplies
- Telephone

Standards: Complete the procedure and all critical steps in _____ minutes with a minimum score of 85% within three attempts.

Scoring: Divide the points earned by the total possible points. Failure to perform a critical step, indicated by an asterisk (*), results in an unsatisfactory overall score.

Time began _____ **Time ended** _____ **Total minutes:** _____

Steps	Possible Points	Attempt 1	Attempt 2	Attempt 3
1. Check the appointment schedule for the next day.	10	_____	_____	_____
2. Confirm all appointments.	10	_____	_____	_____
*3. Document a patient's late arrival in the appointment book or on the computer.	10	_____	_____	_____
*4. Document a "no show" in the appointment book or on the computer.	10	_____	_____	_____
*5. Document a late arrival and a "no show" in the patient's medical record.	10	_____	_____	_____
*6. Attempt to call the patient who did not show for the appointment and document the results of the call in the medical record.	10	_____	_____	_____
*7. Set a new appointment for the "no show" patient.	10	_____	_____	_____
*8. Inform patients that the physician is running behind schedule by 15 minutes.	10	_____	_____	_____
*9. Mark the appointment book or computer when patients arrive for their appointments.	10	_____	_____	_____
*10. Have patients sign in when they arrive for their appointment.	10	_____	_____	_____

Comments:

Points earned _____ ÷ 100 possible points = Score _____ % Score

Instructor's signature _____

Procedure **10-2 Schedule and Monitor Appointments**

PROCEDURE 10-3 Schedule Appointments for New Patients

MAERB/CAAHEP COMPETENCIES: V.P.V.1
ABHES COMPETENCIES: 8.d

TASK: To schedule a new patient for a first office visit.

Equipment and Supplies
- Appointment book or computer
- Scheduling guidelines
- Appointment card
- Telephone

Standards: Complete the procedure and all critical steps in _____ minutes with a minimum score of 85% within three attempts.

Scoring: Divide the points earned by the total possible points. Failure to perform a critical step, indicated by an asterisk (*), results in an unsatisfactory overall score.

Time began _____   Time ended _____   Total minutes: _____

Steps	Possible Points	Attempt 1	Attempt 2	Attempt 3
*1. Obtain the patient's full name (verify the spelling), birth date, address, and telephone number.	10	_____	_____	_____
2. Determine whether the patient was referred by another physician.	10	_____	_____	_____
*3. Determine the patient's chief complaint and when the first symptoms occurred.	10	_____	_____	_____
*4. Search the appointment book for the first available time and an alternate time.	10	_____	_____	_____
*5. Offer the patient a choice of these dates and times.	20	_____	_____	_____
*6. Enter the chosen time in the appointment book, followed by the patient's telephone number, noting NP to indicate the new patient status.	10	_____	_____	_____
*7. Explain the financial arrangements expected of new patients.	10	_____	_____	_____
*8. Offer travel and parking directions and e-mail or mail the paperwork the new patient must complete.	10	_____	_____	_____
*9. Repeat the day, date, and time of the appointment before saying goodbye to the patient.	10	_____	_____	_____

Comments:

Points earned _____ ÷ 100 possible points = Score _____ % Score

Instructor's signature _____

Procedure **10-3 Schedule Appointments for New Patients**

Name _____ Date _____ Score _____

PROCEDURE 10-4 Schedule Appointments for Established Patients or Visitors

MAERB/CAAHEP COMPETENCIES: V.P.V.1
ABHES COMPETENCIES: 8.d

TASK: To schedule a general appointment either by telephone or in person.

Equipment and Supplies
- Appointment book or computer
- Office procedure manual
- Clerical supplies
- Appointment cards
- Telephone

Standards: Complete the procedure and all critical steps in _____ minutes with a minimum score of 85% within three attempts.

Scoring: Divide the points earned by the total possible points. Failure to perform a critical step, indicated by an asterisk (*), results in an unsatisfactory overall score.

Time began _____   Time ended _____   Total minutes: _____

Steps	Possible Points	Attempt 1	Attempt 2	Attempt 3
*1. Answer the phone by the third ring.	10	_____	_____	_____
*2. Identify the patient on the phone and obtain his or her phone number.	10	_____	_____	_____
*3. Ask the reason for making the appointment.	10	_____	_____	_____
4. Determine whether the appointment is for the person on the phone or a family member.	5	_____	_____	_____
5. Determine which provider or employee the person wishes to see.	5	_____	_____	_____
*6. Give the caller a choice of two appointment days.	10	_____	_____	_____
*7. Give the caller a choice of morning or afternoon.	10	_____	_____	_____
*8. Give the caller a choice of times.	10	_____	_____	_____
*9. Write the chosen time in the appointment book or enter it into the computer.	10	_____	_____	_____
*10. Repeat the appointment day, date, and time back to the caller and thank the person for calling.	10	_____	_____	_____
*11. Allow the caller to hang up first.	5	_____	_____	_____
*12. Prepare an appointment card for appointments made in person.	5	_____	_____	_____

37

Comments:

Points earned _____ ÷ 100 possible points = Score _____ % Score

Instructor's signature _____

Procedure **10-4 Schedule Appointments for Established Patients**

Name _____ Date _____ Score _____

PROCEDURE 10-5 Document Appropriately and Accurately

MAERB/CAAHEP COMPETENCIES: IX.P.IX.7
ABHES COMPETENCIES: 4.a

TASK: To document appropriately and accurately on all patient medical records and other office paperwork that concerns the patient.

Equipment and Supplies
- Any medical document
- Clerical supplies
- Computer
- Office policy and procedure manual

Standards: Complete the procedure and all critical steps in _____ minutes with a minimum score of 85% within three attempts.

Scoring: Divide the points earned by the total possible points. Failure to perform a critical step, indicated by an asterisk (*), results in an unsatisfactory overall score.

Time began _____   Time ended _____   Total minutes: _____

Steps	Possible Points	Attempt 1	Attempt 2	Attempt 3
1. Determine the information that needs to be added to the medical document.	10	_____	_____	_____
2. Make sure the information is factual, timely, and accurate.	10	_____	_____	_____
*3. Document the information by writing or typing it into the record.	10	_____	_____	_____
*4. Review the entry for errors, legibility, and clarity.	10	_____	_____	_____
*5. Date and sign the entry.	10	_____	_____	_____
*6. Make sure the entry is made so that it complies with all legal regulations.	10	_____	_____	_____
*7. Make sure the entry is made in such a way that it complies with office policy.	10	_____	_____	_____
*8. If corrections are necessary, make them according to the office policy and procedures manual.	10	_____	_____	_____
*9. Make sure the correction has not obliterated any part of the medical record.	10	_____	_____	_____
*10. Initial and date the entry.	10	_____	_____	_____

Comments:

Points earned _____ ÷ 100 possible points = **Score** _____ **% Score**

Instructor's signature _____

Procedure **10-5 Document Appropriately and Accurately**

Name _____ Date _____ Score _____

PROCEDURE 10-6 Schedule Outpatient Admissions and Procedures

MAERB/CAAHEP COMPETENCIES: V.P.V.2
ABHES COMETENCIES: 8.d

TASK: To schedule a patient for outpatient admission or procedure within the time frame needed by the physician, confirm with the patient, and issue all required instructions.

Equipment and Supplies
- Diagnostic test order from physician
- Name, address, and telephone number of diagnostic facility
- Patient's demographic information
- Patient's medical record
- Test preparation instructions
- Telephone
- Consent form

Standards: Complete the procedure and all critical steps in _____ minutes with a minimum score of 85% within three attempts.

Scoring: Divide the points earned by the total possible points. Failure to perform a critical step, indicated by an asterisk (*), results in an unsatisfactory overall score.

Time began _____ **Time ended** _____ **Total minutes:** _____

Steps	Possible Points	Attempt 1	Attempt 2	Attempt 3
1. Obtain an oral or written order from the physician for the exact procedure to be performed.	10	_____	_____	_____
*2. Determine the patient's availability.	10	_____	_____	_____
*3. Telephone the diagnostic facility to:	20			
a. Order the specific test needed		_____	_____	_____
b. Determine the time and date for the procedure		_____	_____	_____
c. Give the patient's name, age, address, and contact information		_____	_____	_____
d. Determine whether the patient should be given any specific instructions		_____	_____	_____
e. Notify the facility of the urgency of results, if applicable		_____	_____	_____
*4. Notify the patient of the arrangements, including:	20			
a. Name, address, and telephone number of the facility		_____	_____	_____
b. Date and time to report for the test		_____	_____	_____
c. Instructions on preparation for the test (e.g., eating restrictions, fluids, medications, enemas)		_____	_____	_____
d. What to take (e.g., identification, insurance cards, orders)		_____	_____	_____

41

Steps	Possible Points	Attempt 1	Attempt 2	Attempt 3
*5. Ask the patient to repeat the instructions to verify that the person understands them.	10	_____	_____	_____
*6. Note the arrangements in the patient's medical record.	20	_____	_____	_____
*7. If necessary, put a reminder in a "tickler" file to follow up on the patient's testing to ensure that results are received.	10	_____	_____	_____

Comments:

Points earned _____ ÷ 100 possible points = Score _____ % Score

Instructor's signature _____

Name _____ Date _____ Score _____

PROCEDURE 10-7 Schedule Inpatient Admissions

MAERB/CAAHEP COMPETENCIES: V.P.V.2
ABHES COMPETENCIES: 8.d.2

TASK: To schedule a patient for inpatient admission within the time frame needed by the physician, confirm with the patient, and issue all required instructions.

Equipment and Supplies

- Admission orders from the physician
- Name, address, and telephone number of inpatient facility
- Patient's demographic information
- Patient's medical record
- Any preparation instructions for the patient
- Telephone
- Admission packet

Standards: Complete the procedure and all critical steps in _____ minutes with a minimum score of 85% within three attempts.

Scoring: Divide the points earned by the total possible points. Failure to perform a critical step, indicated by an asterisk (*), results in an unsatisfactory overall score.

Time began _____   Time ended _____   Total minutes: _____

Steps	Possible Points	Attempt 1	Attempt 2	Attempt 3
1. Obtain an oral or written order from the physician for the admission.	10	_____	_____	_____
*2. Precertify the admission with the patient's insurance company, if necessary.	20	_____	_____	_____
*3. Determine the physician's and the patient's availability if the admission is not an emergency.	10	_____	_____	_____
*4. Telephone the facility and schedule the admission, providing the following information:	20			
a. Testing to be done		_____	_____	_____
b. Admitting diagnosis		_____	_____	_____
c. Date and time of admission		_____	_____	_____
d. Patient's room preferences		_____	_____	_____
e. Demographic information, including insurance coverage		_____	_____	_____
f. Special instructions for the patient		_____	_____	_____
g. Urgency of test results		_____	_____	_____

Steps	Possible Points	Attempt 1	Attempt 2	Attempt 3
*5. Notify the patient of the arrangements, including:	20			
a. Name, address, and phone number of the facility		_____	_____	_____
b. Date and time to report for admission		_____	_____	_____
c. Instructions on preparation for procedures, if necessary (e.g., diet restrictions, fluids, medications)		_____	_____	_____
d. Preadmission testing requirements		_____	_____	_____
*6. Ask the patient to repeat the instructions to verify that the person understands them.	10	_____	_____	_____
*7. Put a reminder on the physician's calendar. If the physician keeps a list of inpatients, add the patient's name to that list.	10	_____	_____	_____

Comments:

Points earned _____ ÷ 100 possible points = Score _____ % Score

Instructor's signature _____

Name _____ Date _____ Score _____

PROCEDURE 10-8 Schedule Inpatient Procedures

MAERB/CAAHEP COMPETENCIES: V.P.V.2
ABHES COMPETENCIES: 8.d.2

TASK: To schedule a patient for inpatient surgery within the time frame needed by the physician, confirm with the patient, and issue all required instructions.

Equipment and Supplies

- Orders from physician
- Name, address, and telephone number of inpatient facility
- Patient's demographic information
- Patient's medical record
- Any preparation instructions for the patient
- Telephone
- Consent form

Standards: Complete the procedure and all critical steps in _____ minutes with a minimum score of 85% within three attempts.

Scoring: Divide the points earned by the total possible points. Failure to perform a critical step, indicated by an asterisk (*), results in an unsatisfactory overall score.

Time began _____ Time ended _____ Total minutes: _____

Steps	Possible Points	Attempt 1	Attempt 2	Attempt 3
1. Obtain an oral or written order from the physician for the admission.	10	_____	_____	_____
2. Precertify the admission with the patient's insurance company, if necessary.	10	_____	_____	_____
*3. Determine the physician's availability if the surgery is not an emergency. Another physician may be the surgeon, requiring coordination with his or her office.	20	_____	_____	_____
*4. Telephone the hospital surgical or diagnostic department to schedule the procedure and to:	20			
a. Order any specific tests needed		_____	_____	_____
b. Provide the patient's admitting diagnosis		_____	_____	_____
c. Establish the date and time		_____	_____	_____
d. Give the patient's name, age, address, and telephone number		_____	_____	_____
e. Provide demographic information on the patient, including insurance information		_____	_____	_____
f. Determine any special instructions for the patient		_____	_____	_____
g. Notify the facility of the urgency of the surgery or procedure, if applicable		_____	_____	_____

45

Steps	Possible Points	Attempt 1	Attempt 2	Attempt 3
*5. Notify the patient of the arrangements, if the patient has not already been admitted to the hospital, including:	20			
a. Name, address, and telephone number of the facility		_____	_____	_____
b. Date and time to report for admission		_____	_____	_____
c. Instructions on preparation for any procedures, if necessary (e.g., diet restrictions, fluids, medications)		_____	_____	_____
d. Preadmission testing requirements		_____	_____	_____
*6. Ask the patient to repeat the instructions to verify that the person understands them.	10	_____	_____	_____
*7. Put reminder on the physician's calendar. If the physician keeps a list of inpatients, add the patient's name to that list.	10	_____	_____	_____

Comments:

Points earned _____ ÷ 100 possible points = Score _____ % Score

Instructor's signature _____

WORK PRODUCT 10-1

Name: _____

Advance Preparation and Establishing a Matrix

Corresponds to Procedure 10-1

<u>MAERB/CAAHEP COMPETENCIES:</u> V.P.V.1

<u>ABHES COMPETENCIES:</u> 8.d

Complete Appointment Page 1 using the information in Part III.

			DAY							
			DATE							
			8	00						
				10						
				20						
				30						
				40						
				50						
			9	00						
				10						
				20						
				30						
				40						
				50						
			10	00						
				10						
				20						
				30						
				40						
				50						
			11	00						
				10						
				20						
				30						
				40						
				50						
			12	00						
				10						
				20						
				30						
				40						
				50						
			1	00						
				10						
				20						
				30						
				40						
				50						
			2	00						
				10						
				20						
				30						
				40						
				50						
			3	00						
				10						
				20						
				30						
				40						
				50						
			4	00						
				10						
				20						
				30						
				40						
				50						
			5	00						
				10						
				20						
				30						
				40						
				50						

Bibbero Systems Form 56-7310

WORK PRODUCT 10-2

Name: _____

Scheduling Appointments

Corresponds to Procedure 10-1

<u>MAERB/CAAHEP COMPETENCIES:</u> V.P.V.1.

<u>ABHES COMPETENCIES:</u> 8.d

Complete Appointment Page 2 using the information in Part IV.

			DAY							
			DATE							
			8	00 10 20 30 40 50						
			9	00 10 20 30 40 50						
			10	00 10 20 30 40 50						
			11	00 10 20 30 40 50						
			12	00 10 20 30 40 50						
			1	00 10 20 30 40 50						
			2	00 10 20 30 40 50						
			3	00 10 20 30 40 50						
			4	00 10 20 30 40 50						
			5	00 10 20 30 40 50						

Bibbero Systems Form 56-7310

Work Product **10-2**

WORK PRODUCT 10-3

Name: _____

Scheduling Appointments

Corresponds to Procedure 10-1

<u>MAERB/CAAHEP COMPETENCIES:</u> V.P.V.1

<u>ABHES COMPETENCIES:</u> 8.d

Complete Appointment Page 3 using the information in Part IV.

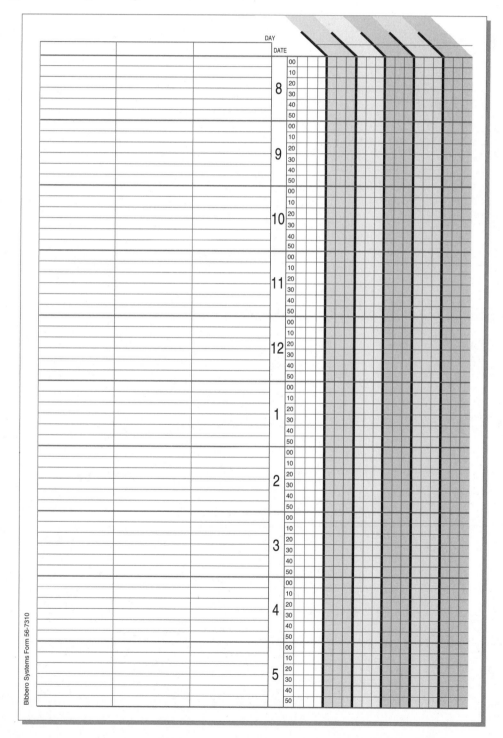

Bibbero Systems Form 56-7310

51

WORK PRODUCT 10-4

Name: _____

Scheduling Appointments

Corresponds to Procedure 10-1

<u>MAERB/CAAHEP COMPETENCIES:</u> V.P.V.1.

<u>ABHES COMPETENCIES:</u> 8.d

Complete Appointment Page 4 using the information in Part IV.

			DAY		
			DATE		
			8	00 10 20 30 40 50	
			9	00 10 20 30 40 50	
			10	00 10 20 30 40 50	
			11	00 10 20 30 40 50	
			12	00 10 20 30 40 50	
			1	00 10 20 30 40 50	
			2	00 10 20 30 40 50	
			3	00 10 20 30 40 50	
			4	00 10 20 30 40 50	
			5	00 10 20 30 40 50	

Bibbero Systems Form 56-7310

53

WORK PRODUCT 10-5

Name: _____

Scheduling Appointments

Corresponds to Procedure 10-1

<u>MAERB/CAAHEP COMPETENCIES:</u> V.P.V.1.

<u>ABHES COMPETENCIES:</u> 8.d

Complete Appointment Page 5 using the information in Part IV.

Bibbero Systems Form 56-7310

WORK PRODUCT 10-6

Name: _____

Document Appropriately and Accurately

Corresponds to Procedure 10-5

<u>MAERB/CAAHEP COMPETENCIES:</u> IX.P.IX.7.

<u>ABHES COMPETENCIES:</u> 4.a

Document the four patients listed in Part VIII using the progress note form. Use the same progress note to document all four patients' activity, although in a medical record, each would be charted in the patients' individual records.

OUTLINE FORMAT PROGRESS NOTES

Patient Name _____

Prob. No. or Letter	DATE	**S** Subjective	**O** Objective	**A** Assess	**P** Plans	Page _____

Start each Progress Note (Subjective, Objective, through the intervening columns to the right

Assessment and Plans) at the appropriate margin of the page.

shaded column to create an outline form. Write

ORDER # 26-7115 ANDRUS CLINI-REC CHART ORGANIZING SYSTEMS • 1976 BIBBERO SYSTEMS, INC. • PETALUMA, CA.
TO REORDER CALL TOLL FREE: (800) BIBBERO (800-242-2376) OR FAX (800) 242-9330 www.bibbero.com Mfg IN U.S.A.

WORK PRODUCT 10-7

Name: _____

Scheduling Inpatient and Outpatient Admissions and Procedures

Corresponds to Procedures 10-6 through 10-8

<u>MAERB/CAAHEP COMPETENCIES:</u> V.P.V.2

<u>ABHES COMPETENCIES:</u> 8.d.1

Complete the referral form using the information in Part VIII, question 1.

BLACKBURN PRIMARY CARE ASSOCIATES, P.C.
1990 Turquoise Drive • Blackburn, WI 54937
Phone 608-459-8857 • Fax 608-459-8860
Referral Form Effective Jan. 1, 20XX

Patient Name _____ **Phone #** _____
SS # _____ **DOB** _____
Diagnosis (ICD-9 Required) _____
Insurance Type _____
Referring Physician _____ **Phone** _____
Office Contact _____ **Fax** _____

REFERRAL FOR:
❑ Consult Only
❑ Evaluation and Treatment
❑ Inpatient Surgery
❑ Inpatient Admission
❑ Outpatient Surgery
❑ Outpatient Lab
❑ Outpatient X-ray
❑ Procedure Only
❑ Chiropractic
❑ Physical Therapy
❑ Back in Action Rehabilitation Program
❑ Psychophysiologic Evaluation
❑ Biofeedback
❑ Other _____

Comments
_____
_____
_____
_____
_____
_____
_____

REFERRAL TIMEFRAME:
❑ First Available Appt (within 5 business days)
❑ Stat (within 24 hr)

PROVIDER:
❑ Ron Lupez, M.D.
❑ Donald Lawler, M.D.
❑ Robert Hughes, D.O.
❑ Neil Stern, D.C.
❑ Joel Lively, P.T.

PLEASE INCLUDE THE FOLLOWING:
❑ Copy of Insurance Card
❑ Demographic Information
❑ Treatment Notes
❑ Diagnostic Reports

HOSPITAL/FACILITY
❑ Mercy Hospital
❑ Presbyterian Hospital
❑ Outpatient Surgical Complex
❑ Health and Wellness Center

Scheduled By _____

Appt Date/Time _____ Physician _____

WORK PRODUCT 10-8

Name: _____

Scheduling Inpatient and Outpatient Admissions and Procedures

Corresponds to Procedures 10-6 through 10-8

MAERB/CAAHEP COMPETENCIES: V.P.V.2

ABHES COMPETENCIES: 8.d

Complete the referral form using the information in Part VIII, question 2.

BLACKBURN PRIMARY CARE ASSOCIATES, P.C.
1990 Turquoise Drive • Blackburn, WI 54937
Phone 608-459-8857 • Fax 608-459-8860
Referral Form Effective Jan. 1, 20XX

Patient Name _____ **Phone #** _____
SS # _____ **DOB** _____
Diagnosis (ICD-9 Required) _____
Insurance Type _____
Referring Physician _____ **Phone** _____
Office Contact _____ **Fax** _____

REFERRAL FOR:
❑ Consult Only
❑ Evaluation and Treatment
❑ Inpatient Surgery
❑ Inpatient Admission
❑ Outpatient Surgery
❑ Outpatient Lab
❑ Outpatient X-ray
❑ Procedure Only
❑ Chiropractic
❑ Physical Therapy
❑ Back in Action Rehabilitation Program
❑ Psychophysiologic Evaluation
❑ Biofeedback
❑ Other _____

Comments
_____
_____
_____
_____
_____
_____
_____
_____

REFERRAL TIMEFRAME:
❑ First Available Appt (within 5 business days)
❑ Stat (within 24 hr)

PROVIDER:
❑ Ron Lupez, M.D.
❑ Donald Lawler, M.D.
❑ Robert Hughes, D.O.
❑ Neil Stern, D.C.
❑ Joel Lively, P.T.

PLEASE INCLUDE THE FOLLOWING:
❑ Copy of Insurance Card
❑ Demographic Information
❑ Treatment Notes
❑ Diagnostic Reports

HOSPITAL/FACILITY
❑ Mercy Hospital
❑ Presbyterian Hospital
❑ Outpatient Surgical Complex
❑ Health and Wellness Center

Scheduled By _____

Appt Date/Time _____ Physician _____

61

WORK PRODUCT 10-9

Name: _____

Scheduling Inpatient and Outpatient Admissions and Procedures

Corresponds to Procedures 10-6 through 10-8

<u>MAERB/CAAHEP COMPETENCIES:</u> V.P.V.2

<u>ABHES COMPETENCIES:</u> 8.d.1

Complete the referral form using the information in Part VIII, question 3.

BLACKBURN PRIMARY CARE ASSOCIATES, P.C.

1990 Turquoise Drive • Blackburn, WI 54937
Phone 608-459-8857 • Fax 608-459-8860
Referral Form Effective Jan. 1, 20XX

Patient Name _____ **Phone #** _____
SS # _____ **DOB** _____
Diagnosis (ICD-9 Required) _____
Insurance Type _____
Referring Physician _____ **Phone** _____
Office Contact _____ **Fax** _____

REFERRAL FOR:
❑ Consult Only
❑ Evaluation and Treatment
❑ Inpatient Surgery
❑ Inpatient Admission
❑ Outpatient Surgery
❑ Outpatient Lab
❑ Outpatient X-ray
❑ Procedure Only
❑ Chiropractic
❑ Physical Therapy
❑ Back in Action Rehabilitation Program
❑ Psychophysiologic Evaluation
❑ Biofeedback
❑ Other _____

Comments
_____
_____
_____
_____
_____
_____
_____

REFERRAL TIMEFRAME:
❑ First Available Appt (within 5 business days)
❑ Stat (within 24 hr)

PROVIDER:
❑ Ron Lupez, M.D.
❑ Donald Lawler, M.D.
❑ Robert Hughes, D.O.
❑ Neil Stern, D.C.
❑ Joel Lively, P.T.

PLEASE INCLUDE THE FOLLOWING:
❑ Copy of Insurance Card
❑ Demographic Information
❑ Treatment Notes
❑ Diagnostic Reports

HOSPITAL/FACILITY
❑ Mercy Hospital
❑ Presbyterian Hospital
❑ Outpatient Surgical Complex
❑ Health and Wellness Center

Scheduled By _____

Appt Date/Time _____ Physician _____

63

WORK PRODUCT 10-10

Name: _____

Scheduling Inpatient and Outpatient Admissions and Procedures

Corresponds to Procedures 10-6 through 10-8

<u>MAERB/CAAHEP COMPETENCIES:</u> V.P.V.2

<u>ABHES COMPETENCIES:</u> 8.d.1

Complete the referral form using the information in Part VIII, question 4.

BLACKBURN PRIMARY CARE ASSOCIATES, P.C.

1990 Turquoise Drive • Blackburn, WI 54937
Phone 608-459-8857 • Fax 608-459-8860
Referral Form Effective Jan. 1, 20XX

Patient Name _____ **Phone #** _____
SS # _____ **DOB** _____
Diagnosis (ICD-9 Required) _____
Insurance Type _____
Referring Physician _____ **Phone** _____
Office Contact _____ **Fax** _____

REFERRAL FOR:
❑ Consult Only
❑ Evaluation and Treatment
❑ Inpatient Surgery
❑ Inpatient Admission
❑ Outpatient Surgery
❑ Outpatient Lab
❑ Outpatient X-ray
❑ Procedure Only
❑ Chiropractic
❑ Physical Therapy
❑ Back in Action Rehabilitation Program
❑ Psychophysiologic Evaluation
❑ Biofeedback
❑ Other _____

Comments
_____
_____
_____
_____
_____
_____
_____
_____

REFERRAL TIMEFRAME:
❑ First Available Appt (within 5 business days)
❑ Stat (within 24 hr)

PROVIDER:
❑ Ron Lupez, M.D.
❑ Donald Lawler, M.D.
❑ Robert Hughes, D.O.
❑ Neil Stern, D.C.
❑ Joel Lively, P.T.

PLEASE INCLUDE THE FOLLOWING:
❑ Copy of Insurance Card
❑ Demographic Information
❑ Treatment Notes
❑ Diagnostic Reports

HOSPITAL/FACILITY
❑ Mercy Hospital
❑ Presbyterian Hospital
❑ Outpatient Surgical Complex
❑ Health and Wellness Center

Scheduled By _____

Appt Date/Time _____ Physician _____

65

Name _____ Date _____ Score _____

PROCEDURE 11-1 Organize a Patient's Medical Record

MAERB/CAAHEP COMPETENCIES: V.P.V.3
ABHES COMPETENCIES: 8.a

TASK: To prepare patients' medical records for the daily appointment schedule and have them ready for the physician before the patients' arrival.

Equipment and Supplies

- Appointment schedule for current date
- Patients' medical records
- Clerical supplies (e.g., pen, tape, stapler)

Standards: Complete the procedure and all critical steps in _____ minutes with a minimum score of 85% within three attempts.

Scoring: Divide the points earned by the total possible points. Failure to perform a critical step, indicated by an asterisk (*), results in an unsatisfactory overall score.

Time began _____   **Time ended** _____   **Total minutes:** _____

Steps	Possible Points	Attempt 1	Attempt 2	Attempt 3
1. Review the list of appointments for the day.	5	_____	_____	_____
*2. Identify each patient by name and/or medical record number.	10	_____	_____	_____
3. Pull the medical records for each established patient.	10	_____	_____	_____
*4. Compare the records with the names on the list to make sure the correct records have been pulled.	20	_____	_____	_____
*5. Make sure the laboratory results for all previously ordered tests are in the medical record.	10	_____	_____	_____
*6. Replenish forms in the record so that the physician has room to write notes and/or add information.	10	_____	_____	_____
*7. Annotate the appointment list with any special concerns.	5	_____	_____	_____
*8. Arrange the medical records in the order the patients will be seen.	20	_____	_____	_____
*9. Put the records in the designated place for easy retrieval once patients begin to arrive.	10	_____	_____	_____

Comments:

Points earned _____ ÷ 100 possible points = Score _____ % Score

Instructor's signature _____

Name _____ Date _____ Score _____

PROCEDURE 11-2 Register a New Patient

MAERB/CAAHEP COMPETENCIES: V.P.V.3
ABHES COMPETENCIES: 8.a

TASK: To complete a registration form for a new patient with information for credit and insurance claims and to inform and orient the patient to the facility.

Equipment and Supplies
- Registration form
- Clerical supplies (e.g., pen, clipboard)
- Private conference area

Standards: Complete the procedure and all critical steps in _____ minutes with a minimum score of 85% within three attempts.

Scoring: Divide the points earned by the total possible points. Failure to perform a critical step, indicated by an asterisk (*), results in an unsatisfactory overall score.

Time began _____ **Time ended** _____ **Total minutes:** _____

Steps	Possible Points	Attempt 1	Attempt 2	Attempt 3
1. Determine whether the patient is new to the practice.	5	_____	_____	_____
*2. Ask the patient to complete the patient information form.	5	_____	_____	_____
3. Enter the information from the form into the computer or add the form to the patient's medical record in the prescribed place.	15	_____	_____	_____
*4. Review the entire form to make sure all information has been completed.	15	_____	_____	_____
*5. Make a copy of the insurance card, front and back.	10	_____	_____	_____
*6. Verify insurance coverage.	15	_____	_____	_____
*7. Construct the record using the materials prescribed by the medical office.	5	_____	_____	_____
*8. Add progress notes so that the physician can document information in the patient's medical record.	15	_____	_____	_____
*9. Attach an encounter form to the chart and give it to the clinical assistant for use during the patient's examination.	15	_____	_____	_____

Comments:

Points earned _____ ÷ 100 possible points = Score _____ % Score

Instructor's signature _____

Name _____ Date _____ Score _____

PROCEDURE 12-1 Explain General Office Policies

MAERB/CAAHEP COMPETENCIES: IV.P.IV.4
ABHES COMPETENCIES: 4.c, 8.f

TASK: To communicate office policies and procedures effectively to patients and visitors in the office.

Equipment and Supplies
- Office policy manual
- Office procedure manual (if not included in the policy manual)
- Patient information sheets
- Office policy brochure

Standards: Complete the procedure and all critical steps in _____ minutes with a minimum score of 85% within three attempts.

Scoring: Divide the points earned by the total possible points. Failure to perform a critical step, indicated by an asterisk (*), results in an unsatisfactory overall score.

Time began _____   Time ended _____   Total minutes: _____

Steps	Possible Points	Attempt 1	Attempt 2	Attempt 3
*1. Design an office policy brochure or Web site that presents general information for patients. At a minimum, the brochure should have the following:	30			
a. Philosophy statement		_____	_____	_____
b. Goals		_____	_____	_____
c. Description of the medical practice		_____	_____	_____
d. Location and/or map		_____	_____	_____
e. Phone numbers		_____	_____	_____
f. Pager numbers		_____	_____	_____
g. E-mail and Web site addresses		_____	_____	_____
h. Staff names and credentials		_____	_____	_____
i. Services offered		_____	_____	_____
j. Hours of operation		_____	_____	_____
k. Appointment system		_____	_____	_____
l. Cancellation policy		_____	_____	_____
m. Prescription refill guidelines		_____	_____	_____
n. Insurances accepted		_____	_____	_____
o. Emergency procedures		_____	_____	_____
p. Alternate physician coverage		_____	_____	_____
q. Referral and records release policies		_____	_____	_____
r. Special needs accommodations		_____	_____	_____
s. Notice of privacy policies		_____	_____	_____

71

Steps	Possible Points	Attempt 1	Attempt 2	Attempt 3
2. Offer the brochure to new patients.	5	_____	_____	_____
*3. Sit with the patient and explain each section of the document.	20	_____	_____	_____
*4. While explaining the brochure, look for body language and verbal statements from the patient that indicate understanding.	30	_____	_____	_____
*5. Ask the patient whether he or she has any questions.	10	_____	_____	_____
*6. Document that the patient received the brochure in the medical record.	5	_____	_____	_____

Comments:

Points earned _____ ÷ 100 possible points = Score _____ % Score

Instructor's signature _____

Procedure **12-1 Explain General Office Policies**

Name _____ Date _____ Score _____

PROCEDURE 12-2 Explain the Physician's Instructions to Patients, Staff Members, and Visitors

MAERB/CAAHEP COMPETENCIES: IV.P.IV.5
ABHES COMPETENCIES: 9.h

TASK: To communicate office policies and procedures effectively to employees, patients, and visitors in the office so that they understand the physician's instructions.

Equipment and Supplies
- Office policy manual
- Office procedures manual (if not included in the policy manual)
- Patient information sheets (if needed)
- Physician's orders, if applicable
- Patient information brochure

Standards: Complete the procedure and all critical steps in _____ minutes with a minimum score of 85% within three attempts.

Scoring: Divide the points earned by the total possible points. Failure to perform a critical step, indicated by an asterisk (*), results in an unsatisfactory overall score.

Time began _____   **Time ended** _____   **Total minutes:** _____

Steps	Possible Points	Attempt 1	Attempt 2	Attempt 3
1. Determine the patient's communication needs.	10	_____	_____	_____
2. Arrange for an interpreter, if applicable. If no employee speaks the patient's language, make sure the patient brings an interpreter to the appointment.	10	_____	_____	_____
*3. Give the patient the physician's instructions.	10	_____	_____	_____
*4. Explain the instructions to the patient using language that the person can understand.	20	_____	_____	_____
*5. While explaining the instructions, look for verbal and nonverbal indications that the patient understands.	20	_____	_____	_____
*6. Have the patient restate the instructions to verify complete understanding.	10	_____	_____	_____
*7. Provide the patient with any written documentation available that reiterates the instructions and/or the physician's orders for tests, procedures, and/or hospital admission.	10	_____	_____	_____
*8. Document the instructions given in the patient's medical record.	10	_____	_____	_____

Comments:

Points earned _____ ÷ 100 possible points = Score _____ % Score

Instructor's signature _____

Name _____ Date _____ Score _____

PROCEDURE 12-3 Inventory Office Supplies and Equipment

MAERB/CAAHEP COMPETENCIES: V.P.V.10
ABHES COMPETENCIES: 8.e

TASK: To establish an inventory of all expendable supplies in the physician's office and to follow an efficient plan or order control using a card system.

Equipment and Supplies
- Computer
- Inventory and order control cards
- Computer spreadsheet or list of supplies on hand
- Pen or pencil

Standards: Complete the procedure and all critical steps in _____ minutes with a minimum score of 85% within three attempts.

Scoring: Divide the points earned by the total possible points. Failure to perform a critical step, indicated by an asterisk (*), results in an unsatisfactory overall score.

Time began _____ Time ended _____ Total minutes: _____

Steps	Possible Points	Attempt 1	Attempt 2	Attempt 3
1. Enter the names of each item to be inventoried into a computer spreadsheet or on a note card.	5	_____	_____	_____
*2. Write the quantity of each item on hand in the space provided.	10	_____	_____	_____
*3. Place a notation or reorder tag at the point where the supply should be replenished.	10	_____	_____	_____
*4. Review the spreadsheet or cards monthly to determine what supplies need to be ordered.	20	_____	_____	_____
*5. Using supplier catalogs and the Internet, shop for the most competitive prices.	20	_____	_____	_____
*6. When the order has been placed, note the date and quantity ordered.	20	_____	_____	_____
*7. When the order has been received, note the date and quantity in the appropriate area on the spreadsheet, checking for backorder information.	10	_____	_____	_____
*8. Stock the supplies, moving older items forward and placing newer items toward the back.	5	_____	_____	_____

Comments:

Points earned _____ ÷ 100 possible points = Score _____ % Score

Instructor's signature _____

Name _____ Date _____ Score _____

PROCEDURE 12-4 Prepare a Purchase Order

ABHES COMPETENCIES: 8.e

TASK: To prepare an accurate purchase order for supplies or equipment.

Equipment and Supplies
- List or spreadsheet of current inventory
- Phone
- Purchase order
- Fax machine
- Pen

Standards: Complete the procedure and all critical steps in _____ minutes with a minimum score of 85% within three attempts.

Scoring: Divide the points earned by the total possible points. Failure to perform a critical step, indicated by an asterisk (*), results in an unsatisfactory overall score.

Time began _____ **Time ended** _____ **Total minutes:** _____

Steps	Possible Points	Attempt 1	Attempt 2	Attempt 3
1. Review the current inventory and determine what items need to be ordered.	10	_____	_____	_____
*2. Complete the purchase order accurately, filling in all applicable spaces and blanks with the information requested.	15	_____	_____	_____
*3. List the items to be ordered, including the quantity, item numbers, size, color, price, and extended price.	15	_____	_____	_____
*4. Provide the physician's signature, DEA certificate, and medical license information when needed.	15	_____	_____	_____
*5. Call in, fax, mail, or submit the order electronically to the vendor. Keep a copy for your records. Keep any verification provided to prove that the vendor received the order.	15	_____	_____	_____
*6. Note on the inventory spreadsheet or list the items that are on order.	15	_____	_____	_____
*7. Keep a copy of the order in the appropriate place in the office filing system or in the computer business files.	15	_____	_____	_____

77

Comments:

Points earned _____ ÷ 100 possible points = Score _____ % Score

Instructor's signature _____

Name _____ Date _____ Score _____

PROCEDURE 12-5 Perform and Document Routine Maintenance of Office Equipment

MAERB/CAAHEP COMPETENCIES: V.P.V.9
ABHES COMPETENCIES: 8.e.1

TASK: To ensure that all office equipment is in good working order at all times.

Equipment and Supplies

- Spreadsheet with information on each piece of office equipment, including serial number and servicing schedule
- Pen or pencil
- Computer
- Access to all office equipment

Standards: Complete the procedure and all critical steps in _____ minutes with a minimum score of 85% within three attempts.

Scoring: Divide the points earned by the total possible points. Failure to perform a critical step, indicated by an asterisk (*), results in an unsatisfactory overall score.

Time began _____ Time ended _____ Total minutes: _____

Steps	Possible Points	Attempt 1	Attempt 2	Attempt 3
*1. Gather information about each piece of equipment, including at least the following:	20			
a. Name of equipment		_____	_____	_____
b. Type of equipment		_____	_____	_____
c. Manufacturer's name		_____	_____	_____
d. Manufacturer's address		_____	_____	_____
e. Contact phone numbers for technical support		_____	_____	_____
f. Contact phone numbers for manufacturer's main office		_____	_____	_____
g. Date purchased		_____	_____	_____
h. Cost of product		_____	_____	_____
i. Original receipt showing where the item was purchased		_____	_____	_____
j. Dates warranty begins and ends		_____	_____	_____
k. Addresses of where to send equipment if under warranty		_____	_____	_____
*2. Enter the information about each piece of equipment into a document or spreadsheet.	20	_____	_____	_____
3. Design a document containing each month of the year.	5	_____	_____	_____

Steps	Possible Points	Attempt 1	Attempt 2	Attempt 3
*4. Mark which equipment needs servicing in which months.	10	_____	_____	_____
5. Check which pieces of equipment need servicing this month.	10	_____	_____	_____
*6. Schedule servicing and maintenance for the equipment on the list for the current month.	10	_____	_____	_____
*7. Make sure servicing appointments are kept.	20	_____	_____	_____
*8. Record new information and scheduling needs into the spreadsheet or list as needed.	5	_____	_____	_____

Comments:

Points earned _____ ÷ 100 possible points = Score _____ % Score

Instructor's signature _____

Name _____ Date _____ Score _____

PROCEDURE 12-6 Use the Internet to Access Information Related to the Medical Office

MAERB/CAAHEP COMPETENCIES: V.P.V.7
ABHES COMPETENCIES: 7.a

TASK: To use the Internet to research any topic related to the medical office.

Equipment and Supplies
- Computer
- Topic for research
- Printer

Standards: Complete the procedure and all critical steps in _____ minutes with a minimum score of 85% within three attempts.

Scoring: Divide the points earned by the total possible points. Failure to perform a critical step, indicated by an asterisk (*), results in an unsatisfactory overall score.

Time began _____   Time ended _____   Total minutes: _____

Steps	Possible Points	Attempt 1	Attempt 2	Attempt 3
1. Start the computer, if necessary.	10	_____	_____	_____
2. Open a Web browser.	10	_____	_____	_____
*3. Open a search engine (make sure you can locate at least five major search engines).	10	_____	_____	_____
*4. Type the subject in the search box.	10	_____	_____	_____
*5. Review the results of the search.	20	_____	_____	_____
*6. Determine which results are from a reliable source.	10	_____	_____	_____
*7. Decide which information is pertinent to the research project.	10	_____	_____	_____
*8. Print the information, if desired.	10	_____	_____	_____
*9. Create a file on the computer for storing the information.	10	_____	_____	_____

Comments:

Points earned _____ ÷ 100 possible points = Score _____ % Score

Instructor's signature _____

Procedure **12-6 Use the Internet to Access Information**

Name _____ Date _____ Score _____

PROCEDURE 12-7 Make Travel Arrangements

ABHES COMPETENCIES: 8.f

TASK: To make travel arrangements for the physician or another staff member.

Equipment and Supplies
- Travel plan or itinerary
- Telephone
- Telephone directory
- Computer with Internet access

Standards: Complete the procedure and all critical steps in _____ minutes with a minimum score of 85% within three attempts.

Scoring: Divide the points earned by the total possible points. Failure to perform a critical step, indicated by an asterisk (*), results in an unsatisfactory overall score.

Time began _____   Time ended _____   Total minutes: _____

Steps	Possible Points	Attempt 1	Attempt 2	Attempt 3
*1. Verify the dates of the planned trip.	10	____	____	____
*2. Obtain the following information:	10			
a. Desired date and time of departure		____	____	____
b. Desired date and time of return		____	____	____
c. Preferred mode of transportation		____	____	____
d. Number in the party		____	____	____
e. Preferred lodging and price range		____	____	____
f. Preferred ticketing method (electronic or paper)		____	____	____
*3. Telephone a trusted travel agency to arrange for transportation and lodging reservations or book using the Internet.	10	____	____	____
4. Arrange for travelers' checks, if needed.	10	____	____	____
5. Pick up tickets, print e-tickets, or arrange for ticket delivery.	10	____	____	____
*6. Check tickets to confirm conformance with the travel plan.	10	____	____	____
*7. Confirm hotel and air reservations.	10	____	____	____

Steps	Possible Points	Attempt 1	Attempt 2	Attempt 3
*8. Prepare an itinerary, including at least the following information:	10			
a. Date and time of departure		_____	_____	_____
b. Flight numbers or identifying information for other modes of transportation		_____	_____	_____
c. Mode of transportation to hotels		_____	_____	_____
d. Name, address, and telephone number of all hotels, with confirmation numbers		_____	_____	_____
e. Name, address, and emergency telephone number of travel agency		_____	_____	_____
f. Date and time of return		_____	_____	_____
*9. Put one copy of the itinerary in the appropriate office file.	10	_____	_____	_____
*10. Give several copies of the itinerary to the traveler.	10	_____	_____	_____

Comments:

Points earned _____ ÷ 100 possible points = Score _____ % Score

Instructor's signature _____

PROCEDURE 12-8 Develop a Personal (Patient and Employee) Safety Plan

MAERB/CAAHEP COMPETENCIES: X.P.XI.3
ABHES COMPETENCIES: 4.e

TASK: To ensure patient and employee safety during any hazard or emergency situation.

Equipment and Supplies

- Hazard assessment for facility
- Office policy manual
- Community resource information
- List of contact information for all employees
- Clerical supplies for emergency action plan

Standards: Complete the procedure and all critical steps in _____ minutes with a minimum score of 85% within three attempts.

Scoring: Divide the points earned by the total possible points. Failure to perform a critical step, indicated by an asterisk (*), results in an unsatisfactory overall score.

Time began _____ **Time ended** _____ **Total minutes:** _____

Steps	Possible Points	Attempt 1	Attempt 2	Attempt 3
*1. Complete a hazard assessment for the facility.	5	_____	_____	_____
2. Determine the roles of other area health care facilities in case of an emergency.	5	_____	_____	_____
*3. Review the information from the hazard assessment.	5	_____	_____	_____
*4. Determine the method employees will use to report their readiness for duty during a hazardous situation or an emergency.	5	_____	_____	_____
*5. Develop an emergency action plan for each type of hazard that can be reasonably anticipated.	10	_____	_____	_____
*6. Provide for patient and employee safety in the plan.	10	_____	_____	_____
*7. Determine the extent of care that can reasonably be provided in a hazardous situation or an emergency.	10	_____	_____	_____
*8. Establish a clear chain of command.	10	_____	_____	_____
*9. Provide for break and rest periods for employees.	10	_____	_____	_____
*10. Make provisions for recognizing the effects of stress on both patients and employees during an emergency.	5	_____	_____	_____
*11. Determine how resources will likely be restored.	5	_____	_____	_____
*12. Consider the facility's vulnerabilities and make a plan to overcome those weaknesses.	10	_____	_____	_____
*13. Conduct regular emergency drills.	10	_____	_____	_____

Did the student:

	Yes	No
Recognize the effects of stress on all persons involved in emergency situations?	_____	_____
Demonstrate self-awareness in responding to emergency situations?	_____	_____

Comments:

Points earned _____ ÷ 100 possible points = Score _____ % Score

Instructor's signature _____

86

Procedure **12-8 Develop a Personal Safety Plan**

Name _____ Date _____ Score _____

PROCEDURE 12-9 Maintain a Current List of Community Resources for Emergency Preparedness

MAERB/CAAHEP COMPETENCIES: X.P.XI.12
ABHES COMPETENCIES: 9.g, 9.i

TASK: To help patients find organizations that can assist with their needs during an emergency and to establish a list of community resources that can be used for referral purposes during any type of emergency.

Equipment and Supplies
- Phone book
- Computer with Internet access
- Library access
- Newspapers
- Local volunteer guides
- Pen or pencil
- Notepad

Standards: Complete the procedure and all critical steps in _____ minutes with a minimum score of 85% within three attempts.

Scoring: Divide the points earned by the total possible points. Failure to perform a critical step, indicated by an asterisk (*), results in an unsatisfactory overall score.

Time began _____ Time ended _____ Total minutes: _____

Steps	Possible Points	Attempt 1	Attempt 2	Attempt 3
*1. Research the resources available in the surrounding area.	25	_____	_____	_____
*2. Prepare a document or spreadsheet containing a list of the various resources. Include the following information:	25			
a. Agency's name		_____	_____	_____
b. Agency's purpose or mission		_____	_____	_____
c. Physical address		_____	_____	_____
d. Mailing address, if different		_____	_____	_____
e. Phone numbers		_____	_____	_____
f. Contact name		_____	_____	_____
g. Hours of operation		_____	_____	_____
h. Services offered or performed		_____	_____	_____
*3. Update the information whenever a change is necessary.	25	_____	_____	_____
*4. Provide referrals to patients as needed.	25	_____	_____	_____

Comments:

Points earned _____ ÷ 100 possible points = Score _____ % Score

Instructor's signature _____

Procedure **12-9 Maintain a Current List of Community Resources**

PROCEDURE 12-10 Use Proper Body Mechanics

MAERB/CAAHEP COMPETENCIES: X.P.XI.11
ABHES COMPETENCIES: 8.e

TASK: To prevent workplace injuries through the use of proper body mechanics.

Equipment and Supplies
- Ergonomic brochures or instruction sheets
- Computer with Internet access
- Web sites concerned with the prevention of workplace injuries

Standards: Complete the procedure and all critical steps in _____ minutes with a minimum score of 85% within three attempts.

Scoring: Divide the points earned by the total possible points. Failure to perform a critical step, indicated by an asterisk (*), results in an unsatisfactory overall score.

Time began _____ Time ended _____ Total minutes: _____

Steps	Possible Points	Attempt 1	Attempt 2	Attempt 3
1. Evaluate the workplace and workstation for ergonomic issues.	25	_____	_____	_____
2. Test the weight of a load to be lifted and determine whether a second person should assist with the task.	25	_____	_____	_____
*3. Lift an item using ergonomic guidelines.	25	_____	_____	_____
*4. Demonstrate appropriate ergonomics while seated at a computer workstation.	25	_____	_____	_____

Comments:

Points earned _____ ÷ 100 possible points = Score _____ % Score

Instructor's signature _____

PROCEDURE 12-11 Develop and Maintain a Current List of Community Resources Related to Patients' Healthcare Needs

MAERB/CAAHEP COMPETENCIES: IV.P.IV.12
ABHES COMPETENCIES: 9.i

TASK: To help patients find organizations that can assist with their needs beyond the physician's office and to establish a list of community resources that can be used for referral purposes.

Equipment and Supplies
- Phone book
- Computer with Internet access
- Library access
- Newspapers
- Local volunteer guides
- Pen or pencil
- Notepad

Standards: Complete the procedure and all critical steps in _____ minutes with a minimum score of 85% within three attempts.

Scoring: Divide the points earned by the total possible points. Failure to perform a critical step, indicated by an asterisk (*), results in an unsatisfactory overall score.

Time began _____ **Time ended** _____ **Total minutes:** _____

Steps	Possible Points	Attempt 1	Attempt 2	Attempt 3
*1. Research the resources available in the local community.	20	____	____	____
*2. Create a document or spreadsheet containing the following information:	20			
a. Agency's name		____	____	____
b. Agency's purpose or mission		____	____	____
c. Physical address		____	____	____
d. Mailing address, if different		____	____	____
e. Phone numbers		____	____	____
f. Web site addresses		____	____	____
g. Contact names and e-mail information		____	____	____
h. Hours of operation		____	____	____
i. Services offered or provided		____	____	____
*3. Update the information whenever necessary and at least annually.	20	____	____	____
*4. Provide referrals to agencies upon the physician's or patient's request.	20	____	____	____
*5. Document referrals in the patient's medical record.	20	____	____	____

Comments:

Points earned _____ ÷ 100 possible points = Score _____ % Score

Instructor's signature _____

Procedure **12-11 Develop and Maintain a Current List**

WORK PRODUCT 12-1

Name: _____

Equipment Inventory

Corresponds to Procedure 12-3

<u>MAERB/CAAHEP COMPETENCIES:</u> V.P.V.10

<u>ABHES COMPETENCIES:</u> 8.e

Complete the form below according to the instructions in Part V.

Blackburn Primary Care
Associates, PC
1990 Turquoise Drive
Blackburn, WI 54937

Phone: 608-459-8857
Fax: 608-459-8860
E-mail:
blackburnom@blackburnpca.com
www.blackburnpca.com

BLACKBURN PRIMARY CARE ASSOCIATES, P.C.

Equipment Inventory List

Purpose:

Date:

Description	Check/P.O. #	Purchased From	Date Purchased	Serial Number	Warranty	Value
					Total	

93

WORK PRODUCT 12-2

Name: _____

Supply Inventory

Corresponds to Procedure 12-3

MAERB/CAAHEP COMPETENCIES: V.P.V.10

ABHES COMPETENCIES: 8.e

Complete the form below page according to the instructions in Part VI.

Blackburn Primary Care
Associates, PC
1990 Turquoise Drive
Blackburn, WI 54937

Phone: 608-459-8857
Fax: 608-459-8860
E-mail:
blackburnom@blackburnpca.com
www.blackburnpca.com

BLACKBURN PRIMARY CARE ASSOCIATES, P.C.

Supply Inventory List

Purpose:

Date:

Description and Item Number	Needed On Hand	Currently On Hand	Date Ordered	Price Per Unit	Total Price	Date Received

WORK PRODUCT 12-3

Name: _____

Equipment Maintenance Log

Corresponds to Procedure 12-5

MAERB/CAAHEP COMPETENCIES: V.P.V.9

ABHES COMPETENCIES: 8.e

Complete the form on the next page according to the instructions in Part VIII.

EQUIPMENT INVENTORY LIST

Physical Condition

Asset or serial number	Item description (make and model)	Location	Condition
820692791P	Laptop Computer	Dr. Lopez's Office	EXC

Financial Information

Vendor	Years of service left	Initial value	Down payment	Date purchased or leased	Loan term in years	Loan rate	Monthly payment	Monthly operating costs	Total monthly cost
Toshiba	5	$1,695.00	n/a	9/15/2001	n/a	n/a	n/a	$27.00	$27.00

Maintenance Schedule

Maintenance Date	Condition of Equipment	Out of Service?	Maintenance Performed	Date in Service
9/25/2006	EXC	no	None needed	9/25/2006

WORK PRODUCT 12-4

Name: _____

Travel Expense Report

Corresponds to Procedure 12-7

<u>ABHES COMPETENCIES:</u> 8.f

Complete the form according to the instructions in Part IX.

Statement number: _____

Expense Statement

Employee information

Name _____   Department _____

Employee ID _____   Manager _____

Position _____

Pay period

| From | |
| To | |

Date	Account	Description	Hotel	Transport	Fuel	Meals	Phone	Entertain.	Misc.	TOTAL

Subtotal _____

Advances _____

TOTAL _____

99

WORK PRODUCT 12-5

Name: _____

Develop a Personal (Patient and Employee) Safety Plan

Corresponds to Procedure 12-8

MAERB/CAAHEP COMPETENCIES: X.P.XI. 3

ABHES COMPETENCIES: 9.g

Location of Facility:	
Date/Time of Inspection:	
Inspector Name:	
Inspector Signature:	

Section A: GENERAL SAFETY ISSUES

		C	NC	NA
1	Emergency phone numbers are clearly posted in the facility.			
2	Emergency procedures are outlined in the policy/procedure manual and are located in a prominent place for reference.			
3	Emergency codes are clearly explained and posted.			
4	Emergency meeting areas are posted.			
5	Aisles, passageways, walkways, and stairwells are clear of all obstructions.			
6	No trip hazards obstruct hallways or walkways.			
7	Stairways and exits are lighted and clearly negotiable.			
8	Walkways that could be slip hazards during inclement weather are clear and mats are available when needed.			
9	Fire extinguishers are properly located and accessible.			
10	Exits and evacuation routes are clearly marked.			
11	Emergency lighting is working properly.			
12	Storage areas are neat and orderly.			
13	Trash bins are available, clean, and have disposable liners.			

Section B: Hazardous Materials

		C	NC	NA
1	Employees have been trained on OSHA/CLIA regulations and documentation is available for review in each employee file for both intial and annual training sessions.			
2	Material Safety Data Sheets (MSDS) are available for all hazardous materials and chemicals in the facility.			
3	Spill kits are available.			
4	Hazardous materials are clearly and properly labeled.			
5	Flammable materials are stored safely.			
6	Compressed gas and oxygen cylinders are stored safely.			
7	Personal Protective Equipment (PPE) is available for all employees.			
8	Eyewash and safety showers are located in appropriate areas.			
9	Documentation is available to prove that eyewash and safety showers are tested monthly and found in good working order.			
10	Hazardous waste is located in appropriate biosafety bins.			

101

Section B: Hazardous Materials (continued)

		C	NC	NA
11	Documentation is available to prove proper disposal of hazardous waste.			
12	Universal waste and hazardous waste are disposed of in separate containers.			
13	Information about hazardous materials is clearly communicated to employees.			
14	The facility's Exposure Control Plan is in use.			
15	Documentation is available to prove that an annual hazard assessment has been completed.			
16	An emergency action plan is available in the facility.			
17	OSHA Form 300 is posted during the required time period.			
18	Records are available to prove that Hepatitis B immunizations were given to employees or declined by the employee.			
19	Employees are aware of procedures for reporting incidents.			
20	Needles are disposed of properly and safely.			
21	Employees are performing procedures only with proper education and training.			

Section C: Electrical Hazards

		C	NC	NA
1	Circuits are not overloaded.			
2	Equipment plugs are properly grounded and in good condition.			
3	Extension cords have a ground plug and are in good condition.			
4	Breaker box switches are clearly labeled.			
5	Surge protectors are clean, free from dust, and not overloaded.			

Section D: Emergency Preparedness

		C	NC	NA
1	An employee and patient safety plan is in place.			
2	Documentation of emergency drills is available.			
3	The role of each employee in emergency situations is delineated and communicated to the employees.			
4	Backup systems are in place for power outages.			
5	Up-to-date information is available regarding community resources.			
6	A stock of emergency supplies is available.			
7	Assessment of naturally-occuring events (e.g. weather) is determined for the geographic area and included in the employee and patient safety plan.			
8	Technological hazards are included in the safety plan.			
9	Human hazards (e.g. mass casualties, bomb threats) are included in drills and safety plans.			

PROCEDURE 13-1 Compose Professional Business Letters

MAERB/CAAHEP COMPETENCIES: IV.P.IV.10
ABHES COMPETENCIES: 7.a, 8.f

TASK: To compose a professional business letter that conveys information in an accurate and concise manner and that is easy for the reader to comprehend.

Equipment and Supplies

- Computer
- Word processing software
- Draft paper
- Letterhead
- Printer
- Pen or pencil
- Highlighter
- Envelope
- Correspondence to be answered
- Other pertinent information needed to compose a letter
- Electronic or paper dictionary and thesaurus
- Writer's handbook
- Portfolio and/or templates

Standards: Complete the procedure and all critical steps in _____ minutes with a minimum score of 85% within three attempts.

Scoring: Divide the points earned by the total possible points. Failure to perform a critical step, indicated by an asterisk (*), results in an unsatisfactory overall score.

Time began _____ **Time ended** _____ **Total minutes:** _____

Steps	Possible Points	Attempt 1	Attempt 2	Attempt 3
1. Determine the reason for sending the correspondence and the intended goals.	10	_____	_____	_____
2. Open a document on the computer to prepare a draft of the letter and save it for future reference.	5	_____	_____	_____
*3. Date the letter.	5	_____	_____	_____
*4. Type the inside address.	5	_____	_____	_____
*5. Type a subject line and list the patient's name or the subject of the correspondence.	10	_____	_____	_____
*6. Type the body of the letter, paying strict attention to its goals.	10	_____	_____	_____
*7. Type the closing of the letter and use the name of the person who will be considered the author.	10	_____	_____	_____
*8. Proofread the document for accuracy and spelling.	10	_____	_____	_____

Steps	Possible Points	Attempt 1	Attempt 2	Attempt 3
*9. Make any necessary corrections to the letter.	10	_____	_____	_____
*10. Reread the letter to ensure that the goals have been met.	5	_____	_____	_____
*11. Address the envelope according to USPS OCR guidelines.	10	_____	_____	_____
*12. Affix the correct postage and mail the letter.	10	_____	_____	_____

Comments:

Points earned _____ ÷ 100 possible points = Score _____ % Score

Instructor's signature _____

PROCEDURE 13-2 Organize Technical Information and Summaries

MAERB/CAAHEP COMPETENCIES: IV.P.IV.2
ABHES COMPETENCIES: 8.f

TASK: To compose a clearly written, grammatically correct business letter or memo that can be easily understood by the reader and to eliminate spelling and grammatical errors.

Equipment and Supplies
- Stationery
- Computer
- Correspondence to be answered or notes
- Proofreader's marks guide

Standards: Complete the procedure and all critical steps in _____ minutes with a minimum score of 85% within three attempts.

Scoring: Divide the points earned by the total possible points. Failure to perform a critical step, indicated by an asterisk (*), results in an unsatisfactory overall score.

Time began _____ **Time ended** _____ **Total minutes:** _____

Steps	Possible Points	Attempt 1	Attempt 2	Attempt 3
1. Scan the letter to be answered or the notes for the memo to be composed.	10	_____	_____	_____
*2. Compose the letter or memo, using good grammar.	10	_____	_____	_____
*3. Print a draft of the letter or memo.	10	_____	_____	_____
*4. Proofread the draft carefully, highlighting changes and noting additions to be made.	10	_____	_____	_____
*5. Revise the letter according to the notes.	20	_____	_____	_____
*6. Proofread the final draft.	10	_____	_____	_____
*7. Print the final draft.	10	_____	_____	_____
*8. Allow a co-worker to proofread the letter and make any necessary corrections.	10	_____	_____	_____
*9. Make a file copy of the letter or memo and distribute it appropriately.	10	_____	_____	_____

Comments:

Points earned _____ ÷ 100 possible points = Score _____ % Score

Instructor's signature _____

Name _____ Date _____ Score _____

PROCEDURE 13-3 Receive, Organize, Prioritize, and Transmit Information Expediently

MAERB/CAAHEP COMPETENCIES: IV.P.IV.10, IV.P.IV.2
ABHES COMPETENCIES: 8.a

TASK: To efficiently sort through the mail that arrives in the medical office on a daily basis.

Equipment and Supplies
- Computer
- Draft paper
- Letterhead stationery
- Pen or pencil
- Highlighter
- Staple remover
- Paper clips
- Letter opener
- Stapler
- Transparent tape
- Date stamp

Standards: Complete the procedure and all critical steps in _____ minutes with a minimum score of 85% within three attempts.

Scoring: Divide the points earned by the total possible points. Failure to perform a critical step, indicated by an asterisk (*), results in an unsatisfactory overall score.

Time began _____ Time ended _____ Total minutes: _____

Steps	Possible Points	Attempt 1	Attempt 2	Attempt 3
1. Clear work space on the desk.	10	_____	_____	_____
2. Sort the mail according to importance and urgency so that the most important issues can be addressed first.	10	_____	_____	_____
3. Stack the envelopes so that they all face the same direction and open them along the top edge.	10	_____	_____	_____
*4. Open the mail neatly and in an organized manner.	10	_____	_____	_____
*5. Remove the contents and paper clip the documents together, if necessary. Hold the envelope to the light or visually examine it to make sure all documents have been removed.	20	_____	_____	_____
*6. Make a note of the postmark, if necessary.	10	_____	_____	_____
*7. Date stamp the letter and secure any enclosures.	20	_____	_____	_____
*8. Organize the mail for transmission to each person and distribute it at the appropriate time. Make additions to patients' medical records where indicated and/or required according to office policy and legislation.	10	_____	_____	_____

Comments:

Points earned _____ **÷ 100 possible points = Score** _____ **% Score**

Instructor's signature _____

Procedure 13-3 **Receive, Organize, Prioritize and Transmit Information**

PROCEDURE 13-4 Address an Envelope According to Postal Service Optical Character Reader Guidelines

MAERB/CAAHEP COMPETENCIES: IV.P.IV.10, IV.P.IV.2
ABHES COMPETENCIES: 7.a, 8.f

TASK: To correctly address business correspondence so that the mail arrives at the post office and is processed by the U.S. Postal Service as efficiently as possible.

Equipment and Supplies

- Envelopes
- Computer
- Correspondence

Standards: Complete the procedure and all critical steps in _____ minutes with a minimum score of 85% within three attempts.

Scoring: Divide the points earned by the total possible points. Failure to perform a critical step, indicated by an asterisk (*), results in an unsatisfactory overall score.

Time began _____ **Time ended** _____ **Total minutes:** _____

Steps	Possible Points	Attempt 1	Attempt 2	Attempt 3
1. Place the envelope in the printer.	10	_____	_____	_____
*2. Enter the word processing program and check the TOOLS section for envelopes. The address block should start no higher than 2¼ inches from the bottom. Leave a bottom margin of at least ⅝ inch and left and right margins of at least 1 inch.	20	_____	_____	_____
*3. Use dark type on a light background, no script or italics, and capitalize everything in the address.	10	_____	_____	_____
*4. Type the address in block format, using only approved abbreviations and eliminating all punctuation.	20	_____	_____	_____
*5. Type the city, state, and ZIP code on the last line of the address.	10	_____	_____	_____
*6. No line should have more than 27 total characters, including spaces.	10	_____	_____	_____
*7. Leave a ⅝ × 4¾-inch blank space in the bottom right corner of the envelope.	10	_____	_____	_____
*8. Make sure the envelope is addressed accurately, considering the requirements for overseas mailing if applicable.	10	_____	_____	_____

Comments:

Points earned _____ ÷ 100 possible points = **Score** _____ **% Score**

Instructor's signature _____

Procedure 13-4 **Address an Envelope According to Postal Service**

WORK PRODUCT 13-1

Name: _____

Addressing an Envelope

Corresponds to Procedures 13-1, 13-2, and 13-4

<u>MAERB/CAAHEP COMPETENCIES:</u> IV.P.IV.10, IV.P.IV.2

<u>ABHES COMPETENCIES:</u> 7.a, 8.a, 8.f

Complete the envelopes below according to the directions in Part I, questions 1-3.

Blackburn Primary Care Associates, P.C.
1990 Turquoise Drive
Blackburn, WI 54937

Blackburn Primary Care Associates, P.C.
1990 Turquoise Drive
Blackburn, WI 54937

Blackburn Primary Care Associates, P.C.
1990 Turquoise Drive
Blackburn, WI 54937

WORK PRODUCT 13-2

Name: _____

Initiating Correspondence

Corresponds to Procedures 13-1, 13-2, and 13-4

<u>CAAHEP COMPETENCIES:</u> IV.P.IV.10, IV.P.IV.2

<u>ABHES COMPETENCIES:</u> 7.a, 8.f

Using the form below, write a letter according to the directions in Part III, question A.

Blackburn Primary Care Associates
1990 Turquoise Drive
Blackburn, WI 54937
(555) 555-1234

WORK PRODUCT 13-3

Name: _____

Initiating a Memo

Corresponds to Procedures 13-1, 13-2, and 13-4

<u>CAAHEP COMPETENCIES:</u> IV.P.IV.10, IV.P.IV.2

<u>ABHES COMPETENCIES:</u> 7.a, 8.f

Using the form below, write a memo according to the directions in Part III, question B.

MEMORANDUM

Date:

To:

From:

Subject:

115

WORK PRODUCT 13-4

Name: _____

Responding to Correspondence

Corresponds to Procedures 13-1, 13-2, and 13-3

<u>CAAHEP COMPETENCIES:</u> IV.P.IV.10, IV.P.IV.2

<u>ABHES COMPETENCIES:</u> 7.a, 8.f

Using the form below, write a letter according to the directions in Part III, question C.

Blackburn Primary Care Associates
1990 Turquoise Drive
Blackburn, WI 54937
(555) 555-1234

WORK PRODUCT 13-5

Name: _____

Responding to a Memo

Corresponds to Procedures 13-1, 13-2, and 13-3

<u>CAAHEP COMPETENCIES:</u> IV.P.IV.10, IV.P.IV.2

<u>ABHES COMPETENCIES:</u> 7.a, 8.f

Using the form below, write a memo according to the directions in Part III, question D.

M E M O R A N D U M

    Date:

    To:

    From:

    Subject:

- -

WORK PRODUCT 13-6

Name: _____

Initiating a Fax

Corresponds to Procedures 13-1, 13-2, and 13-3

<u>CAAHEP COMPETENCIES:</u> IV.P.IV.10, IV.P.IV.2

<u>ABHES COMPETENCIES:</u> 7.a, 8.f

Design a coversheet for a fax message using the form below according to the directions in Part III, question E.

Blackburn Primary Care Associates
1990 Turquoise Drive
Blackburn, WI 54937
(555) 555-1234

PROCEDURE 14-1 Document Patient Care Accurately

MAERB/CAAHEP COMPETENCIES: IV.P.IV.8
ABHES COMPETENCIES: 4.a

TASK: To document appropriately and accurately in all medical records and other office paperwork that concerns the patient.

Equipment and Supplies

- Any medical document
- Clerical supplies
- Computer
- Office policy and procedures manual
- Progress notes

Standards: Complete the procedure and all critical steps in _____ minutes with a minimum score of 85% within three attempts.

Scoring: Divide the points earned by the total possible points. Failure to perform a critical step, indicated by an asterisk (*), results in an unsatisfactory overall score.

Time began _____   **Time ended** _____   **Total minutes:** _____

Steps	Possible Points	Attempt 1	Attempt 2	Attempt 3
*1. Determine the entry to be made into the document.	5	_____	_____	_____
*2. Make the entry in legible handwriting.	20	_____	_____	_____
*3. Check the entry for accuracy.	20	_____	_____	_____
*4. Authenticate the entry.	20	_____	_____	_____
*5. Make a correction to the same entry.	10	_____	_____	_____
*6. Authenticate the corrected entry.	10	_____	_____	_____
*7. Check the entry for accuracy.	10	_____	_____	_____
*8. Put the document in the appropriate record or file.	5	_____	_____	_____

123

Comments:

Points earned _____ ÷ 100 possible points = Score _____ % Score

Instructor's signature _____

Procedure **14-1 Document Patient Care Accurately**

Name _____ Date _____ Score _____

PROCEDURE 14-2 Organize a Patient's Medical Record

MAERB/CAAHEP COMPETENCIES: V.P.V.3
ABHES COMPETENCIES: 8.a

TASK: To create a medical file for a new patient that will contain all the personal data necessary for a complete record and any other information required by the facility.

Equipment and Supplies
- Computer
- Clerical supplies (pen, clipboard)
- Registration form
- File folder
- Color-coded labels for folder
- Index label for folder tab
- Identification (ID) card, if using a numeric system
- Cross-reference card, if needed
- Financial ledger, if needed
- Routing slip
- Private conference area

Standards: Complete the procedure and all critical steps in _____ minutes with a minimum score of 85% within three attempts.

Scoring: Divide the points earned by the total possible points. Failure to perform a critical step, indicated by an asterisk (*), results in an unsatisfactory overall score.

Time began _____   Time ended _____   Total minutes: _____

Steps	Possible Points	Attempt 1	Attempt 2	Attempt 3
1. Determine that the patient is new to the office.	10	_____	_____	_____
*2. Obtain and record the required personal data.	10	_____	_____	_____
*3. Enter the information on the patient history form.	10	_____	_____	_____
*4. Review the entire form.	10	_____	_____	_____
*5. Select the label and file folder for the record.	10	_____	_____	_____
*6. Type the caption on the label and put it on the folder.	10	_____	_____	_____
*7. For numeric filing, prepare a cross-reference.	10	_____	_____	_____
*8. Prepare the financial card or enter the data into a computerized ledger.	10	_____	_____	_____
*9. Put the patient history form and other required forms in the folder.	10	_____	_____	_____
*10. Clip an encounter form on the outside of the folder.	10	_____	_____	_____
11. Prepare electronic records as prescribed by the software system.	N/A	_____	_____	_____

125

Comments:

Points earned _____ ÷ 100 possible points = Score _____ % Score

Instructor's signature _____

Procedure **14-2 Organize a Patient's Medical Record**

Name _____ Date _____ Score _____

PROCEDURE 14-3 Prepare an Informed Consent for Treatment Form

MAERB/CAAHEP COMPETENCIES: V.P.V.3
ABHES COMPETENCIES: 8.a

TASK: To adequately and completely inform the patient about the treatment or procedure the person is to receive and to provide legal protection for the facility and the provider.

Equipment and Supplies
- Pen
- Consent form

Standards: Complete the procedure and all critical steps in _____ minutes with a minimum score of 85% within three attempts.

Scoring: Divide the points earned by the total possible points. Failure to perform a critical step, indicated by an asterisk (*), results in an unsatisfactory overall score.

Time began _____   **Time ended** _____   **Total minutes:** _____

Steps	Possible Points	Attempt 1	Attempt 2	Attempt 3
1. After the physician provides the details of the procedure to be done, prepare the consent form. Make sure the form addresses the following:	20			
a. Nature of the procedure or treatment		_____	_____	_____
b. Risks and/or benefits of the procedure or treatment		_____	_____	_____
c. Any reasonable alternatives to the procedure or treatment		_____	_____	_____
d. Risks and/or benefits of each alternative		_____	_____	_____
e. Risks and/or benefits of not performing the procedure or treatment		_____	_____	_____
2. Personalize the form with the patient's name and any other demographic information the form requires.	10	_____	_____	_____
*3. Give the form to the physician to use in counseling the patient about the procedure.	10	_____	_____	_____
4. Witness the patient's signature on the form, if necessary. The physician usually signs the form as well.	10	_____	_____	_____
*5. Provide the patient with a copy of the consent form.	10	_____	_____	_____
6. Put the consent form in the patient's chart. The facility where the procedure is to be performed may require a copy.	10	_____	_____	_____
*7. Ask the patient if he or she has any questions about the procedure. Refer questions that you, as the medical assistant, cannot or should not answer to the physician. Make sure all the patient's questions are answered.	20	_____	_____	_____
*8. Provide the patient with the information about the date and time of the procedure.	10	_____	_____	_____

127

Comments:

Points earned _____ ÷ 100 possible points = Score _____ % Score

Instructor's signature _____

128

PROCEDURE 14-4 Add Supplementary Items to Patients' Records

MAERB/CAAHEP COMPETENCIES: V.P.V.3
ABHES COMPETENCIES: 8.a

TASK: To add supplementary documents and progress notes to patients' histories, observing standard steps in filing while creating an orderly file that facilitates ready reference to any item of information.

Equipment and Supplies
- Assorted correspondence, diagnostic reports, and progress notes
- Patients' files
- Computer
- Mending tape
- FILE stamp or pen
- Sorter
- Stapler

Standards: Complete the procedure and all critical steps in _____ minutes with a minimum score of 85% within three attempts.

Scoring: Divide the points earned by the total possible points. Failure to perform a critical step, indicated by an asterisk (*), results in an unsatisfactory overall score.

Time began _____ **Time ended** _____ **Total minutes:** _____

Steps	Possible Points	Attempt 1	Attempt 2	Attempt 3
*1. Group all papers according to the patients' names.	20	_____	_____	_____
*2. Remove any staples or paper clips.	10	_____	_____	_____
*3. Mend any damaged or torn records.	10	_____	_____	_____
*4. Attach any small items to standard-size paper.	10	_____	_____	_____
*5. Group any related papers together.	10	_____	_____	_____
*6. Put your initials or FILE stamp in the upper left corner.	10	_____	_____	_____
*7. Code the document by underlining or writing the patient's name in the upper right corner.	10	_____	_____	_____
*8. Continue steps 2 through 7 until all documents have been conditioned, released, indexed, and coded.	10	_____	_____	_____
*9. Place all documents in the sorter in filing sequence.	10	_____	_____	_____

Comments:

Points earned _____ ÷ 100 possible points = Score _____ % Score

                        Instructor's signature _____

Procedure **14-4 Add Supplementary Items to Patients' Records**

Name _____ Date _____ Score _____

PROCEDURE 14-5 Prepare a Record Release Form

MAERB/CAAHEP COMPETENCIES: IX.P. IX.3
ABHES COMPETENCIES: 4.c

TASK: To provide a legal document indicating the patient's consent to the release of his or her medical records to another provider or healthcare facility following HIPAA regulations.

Equipment and Supplies
- Medical record release form
- Pen
- Envelope

Standards: Complete the procedure and all critical steps in _____ minutes with a minimum score of 85% within three attempts.

Scoring: Divide the points earned by the total possible points. Failure to perform a critical step, indicated by an asterisk (*), results in an unsatisfactory overall score.

Time began _____ Time ended _____ Total minutes: _____

Steps	Possible Points	Attempt 1	Attempt 2	Attempt 3
1. Explain to the patient that a medical record release form will be necessary to obtain records from another provider. If the patient is having records sent to another provider, a release will also be required.	20	_____	_____	_____
*2. Review the record release form with the patient and ask if the person understands the form and if he or she has any questions about it.	20	_____	_____	_____
*3. Have the patient sign the form in the space indicated. If other demographic information is required, (e.g., Social Security number or other names used), complete that information as well.	20	_____	_____	_____
*4. Make a copy of the form for the file and then mail the form to the appropriate facility. Note the date the form was sent. Provide a copy to the patient if requested.	20	_____	_____	_____
5. Follow up to make sure the requested records actually arrive.	20	_____	_____	_____

Comments:

Points earned _____ ÷ 100 possible points = Score _____ % Score

Instructor's signature _____

Name _____ Date _____ Score _____

PROCEDURE 14-6 File Medical Records Using an Alphabetic System

MAERB/CAAHEP COMPETENCIES: V.P.V.4
ABHES COMPETENCIES: 8.a

TASK: To file records efficiently using an alphabetic system and to ensure that the records can be retrieved easily and quickly.

Equipment and Supplies
- Medical records
- Physical filing equipment
- Cart to carry records, if needed
- Alphabetic file guide
- Staple remover
- Stapler

Standards: Complete the procedure and all critical steps in _____ minutes with a minimum score of 85% within three attempts.

Scoring: Divide the points earned by the total possible points. Failure to perform a critical step, indicated by an asterisk (*), results in an unsatisfactory overall score.

Time began _____   **Time ended** _____   **Total minutes:** _____

Steps	Possible Points	Attempt 1	Attempt 2	Attempt 3
*1. Using alphabetic guidelines, put the records to be filed in alphabetic order. If a stack of documents is to be filed, place them in alphabetic order inside an alphabetic file guide or sorter. Use rules for filing documents alphabetically.	20	_____	_____	_____
*2. Go to the filing storage equipment (shelves, cabinets, or drawers) and locate the spot in the alphabet for the first file.	20	_____	_____	_____
*3. Put the file in the cabinet or drawer in correct alphabetic order.	20	_____	_____	_____
*4. If you are adding a document to a file, put it on top so that the most recent information is seen first. This puts the information in the file in reverse chronologic order.	20	_____	_____	_____
*5. Securely fasten all documents to the medical record; do not just drop the documents inside it. Refile the medical record in its proper place.	20	_____	_____	_____

Comments:

Points earned _____ ÷ 100 possible points = **Score** _____ **% Score**

Instructor's signature _____

Name _____ Date _____ Score _____

PROCEDURE 14-7 File Medical Records Using a Numeric System

MAERB/CAAHEP COMPETENCIES: V.P.V.4
ABHES COMPETENCIES: 8.a

TASK: To file records efficiently using a numeric system and ensure that the records can be easily and quickly retrieved.

Equipment and Supplies

- Medical records
- Physical filing equipment
- Cart to carry records, if needed
- Numeric file guide
- Staple remover
- Stapler
- Paper clips

Standards: Complete the procedure and all critical steps in _____ minutes with a minimum score of 85% within three attempts.

Scoring: Divide the points earned by the total possible points. Failure to perform a critical step, indicated by an asterisk (*), results in an unsatisfactory overall score.

Time began _____   Time ended _____   Total minutes: _____

Steps	Possible Points	Attempt 1	Attempt 2	Attempt 3
*1. Using numeric guidelines, put the records to be filed in numeric order. If a stack of documents is to be filed, write the chart number on the document. Use rules for filing documents alphabetically.	20	____	____	____
*2. Go to the filing storage equipment (shelves, cabinets, or drawers) and locate the numeric spot for the first file.	20	____	____	____
*3. Put the file in the cabinet or drawer in correct numeric order.	20	____	____	____
*4. If you are adding a document to a file, put it on top so that the most recent information is seen first. This puts the information in the file in reverse chronologic order.	20	____	____	____
*5. Securely fasten all documents to the medical record. Do not just drop the documents inside the medical record. Refile the medical record in its proper place.	20	____	____	____

Comments:

Points earned _____ ÷ 100 possible points = Score _____ % Score

Instructor's signature _____

Procedure **14-7 File Medical Records**

PROCEDURE 14-8 Maintain Organization by Filing

MAERB/CAAHEP COMPETENCIES: V.P.V.8, V.A.V.1
ABHES COMPETENCIES: 8.a

TASK: To make sure various office filing systems are maintained and can be used by all staff members at the medical facility.

Equipment and Supplies
- Documents to be filed
- Various file folders
- Office filing systems (e.g., equipment maintenance, general office, and so on, if the facility's files are not kept in one general grouping)
- Clerical supplies

Standards: Complete the procedure and all critical steps in _____ minutes with a minimum score of 85% within three attempts.

Scoring: Divide the points earned by the total possible points. Failure to perform a critical step, indicated by an asterisk (*), results in an unsatisfactory overall score.

Time began _____   **Time ended** _____   **Total minutes:** _____

Steps	Possible Points	Attempt 1	Attempt 2	Attempt 3
1. Identify the correct filing system for the document.	20	_____	_____	_____
*2. Inspect the document to be added.	20	_____	_____	_____
*3. Add the document to the proper file in the correct filing system.	20	_____	_____	_____
*4. Attach the document to the file permanently or according to office policy.	20	_____	_____	_____
*5. Attach documents in the file with the most recent on top. Then place the record in the designated place in the filing system.	10	_____	_____	_____
*6. Continue the process until all documents have been filed.	10	_____	_____	_____

Did the student:	Yes	No
Consider the staff's needs and limitations in establishing a filing system?	_____	_____

137

Comments:

Points earned _____ ÷ 100 possible points = Score _____ % Score

Instructor's signature _____

WORK PRODUCT 14-1

Name: _____

Document Patient Care Accurately

Corresponds to Procedure 14-8

<u>MAERB/CAAHEP COMPETENCIES:</u> IV.P.IV.8

<u>ABHES COMPETENCIES:</u> 8.a

OUTLINE FORMAT PROGRESS NOTES

Patient Name _____

Prob. No. or Letter	DATE	S Subjective	O Objective	A Assess	P Plans	Page _____

Start each Progress Note (Subjective, Objective, through the intervening columns to the right   Assessment and Plans) at the appropriate margin of the page.   shaded column to create an outline form. Write

ORDER # 26-7115 ANDRUS CLINI-REC   CHART ORGANIZING SYSTEMS •   1976 BIBBERO SYSTEMS, INC. • PETALUMA, CA.
TO REORDER CALL TOLL FREE: (800) BIBBERO (800-242-2376) OR FAX (800) 242-9330   www.bibbero.com   Mfg In U.S.A.

139

Name _____ Date _____ Score _____

PROCEDURE 15-1 Execute Data Management Using Electronic Healthcare Records such as the EMR

CAAHEP COMPETENCIES: V.P.V.5
ABHES COMPETENCIES: 7.b, 8.a

TASK: To obtain and enter patient data using the electronic health record (EHR) and/or the electronic medical record (EMR).

Equipment and Supplies

- Patient's medical records
- Data to be included in medical records
- Computer

Standards: Complete the procedure and all critical steps in _____ minutes with a minimum score of 85% within three attempts.

Scoring: Divide the points earned by the total possible points. Failure to perform a critical step, indicated by an asterisk (*), results in an unsatisfactory overall score.

Time began _____   **Time ended** _____   **Total minutes:** _____

Steps	Possible Points	Attempt 1	Attempt 2	Attempt 3
*1. Welcome the patient warmly, maintaining eye contact.	10	_____	_____	_____
*2. Open the EMR.	10	_____	_____	_____
*3. Position yourself so that the computer is not between you and the patient.	10	_____	_____	_____
*4. Verify the patient's demographics.	10	_____	_____	_____
*5. Discuss the reason for the patient's visit to the physician and document the data in the EMR.	10	_____	_____	_____
*6. Keep eye contact with the patient, not the computer keyboard, especially while talking.	10	_____	_____	_____
*7. Use proper techniques for entering information into the EMR.	10	_____	_____	_____
*8. Ask the patient whether information about any other concerns should be added to the EMR.	10	_____	_____	_____
*9. Review the information entered with the patient for clarity.	10	_____	_____	_____
*10. Electronically sign all entries and save the data.	10	_____	_____	_____

141

Comments:

Points earned _____ ÷ 100 possible points = Score _____ % Score

Instructor's signature _____

Procedure **15-1 Execute Data Management**

WORK PRODUCT 15-1

Name: _____

Document Patient Education Accurately

Corresponds to Procedure 15-1

<u>CAAHEP COMPETENCIES:</u> IV.P.IV.9

<u>ABHES COMPETENCIES:</u> 4.a, 9.h

OUTLINE FORMAT PROGRESS NOTES

Patient Name _____

Prob. No. or Letter	DATE	**S** Subjective	**O** Objective	**A** Assess	**P** Plans	Page _____

Start each Progress Note (Subjective, Objective, Assessment and Plans) at the appropriate margin of the page. shaded column to create an outline form. Write through the intervening columns to the right

ORDER # **26-7115**   ANDRUS CLINI-REC   CHART ORGANIZING SYSTEMS •   1976 BIBBERO SYSTEMS, INC. • PETALUMA, CA.
TO REORDER CALL TOLL FREE: (800) BIBBERO (800-242-2376) OR FAX (600) 242-9330 www.bibbero.com   MFG IN U.S.A.

143

Work Product **15-1**

Name _____ Date _____ Score _____

PROCEDURE 17-1 Apply HIPAA Rules in Regard to Privacy/Release of Information

MAERB/CAAHEP COMPETENCIES: IX.P.IX.3
ABHES COMPETENCIES: 4.b

TASK: To follow guidelines established by the Health Insurance Portability and Accountability Act (HIPAA) to keep patient confidentiality and to protect the patient's health information.

Equipment and Supplies
- HIPAA Privacy Rule
- Office policy and procedures manual
- Release of information forms
- Notice of privacy policy

Standards: Complete the procedure and all critical steps in _____ minutes with a minimum score of 85% within three attempts.

Scoring: Divide the points earned by the total possible points. Failure to perform a critical step, indicated by an asterisk (*), results in an unsatisfactory overall score.

Time began _____ **Time ended** _____ **Total minutes:** _____

Steps	Possible Points	Attempt 1	Attempt 2	Attempt 3
1. Review HIPAA rules and office policy regarding the release of patient information and confidentiality in the facility.	10	_____	_____	_____
*2. Review the notice of privacy practices for the facility.	10	_____	_____	_____
*3. Review the facility's authorization to release medical records form.	10	_____	_____	_____
*4. Thoroughly read the request for information.	10	_____	_____	_____
*5. Determine whether the document is valid.	10	_____	_____	_____
*6. Determine the exact information being requested.	10	_____	_____	_____
7. Make sure the release of information form is one designated by the facility or one that contains all the same information.	10	_____	_____	_____
8. Make the requestor complete one of the facility's request forms, if necessary.	10	_____	_____	_____
*9. Forward only the information requested to the person or representative of the organization who presented the authorization for release of information.	10	_____	_____	_____
*10. Release the information by mail or to the agent of the requestor.	10	_____	_____	_____

Comments:

Points earned _____ ÷ 100 possible points = Score _____ % Score

Instructor's signature _____

Procedure **17-1 Apply HIPAA Rules in Regard to Privacy/Release of Information**

Name _____ Date _____ Score _____

PROCEDURE 17-2 Perform Risk Management Procedures

ABHES COMPETENCIES: 4.e

TASK: To prevent situations that may result in risks and liability in the physician's office.

Equipment and Supplies
- Copy of laws affecting the physician's practice
- Computer with Internet access
- Office policy and procedure manual

Standards: Complete the procedure and all critical steps in _____ minutes with a minimum score of 85% within three attempts.

Scoring: Divide the points earned by the total possible points. Failure to perform a critical step, indicated by an asterisk (*), results in an unsatisfactory overall score.

Time began _____   Time ended _____   Total minutes: _____

Steps	Possible Points	Attempt 1	Attempt 2	Attempt 3
*1. Become familiar with laws affecting medical practice.	20	_____	_____	_____
*2. Become familiar with office policies and procedures.	20	_____	_____	_____
*3. Choose one law to research and present risk management procedures to help the practice remain in compliance.	20	_____	_____	_____
*4. Present the report to the class.	20	_____	_____	_____
*5. Provide the instructor with a copy of the report.	20	_____	_____	_____

Comments:

Points earned _____ ÷ 100 possible points = Score _____ % Score

Instructor's signature _____

148

Name _____ Date _____ Score _____

PROCEDURE 18-1 Perform ICD-9-CM Coding

MAERB/CAAHEP COMPETENCIES: IV.P.IV.3, VII.P.VII.2, VIII.P.VIII.2, VIII.A.VIII.1
ABHES COMPETENCIES: 8.c.3

TASK: To perform accurate diagnosis coding using the ICD-9-CM manual.

Equipment and Supplies
- ICD-9-CM manual (volumes 1 and 2, current year)
- Encounter form or charge ticket
- Medical record
- Paper
- Pen or pencil

Standards: Complete the procedure and all critical steps in _____ minutes with a minimum score of 85% within three attempts.

Scoring: Divide the points earned by the total possible points. Failure to perform a critical step, indicated by an asterisk (*), results in an unsatisfactory overall score.

Time began _____ Time ended _____ Total minutes: _____

Steps	Possible Points	Attempt 1	Attempt 2	Attempt 3
Preparation				
*1. Abstract the diagnostic statement or statements from the encounter form and/or the patient's medical record.	10	_____	_____	_____
From the Alphabetic Index				
*2. Locate the main terms taken from the diagnostic statement in the Alphabetic Index (volume 2) of the ICD-9-CM manual.	10	_____	_____	_____
3. Locate the modifying words listed under the main term in the ICD-9-CM manual.	10	_____	_____	_____
4. Review the conventions, punctuation, and notes in the Alphabetic Index.	10	_____	_____	_____
5. Choose a tentative code, codes, or code range from the Alphabetic Index that matches the diagnostic statement as closely as possible.	10	_____	_____	_____
From the Tabular Index				
6. Look up the codes chosen from the Alphabetic Index in the Tabular Index (volume 1).	10	_____	_____	_____
7. Review the notes, conventions, and ICD-9-CM Official Coding Guidelines associated with the code and code description in the Tabular Index.	10	_____	_____	_____
*8. Verify the tentative code's accuracy in the Tabular Index.	10	_____	_____	_____
*9. Carry the codes to the highest level of specificity.	10	_____	_____	_____
*10. Assign the code.	10	_____	_____	_____

Did the student:

Yes   No

Demonstrate an ability to work with the physician to achieve the maximum reimbursement?   _____   _____

Comments:

Points earned _____ ÷ 100 possible points = Score _____ % Score

Instructor's signature _____

Procedure **18-1 Perform ICD-9-CM Coding**

Name _____ Date _____ Score _____

PROCEDURE 19-1 Perform Procedural Coding: CPT Coding

MAERB/CAAHEP COMPETENCIES: IV.P.IV.3, VIII.P.VIII.1, VIII.A.VIII.1
ABHES COMPETENCIES: 8.c.3

TASK: To use the steps for procedure and service coding to find the most accurate and specific CPT Category I code.

Equipment and Supplies
- CPT coding manual (current year)
- Encounter form (charge ticket)
- Medical record
- Paper
- Pen or pencil
- Medical dictionary or medical terminology reference book

Standards: Complete the procedure and all critical steps in _____ minutes with a minimum score of 85% within three attempts.

Scoring: Divide the points earned by the total possible points. Failure to perform a critical step, indicated by an asterisk (*), results in an unsatisfactory overall score.

Time began _____ Time ended _____ Total minutes: _____

Steps	Possible Points	Attempt 1	Attempt 2	Attempt 3
*1. Abstract the procedures and/or services performed from the medical documentation.	10	_____	_____	_____
2. Select the most appropriate main term to begin the search in the Alphabetic Index.	10	_____	_____	_____
3. Determine the main and modifying terms from the abstracted information.	10	_____	_____	_____
*4. Select a modifying term (or terms), if needed, once the main term has been located. If no modifying term produces an appropriate code or code range, repeat steps 2 and 3 using a different main term classification.	10	_____	_____	_____
5. Find the code or code ranges that include all or most of the medical record procedure or service description. Disregard any code containing descriptions or wording not included in the medical record.	5	_____	_____	_____
6. Write down the code or code ranges that best match medical documentation.	5	_____	_____	_____
*7. Turn to the main text (Tabular Index) and find the first code or code range chosen from the Alphabetic Index.	10	_____	_____	_____
8. Compare the description of the code with the medical documentation. Verify that all or most of the medical record documentation matches the code description.	10	_____	_____	_____
9. Read the guidelines and notes for the section, subsection, and code to ensure that no contraindications prevent use of the code.	5	_____	_____	_____

151

Steps	Possible Points	Attempt 1	Attempt 2	Attempt 3
10. Evaluate the conventions.	5	_____	_____	_____
11. Determine whether special circumstances require a modifier. Determine whether a Special Report is required.	10	_____	_____	_____
*12. Assign the code.	10	_____	_____	_____

Did the student:	Yes	No
Demonstrate an ability to work with the physician to achieve the maximum reimbursement?	_____	_____

Comments:

Points earned _____ ÷ 100 possible points = Score _____ % Score

Instructor's signature _____

Procedure **19-1 Perform Procedural Coding: CPT Coding**

Name _____ Date _____ Score _____

PROCEDURE 19-2 Perform Procedural Coding: Evaluation and Management Coding

MAERB/CAAHEP COMPETENCIES: IV.P.IV.3, VIII.P.VIII.1, VIII.A.VIII.1
ABHES COMPETENCIES: 8.c.3

TASK: To use the steps for Evaluation and Management (E&M) coding to find the most accurate and specific CPT Category I E&M section code.

Equipment and Supplies
- CPT coding manual (current year)
- Encounter form (charge ticket)
- Medical record
- Paper
- Pen or pencil
- Medical dictionary or medical terminology reference book

Standards: Complete the procedure and all critical steps in _____ minutes with a minimum score of 85% within three attempts.

Scoring: Divide the points earned by the total possible points. Failure to perform a critical step, indicated by an asterisk (*), results in an unsatisfactory overall score.

Time began _____   Time ended _____   Total minutes: _____

Steps	Possible Points	Attempt 1	Attempt 2	Attempt 3
*1. Determine the place of service.	10	____	____	____
2. Determine the patient's status.	10	____	____	____
3. Review the guidelines and notes for the selected subsection, category, or subcategory.	10	____	____	____
*4. Identify the subsection, category, or subcategory of service in the E&M section.	20	____	____	____
*5. Review the level of E&M service descriptions for each code in the subsection, category, or subcategory chosen.	10	____	____	____
6. Determine the level of service:	20			
a. Determine the extent of the history obtained.		____	____	____
b. Determine the extent of the examination performed.		____	____	____
c. Determine the complexity of medical decision making.		____	____	____
7. If necessary, compare the medical documentation against the examples in Appendix C (Clinical Examples) of the CPT manual.	10	____	____	____
*8. Select the appropriate level of E&M service code and document it in the medical record or on the encounter form.	10	____	____	____

Did the student:

	Yes	No
Demonstrate an ability to work with the physician to achieve the maximum reimbursement?	_____	_____

Comments:

Points earned _____ **÷ 100 possible points = Score** _____ **% Score**

Instructor's signature _____

Name _____ Date _____ Score _____

PROCEDURE 19-3 Perform Procedural Coding: Anesthesia Coding

MAERB/CAAHEP COMPETENCIES: IV.P.IV.3, VIII.P.VIII.1, VIII.A.VIII.1
ABHES COMPETENCIES: 8.c.3

TASK: To use the steps to select the most accurate and specific anesthesia code and perform the anesthesia formula calculation to determine the charge for the service.

Equipment and Supplies
- CPT coding manual (current year)
- Encounter form (charge ticket)
- Medical record
- Conversion factor list
- Paper
- Pen or pencil
- Calculator

Standards: Complete the procedure and all critical steps in _____ minutes with a minimum score of 85% within three attempts.

Scoring: Divide the points earned by the total possible points. Failure to perform a critical step, indicated by an asterisk (*), results in an unsatisfactory overall score.

Time began _____ Time ended _____ Total minutes: _____

Steps	Possible Points	Attempt 1	Attempt 2	Attempt 3
*1. Read the medical documentation to determine what procedure or service was provided.	10	_____	_____	_____
*2. Determine the anatomic site or organ system involved.	10	_____	_____	_____
3. In the Alphabetic Index, go to the heading "Anesthesia" and find the code or code range that includes all or most of the procedure or service documented in the medical record.	5	_____	_____	_____
4. Write down the code or code range found in the Alphabetic Index, under the Anesthesia heading, that best matches the medical documentation.	5	_____	_____	_____
*5. Turn to the main text (Tabular Index), Anesthesia section, and find the code or code range chosen from the Alphabetic Index.	10	_____	_____	_____
6. Read the guidelines and notes for the section, subsection, category, or subcategory.	5	_____	_____	_____
7. Evaluate the conventions, especially add-on codes (+) and exemptions from modifier −51.	5	_____	_____	_____
*8. Document the code selected.	5	_____	_____	_____
9. Determine the basic unit value from the Relative Value Guide.	5	_____	_____	_____
10. Determine the patient's physical status and document the appropriate modifier.	5	_____	_____	_____

155

Steps	Possible Points	Attempt 1	Attempt 2	Attempt 3
11. Determine whether a qualifying circumstance modifier should be used. If so, document the modifier.	5	_____	_____	_____
*12. Determine the total anesthesia time, divide by 15 minutes, and document the time.	10	_____	_____	_____
13. Select the appropriate geographic conversion factor.	5	_____	_____	_____
*14. Calculate the charge for the anesthesia service using the anesthesia formula.	10	_____	_____	_____
*15. Read medical documentation to determine what procedure or service was provided	5	_____	_____	_____

Did the student:

	Yes	No
Did the student demonstrate an ability to work with the physician to achieve the maximum reimbursement?	_____	_____

Comments:

Points earned _____ ÷ 100 possible points = Score _____ % Score

Instructor's signature _____

Name _____ Date _____ Score _____

PROCEDURE 19-4 Perform Procedural Coding: HCPCS Coding

MAERB/CAAHEP COMPETENCIES: IV.P.IV.3, VIII.P.VIII.1, VIII.A.VIII.1
ABHES COMPETENCIES: 8.c.3

TASK: To use the steps for the procedure and service coding to find the most accurate and specific HCPCS code.

Equipment and Supplies
- HCPCS coding manual (current year)
- Medical record
- Encounter form (charge ticket)
- Paper
- Pen or pencil

Standards: Complete the procedure and all critical steps in _____ minutes with a minimum score of 85% within three attempts.

Scoring: Divide the points earned by the total possible points. Failure to perform a critical step, indicated by an asterisk (*), results in an unsatisfactory overall score.

Time began _____ Time ended _____ Total minutes: _____

Steps	Possible Points	Attempt 1	Attempt 2	Attempt 3
*1. Read the medical documentation to determine the procedures or services provided.	10	_____	_____	_____
*2. Determine the main and modifying terms from the abstracted information.	10	_____	_____	_____
3. Select modifying terms, if needed.	5	_____	_____	_____
4. Select the most appropriate main term to begin the search in the Alphabetic Index.	5	_____	_____	_____
*5. If no modifying term produces an appropriate code or code range, repeat steps 2 and 3 using a different main term classification.	10	_____	_____	_____
6. Find the code or code ranges that include all or most of the description of the procedure or service found in the medical record.	10	_____	_____	_____
7. Disregard any code or code range containing additional descriptions or modifying terms not found in the medical record.	5	_____	_____	_____
*8. Write down the code that best matches the description in the medical record.	5	_____	_____	_____
9. Turn to the Main Text and find the code or code range chosen from the Alphabetic Index.	5	_____	_____	_____
*10. Compare the description of the code with the medical documentation. Verify that all or most of the medical record documentation matches the code description and that no additional element or information is present in the code description that is not found in the documentation.	10	_____	_____	_____

157

Steps	Possible Points	Attempt 1	Attempt 2	Attempt 3
*11. Read the guidelines for the section, subsection, and code to make sure no contraindications prevent use of the code.	10	_____	_____	_____
12. Evaluate the HCPCS manual conventions.	5	_____	_____	_____
13. Determine whether special circumstances require a modifier.	5	_____	_____	_____
*14. Record the HCPCS code selected.	5	_____	_____	_____

Did the student: Yes   No

Did the student demonstrate an ability to work with the physician to achieve the maximum reimbursement?   _____   _____

Comments:

Points earned _____ ÷ 100 possible points = Score _____ % Score

Instructor's signature _____

Name _____ Date _____ Score _____

PROCEDURE 20-1 Apply Managed Care Policies and Procedures

MAERB/CAAHEP COMPETENCIES: IV.P.IV.3, VII.P.VII.1, IX.A.IX.2
ABHES COMPETENCIES: 4.f., 8.2

TASK: To act within the guidelines of the managed care contracts the physician and/or medical facility officials have signed.

Equipment and Supplies
- Managed care contracts (sample provided in the student workbook)
- Managed care handbooks (sample excerpt provided in the student workbook)
- Forms from managed care organizations

Standards: Complete the procedure and all critical steps in _____ minutes with a minimum score of 85% within three attempts.

Scoring: Divide the points earned by the total possible points. Failure to perform a critical step, indicated by an asterisk (*), results in an unsatisfactory overall score.

Time began _____ **Time ended** _____ **Total minutes:** _____

Steps	Possible Points	Attempt 1	Attempt 2	Attempt 3
1. Determine the managed care organization to which the patient subscribes.	10	_____	_____	_____
*2. Read and study the policies and procedures set forth by the managed care organization.	10	_____	_____	_____
3. Make sure a signature is on file for the patient.	10	_____	_____	_____
*4. Determine what procedures and services are to be billed on the claim.	20	_____	_____	_____
5. Determine whether all procedures and services to be billed are covered by the managed care plan.	20	_____	_____	_____
*6. Obtain any forms needed to process the patient's claims.	10	_____	_____	_____
7. Become familiar with the information in managed care policy manuals and handbooks.	10	_____	_____	_____
8. Determine whom to contact if questions arise about the various managed care organizations.	10	_____	_____	_____

Did the student:	Yes	No
Demonstrate awareness of the consequences of not working within the legal scope of practice?	_____	_____

159

Comments:

Points earned _____ ÷ 100 possible points = Score _____ % Score

Instructor's signature _____

Name _____ Date _____ Score _____

PROCEDURE 20-2 Apply Third-Party Guidelines

MAERB/CAAHEP COMPETENCIES: IV.P.IV.3, VII.P.VII.2
ABHES COMPETENCIES: 4.f., 8.2

TASK: To ensure that claims are processed quickly and result in the highest allowable reimbursement.

Equipment and Supplies

- Insurance carrier contracts
- Insurance carrier handbooks
- Clerical supplies
- Forms from insurance carrier
- Insurance claim forms (CMS-1500)

Standards: Complete the procedure and all critical steps in _____ minutes with a minimum score of 85% within three attempts.

Scoring: Divide the points earned by the total possible points. Failure to perform a critical step, indicated by an asterisk (*), results in an unsatisfactory overall score.

Time began _____   **Time ended** _____   **Total minutes:** _____

Steps	Possible Points	Attempt 1	Attempt 2	Attempt 3
*1. Determine the patient's health insurance plan.	10	_____	_____	_____
2. Review the rules and regulations that govern that particular organization.	10	_____	_____	_____
*3. Make sure a signature is on file for the patient.	10	_____	_____	_____
*4. Determine the procedures and/or services to be billed on the claim.	20	_____	_____	_____
*5. Determine whether all the procedures and/or services to be billed are covered by the health insurance plan.	20	_____	_____	_____
*6. Inform the patient of any procedures and/or services that will not be covered.	10	_____	_____	_____
7. Determine whether any information needs to be added to the blocks designated "for local use."	10	_____	_____	_____
*8. Submit the claim to the correct insurance company address or clearinghouse.	10	_____	_____	_____

Comments:

Points earned _____ ÷ 100 possible points = **Score** _____ **% Score**

Instructor's signature _____

162

Name _____ Date _____ Score _____

PROCEDURE 20-3 Perform Verification of Eligibility and Benefits

MAERB/CAAHEP COMPETENCIES: IV.P.IV.3; VII.P.VII.6; IX.A.IX.2
ABHES COMPETENCIES: 4.f; 8.2

TASK: To confirm that the patient's insurance is in effect and to determine what benefits are covered and what exclusions, noncovered procedures and services, and precertifications are included or required.

Equipment and Supplies
- Patient's record
- Verification of eligibility and benefits form
- Patient's insurance information
- Telephone and fax machine
- Pen

Standards: Complete the procedure and all critical steps in _____ minutes with a minimum score of 85% within three attempts.

Scoring: Divide the points earned by the total possible points. Failure to perform a critical step, indicated by an asterisk (*), results in an unsatisfactory overall score.

Time began _____ Time ended _____ Total minutes: _____

Steps	Possible Points	Attempt 1	Attempt 2	Attempt 3
*1. Determine the patient's insurance company when he or she makes the initial call for an appointment.	15	_____	_____	_____
*2. Make a copy of the front and back of the patient's insurance card (or cards).	15	_____	_____	_____
3. Complete the patient portion of the verification of eligibility and benefit form, including demographic and insurance information for the patient, and the contact information for the insurance plan. Complete one form for each of the patient's insurance plans.	15	_____	_____	_____
*4. Contact the insurance carrier by phone to:	15	_____	_____	_____
a. Verify that the patient is eligible for benefits and the insurance is in effect.		_____	_____	_____
b. Determine the basic benefits, exclusions, or noncovered services of the insurance plan.		_____	_____	_____
c. Determine whether there are deductibles, co-payments, or any other out-of-pocket expenses the patient is responsible for paying.		_____	_____	_____
d. Determine whether preauthorization is required for referral to a specialist or for any procedures and/or services.		_____	_____	_____
5. Obtain the name, title, and phone number of the person contacted.	20	_____	_____	_____
*6. Document all verification information in the patient's medical record.	20	_____	_____	_____

163

Did the student:

	Yes	No
Demonstrate awareness of the consequences of not working within the legal scope of practice?	_____	_____

Comments:

Points earned _____ ÷ 100 possible points = Score _____ % Score

Instructor's signature _____

Name _____ Date _____ Score _____

PROCEDURE 20-4 Perform Preauthorization (Precertification) and/or Referral Procedures

MAERB/CAAHEP COMPETENCIES: IV.P.IV.3; VII.P.VII.4; VII.P.VII.5
ABHES COMPETENCIES: 8.c.2

TASK: To use the information in the case study to obtain precertification from a patient's HMO for requested services or procedures.

Equipment and Supplies
- Patient's record
- Precertification/preauthorization form
- Referral form
- Patient's insurance information, including telephone and fax numbers of the insurance carrier
- Telephone and fax machine
- Pen

Standards: Complete the procedure and all critical steps in _____ minutes with a minimum score of 85% within three attempts.

Scoring: Divide the points earned by the total possible points. Failure to perform a critical step, indicated by an asterisk (*), results in an unsatisfactory overall score.

Time began _____ Time ended _____ Total minutes: _____

Steps	Possible Points	Attempt 1	Attempt 2	Attempt 3
*1. Gather the necessary documents and forms.	15	_____	_____	_____
*2. Examine the patient's record and determine the service or procedure for which preauthorization is being requested, including, if applicable, the specialist's name and phone number and the reason for the request.	15	_____	_____	_____
*3. Complete the referral form.	25	_____	_____	_____
*4. Proofread the completed form.	15	_____	_____	_____
*5. Fax the completed form to the patient's insurance carrier.	15	_____	_____	_____
*6. Place a copy of the returned approval form in the patient's medical record.	15	_____	_____	_____

Comments:

Points earned _____ ÷ 100 possible points = Score _____ % Score

Instructor's signature _____

Procedure **20-4 Perform Preauthorization**

Name _____ Date _____ Score _____

PROCEDURE 20-5 Perform Deductible, Co-Insurance, and Allowable Amount Calculations

CAAHEP COMPETENCIES: IV.P.IV.3; VII.P.VII.2
ABHES COMPETENCIES: 8.c.2, 8.c.3

TASK: To calculate the patient's out-of-pocket expenses or the amount to be billed to a secondary insurance carrier and to determine what amounts, if any, are to be written off or passed on to the patient for payment.

Equipment and Supplies

- Explanation of benefits (EOB) form, explanation of Medicare benefits (EOMB) form, remittance advice (RA), or verification of eligibility and benefits form
- Patient accounts receivable ledger
- Calculator
- Pen
- Paper

Standards: Complete the procedure and all critical steps in _____ minutes with a minimum score of 85% within three attempts.

Scoring: Divide the points earned by the total possible points. Failure to perform a critical step, indicated by an asterisk (*), results in an unsatisfactory overall score.

Time began _____ Time ended _____ Total minutes: _____

Steps	Possible Points	Attempt 1	Attempt 2	Attempt 3
1. Assemble the required materials and equipment.	15	____	____	____
*2. Using the EOB, EOMB, and/or RA and/or the verification of eligibility and benefits form, as well as the patient accounts receivable ledger:	25			
a. Enter the total charge from the EOB and/or the patient accounts receivable ledger.		____	____	____
b. Subtract the deductible amount from the total charge.		____	____	____
*3. If the patient has met the deductible, determine the co-insurance payment due.	15	____	____	____
*4. Record the deductible and, if applicable, co-insurance amounts on separate lines in the patient balance due column of the patient ledger.	15	____	____	____
5. Subtract the allowable amount of each charge from the actual billed charge.	15	____	____	____
*6. Record the difference in either the adjustments or the balance due column.	15	____	____	____

167

Comments:

Points earned _____ ÷ **100 possible points = Score** _____ **% Score**

Instructor's signature _____

Name _____ Date _____ Score _____

PROCEDURE 21-1 Gather Data to Complete CMS-1500 Form

MAERB/CAAHEP COMPETENCIES: IV.P.IV.3; VII.P.VII.1; VII.P.VII.2; VII.P.VII.3; VII.P.VII.4; VII.P.VII.5; VII.P.VII.6; VIII.P.VIII.1; VIII.P.VIII.2
ABHES COMPETENCIES: 8.c.1, 8.c.2, 8.c.3

TASK: To gather all information and documentation required for completing an insurance claim.

Equipment and Supplies

- Patient registration form
- Photocopy of patient's insurance card or cards, driver's license or state-issued identification card, and student ID (if applicable)
- Verification of Eligibility and Benefits form
- Preauthorization and/or referral form
- Encounter form (charge ticket or superbill)
- ICD-9-CM coding manual
- CPT coding manual
- HCPCS coding manual

Standards: Complete the procedure and all critical steps in _____ minutes with a minimum score of 85% within three attempts.

Scoring: Divide the points earned by the total possible points. Failure to perform a critical step, indicated by an asterisk (*), results in an unsatisfactory overall score.

Time began _____   **Time ended** _____   **Total minutes:** _____

Steps	Possible Points	Attempt 1	Attempt 2	Attempt 3
*1. Have the patient or the patient's guardian complete the patient registration, release of information, and authorization of benefits forms in full and return them to you.	10	_____	_____	_____
*2. Ask for the patient's and the insured's driver's license and insurance card (or cards). If the patient is a student, ask for a student ID. If the patient has more than one insurance policy, get the name, address, and group and policy numbers for each company.	10	_____	_____	_____
*3. Photocopy the back and front of the patient's insurance card (or cards) and place the photocopy in the medical record and/or in the patient's insurance file.	5	_____	_____	_____
*4. Confirm the patient's and the insured's full name, address, phone number, date of birth, and gender by comparing the patient registration form with the driver's license or identification card.	5	_____	_____	_____
*5. Determine whether someone other than the patient is the guarantor.	5	_____	_____	_____
*6. Call the employer and confirm the patient's employment (optional). If the patient is insured under a group health plan, workers' compensation, TRICARE, and some other types of insurance, this information can be confirmed when eligibility and benefits are verified.	5	_____	_____	_____

Steps	Possible Points	Attempt 1	Attempt 2	Attempt 3
*7. Confirm that the patient has signed and dated the release of information form.	5	_____	_____	_____
*8. Confirm that the insured has signed the authorization of benefits form. Signatures to authorize insurance billing, supplying information to insurance companies, and acceptance of assignments of benefits (if appropriate) should be obtained from all new patients and at the beginning of each new calendar year.	10	_____	_____	_____
*9. Contact the insurance carrier and verify benefits and insurance coverage.	10	_____	_____	_____
*10. Obtain any precertification or referral authorizations required by the insurance carrier or payer.	10	_____	_____	_____
11. Code the diagnosis or diagnoses for the encounter using the ICD-9-CM coding manual.	5	_____	_____	_____
12. Select any qualifying circumstance, physical or patient status, or other modifiers as appropriate.	5	_____	_____	_____
13. Code the procedures and services provided during the encounter using the CPT and/or HCPCS coding manual.	5	_____	_____	_____
14. Select any CPT and/or HCPCS modifiers as appropriate.	5	_____	_____	_____
15. Using Table 21-1 in the textbook or a similar list of information to gather in preparation for insurance claim submission, confirm that all information needed has been obtained.	5	_____	_____	_____

Comments:

Points earned _____ ÷ 100 possible points = Score _____ % Score

Instructor's signature _____

WORK PRODUCT 21-1

Name: _____

Completing a CMS-1500 Claim Form

Corresponds to Procedure 21-2

CAAHEP COMPETENCIES: IV.P.IV.3; VII.P.VII.1; VII.P.VII.2; VII.P.VII.3; VII.P.VII.4; VII.P.VII.5; VII.P.VII.6; VIII.P.VIII.1; VIII.P.VIII.2

ABHES COMPETENCIES: 8.c.1, 8.c.2, 8.c.3

Complete Claim Form 1 using the information in Part I, question 1.

HEALTH INSURANCE CLAIM FORM

APPROVED BY NATIONAL UNIFORM CLAIM COMMITTEE (NUCC) 02/12

PICA										PICA	

1. MEDICARE (Medicare#) MEDICAID (Medicaid#) TRICARE (ID#DoD#) CHAMPVA (Member ID#) GROUP HEALTH PLAN (ID#) FECA BLK LUNG (ID#) OTHER (ID#) **1a.** INSURED'S I.D. NUMBER (For Program in Item 1)

2. PATIENT'S NAME (Last Name, First Name, Middle Initial) **3.** PATIENT'S BIRTH DATE MM DD YY SEX M F **4.** INSURED'S NAME (Last Name, First Name, Middle Initial)

5. PATIENT'S ADDRESS (No., Street) **6.** PATIENT RELATIONSHIP TO INSURED Self Spouse Child Other **7.** INSURED'S ADDRESS (No., Street)

CITY STATE **8.** RESERVED FOR NUCC USE CITY STATE

ZIP CODE TELEPHONE (Include Area Code) ( ) ZIP CODE TELEPHONE (Include Area Code) ( )

9. OTHER INSURED'S NAME (Last Name, First Name, Middle Initial) **10.** IS PATIENT'S CONDITION RELATED TO: **11.** INSURED'S POLICY GROUP OR FECA NUMBER

a. OTHER INSURED'S POLICY OR GROUP NUMBER **a.** EMPLOYMENT? (Current or Previous) YES NO **a.** INSURED'S DATE OF BIRTH MM DD YY SEX M F

b. RESERVED FOR NUCC USE **b.** AUTO ACCIDENT? PLACE (State) YES NO **b.** OTHER CLAIM ID (Designated by NUCC)

c. RESERVED FOR NUCC USE **c.** OTHER ACCIDENT? YES NO **c.** INSURANCE PLAN NAME OR PROGRAM NAME

d. INSURANCE PLAN NAME OR PROGRAM NAME **10d.** CLAIM CODES (Designated by NUCC) **d.** IS THERE ANOTHER HEALTH BENEFIT PLAN? YES NO *If yes*, complete items 9, 9a, and 9d.

READ BACK OF FORM BEFORE COMPLETING & SIGNING THIS FORM.

12. PATIENT'S OR AUTHORIZED PERSON'S SIGNATURE I authorize the release of any medical or other information necessary to process this claim. I also request payment of government benefits either to myself or to the party who accepts assignment below.

SIGNED _____ DATE _____

13. INSURED'S OR AUTHORIZED PERSON'S SIGNATURE I authorize payment of medical benefits to the undersigned physician or supplier for services described below.

SIGNED _____

14. DATE OF CURRENT ILLNESS, INJURY, or PREGNANCY(LMP) MM DD YY QUAL. **15.** OTHER DATE MM DD YY QUAL. **16.** DATES PATIENT UNABLE TO WORK IN CURRENT OCCUPATION MM DD YY FROM TO MM DD YY

17. NAME OF REFERRING PROVIDER OR OTHER SOURCE 17a. 17b. NPI **18.** HOSPITALIZATION DATES RELATED TO CURRENT SERVICES MM DD YY FROM TO MM DD YY

19. ADDITIONAL CLAIM INFORMATION (Designated by NUCC) **20.** OUTSIDE LAB? YES NO $ CHARGES

21. DIAGNOSIS OR NATURE OF ILLNESS OR INJURY Relate A-L to service line below (24E) ICD Ind. **22.** RESUBMISSION CODE ORIGINAL REF. NO.

A. ___ B. ___ C. ___ D. ___
E. ___ F. ___ G. ___ H. ___
I. ___ J. ___ K. ___ L. ___

23. PRIOR AUTHORIZATION NUMBER

24. A. DATE(S) OF SERVICE From / To MM DD YY MM DD YY	B. PLACE OF SERVICE	C. EMG	D. PROCEDURES, SERVICES, OR SUPPLIES (Explain Unusual Circumstances) CPT/HCPCS / MODIFIER	E. DIAGNOSIS POINTER	F. $ CHARGES	G. DAYS OR UNITS	H. EPSDT Family Plan	I. ID. QUAL.	J. RENDERING PROVIDER ID. #
1								NPI	
2								NPI	
3								NPI	
4								NPI	
5								NPI	
6								NPI	

25. FEDERAL TAX I.D. NUMBER SSN EIN **26.** PATIENT'S ACCOUNT NO. **27.** ACCEPT ASSIGNMENT? (For govt. claims, see back) YES NO **28.** TOTAL CHARGE $ **29.** AMOUNT PAID $ **30.** Rsvd for NUCC Use $

31. SIGNATURE OF PHYSICIAN OR SUPPLIER INCLUDING DEGREES OR CREDENTIALS (I certify that the statements on the reverse apply to this bill and are made a part thereof.)

SIGNED _____ DATE _____

32. SERVICE FACILITY LOCATION INFORMATION a. NPI b.

33. BILLING PROVIDER INFO & PH # ( ) a. NPI b.

NUCC Instruction Manual available at: www.nucc.org *PLEASE PRINT OR TYPE* APPROVED OMG-098-1197 FORM 1500 (02-12) PENDING

CARRIER

PATIENT AND INSURED INFORMATION

PHYSICIAN OR SUPPLIER INFORMATION

171

WORK PRODUCT 21-2

Name: _____

Completing a CMS-1500 Claim Form

Corresponds to Procedure 21-2

<u>CAAHEP COMPETENCIES:</u> IV.P.IV.3; VII.P.VII.1; VII.P.VII.2; VII.P.VII.3; VII.P.VII.4; VII.P.VII.5; VII.P.VII.6; VIII.P.VIII.1; VIII.P.VIII.2

<u>ABHES COMPETENCIES:</u> 8.c.1, 8.c.2, 8.c.3

Complete Claim Form 2 using the information in Part I, question 2.

HEALTH INSURANCE CLAIM FORM

APPROVED BY NATIONAL UNIFORM CLAIM COMMITTEE (NUCC) 02/12

CARRIER

PICA | | | | PICA | |

1. MEDICARE (Medicare#) MEDICAID (Medicaid#) TRICARE (ID#DoD#) CHAMPVA (Member ID#) GROUP HEALTH PLAN (ID#) FECA BLK LUNG (ID#) OTHER (ID#)
1a. INSURED'S I.D. NUMBER (For Program in Item 1)

2. PATIENT'S NAME (Last Name, First Name, Middle Initial)
3. PATIENT'S BIRTH DATE MM | DD | YY SEX M F
4. INSURED'S NAME (Last Name, First Name, Middle Initial)

5. PATIENT'S ADDRESS (No., Street)
6. PATIENT RELATIONSHIP TO INSURED Self Spouse Child Other
7. INSURED'S ADDRESS (No., Street)

CITY STATE
8. RESERVED FOR NUCC USE
CITY STATE

ZIP CODE TELEPHONE (Include Area Code) ( )
ZIP CODE TELEPHONE (Include Area Code) ( )

9. OTHER INSURED'S NAME (Last Name, First Name, Middle Initial)
10. IS PATIENT'S CONDITION RELATED TO:
11. INSURED'S POLICY GROUP OR FECA NUMBER

a. OTHER INSURED'S POLICY OR GROUP NUMBER
a. EMPLOYMENT? (Current or Previous) YES NO
a. INSURED'S DATE OF BIRTH MM | DD | YY SEX M F

b. RESERVED FOR NUCC USE
b. AUTO ACCIDENT? YES NO PLACE (State)
b. OTHER CLAIM ID (Designated by NUCC)

c. RESERVED FOR NUCC USE
c. OTHER ACCIDENT? YES NO
c. INSURANCE PLAN NAME OR PROGRAM NAME

d. INSURANCE PLAN NAME OR PROGRAM NAME
10d. CLAIM CODES (Designated by NUCC)
d. IS THERE ANOTHER HEALTH BENEFIT PLAN? YES NO *If yes,* complete items 9, 9a, and 9d.

READ BACK OF FORM BEFORE COMPLETING & SIGNING THIS FORM.
12. PATIENT'S OR AUTHORIZED PERSON'S SIGNATURE I authorize the release of any medical or other information necessary to process this claim. I also request payment of government benefits either to myself or to the party who accepts assignment below.

SIGNED _____ DATE _____

13. INSURED'S OR AUTHORIZED PERSON'S SIGNATURE I authorize payment of medical benefits to the undersigned physician or supplier for services described below.

SIGNED _____

PATIENT AND INSURED INFORMATION

14. DATE OF CURRENT ILLNESS, INJURY, or PREGNANCY(LMP) MM | DD | YY QUAL.
15. OTHER DATE QUAL. MM | DD | YY
16. DATES PATIENT UNABLE TO WORK IN CURRENT OCCUPATION FROM MM | DD | YY TO MM | DD | YY

17. NAME OF REFERRING PROVIDER OR OTHER SOURCE
17a.
17b. NPI
18. HOSPITALIZATION DATES RELATED TO CURRENT SERVICES FROM MM | DD | YY TO MM | DD | YY

19. ADDITIONAL CLAIM INFORMATION (Designated by NUCC)
20. OUTSIDE LAB? YES NO $ CHARGES

21. DIAGNOSIS OR NATURE OF ILLNESS OR INJURY Relate A-L to service line below (24E) ICD Ind.
A. B. C. D.
E. F. G. H.
I. J. K. L.
22. RESUBMISSION CODE ORIGINAL REF. NO.
23. PRIOR AUTHORIZATION NUMBER

24. A. DATE(S) OF SERVICE From MM DD YY To MM DD YY | B. PLACE OF SERVICE | C. EMG | D. PROCEDURES, SERVICES, OR SUPPLIES (Explain Unusual Circumstances) CPT/HCPCS | MODIFIER | E. DIAGNOSIS POINTER | F. $ CHARGES | G. DAYS OR UNITS | H. EPSDT Family Plan | I. ID. QUAL. | J. RENDERING PROVIDER ID. #

1 NPI

2 NPI

3 NPI

4 NPI

5 NPI

6 NPI

PHYSICIAN OR SUPPLIER INFORMATION

25. FEDERAL TAX I.D. NUMBER SSN EIN
26. PATIENT'S ACCOUNT NO.
27. ACCEPT ASSIGNMENT? (For govt. claims, see back) YES NO
28. TOTAL CHARGE $
29. AMOUNT PAID $
30. Rsvd for NUCC Use $

31. SIGNATURE OF PHYSICIAN OR SUPPLIER INCLUDING DEGREES OR CREDENTIALS (I certify that the statements on the reverse apply to this bill and are made a part thereof.) SIGNED _____ DATE _____
32. SERVICE FACILITY LOCATION INFORMATION a. **NPI** b.
33. BILLING PROVIDER INFO & PH # ( ) a. **NPI** b.

NUCC Instruction Manual available at: www.nucc.org   *PLEASE PRINT OR TYPE*   APPROVED OMG-098-1197 FORM 1500 (02-12) PENDING

173

WORK PRODUCT 21-3

Name: _____

Completing a CMS-1500 Claim Form

Corresponds to Procedure 21-2

<u>CAAHEP COMPETENCIES:</u> IV.P.IV.3; VII.P.VII.1; VII.P.VII.2; VII.P.VII.3; VII.P.VII.4; VII.P.VII.5; VII.P.VII.6; VIII.P.VIII.1; VIII.P.VIII.2

<u>ABHES COMPETENCIES:</u> 8.c.1, 8.c.2, 8.c.3

Complete Claim Form 3 using the information in Part I, question 3.

HEALTH INSURANCE CLAIM FORM
APPROVED BY NATIONAL UNIFORM CLAIM COMMITTEE (NUCC) 02/12

CARRIER

PICA		PICA

1. MEDICARE ☐ (Medicare#) MEDICAID ☐ (Medicaid#) TRICARE ☐ (ID#DoD#) CHAMPVA ☐ (Member ID#) GROUP HEALTH PLAN ☐ (ID#) FECA BLK LUNG ☐ (ID#) OTHER ☐ (ID#)   1a. INSURED'S I.D. NUMBER (For Program in Item 1)

2. PATIENT'S NAME (Last Name, First Name, Middle Initial)   3. PATIENT'S BIRTH DATE MM | DD | YY   SEX M ☐ F ☐   4. INSURED'S NAME (Last Name, First Name, Middle Initial)

5. PATIENT'S ADDRESS (No., Street)   6. PATIENT RELATIONSHIP TO INSURED Self ☐ Spouse ☐ Child ☐ Other ☐   7. INSURED'S ADDRESS (No., Street)

CITY   STATE   8. RESERVED FOR NUCC USE   CITY   STATE

ZIP CODE   TELEPHONE (Include Area Code) ( )   ZIP CODE   TELEPHONE (Include Area Code) ( )

9. OTHER INSURED'S NAME (Last Name, First Name, Middle Initial)   10. IS PATIENT'S CONDITION RELATED TO: 11. INSURED'S POLICY GROUP OR FECA NUMBER

a. OTHER INSURED'S POLICY OR GROUP NUMBER   a. EMPLOYMENT? (Current or Previous) ☐ YES ☐ NO   a. INSURED'S DATE OF BIRTH MM | DD | YY   SEX M ☐ F ☐

b. RESERVED FOR NUCC USE   b. AUTO ACCIDENT? ☐ YES ☐ NO PLACE (State)   b. OTHER CLAIM ID (Designated by NUCC)

c. RESERVED FOR NUCC USE   c. OTHER ACCIDENT? ☐ YES ☐ NO   c. INSURANCE PLAN NAME OR PROGRAM NAME

d. INSURANCE PLAN NAME OR PROGRAM NAME   10d. CLAIM CODES (Designated by NUCC)   d. IS THERE ANOTHER HEALTH BENEFIT PLAN? ☐ YES ☐ NO *If yes*, complete items 9, 9a, and 9d.

READ BACK OF FORM BEFORE COMPLETING & SIGNING THIS FORM.
12. PATIENT'S OR AUTHORIZED PERSON'S SIGNATURE I authorize the release of any medical or other information necessary to process this claim. I also request payment of government benefits either to myself or to the party who accepts assignment below.
SIGNED _____ DATE _____

13. INSURED'S OR AUTHORIZED PERSON'S SIGNATURE I authorize payment of medical benefits to the undersigned physician or supplier for services described below.
SIGNED _____

14. DATE OF CURRENT ILLNESS, INJURY, or PREGNANCY(LMP) MM | DD | YY QUAL. | 15. OTHER DATE QUAL. | MM | DD | YY   16. DATES PATIENT UNABLE TO WORK IN CURRENT OCCUPATION FROM MM | DD | YY TO MM | DD | YY

17. NAME OF REFERRING PROVIDER OR OTHER SOURCE   17a. | 17b. NPI   18. HOSPITALIZATION DATES RELATED TO CURRENT SERVICES FROM MM | DD | YY TO MM | DD | YY

19. ADDITIONAL CLAIM INFORMATION (Designated by NUCC)   20. OUTSIDE LAB? ☐ YES ☐ NO $ CHARGES

21. DIAGNOSIS OR NATURE OF ILLNESS OR INJURY Relate A-L to service line below (24E) ICD Ind. |
A. |___ B. |___ C. |___ D. |___
E. |___ F. |___ G. |___ H. |___
I. |___ J. |___ K. |___ L. |___

22. RESUBMISSION CODE | ORIGINAL REF. NO.

23. PRIOR AUTHORIZATION NUMBER

24. A. DATE(S) OF SERVICE From MM DD YY To MM DD YY	B. PLACE OF SERVICE	C. EMG	D. PROCEDURES, SERVICES, OR SUPPLIES (Explain Unusual Circumstances) CPT/HCPCS	MODIFIER	E. DIAGNOSIS POINTER	F. $ CHARGES	G. DAYS OR UNITS	H. EPSDT Family Plan	I. ID. QUAL.	J. RENDERING PROVIDER ID. #
1										NPI
2										NPI
3										NPI
4										NPI
5										NPI
6										NPI

25. FEDERAL TAX I.D. NUMBER ☐ SSN ☐ EIN   26. PATIENT'S ACCOUNT NO.   27. ACCEPT ASSIGNMENT? (For govt. claims, see back) ☐ YES ☐ NO   28. TOTAL CHARGE $ 29. AMOUNT PAID $ 30. Rsvd for NUCC Use

31. SIGNATURE OF PHYSICIAN OR SUPPLIER INCLUDING DEGREES OR CREDENTIALS (I certify that the statements on the reverse apply to this bill and are made a part thereof.)
SIGNED _____ DATE _____

32. SERVICE FACILITY LOCATION INFORMATION
a. **NPI** b.

33. BILLING PROVIDER INFO & PH # ( )
a. **NPI** b.

NUCC Instruction Manual available at: www.nucc.org   *PLEASE PRINT OR TYPE*   APPROVED OMG-098-1197 FORM 1500 (02-12) PENDING

PATIENT AND INSURED INFORMATION

PHYSICIAN OR SUPPLIER INFORMATION

175

WORK PRODUCT 21-4

Name: _____

Completing a CMS-1500 Claim Form

Corresponds to Procedure 21-2

<u>CAAHEP COMPETENCIES:</u> IV.P.IV.3; VII.P.VII.1; VII.P.VII.2; VII.P.VII.3; VII.P.VII.4; VII.P.VII.5; VII.P.VII.6; VIII.P.VIII.1; VIII.P.VIII.2

<u>ABHES COMPETENCIES:</u> 8.c.1, 8.c.2, 8.c.3

Complete Claim Form 4 using the information in Part I, question 4.

HEALTH INSURANCE CLAIM FORM

APPROVED BY NATIONAL UNIFORM CLAIM COMMITTEE (NUCC) 02/12

| PICA | | | | | | | | PICA | |

1. MEDICARE (Medicare#)   **MEDICAID** (Medicaid#)   **TRICARE** (ID#DoD#)   **CHAMPVA** (Member ID#)   **GROUP HEALTH PLAN** (ID#)   **FECA BLK LUNG** (ID#)   **OTHER** (ID#)   **1a. INSURED'S I.D. NUMBER** (For Program in Item 1)

2. PATIENT'S NAME (Last Name, First Name, Middle Initial)

3. PATIENT'S BIRTH DATE MM DD YY SEX M F

4. INSURED'S NAME (Last Name, First Name, Middle Initial)

5. PATIENT'S ADDRESS (No., Street)

6. PATIENT RELATIONSHIP TO INSURED Self Spouse Child Other

7. INSURED'S ADDRESS (No., Street)

CITY   STATE

8. RESERVED FOR NUCC USE

CITY   STATE

ZIP CODE   TELEPHONE (Include Area Code) ( )

ZIP CODE   TELEPHONE (Include Area Code) ( )

9. OTHER INSURED'S NAME (Last Name, First Name, Middle Initial)

10. IS PATIENT'S CONDITION RELATED TO:

11. INSURED'S POLICY GROUP OR FECA NUMBER

a. OTHER INSURED'S POLICY OR GROUP NUMBER

a. EMPLOYMENT? (Current or Previous) YES NO

a. INSURED'S DATE OF BIRTH MM DD YY SEX M F

b. RESERVED FOR NUCC USE

b. AUTO ACCIDENT? YES NO PLACE (State)

b. OTHER CLAIM ID (Designated by NUCC)

c. RESERVED FOR NUCC USE

c. OTHER ACCIDENT? YES NO

c. INSURANCE PLAN NAME OR PROGRAM NAME

d. INSURANCE PLAN NAME OR PROGRAM NAME

10d. CLAIM CODES (Designated by NUCC)

d. IS THERE ANOTHER HEALTH BENEFIT PLAN? YES NO *If yes*, complete items 9, 9a, and 9d.

READ BACK OF FORM BEFORE COMPLETING & SIGNING THIS FORM.

12. PATIENT'S OR AUTHORIZED PERSON'S SIGNATURE I authorize the release of any medical or other information necessary to process this claim. I also request payment of government benefits either to myself or to the party who accepts assignment below.

SIGNED _____ DATE _____

13. INSURED'S OR AUTHORIZED PERSON'S SIGNATURE I authorize payment of medical benefits to the undersigned physician or supplier for services described below.

SIGNED _____

14. DATE OF CURRENT ILLNESS, INJURY, or PREGNANCY(LMP) MM DD YY QUAL.

15. OTHER DATE QUAL. MM DD YY

16. DATES PATIENT UNABLE TO WORK IN CURRENT OCCUPATION MM DD YY FROM TO MM DD YY

17. NAME OF REFERRING PROVIDER OR OTHER SOURCE

17a.   17b. NPI

18. HOSPITALIZATION DATES RELATED TO CURRENT SERVICES MM DD YY FROM TO MM DD YY

19. ADDITIONAL CLAIM INFORMATION (Designated by NUCC)

20. OUTSIDE LAB? YES NO $ CHARGES

21. DIAGNOSIS OR NATURE OF ILLNESS OR INJURY Relate A-L to service line below (24E) ICD Ind.

A. ___ B. ___ C. ___ D. ___
E. ___ F. ___ G. ___ H. ___
I. ___ J. ___ K. ___ L. ___

22. RESUBMISSION CODE   ORIGINAL REF. NO.

23. PRIOR AUTHORIZATION NUMBER

24. A. DATE(S) OF SERVICE From MM DD YY To MM DD YY	B. PLACE OF SERVICE	C. EMG	D. PROCEDURES, SERVICES, OR SUPPLIES (Explain Unusual Circumstances) CPT/HCPCS MODIFIER	E. DIAGNOSIS POINTER	F. $ CHARGES	G. DAYS OR UNITS	H. EPSDT Family Plan	I. ID. QUAL.	J. RENDERING PROVIDER ID. #
1									NPI
2									NPI
3									NPI
4									NPI
5									NPI
6									NPI

25. FEDERAL TAX I.D. NUMBER   SSN EIN

26. PATIENT'S ACCOUNT NO.

27. ACCEPT ASSIGNMENT? (For govt. claims, see back) YES NO

28. TOTAL CHARGE $

29. AMOUNT PAID $

30. Rsvd for NUCC Use $

31. SIGNATURE OF PHYSICIAN OR SUPPLIER INCLUDING DEGREES OR CREDENTIALS (I certify that the statements on the reverse apply to this bill and are made a part thereof.)

SIGNED _____ DATE _____

32. SERVICE FACILITY LOCATION INFORMATION

a. **NPI**   b.

33. BILLING PROVIDER INFO & PH # ( )

a. **NPI**   b.

NUCC Instruction Manual available at: www.nucc.org   *PLEASE PRINT OR TYPE*   APPROVED OMG-098-1197 FORM 1500 (02-12) PENDING

CARRIER

PATIENT AND INSURED INFORMATION

PHYSICIAN OR SUPPLIER INFORMATION

177

WORK PRODUCT 21-5

Name: _____

Completing a CMS-1500 Claim Form

Corresponds to Procedure 21-2

<u>CAAHEP COMPETENCIES:</u> IV.P.IV.3; VII.P.VII.1; VII.P.VII.2; VII.P.VII.3; VII.P.VII.4; VII.P.VII.5; VII.P.VII.6; VIII.P.VIII.1; VIII.P.VIII.2

<u>ABHES COMPETENCIES:</u> 8.c.1, 8.c.2, 8.c.3

Complete Claim Form 5 using the information in Part I, question 5.

HEALTH INSURANCE CLAIM FORM
APPROVED BY NATIONAL UNIFORM CLAIM COMMITTEE (NUCC) 02/12

□□ PICA	PICA □□

1. MEDICARE MEDICAID TRICARE CHAMPVA GROUP HEALTH PLAN FECA BLK LUNG OTHER	1a. INSURED'S I.D. NUMBER (For Program in Item 1)
□ (Medicare#) □ (Medicaid#) □ (ID#DoD#) □ (Member ID#) □ (ID#) □ (ID#) □	

2. PATIENT'S NAME (Last Name, First Name, Middle Initial) | 3. PATIENT'S BIRTH DATE MM DD YY SEX M□ F□ | 4. INSURED'S NAME (Last Name, First Name, Middle Initial)

5. PATIENT'S ADDRESS (No., Street) | 6. PATIENT RELATIONSHIP TO INSURED Self□ Spouse□ Child□ Other□ | 7. INSURED'S ADDRESS (No., Street)

CITY | STATE | 8. RESERVED FOR NUCC USE | CITY | STATE

ZIP CODE | TELEPHONE (Include Area Code) ( ) | | ZIP CODE | TELEPHONE (Include Area Code) ( )

9. OTHER INSURED'S NAME (Last Name, First Name, Middle Initial) | 10. IS PATIENT'S CONDITION RELATED TO: | 11. INSURED'S POLICY GROUP OR FECA NUMBER

a. OTHER INSURED'S POLICY OR GROUP NUMBER | a. EMPLOYMENT? (Current or Previous) □ YES □ NO | a. INSURED'S DATE OF BIRTH MM DD YY SEX M□ F□

b. RESERVED FOR NUCC USE | b. AUTO ACCIDENT? PLACE (State) □ YES □ NO | b. OTHER CLAIM ID (Designated by NUCC)

c. RESERVED FOR NUCC USE | c. OTHER ACCIDENT? □ YES □ NO | c. INSURANCE PLAN NAME OR PROGRAM NAME

d. INSURANCE PLAN NAME OR PROGRAM NAME | 10d. CLAIM CODES (Designated by NUCC) | d. IS THERE ANOTHER HEALTH BENEFIT PLAN? □ YES □ NO *If yes,* complete items 9, 9a, and 9d.

READ BACK OF FORM BEFORE COMPLETING & SIGNING THIS FORM.
12. PATIENT'S OR AUTHORIZED PERSON'S SIGNATURE I authorize the release of any medical or other information necessary to process this claim. I also request payment of government benefits either to myself or to the party who accepts assignment below.

SIGNED _____ DATE _____

13. INSURED'S OR AUTHORIZED PERSON'S SIGNATURE I authorize payment of medical benefits to the undersigned physician or supplier for services described below.

SIGNED _____

14. DATE OF CURRENT ILLNESS, INJURY, or PREGNANCY(LMP) MM DD YY QUAL. | 15. OTHER DATE QUAL. MM DD YY | 16. DATES PATIENT UNABLE TO WORK IN CURRENT OCCUPATION FROM MM DD YY TO MM DD YY

17. NAME OF REFERRING PROVIDER OR OTHER SOURCE | 17a. 17b. NPI | 18. HOSPITALIZATION DATES RELATED TO CURRENT SERVICES FROM MM DD YY TO MM DD YY

19. ADDITIONAL CLAIM INFORMATION (Designated by NUCC) | 20. OUTSIDE LAB? □ YES □ NO $ CHARGES

21. DIAGNOSIS OR NATURE OF ILLNESS OR INJURY Relate A-L to service line below (24E) ICD Ind. | 22. RESUBMISSION CODE ORIGINAL REF. NO.

A. |___| B. |___| C. |___| D. |___|
E. |___| F. |___| G. |___| H. |___|
I. |___| J. |___| K. |___| L. |___|

23. PRIOR AUTHORIZATION NUMBER

24. A. DATE(S) OF SERVICE From To MM DD YY MM DD YY	B. PLACE OF SERVICE	C. EMG	D. PROCEDURES, SERVICES, OR SUPPLIES (Explain Unusual Circumstances) CPT/HCPCS MODIFIER	E. DIAGNOSIS POINTER	F. $ CHARGES	G. DAYS OR UNITS	H. EPSDT Family Plan	I. ID. QUAL.	J. RENDERING PROVIDER ID. #
1									NPI
2									NPI
3									NPI
4									NPI
5									NPI
6									NPI

25. FEDERAL TAX I.D. NUMBER SSN□ EIN□ | 26. PATIENT'S ACCOUNT NO. | 27. ACCEPT ASSIGNMENT? (For govt. claims, see back) □ YES □ NO | 28. TOTAL CHARGE $ | 29. AMOUNT PAID $ | 30. Rsvd for NUCC Use $

31. SIGNATURE OF PHYSICIAN OR SUPPLIER INCLUDING DEGREES OR CREDENTIALS (I certify that the statements on the reverse apply to this bill and are made a part thereof.)

SIGNED _____ DATE _____

32. SERVICE FACILITY LOCATION INFORMATION a. **NPI** b.

33. BILLING PROVIDER INFO & PH # ( ) a. **NPI** b.

NUCC Instruction Manual available at: www.nucc.org | *PLEASE PRINT OR TYPE* | APPROVED OMG-098-1197 FORM 1500 (02-12) PENDING

CARRIER — PATIENT AND INSURED INFORMATION — PHYSICIAN OR SUPPLIER INFORMATION

179

Name _____ Date _____ Score _____

PROCEDURE 22-1 Use Computerized Office Billing Systems

CAAHEP COMPETENCIES: VI.P.VI.3
ABHES COMPETENCIES: 8.b

TASK: To use the computer in such a way that office billing functions are done efficiently, accurately, and in a timely manner.

Equipment and Supplies
- Computer with billing software installed
- Physician's fee schedule
- Encounter forms
- Calculator

Standards: Complete the procedure and all critical steps in _____ minutes with a minimum score of 85% within three attempts.

Scoring: Divide the points earned by the total possible points. Failure to perform a critical step, indicated by an asterisk (*), results in an unsatisfactory overall score.

Time began _____ **Time ended** _____ **Total minutes:** _____

Steps	Possible Points	Attempt 1	Attempt 2	Attempt 3
1. Open the billing program software.	10	_____	_____	_____
*2. Generate an aging report to determine which patients need to be billed in the billing cycle.	20	_____	_____	_____
3. Review the accounts to determine whether any should be referred to a collection agency.	20	_____	_____	_____
*4. Run the software to print billing statements.	20	_____	_____	_____
*5. Determine whether any of the accounts need special handling.	10	_____	_____	_____
*6. Prepare the statements for mailing according to the billing cycle.	10	_____	_____	_____
*7. Determine the postage rate and mail the statements.	10	_____	_____	_____

Comments:

Points earned _____ ÷ 100 possible points = Score _____ % Score

Instructor's signature _____

Name _____ Date _____ Score _____

PROCEDURE 22-2 Post Entries on a Day Sheet

CAAHEP COMPETENCIES: VI.P.VI.2.a
ABHES COMPETENCIES: 8.b.1

TASK: To post 1 day's charges and payments and compute the daily bookkeeping cycle using a pegboard.

Equipment and Supplies
- Pegboard
- Calculator
- Pen
- Day sheet
- Receipts
- Ledger cards
- Balances from previous day

Standards: Complete the procedure and all critical steps in _____ minutes with a minimum score of 85% within three attempts.

Scoring: Divide the points earned by the total possible points. Failure to perform a critical step, indicated by an asterisk (*), results in an unsatisfactory overall score.

Time began _____   Time ended _____   Total minutes: _____

Steps	Possible Points	Attempt 1	Attempt 2	Attempt 3
1. Prepare the board:	5			
a. Place a new day sheet on the board.		_____	_____	_____
b. Place receipts over the pegs, aligning the top receipt with the first open line on the day sheet. If you are using a computer, open the accounting program.		_____	_____	_____
*2. Carry forward the balances from the previous day.	5	_____	_____	_____
3. Pull the ledger cards for the patients being seen that day.	5	_____	_____	_____
*4. Insert the ledger card under the first receipt, aligning the first available writing line with the carbonized strip on the receipt.	5	_____	_____	_____
*5. Enter the patient's name, the date, the receipt number, and any existing balance from the ledger card.	5	_____	_____	_____
*6. Detach the charge slip from the receipt and clip it to the patient's medical record.	5	_____	_____	_____
*7. Accept the returned charge slip at the end of the visit.	5	_____	_____	_____
*8. Line up the receipt with the ledger card and day sheet.	5	_____	_____	_____
*9. Write the service code number and fee on the receipt or, with a computer system, enter the fees in the appropriate field.	5	_____	_____	_____
*10. Accept the patient's payment and record the amount of the payment and the new balance.	5	_____	_____	_____

183

Steps	Possible Points	Attempt 1	Attempt 2	Attempt 3
*11. Give the completed receipt to the patient or, with a computer system, print a receipt.	5	_____	_____	_____
*12. Repeat steps 4 through 11 for each transaction of the day.	25	_____	_____	_____
*13. Total all columns of the day sheet at the end of the day.	5	_____	_____	_____
*14. Write preliminary totals in pencil where indicated at the bottom of the day sheet or, with a computer system, print an end of day summary.	5	_____	_____	_____
*15. Complete the proof of totals and enter the totals in ink.	5	_____	_____	_____
*16. Enter the figures for accounts receivable control.	5	_____	_____	_____

Comments:

Points earned _____ ÷ 100 possible points = Score _____ % Score

Instructor's signature _____

Name _____ Date _____ Score _____

PROCEDURE 22-3 Post Adjustments

CAAHEP COMPETENCIES: VI.P.VI.2.d
ABHES COMPETENCIES: 8.b.2

TASK: To process adjustments to patients' accounts accurately.

Equipment and Supplies
- Patient ledgers
- Office policy and procedures manual
- Explanation of benefits (EOB) or remittance advice (RA)
- Bookkeeping system
- Clerical supplies
- Payments
- Calculator

Standards: Complete the procedure and all critical steps in _____ minutes with a minimum score of 85% within three attempts.

Scoring: Divide the points earned by the total possible points. Failure to perform a critical step, indicated by an asterisk (*), results in an unsatisfactory overall score.

Time began _____   Time ended _____   Total minutes: _____

Steps	Possible Points	Attempt 1	Attempt 2	Attempt 3
1. Open the mail and set the payments aside with their corresponding EOB/RA.	10	_____	_____	_____
*2. Paper-clip the EOB/RA to the check that arrived with it as payment.	10	_____	_____	_____
*3. Post the payment to the patient's account.	10	_____	_____	_____
*4. Determine whether an adjustment is necessary on the account.	10	_____	_____	_____
*5. Review the current procedure to follow in adjusting the account.	10	_____	_____	_____
*6. If a manual system is used, make sure the ledger card is aligned properly with the day sheet.	10	_____	_____	_____
*7. Post the adjustment in the adjustment column or other specified place on the day sheet or in the computer application.	20	_____	_____	_____
*8. Check the math calculations to make sure the adjustment was figured correctly.	10	_____	_____	_____
*9. Determine the current balance on the patient's account.	10	_____	_____	_____

Comments:

Points earned _____ ÷ 100 possible points = Score _____ % Score

Instructor's signature _____

Procedure **22-3 Post Adjustments**

PROCEDURE 22-4 Process a Credit Balance

CAAHEP COMPETENCIES: VI.P.VI.2.e
ABHES COMPETENCIES: 8.b.3

TASK: To return overpayments to patients in a timely manner.

Equipment and Supplies
- Patient ledgers
- Office policy and procedures manual
- Explanation of benefits (EOB) or remittance advice (RA)
- Bookkeeping system
- Clerical supplies
- Payments
- Calculator

Standards: Complete the procedure and all critical steps in _____ minutes with a minimum score of 85% within three attempts.

Scoring: Divide the points earned by the total possible points. Failure to perform a critical step, indicated by an asterisk (*), results in an unsatisfactory overall score.

Time began _____   **Time ended** _____   **Total minutes:** _____

Steps	Possible Points	Attempt 1	Attempt 2	Attempt 3
1. Review the office policy and procedures manual to determine the correct procedure for refunding a credit balance.	10	_____	_____	_____
*2. Evaluate the payment received and the EOB/RA.	20	_____	_____	_____
*3. Post the payment to the patient's account.	20	_____	_____	_____
*4. Determine whether an overpayment has been made.	10	_____	_____	_____
*5. Review the account to determine whether more insurance payments are expected on the account.	20	_____	_____	_____
*6. Adjust the credit balance off of the patient's account.	20	_____	_____	_____

Comments:

Points earned _____ ÷ 100 possible points = Score _____ % Score

Instructor's signature _____

Procedure **22-4 Process a Credit Balance**

Name _____ Date _____ Score _____

PROCEDURE 22-5 Process Refunds

CAAHEP COMPETENCIES: VI.P.VI.2.f
ABHES COMPETENCIES: 8.b.3

TASK: To return patient refunds in a timely manner.

Equipment and Supplies
- Patient ledgers
- Office policy and procedures manual
- Explanation of benefits (EOB) or remittance advice (RA)
- Bookkeeping system
- Clerical supplies
- Payments
- Calculator

Standards: Complete the procedure and all critical steps in _____ minutes with a minimum score of 85% within three attempts.

Scoring: Divide the points earned by the total possible points. Failure to perform a critical step, indicated by an asterisk (*), results in an unsatisfactory overall score.

Time began _____ **Time ended** _____ **Total minutes:** _____

Steps	Possible Points	Attempt 1	Attempt 2	Attempt 3
*1. Determine the amount of the refund to be processed.	20	_____	_____	_____
*2. Write a check for the amount of the refund.	20	_____	_____	_____
3. Present the check to the physician for a signature.	10	_____	_____	_____
*4. Determine the patient's correct mailing address.	20	_____	_____	_____
*5. Make a copy of the refund check and put it in the patient's medical record.	20	_____	_____	_____
*6. Mail the refund to the patient.	10	_____	_____	_____

Comments:

Points earned _____ ÷ 100 possible points = Score _____ % Score

Instructor's signature _____

Name _____ Date _____ Score _____

PROCEDURE 22-6 Post Nonsufficient Funds Checks

CAAHEP COMPETENCIES: VI.P.VI.2.g
ABHES COMPETENCIES: 8.b.3

TASK: To correctly note that a patient's check was returned because of insufficient funds.

Equipment and Supplies
- Patient ledgers
- Office policy and procedures manual
- Bookkeeping system
- Clerical supplies
- Calculator

Standards: Complete the procedure and all critical steps in _____ minutes with a minimum score of 85% within three attempts.

Scoring: Divide the points earned by the total possible points. Failure to perform a critical step, indicated by an asterisk (*), results in an unsatisfactory overall score.

Time began _____ **Time ended** _____ **Total minutes:** _____

Steps	Possible Points	Attempt 1	Attempt 2	Attempt 3
1. Pull the ledger card for the patient who wrote the check.	10	_____	_____	_____
*2. Determine the amount to be added back to the ledger card as a result of the returned check (usually the amount of the check plus the office returned check fee).	20	_____	_____	_____
*3. Post that amount to the patient's ledger card.	20	_____	_____	_____
*4. Send a certified letter to the patient requiring timely payment of the check and any fees assessed to the patient's account for processing.	20	_____	_____	_____
*5. Note this collection activity in the patient's financial records.	20	_____	_____	_____
*6. When the patient pays the check and fees, process it as a regular payment and return the check to the patient.	10	_____	_____	_____

Comments:

Points earned _____ ÷ 100 possible points = Score _____ % Score

Instructor's signature _____

Procedure **22-6 Post Nonsufficient Funds Checks**

Name _____ Date _____ Score _____

PROCEDURE 22-7 Explain Professional Fees and Make Credit Arrangements with a Patient

CAAHEP COMPETENCIES: VI.C.VI.12
ABHES COMPETENCIES: 8.f, 11.b

TASK: To assist the patient in paying for services by making mutually beneficial credit arrangements according to established office policy.

Equipment and Supplies
- Patient ledger
- Calendar
- Truth in lending form
- Credit application
- Assignment of benefits form
- Private area for interview

Standards: Complete the procedure and all critical steps in minutes with a minimum score of 85% within three attempts.

Scoring: Divide the points earned by the total possible points. Failure to perform a critical step, indicated by an asterisk (*), results in an unsatisfactory overall score.

Time began _____   Time ended _____   Total minutes: _____

Steps	Possible Points	Attempt 1	Attempt 2	Attempt 3
1. Answer all the patient's questions about credit thoroughly and kindly.	10	____	____	____
*2. Inform the patient of the office policy regarding credit:	20			
a. Payment at the time of the first visit		____	____	____
b. Payment by bank card		____	____	____
c. Credit application		____	____	____
3. Have the patient complete a credit application.	10	____	____	____
*4. Check the credit application.	10	____	____	____
*5. Discuss with the patient the arrangements that are possible and allow the patient to decide which arrangement is most suitable.	10	____	____	____
*6. Prepare the truth in lending form and have the patient sign it if the agreement requires more than four installments.	10	____	____	____
*7. Have the patient execute an assignment of insurance benefits.	10	____	____	____
*8. Make a copy of the patient's insurance ID and have the patient sign an assignment of benefits and release of information form, if necessary.	10	____	____	____
*9. Keep the patient's credit information confidential.	10	____	____	____

193

Comments:

Points earned _____ ÷ 100 possible points = **Score** _____ **% Score**

Instructor's signature _____

PROCEDURE 22-8 Perform Billing Procedures

CAAHEP COMPETENCIES: VI.P.VI.2.b
ABHES COMPETENCIES: 8.b

TASK: To bill insurance companies for patient procedures and services and to obtain the maximum legal reimbursement.

Equipment and Supplies
- Patient ledgers
- Accounting system
- Calculator
- Claim forms
- Encounter forms
- Clerical supplies

Standards: Complete the procedure and all critical steps in _____ minutes with a minimum score of 85% within three attempts.

Scoring: Divide the points earned by the total possible points. Failure to perform a critical step, indicated by an asterisk (*), results in an unsatisfactory overall score.

Time began _____   **Time ended** _____   **Total minutes:** _____

Steps	Possible Points	Attempt 1	Attempt 2	Attempt 3
*1. Determine the procedures and/or services to be billed by reading the patient's medical record.	20	____	____	____
*2. Determine the diagnosis code or codes applicable to the claim.	10	____	____	____
*3. Determine the procedure code or codes applicable to the claim.	10	____	____	____
*4. Complete the CMS-1500 claim form, following the directions provided for each block.	20	____	____	____
5. Insert the correct amount of money to bill in the appropriate block on the claim form.	10	____	____	____
6. Address the claim to the carrier's correct address for claim submissions.	10	____	____	____
7. Mail the claim form.	10	____	____	____
8. Follow up on the claim to ensure timely payment.	10	____	____	____

Comments:

Points earned _____ ÷ 100 possible points = Score _____ % Score

Instructor's signature _____

Procedure **22-8 Perform Billing Procedures**

Name _____ Date _____ Score _____

PROCEDURE 22-9 Perform Collection Procedures

CAAHEP COMPETENCIES: VI.P.VI.2.c
ABHES COMPETENCIES: 8.b, 8.f

TASK: To collect the maximum amount of funds on each account.

Equipment and Supplies

- Patient ledger
- Office policy and procedures manual
- Clerical supplies
- Scripts for telephone collections
- Letters for collection efforts
- Telephone
- Letterhead and envelopes
- Copies of claim forms previously filed

Standards: Complete the procedure and all critical steps in _____ minutes with a minimum score of 85% within three attempts.

Scoring: Divide the points earned by the total possible points. Failure to perform a critical step, indicated by an asterisk (*), results in an unsatisfactory overall score.

Time began _____ Time ended _____ Total minutes: _____

Steps	Possible Points	Attempt 1	Attempt 2	Attempt 3
1. Review the office policy for collection procedures.	10	_____	_____	_____
*2. Evaluate the patient's ledger to determine whether it needs collection activity.	10	_____	_____	_____
*3. Determine the appropriate collection activity for the account.	10	_____	_____	_____
*4. Telephone the patient or guarantor to initiate payment on the account.	10	_____	_____	_____
*5. If the patient or guarantor cannot be reached by phone, send a postcard or collection letter.	10	_____	_____	_____
*6. Send a more demanding collection letter if past efforts by phone or letter have not produced results.	10	_____	_____	_____
*7. Once all collection efforts have failed, present the account to the physician for a decision on further disposition.	10	_____	_____	_____
*8. With the physician's approval, send the account to a collection agency.	10	_____	_____	_____
*9. If further payments arrive on the account, send them directly to the collection agency.	10	_____	_____	_____
*10. Document the final collection activity in the patient's medical record.	10	_____	_____	_____

Comments:

Points earned _____ ÷ 100 possible points = Score _____ % Score

Instructor's signature _____

PROCEDURE 22-10 Post Collection Agency Payments

CAAHEP COMPETENCIES: VI.P.VI.2.h
ABHES COMPETENCIES: 8.b

TASK: To post payments received on an account after it has been turned over to a collection agency.

Equipment and Supplies
- Patient ledger
- Office policy and procedures manual
- Bookkeeping system
- Clerical supplies
- Calculator

Standards: Complete the procedure and all critical steps in _____ minutes with a minimum score of 85% within three attempts.

Scoring: Divide the points earned by the total possible points. Failure to perform a critical step, indicated by an asterisk (*), results in an unsatisfactory overall score.

Time began _____ **Time ended** _____ **Total minutes:** _____

Steps	Possible Points	Attempt 1	Attempt 2	Attempt 3
*1. Determine that a payment received is for an account that is currently being serviced by a collection agency.	25	_____	_____	_____
*2. Notify the collection agency that a payment has been made on the account. Mail the payment to the collection agency.	25	_____	_____	_____
3. Notify the patient that the payment has been forwarded to the collection agency.	25	_____	_____	_____
*4. Instruct the patient to send any future payments to the collection agency.	25	_____	_____	_____

Comments:

Points earned _____ ÷ 100 possible points = Score _____ % Score

Instructor's signature _____

Procedure **22-10 Post Collection Agency Payments**

WORK PRODUCT 22-1

Name: _____

Perform Billing Procedures

Corresponds to Procedure 22-8

<u>CAAHEP COMPETENCIES:</u> VI.P.VI.2.b

<u>ABHES COMPETENCIES:</u> 8.a

Complete the billing form below using the information in Part I, question 2.

Blackburn Primary Care Associates, PC
1990 Turquoise Drive
Blackburn, WI 54937
(608) 459-8857

Howard M. Lawler, MD   11
Joanne R. Hughes, MD   21
Ralph Garcia Lopez, MD   31
TAX ID NO. 00-00000000

GUARANTOR NAME AND ADDRESS	PATIENT NO.	PATIENT NAME	DOCTOR NO.	DATE
	DATE OF BIRTH / TELEPHONE NO.	INSURANCE — CODE / DESCRIPTION	CERTIFICATE NO.	

OFFICE - NEW

X	CPT	SERVICE	FEE
	99201	Prob Foc/Straight	
	99202	Exp Prob/Straight	
	99203	Detailed/Low	
	99204	Compre/Moderate	
	99205	Compre/High	

OFFICE - ESTABLISHED

X	CPT	SERVICE	FEE
	99211	Nurse/Minimal	
	99212	Prob Foc/Straight	
	99213	Exp Prob/Low	
	99214	Detailed/Moderate	
	99215	Compre/High	

OFFICE - CONSULT

X	CPT	SERVICE	FEE
	99241	Prob/Foc/Straight	
	99242	Exp Prob/Straight	
	99243	Detailed/Low	
	99244	Compre/Moderate	
	99245	Compre/High	

PREVENTIVE CARE - ADULT

X	CPT	SERVICE	FEE
	99385	18-39 Initial	
	99386	40-64 Initial	
	99387	65+ Initial	
	99395	18-39 Periodic	
	99396	40-64 Periodic	
	99397	65+ Periodic	

GASTROENEROLOGY

X	CPT	SERVICE	FEE
	45300	Sigmoidoscopy Rig	
	45305	Sigmoid Rig w/bx	
	45330	Sigmoidoscopy Flex	
	45331	Sigmoid Flex w/bx	
	45378	Colonoscopy Diag	
	45380	Colonoscopy w/bx	
	46600	Anoscopy	

CARDIOLOGY & HEARING

X	CPT	SERVICE	FEE
	93000	EKG (Global)	
	93015	Stress Test (Global)	
	93224	Holter (Global)	
	93225	Holter Hook Up	
	93227	Holter Interpretation	
	94010	Pulm Function Test	
	92551	Audiometry Screen	

INJECTIONS & IMMUNIZATION

X	CPT	SERVICE	FEE
	86585	TB Skin Test	
	90716	Varicella Vaccine	
	90724	Flu Vaccine	
	90732	Pneumovax	
	90718	TD Immunization	
	90782	Injection IM*	
	90788	Injection IM Antibiot*	
		Injection joint*	

SM   MED   MAJOR
(circle one)

FOR ALL INJECTIONS, SUPPLY DRUG INFORMATION

REPAIR & DERMATOLOGY

X	CPT	SERVICE	FEE
	17110	Warts: #	
		Tags: #	
		Lesion Excis	
		Lesion Destruct	

SIZE CM: SITE:
MALIG: PREMAL/BEN:
(Check One Above)

Simple Closure
Intermed Closure

SIZE CM: SITE:

| | 10060 | I&D Abscess | |
| | 10080 | I&D Cyst | |

OTHER

SUPPLIES/DRUGS*

DRUG NAME:
UNIT/MEASURE:
QUANTITY

DIAGNOSTIC CODES: ICD-9-CM

☐ 789.0 Abdominal Pain	☐ 782.3 Edema	☐ 614.9 Pelvic Inflammatory Disease	☐ 474.0 Tonsillitis, Chronic
☐ 795.0 Abnormal Pap Smear	☐ 492.8 Emphysema	☐ 685.1 Pilonidal Cyst	☐ 465.9 Upper Respiratory Infection, Acute
☐ 706.1 Acne Vulgaris	☐ V16.0 Family History Of Diabetes	☐ 462 Pharyngitis, Acute	☐ 599.0 Urinary Tract Infection
☐ 477.0 Allergic Rhinitis	☐ 780.6 Fever of Undetermined Origin	☐ 627.1 Postmenopausal Bleeding	☐ V03.9 Vaccination/Bacterial Dis.
☐ 285.9 Anemia, NOS	☐ 578.9 G.I. Bleeding, Unspecified	☐ 625.4 Premenstrual Tension	☐ V06.8 Vaccination/Combination
☐ 281.0 Pernicious	☐ 727.41 Ganglion of Joint	☐ 782.1 Rash	☐ V04.8 Vaccination, Influenza
☐ 411.1 Angina, Unstable	☐ 535.0 Gastritis, Acute	☐ 569.3 Rectal Bleeding	☐ 616.10 Vaginitis, Vulvitis, NOS
☐ 427.9 Arythmia, NOS	☐ V72.3 Arythmia, NOS	☐ 398.90 Rheumatic Heart Disease, NOS	☐ 780.4 Vertigo
☐ 440.9 Arteriosclerosis	☐ 748.0 Headache	☐ 431.9 Sinusitis, Acute, NOS	☐ 787.0 Vomiting, Nausea
☐ 714.0 Arthritis, Rheumatoid	☐ 550.90 Hernia, Inguinal, NOS	☐ 782.1 Skin Eruption, Rash	☐ _____
☐ 414.0 ASHD	☐ 054.9 Herpes Simplex	☐ 845.00 Sprain, Acute	☐ _____
☐ 493.90 Asthma, Bronchial W/O Status Ast.	☐ 053.9 Herpes Zoster	☐ 848.9 Sprain, Muscle, Unspec. Site	☐ _____
☐ 493.91 Asthma, Bronchial W/Status Ast.	☐ 708.9 Hives/Urticaria	☐ 785.6 Swollen Glands	☐ _____
☐ 466.1 Bronchiolitis, Acute	☐ 401.1 Hypertension, Benign	☐ 246.9 Thyroid Disease, Unspecified	☐ _____
☐ 466.0 Bronchitis, Acute	☐ 401.0 Hypertension, Malignant	☐ 463 Tonsillitis, Acute	
☐ 727.3 Bursitis	☐ 402.90 Hypertension, W/O CHF		
☐ 786.50 Chest Pain	☐ 244.9 Hypothyroidism, Primary		
☐ 574.20 Cholelithiasis	☐ 380.4 Impacted Cerumen		
☐ 372.30 Conjunctivitis, Unspecified	☐ 487.1 Influenza		
☐ 564.0 Constipation	☐ 564.1 Irritable Bowel Syndrome		
☐ 496 COPD	☐ 464.0 Laryngitis, Acute		
☐ 692.9 Dermatitis, Allergic	☐ 454.9 Leg Varicose Veins		
☐ 250.01 Diabetes Mellitus, ID	☐ 424.0 Mitral Valve Prolapse		
☐ 250.00 Diabetes Mellitus, NID	☐ 412 Myocardial Infarction, Old		
☐ 558.9 Diarrhea	☐ 715.90 Osteoarthritis, Unspec. Site		
☐ 562.11 Diverticulitis	☐ 620.2 Ovarian Cyst		
☐ 562.10 Diverticulosis			

RETURN APPOINTMENT

_____ Days
_____ Weeks
_____ Months

Authorization Number:
▶ _____

BALANCE DUE

DATE OF SERVICE	CPT CODE	DIAGNOSIS CODE(S)	CHARGE

Place of Service:
( ) Office
( ) Emergency Room
( ) Inpatient Hospital
( ) Outpatient Hospital
( ) Nursing Home

TOTAL CHARGE	$
AMOUNT PAID	$
PREVIOUS BAL	$
BALANCE DUE	$

Check #: _____

(Circle Method of Payment)
CASH   CHECK   MC   VISA

Physician's Signature
▶ _____

201

WORK PRODUCT 22-2

Name: _____

Perform Billing Procedures

Corresponds to Procedure 22-8

<u>CAAHEP COMPETENCIES:</u> VI.P.VI.2.b

<u>ABHES COMPETENCIES:</u> 8.a

Complete the billing form below using the information in Part I, question 3.

Blackburn Primary Care Associates, PC
1990 Turquoise Drive
Blackburn, WI 54937
(608) 459-8857

Howard M. Lawler, MD   11
Joanne R. Hughes, MD   21
Ralph Garcia Lopez, MD 31
TAX ID NO. 00-00000000

GUARANTOR NAME AND ADDRESS	PATIENT NO.	PATIENT NAME	DOCTOR NO.	DATE

	DATE OF BIRTH	TELEPHONE NO.	INSURANCE		
			CODE	DESCRIPTION	CERTIFICATE NO.

OFFICE - NEW

X	CPT	SERVICE	FEE
	99201	Prob Foc/Straight	
	99202	Exp Prob/Straight	
	99203	Detailed/Low	
	99204	Compre/Moderate	
	99205	Compre/High	

OFFICE - ESTABLISHED

X	CPT	SERVICE	FEE
	99211	Nurse/Minimal	
	99212	Prob Foc/Straight	
	99213	Exp Prob/Low	
	99214	Detailed/Moderate	
	99215	Compre/High	

OFFICE - CONSULT

X	CPT	SERVICE	FEE
	99241	Prob Foc/Straight	
	99242	Exp Prob/Straight	
	99243	Detailed/Low	
	99244	Compre/Moderate	
	99245	Compre/High	

PREVENTIVE CARE - ADULT

X	CPT	SERVICE	FEE
	99385	18-39 Initial	
	99386	40-64 Initial	
	99387	65+ Initial	
	99395	18-39 Periodic	
	99396	40-64 Periodic	
	99397	65+ Periodic	

GASTROENEROLOGY

X	CPT	SERVICE	FEE
	45300	Sigmoidoscopy Rig	
	45305	Sigmoid Rig w/bx	
	45330	Sigmoidoscopy Flex	
	45331	Sigmoid Flex w/bx	
	45378	Colonoscopy Diag	
	45380	Colonoscopy w/bx	
	46600	Anoscopy	

CARDIOLOGY & HEARING

X	CPT	SERVICE	FEE
	93000	EKG (Global)	
	93015	Stress Test (Global)	
	93224	Holter (Global)	
	93225	Holter Hook Up	
	93227	Holter Interpretation	
	94010	Pulm Function Test	
	92551	Audiometry Screen	

INJECTIONS & IMMUNIZATION

X	CPT	SERVICE	FEE
	86585	TB Skin Test	
	90716	Varicella Vaccine	
	90724	Flu Vaccine	
	90732	Pneumovax	
	90718	TD Immunization	
	90782	Injection IM*	
	90788	Injection IM Antibiot*	
		Injection joint*	

REPAIR & DERMATOLOGY

X	CPT	SERVICE	FEE
	17110	Warts: #	
		Tags: #	
		Lesion Excis	
		Lesion Destruct	

SIZE CM: SITE:
MALIG: PREMAL/BEN:
(Check One Above)
Simple Closure
Intermed Closure
SIZE CM: SITE:

OTHER

SUPPLIES/DRUGS*

DRUG NAME:
UNIT/MEASURE:
QUANTITY

SM   MED   MAJOR
(circle one)
FOR ALL INJECTIONS, SUPPLY DRUG
INFORMATION

	10060	I&D Abscess	
	10080	I&D Cyst	

DIAGNOSTIC CODES: ICD-9-CM

☐ 789.0 Abdominal Pain	☐ 782.3 Edema	☐ 614.9 Pelvic Inflammatory Disease	☐ 474.0 Tonsillitis, Chronic
☐ 795.0 Abnormal Pap Smear	☐ 492.8 Emphysema	☐ 685.1 Pilonidal Cyst	☐ 465.9 Upper Respiratory Infection, Acute
☐ 706.1 Acne Vulgaris	☐ V16.0 Family History Of Diabetes	☐ 462 Pharyngitis, Acute	☐ 599.0 Urinary Tract Infection
☐ 477.0 Allergic Rhinitis	☐ 780.6 Fever of Undetermined Origin	☐ 627.1 Postmenopausal Bleeding	☐ V03.9 Vaccination/Bacterial Dis.
☐ 285.9 Anemia, NOS	☐ 578.9 G.I. Bleeding, Unspecified	☐ 625.4 Premenstrual Tension	☐ V06.8 Vaccination/Combination
☐ 281.0 Pernicious	☐ 727.41 Ganglion of Joint	☐ 782.1 Rash	☐ V04.8 Vaccination, Influenza
☐ 411.1 Angina, Unstable	☐ 535.0 Gastritis, Acute	☐ 569.3 Rectal Bleeding	☐ 616.10 Vaginitis, Vulvitis, NOS
☐ 427.9 Arythmia, NOS	☐ V72.3 Arythmia, NOS	☐ 398.90 Rheumatic Heart Disease, NOS	☐ 780.4 Vertigo
☐ 440.9 Arteriosclerosis	☐ 748.0 Headache	☐ 431.9 Sinusitis, Acute, NOS	☐ 787.0 Vomiting, Nausea
☐ 714.0 Arthritis, Rheumatoid	☐ 550.90 Hernia, Inguinal, NOS	☐ 782.1 Skin Eruption, Rash	☐ _____
☐ 414.0 ASHD	☐ 054.9 Herpes Simplex	☐ 845.00 Sprain, Ankle	☐ _____
☐ 493.90 Asthma, Bronchial W/O Status Ast.	☐ 053.9 Herpes Zoster	☐ 848.9 Sprain, Muscle, Unspec. Site	☐ _____
☐ 493.91 Asthma, Bronchial W/Status Ast.	☐ 708.9 Hives/Urticaria	☐ 785.6 Swollen Glands	☐ _____
☐ 466.1 Bronchiolitis, Acute	☐ 401.1 Hypertension, Benign	☐ 246.9 Thyroid Disease, Unspecified	
☐ 466.0 Bronchitis, Acute	☐ 401.0 Hypertension, Malignant	☐ 463 Tonsillitis, Acute	
☐ 727.3 Bursitis	☐ 402.90 Hypertension, W/O CHF		
☐ 786.50 Chest Pain	☐ 244.9 Hypothyroidism, Primary		
☐ 574.20 Cholelithiasis	☐ 380.4 Impacted Cerumen		
☐ 372.30 Conjunctivitis, Unspecified	☐ 487.1 Influenza		
☐ 564.0 Constipation	☐ 564.1 Irritable Bowel Syndrome		
☐ 496 COPD	☐ 464.0 Laryngitis, Acute		
☐ 692.9 Dermatitis, Allergic	☐ 454.9 Leg Varicose Veins		
☐ 250.01 Diabetes Mellitus, ID	☐ 424.0 Mitral Valve Prolapse		
☐ 250.00 Diabetes Mellitus, NID	☐ 412 Myocardial Infarction, Old		
☐ 558.9 Diarrhea	☐ 715.90 Osteoarthritis, Unspec. Site		
☐ 562.11 Diverticulitis	☐ 620.2 Ovarian Cyst		
☐ 562.10 Diverticulosis			

RETURN APPOINTMENT

_____ Days
_____ Weeks
_____ Months

Authorization Number:
▶
_____

BALANCE DUE

DATE OF SERVICE	CPT CODE	DIAGNOSIS CODE(S)	CHARGE

Place of Service:
( ) Office
( ) Emergency Room
( ) Inpatient Hospital
( ) Outpatient Hospital
( ) Nursing Home

TOTAL CHARGE	$
AMOUNT PAID	$
PREVIOUS BAL	$
BALANCE DUE	$

Check #: _____
(Circle Method of Payment)
CASH   CHECK   MC   VISA

Physician's Signature
▶ _____

WORK PRODUCT 22-3

Name: ______________________________

Perform Billing Procedures

Corresponds to Procedure 22-8

CAAHEP COMPETENCIES: VI.P.VI.2.b

ABHES COMPETENCIES: 8.a

Complete the billing form below using the information in Part I, question 4.

Blackburn Primary Care Associates, PC
1990 Turquoise Drive
Blackburn, WI 54937
(608) 459-8857

Howard M. Lawler, MD 11
Joanne R. Hughes, MD 21
Ralph Garcia Lopez, MD 31
TAX ID NO. 00-00000000

GUARANTOR NAME AND ADDRESS	PATIENT NO.	PATIENT NAME			DOCTOR NO.	DATE
	DATE OF BIRTH	TELEPHONE NO.	INSURANCE			
			CODE	DESCRIPTION	CERTIFICATE NO.	

OFFICE - NEW

X	CPT	SERVICE	FEE
	99201	Prob Foc/Straight	
	99202	Exp Prob/Straight	
	99203	Detailed/Low	
	99204	Compre/Moderate	
	99205	Compre/High	

OFFICE - ESTABLISHED

X	CPT	SERVICE	FEE
	99211	Nurse/Minimal	
	99212	Prob Foc/Straight	
	99213	Exp Prob/Low	
	99214	Detailed/Moderate	
	99215	Compre/High	

OFFICE - CONSULT

X	CPT	SERVICE	FEE
	99241	Prob/Foc/Straight	
	99242	Exp Prob/Straight	
	99243	Detailed/Low	
	99244	Compre/Moderate	
	99245	Compre/High	

PREVENTIVE CARE - ADULT

X	CPT	SERVICE	FEE
	99385	18-39 Initial	
	99386	40-64 Initial	
	99387	65+ Initial	
	99395	18-39 Periodic	
	99396	40-64 Periodic	
	99397	65+ Periodic	

GASTROENEROLOGY

X	CPT	SERVICE	FEE
	45300	Sigmoidoscopy Rig	
	45305	Sigmoid Rig w/bx	
	45330	Sigmoidoscopy Flex	
	45331	Sigmoid Flex w/bx	
	45378	Colonoscopy Diag	
	45380	Colonoscopy w/bx	
	46600	Anoscopy	

CARDIOLOGY & HEARING

X	CPT	SERVICE	FEE
	93000	EKG (Global)	
	93015	Stress Test (Global)	
	93224	Holter (Global)	
	93225	Holter Hook Up	
	93227	Holter Interpretation	
	94010	Pulm Function Test	
	92551	Audiometry Screen	

INJECTIONS & IMMUNIZATION

X	CPT	SERVICE	FEE
	86585	TB Skin Test	
	90716	Varicella Vaccine	
	90724	Flu Vaccine	
	90732	Pneumovax	
	90718	TD Immunization	
	90782	Injection IM*	
	90788	Injection IM Antibiot*	
		Injection joint*	
	SM	MED MAJOR (circle one)	

FOR ALL INJECTIONS, SUPPLY DRUG INFORMATION

REPAIR & DERMATOLOGY

X	CPT	SERVICE	FEE
	17110	Warts: #	
		Tags: #	
		Lesion Excis	
		Lesion Destruct	
	SIZE CM:	SITE:	
	MALIG:	PREMAL/BEN:	
		(Check One Above)	
		Simple Closure	
		Intermed Closure	
	SIZE CM:	SITE:	
	10060	I&D Abscess	
	10080	I&D Cyst	

OTHER

SUPPLIES/DRUGS*

DRUG NAME:
UNIT/MEASURE:
QUANTITY

DIAGNOSTIC CODES: ICD-9-CM

- ☐ 789.0 Abdominal Pain
- ☐ 795.0 Abnormal Pap Smear
- ☐ 706.1 Acne Vulgaris
- ☐ 477.0 Allergic Rhinitis
- ☐ 285.9 Anemia, NOS
- ☐ 281.0 Pernicious
- ☐ 411.1 Angina, Unstable
- ☐ 427.9 Arythmia, NOS
- ☐ 440.9 Arteriosclerosis
- ☐ 714.0 Arthritis, Rheumatoid
- ☐ 414.0 ASHD
- ☐ 493.90 Asthma, Bronchial W/O Status Ast.
- ☐ 493.91 Asthma, Bronchial W/Status Ast.
- ☐ 466.1 Bronchiolitis, Acute
- ☐ 466.0 Bronchitis, Acute
- ☐ 727.3 Bursitis
- ☐ 786.50 Chest Pain
- ☐ 574.20 Cholelithiasis
- ☐ 372.30 Conjunctivitis, Unspecified
- ☐ 564.0 Constipation
- ☐ 496 COPD
- ☐ 692.9 Dermatitis, Allergic
- ☐ 250.01 Diabetes Mellitus, ID
- ☐ 250.00 Diabetes Mellitus, NID
- ☐ 558.9 Diarrhea
- ☐ 562.11 Diverticulitis
- ☐ 562.10 Diverticulosis
- ☐ 782.3 Edema
- ☐ 492.8 Emphysema
- ☐ V16.0 Family History Of Diabetes
- ☐ 780.6 Fever of Undetermined Origin
- ☐ 578.9 G.I. Bleeding, Unspecified
- ☐ 727.41 Ganglion of Joint
- ☐ 535.0 Gastritis, Acute
- ☐ V72.3 Arythmia, NOS
- ☐ 748.0 Headache
- ☐ 550.90 Hernia, Inguinal, NOS
- ☐ 054.9 Herpes Simplex
- ☐ 053.9 Herpes Zoster
- ☐ 708.9 Hives/Urticaria
- ☐ 401.1 Hypertension, Benign
- ☐ 401.0 Hypertension, Malignant
- ☐ 402.90 Hypertension, W/O CHF
- ☐ 244.9 Hypothyroidism, Primary
- ☐ 380.4 Impacted Cerumen
- ☐ 487.1 Influenza
- ☐ 564.1 Irritable Bowel Syndrome
- ☐ 464.0 Laryngitis, Acute
- ☐ 454.9 Leg Varicose Veins
- ☐ 424.0 Mitral Valve Prolapse
- ☐ 412 Myocardial Infarction, Old
- ☐ 715.90 Osteoarthritis, Unspec. Site
- ☐ 620.2 Ovarian Cyst
- ☐ 614.9 Pelvic Inflammatory Disease
- ☐ 685.1 Pilonidal Cyst
- ☐ 462 Pharyngitis, Acute
- ☐ 627.1 Postmenopausal Bleeding
- ☐ 625.4 Premenstrual Tension
- ☐ 782.1 Rash
- ☐ 569.3 Rectal Bleeding
- ☐ 398.90 Rheumatic Heart Disease, NOS
- ☐ 431.9 Sinusitis, Acute, NOS
- ☐ 782.1 Skin Eruption, Rash
- ☐ 845.00 Sprain, Ankle
- ☐ 848.9 Sprain, Muscle, Unspec. Site
- ☐ 785.6 Swollen Glands
- ☐ 246.9 Thyroid Disease, Unspecified
- ☐ 463 Tonsillitis, Acute
- ☐ 474.0 Tonsillitis, Chronic
- ☐ 465.9 Upper Respiratory Infection, Acute
- ☐ 599.0 Urinary Tract Infection
- ☐ V03.9 Vaccination/Bacterial Dis.
- ☐ V06.8 Vaccination/Combination
- ☐ V04.8 Vaccination, Influenza
- ☐ 616.10 Vaginitis, Vulvitis, NOS
- ☐ 780.4 Vertigo
- ☐ 787.0 Vomiting, Nausea
- ☐ ____ ________________
- ☐ ____ ________________
- ☐ ____ ________________
- ☐ ____ ________________

RETURN APPOINTMENT

________ Days
________ Weeks
________ Months

Authorization Number:
▶ ____________________

BALANCE DUE

DATE OF SERVICE	CPT CODE	DIAGNOSIS CODE(S)	CHARGE

Place of Service:
( ) Office
( ) Emergency Room
( ) Inpatient Hospital
( ) Outpatient Hospital
( ) Nursing Home

TOTAL CHARGE	$
AMOUNT PAID	$
PREVIOUS BAL	$
BALANCE DUE	$

Check #: ____________

(Circle Method of Payment)
CASH CHECK MC VISA

Physician's Signature
▶ ________________________________

WORK PRODUCT 22-4

Name: _____

Posting to Patient Accounts

Corresponds to Procedures 22-3 through 22-6, 22-10

<u>CAAHEP COMPETENCIES:</u> VI.P.VI.2.d., VI.P.VI.2.e., VI.P.VI.2.f., VI.P.VI.2.g., VI.P.VI.2.h

<u>ABHES COMPETENCIES:</u> 8.b.2, 8.b.3

Fill out the ledger using the information in Part II, ledger 1.

Blackburn Primary Care Associates, PC
1990 Turquoise Drive
Blackburn, WI 54937
Phone: 608-459-8857
Fax: 608-459-8860
E-mail: blackburnom@blackburnpca.com
www.blackburnpca.com

Patient Name _____

Address _____

City _____ State _____ Zip _____

Home Phone _____ Cell Phone _____

Email _____ MR# _____

Account Ledger

Entry #	Date	Reference	Service	Charge	Payment	Adj	Current Balance
1							
2							
3							
4							
5							
6							
7							
8							
9							
10							
11							
12							
13							
14							
15							
16							

207

WORK PRODUCT 22-5

Name: _____

Posting to Patient Accounts

Corresponds to Procedures 22-3 through 22-6, 22-10

<u>CAAHEP COMPETENCIES:</u> VI.P.VI.2.d., VI.P.VI.2.e., VI.P.VI.2.f., VI.P.VI.2.g., VI.P.VI.2.h

<u>ABHES COMPETENCIES:</u> 8.b.2, 8.b.3

Fill out the ledger using the information in Part II, ledger 2.

Blackburn Primary Care Associates, PC
1990 Turquoise Drive
Blackburn, WI 54937
Phone: 608-459-8857
Fax: 608-459-8860
E-mail: blackburnom@blackburnpca.com
www.blackburnpca.com

Patient Name _____

Address _____

City _____ State _____ Zip _____

Home Phone _____ Cell Phone _____

Email _____ MR# _____

Account Ledger							
Entry #	Date	Reference	Service	Charge	Payment	Adj	Current Balance
1							
2							
3							
4							
5							
6							
7							
8							
9							
10							
11							
12							
13							
14							
15							
16							

WORK PRODUCT 22-6

Name: _____

Posting to Patient Accounts

Corresponds to Procedures 22-3 through 22-6, 22-10

<u>CAAHEP COMPETENCIES:</u> VI.P.VI.2.d., VI.P.VI.2.e., VI.P.VI.2.f., VI.P.VI.2.g., VI.P.VI.2.h

<u>ABHES COMPETENCIES:</u> 8.b.2, 8.b.3

Fill out the ledger using the information in Part II, ledger 3.

Blackburn Primary Care Associates, PC
1990 Turquoise Drive
Blackburn, WI 54937
Phone: 608-459-8857
Fax: 608-459-8860
E-mail: blackburnom@blackburnpca.com
www.blackburnpca.com

Patient Name _____

Address _____

City _____ State _____ Zip _____

Home Phone _____ Cell Phone _____

Email _____ MR# _____

Account Ledger

Entry #	Date	Reference	Service	Charge	Payment	Adj	Current Balance
1							
2							
3							
4							
5							
6							
7							
8							
9							
10							
11							
12							
13							
14							
15							
16							

WORK PRODUCT 22-7

Name: _____

Proof of Posting

Corresponds to Procedures 22-3 through 22-6, 22-10

<u>CAAHEP COMPETENCIES:</u> VI.P.VI.2.d., VI.P.VI.2.e., VI.P.VI.2.f., VI.P.VI.2.g., VI.P.VI.2.h

<u>ABHES COMPETENCIES:</u> 8.b.2, 8.b.3

Today's Totals

Column A	Fees/Charges	$896.00
Column B	Payments	$1643.00
Column C	Adjustments	$36.00
Column D	New Balance	$3526.00
Column E	Old Balance	$4309.00

Daily Proof - Box One
Arithmetic Posting Proof

Column E	
Plus Column A	
Subtotal	
Minus Column B	
Subtotal	
Minus Column C	
Equals Column D	

Accounts Receivable
Beginning of Month $9071.00
Column A MTD $6589.00
Column B MTD $8226.00
Column C MTD $294.00
Year to Date – Box Three
Accounts Receivable Proof

Accounts Receivable
Previous Day 7923.00
Month to Date – Box Two
Accounts Receivable Proof

Accounts Receivable Previous Day	
Plus Column A	
Subtotal	
Minus Column B	
Subtotal	
Minus Column C	
Accounts Receivable End of Day	

Accounts Receivable Beginning of Month	
Plus Column A Month to Date	
Subtotal	
Minus Column B Month to Date	
Subtotal	
Minus Column C Month to Date	
Accounts Receivable Month to Date	

↑——— TOTALS MUST EQUAL ———↑

213

WORK PRODUCT 22-8

Name: _____

Perform Collection Procedures

Corresponds to Procedure 22-9

<u>CAAHEP COMPETENCIES:</u> VI.P.VI.2.c

Blackburn Primary Care Associates
1990 Turquoise Drive
Blackburn, WI 54937
(555) 555-1234

WORK PRODUCT 22-9

Name: _____

Perform Collection Procedures

Corresponds to Procedure 22-9

<u>CAAHEP COMPETENCIES:</u> VI.P.VI.2.c

Blackburn Primary Care Associates
1990 Turquoise Drive
Blackburn, WI 54937
(555) 555-1234

Name _____ Date _____ Score _____

PROCEDURE 23-1 Write Checks in Payment of Bills

CAAHEP COMPETENCIES: VI.P.VI.2
ABHES COMPETENCIES: 8.b.1

TASK: To write checks correctly for the payment of bills.

Equipment and Supplies
- Checkbook
- Bills to be paid

Standards: Complete the procedure and all critical steps in _____ minutes with a minimum score of 85% within three attempts.

Scoring: Divide the points earned by the total possible points. Failure to perform a critical step, indicated by an asterisk (*), results in an unsatisfactory overall score.

Time began _____ Time ended _____ Total minutes: _____

Steps	Possible Points	Attempt 1	Attempt 2	Attempt 3
*1. Locate the bill to be paid. Then fill out the check stub first.	10	_____	_____	_____
*2. Complete the check stub and the check with a pen or use computer software.	10	_____	_____	_____
*3. Date the check.	10	_____	_____	_____
*4. Write the payee's name on the appropriate line.	10	_____	_____	_____
*5. Leave no space before the name and follow with dashes or a line so that information cannot be added to the check.	10	_____	_____	_____
6. Enter the amount correctly and in a way that prevents alteration.	20	_____	_____	_____
*7. Verify the amount with the check stub.	20	_____	_____	_____
8. On the bill being paid, note the date it was paid and the check number. Then file the bill.	10	_____	_____	_____

Comments:

Points earned _____ ÷ 100 possible points = Score _____ % Score

Instructor's signature _____

Procedure **23-1 Write Checks in Payment of Bills**

Name _____ Date _____ Score _____

PROCEDURE 23-2 Prepare a Bank Deposit

CAAHEP COMPETENCIES: VI.P.VI.1
ABHES COMPETENCIES: 8.a

TASK: To prepare a bank deposit for the day's receipts and to complete appropriate office records related to the deposit.

Equipment and Supplies
- Currency
- Checks for deposit
- Deposit slip
- Endorsement stamp
- Envelope
- Pen

Standards: Complete the procedure and all critical steps in _____ minutes with a minimum score of 85% within three attempts.

Scoring: Divide the points earned by the total possible points. Failure to perform a critical step, indicated by an asterisk (*), results in an unsatisfactory overall score.

Time began _____ Time ended _____ Total minutes: _____

Steps	Possible Points	Attempt 1	Attempt 2	Attempt 3
1. Organize the currency.	10	_____	_____	_____
*2. Total the currency and record the amount on the deposit slip.	10	_____	_____	_____
*3. Put a restrictive endorsement on the back of each check.	20	_____	_____	_____
*4. List each check separately on the deposit slip by ABA number or the patient's last name.	20	_____	_____	_____
*5. Total the amount of currency and checks and enter the total on the deposit slip.	10	_____	_____	_____
*6. Enter the amount of the deposit in the checkbook.	10	_____	_____	_____
*7. Keep a copy of the deposit slip for office records.	10	_____	_____	_____
*8. Put the currency, checks, and deposit slip in an envelope or deposit bag for transport to the bank.	10	_____	_____	_____

Comments:

Points earned _____ ÷ 100 possible points = Score _____ % Score

Instructor's signature _____

222

Name _____ Date _____ Score _____

PROCEDURE 23-3 Reconcile a Bank Statement

ABHES COMPETENCIES: 8.a
TASK: To reconcile a bank statement with the checking account.

Equipment and Supplies
- Ending balance of previous statement
- Current bank statement
- Cancelled checks for current month
- Checkbook stubs
- Calculator
- Pen

Standards: Complete the procedure and all critical steps in _____ minutes with a minimum score of 85% within three attempts.

Scoring: Divide the points earned by the total possible points. Failure to perform a critical step, indicated by an asterisk (*), results in an unsatisfactory overall score.

Time began _____   Time ended _____   Total minutes: _____

Steps	Possible Points	Attempt 1	Attempt 2	Attempt 3
*1. Compare the opening balance of the new statement with the closing balance of the previous statement.	10	_____	_____	_____
*2. Compare debits and/or cancelled checks with the items on the statement.	10	_____	_____	_____
*3. Arrange the checks in numeric order and compare them with the stubs.	10	_____	_____	_____
*4. Put a checkmark on the matching stub.	10	_____	_____	_____
*5. List and total the outstanding checks.	10	_____	_____	_____
*6. Verify that all previous outstanding checks have cleared.	10	_____	_____	_____
*7. Subtract the total of the outstanding checks from the statement balance.	10	_____	_____	_____
*8. To the total in step 7, add any deposits made but not included on the statement balance.	10	_____	_____	_____
*9. Total any bank charges that appear on the bank statement and subtract them from the checkbook balance.	10	_____	_____	_____
*10. If the checkbook and statement do not agree, match the bank statement entries with the checkbook entries to find the errors. Redo all math to check for errors.	10	_____	_____	_____

Comments:

Points earned _____ ÷ 100 possible points = Score _____ % Score

Instructor's signature _____

Procedure **23-3 Reconcile a Bank Statement**

WORK PRODUCT 23-1

Name: _____

Prepare a Bank Deposit

Corresponds to Procedure 23-2

<u>CAAHEP COMPETENCIES:</u> VI.P.VI.2

<u>ABHES COMPETENCIES:</u> 8.b.1

Fill in the bank deposit figure using the information in Part IV, questions 1-4.

BANK DEPOSIT DETAIL			
PAYMENTS			
BANK NUMBER	BY CHECK OR PMO	BY COIN OR CURRENCY	CREDIT CARD
TOTALS			

CURRENCY	
COIN	
CHECKS	
CREDIT CARDS	
TOTAL RECEIPTS	
LESS CREDIT CARD $	
TOTAL DEPOSITS	

DEPOSIT DATE: _____ FIRM: _____

PROCEDURE 24-1 Perform Accounts Receivable Procedures

CAAHEP COMPETENCIES: VI.P.VI.2
ABHES COMPETENCIES: 8.b.1

TASK: To collect amounts due to the physician or medical facility.

Equipment and Supplies
- Patient ledgers
- Office policy and procedures manual
- Telephone
- Letterhead and envelopes
- Clerical supplies

Standards: Complete the procedure and all critical steps in _____ minutes with a minimum score of 85% within three attempts.

Scoring: Divide the points earned by the total possible points. Failure to perform a critical step, indicated by an asterisk (*), results in an unsatisfactory overall score.

Time began _____   Time ended _____   Total minutes: _____

Steps	Possible Points	Attempt 1	Attempt 2	Attempt 3
*1. Prompt the computer to compile a report on the age of accounts receivables.	10	_____	_____	_____
*2. Divide the accounts into the following categories:	20			
a. 0-30 days		_____	_____	_____
b. 30-60 days		_____	_____	_____
c. 60-90 days		_____	_____	_____
d. 90-120 days		_____	_____	_____
e. over 120 days		_____	_____	_____
*3. If the computer program does not perform this function, manually pull all ledger cards with a balance due and divide them into the categories in step 2.	10	_____	_____	_____
*4. Examine the accounts to see which are awaiting an insurance payment or other activity. If insurance is pending and the account is not long overdue, do not take action. File these ledger cards back in the tray.	10	_____	_____	_____
*5. Follow office procedure in taking collection activity on the account. Put collection stickers or messages on the inside of the mailing envelope.	10	_____	_____	_____
6. Attempt to call the patient and make payment arrangements.	10	_____	_____	_____

Steps	Possible Points	Attempt 1	Attempt 2	Attempt 3
7. Bill the patient once monthly according to the individual's billing cycle.	10	_____	_____	_____
8. Post payments on the day they arrive at the office.	10	_____	_____	_____
9. Demonstrate sensitivity and professionalism when handling accounts.	10	_____	_____	_____

Comments:

Points earned _____ ÷ **100 possible points = Score** _____ **% Score**

Instructor's signature _____

PROCEDURE 24-2 Perform Accounts Payable Procedures

CAAHEP COMPETENCIES: VI.P.VI.2
ABHES COMPETENCIES: 8.b.1

TASK: To determine the age of accounts and decide what collection activity is needed.

Equipment and Supplies

- Patient ledger cards with a balance due
- Pen
- Computer
- Calculator

Standards: Complete the procedure and all critical steps in _____ minutes with a minimum score of 85% within three attempts.

Scoring: Divide the points earned by the total possible points. Failure to perform a critical step, indicated by an asterisk (*), results in an unsatisfactory overall score.

Time began _____ **Time ended** _____ **Total minutes:** _____

Steps	Possible Points	Attempt 1	Attempt 2	Attempt 3
1. Pull all ledger cards with a balance due and divide them into the following categories:	10			
a. 0-30 days		_____	_____	_____
b. 30-60 days		_____	_____	_____
c. 60-90 days		_____	_____	_____
d. 90-120 days		_____	_____	_____
e. over 120 days		_____	_____	_____
*2. Determine which accounts are awaiting an insurance payment. Return those ledgers to the ledger tray.	20	_____	_____	_____
*3. For the accounts that remain, follow the office procedure for collections. Put collection reminder stickers on the statements sent to the patient or send a collection letter. Make sure the stickers are inside the envelope, not on the outside.	10	_____	_____	_____
*4. Call patients whose accounts are more than 90 days old. Attempt to make payment arrangements.	20	_____	_____	_____
*5. Send a collection letter to patients whose accounts are more than 120 days old.	20	_____	_____	_____
*6. Add the total accounts receivable for each category and arrive at a figure outstanding for each.	10	_____	_____	_____
7. Note in the chart and/or on the ledger any arrangements made with patients regarding payment of the accounts. Send a follow-up letter to remind the patients of their payment agreements.	10	_____	_____	_____

Comments:

Points earned _____ ÷ 100 possible points = Score _____ % Score

Instructor's signature _____

230

Procedure **24-2 Perform Accounts Payable Procedures**

Name _____ Date _____ Score _____

PROCEDURE 24-3 Account for Petty Cash

ABHES COMPETENCIES: 8.e

TASK: To establish a petty cash fund, maintain an accurate record of expenditures for 1 month, and replenish the fund as necessary.

Equipment and Supplies
- Form for petty cash fund
- Pad of vouchers
- Disbursement journal
- Two checks
- List of petty cash expenditures

Standards: Complete the procedure and all critical steps in _____ minutes with a minimum score of 85% within three attempts.

Scoring: Divide the points earned by the total possible points. Failure to perform a critical step, indicated by an asterisk (*), results in an unsatisfactory overall score.

Time began _____ Time ended _____ Total minutes: _____

Steps	Possible Points	Attempt 1	Attempt 2	Attempt 3
1. Determine the amount needed in the petty cash fund.	10	_____	_____	_____
*2. Write a check in the determined amount.	10	_____	_____	_____
*3. Record the beginning balance in the petty cash fund.	10	_____	_____	_____
*4. Post the amount to miscellaneous on the disbursement record.	10	_____	_____	_____
*5. Prepare a petty cash voucher for each amount withdrawn from the fund.	10	_____	_____	_____
*6. Record each voucher in the petty cash record and enter the new balance.	10	_____	_____	_____
*7. Write a check to replenish the fund as necessary, keeping in mind that the total of the vouchers plus the fund balance must equal the beginning amount in petty cash.	10	_____	_____	_____
*8. Total the expense columns and post to the appropriate accounts in the disbursement journal.	10	_____	_____	_____
*9. Record the amount added to the fund.	10	_____	_____	_____
*10. Record the new balance in the petty cash fund.	10	_____	_____	_____

Comments:

Points earned _____ ÷ 100 possible points = Score _____ % Score

Instructor's signature _____

Procedure **24-3 Account for Petty Cash**

Name _____ Date _____ Score _____

PROCEDURE 24-4 Process an Employee Payroll

ABHES COMPETENCIES: 8.a

TASK: To process payroll and compensate employees, making deductions accurately.

Equipment and Supplies
- Checkbook
- Computer and payroll software, if applicable
- Pen
- Tax withholding tables
- Federal Employers Tax Guide

Standards: Complete the procedure and all critical steps in _____ minutes with a minimum score of 85% within three attempts.

Scoring: Divide the points earned by the total possible points. Failure to perform a critical step, indicated by an asterisk (*), results in an unsatisfactory overall score.

Time began _____ **Time ended** _____ **Total minutes:** _____

Steps	Possible Points	Attempt 1	Attempt 2	Attempt 3
*1. Make sure all information has been collected on the employees, including a copy of the Social Security card, a W-4 form, and an I-9 form.	20	_____	_____	_____
*2. Review the time cards for all employees. Determine whether any employees need counseling because of late arrivals or habitual absences.	20	_____	_____	_____
*3. Figure the salary or hourly wages due the employee for the period worked.	20	_____	_____	_____
*4. Figure the deductions that must be taken from the paycheck. These usually include but are not limited to:	20			
a. Federal, state, and local taxes		_____	_____	_____
b. Social Security withholdings		_____	_____	_____
c. Medicare withholdings		_____	_____	_____
d. Other deductions (e.g., insurance, savings)		_____	_____	_____
e. Donations to organizations (e.g., the United Way)		_____	_____	_____
*5. Write the check for the balance due the employee. Most software can print the checks and explanations of deductions. Put a copy in the employee's file.	20	_____	_____	_____

Comments:

Points earned _____ ÷ 100 possible points = Score _____ % Score

Instructor's signature _____

Procedure **24-4 Process an Employee Payroll**

Name _____ Date _____ Score _____

PROCEDURE 25-1 Interview Job Candidates Effectively

ABHES COMPETENCIES: 8.f

TASK: To evaluate job candidates fairly and choose the best person to fill an available position in the medical facility.

Equipment and Supplies
- Candidate's completed job application
- Candidate's resume
- Private area in the medical office
- Clerical supplies

Standards: Complete the procedure and all critical steps in _____ minutes with a minimum score of 85% within three attempts.

Scoring: Divide the points earned by the total possible points. Failure to perform a critical step, indicated by an asterisk (*), results in an unsatisfactory overall score.

Time began _____   Time ended _____   Total minutes: _____

Steps	Possible Points	Attempt 1	Attempt 2	Attempt 3
*1. Review the duties the candidate will be required to perform.	5	_____	_____	_____
*2. Match each job application with the corresponding resumé.	5	_____	_____	_____
*3. Separate strong candidates from the moderate and the weak candidates.	5	_____	_____	_____
*4. Call each strong candidate and schedule an appointment for an interview.	5	_____	_____	_____
*5. Evaluate the applicant's speaking voice while making the appointment for the interview.	2	_____	_____	_____
6. Select several interview questions in advance to ask all the applicants.	5	_____	_____	_____
*7. Note whether the applicant arrives on time for the interview.	2	_____	_____	_____
*8. Introduce yourself to the applicant and proceed to a private area for the interview.	5	_____	_____	_____
*9. Make the applicant feel as much at ease as possible.	5	_____	_____	_____
*10. Ask the applicant the chosen questions.	5	_____	_____	_____
*11. Evaluate the answers and make notations about the candidate that are not demeaning or unprofessional.	10	_____	_____	_____
*12. Ask the candidate whether he or she has any questions.	2	_____	_____	_____
*13. Offer the candidate a brief tour of the facility.	2	_____	_____	_____
*14. Provide a date by which a hiring decision will be made and suggest that the candidate call the facility that day, if desired.	2	_____	_____	_____

Steps	Possible Points	Attempt 1	Attempt 2	Attempt 3
*15. Evaluate all applicants fairly according to their experience and training.	5	_____	_____	_____
*16. Select the best three candidates and call them for a second interview, if desired.	5	_____	_____	_____
*17. Discuss the final hiring decision with the physician or others who might be involved in the hiring process.	5	_____	_____	_____
*18. Make the final hiring decision.	5	_____	_____	_____
*19. Call the candidate to ask him or her to come to the office to discuss the position.	5	_____	_____	_____
*20. Negotiate salary and benefits.	5	_____	_____	_____
*21. Offer the position.	5	_____	_____	_____
*22. If the offer is declined, call the next candidate to the office to discuss the position; repeat until a satisfactory candidate accepts and agrees to a start date.	5	_____	_____	_____

Comments:

Points earned _____ ÷ 100 possible points = Score _____ % Score

Instructor's signature _____

Name _____ Date _____ Score _____

PROCEDURE 25-2 Conduct a Performance Review

ABHES COMPETENCIES: 4.a

TASK: To evaluate job performance fairly and determine the strengths and weaknesses of employees using accurate documentation.

Equipment and Supplies
- Employee's file
- Past evaluations of employee
- Notes and/or reports on employee's behavior
- Private area in the medical office
- Clerical supplies

Standards: Complete the procedure and all critical steps in _____ minutes with a minimum score of 85% within three attempts.

Scoring: Divide the points earned by the total possible points. Failure to perform a critical step, indicated by an asterisk (*), results in an unsatisfactory overall score.

Time began _____ Time ended _____ Total minutes: _____

Steps	Possible Points	Attempt 1	Attempt 2	Attempt 3
1. Set an appointment for the review with the employee.	10	_____	_____	_____
*2. Allow the employee to complete a self-evaluation of his or her own work.	10	_____	_____	_____
*3. Review the self-evaluation, then document additional information about the employee and his or her performance.	15	_____	_____	_____
4. Share the information with any other supervisor or the physician, if dictated by office policy or if needed for additional input.	10	_____	_____	_____
*5. Complete the final written review and proofread it for accuracy and completeness.	10	_____	_____	_____
*6. Discuss the review with the employee during the evaluation appointment.	10	_____	_____	_____
*7. Progress through the interview and explain the results of the evaluation to the employee.	10	_____	_____	_____
*8. Allow the employee to respond to any of the points raised during the evaluation, but do not allow an argumentative attitude.	5	_____	_____	_____
*9. Allow the employee to respond to the evaluation in writing within a limited period (e.g., 5 days).	5	_____	_____	_____
*10. Ask the employee to sign the evaluation to document that it was reviewed with the individual (the employee does not have to agree with the evaluation to sign it).	5	_____	_____	_____
*11. Give a copy of the evaluation to the employee.	5	_____	_____	_____
*12. Put a copy of the evaluation in the employee's file.	5	_____	_____	_____

237

Comments:

Points earned _____ ÷ 100 possible points = Score _____ % Score

Instructor's signature _____

238

PROCEDURE 25-3 Arrange a Group Meeting

ABHES COMPETENCIES: 8.f

TASK: To plan and conduct a productive meeting that will result in achieved goals and apply concepts for office Procedures.

Equipment and Supplies
- Meeting room
- Agenda
- Visual aids and equipment
- Handouts
- Stopwatch or clock
- Computer
- Paper
- List of items for the agenda

Standards: Complete the procedure and all critical steps in _____ minutes with a minimum score of 85% within three attempts.

Scoring: Divide the points earned by the total possible points. Failure to perform a critical step, indicated by an asterisk (*), results in an unsatisfactory overall score.

Time began _____ **Time ended** _____ **Total minutes:** _____

Steps	Possible Points	Attempt 1	Attempt 2	Attempt 3
1. Determine the purpose of the meeting and draft a list of the items to be discussed; include the desired results of the meeting.	10	_____	_____	_____
*2. Determine where the meeting will be held, the time and date of the meeting, and the individuals who should attend.	10	_____	_____	_____
*3. Send a memo, e-mail, or letter to the individuals who should attend the meeting at least 10 days in advance, if possible. Send a copy to any supervisors who should be kept informed about the issues to be raised at the meeting.	10	_____	_____	_____
*4. Make sure the notice includes the following information:	10			
a. Date		_____	_____	_____
b. Time		_____	_____	_____
c. Place		_____	_____	_____
d. Directions (if not a common meeting room or if held away from the office)		_____	_____	_____
e. Speakers and/or meeting topics		_____	_____	_____
f. Cost and registration information, if applicable		_____	_____	_____
g. List of items individuals should bring to the meeting		_____	_____	_____
*5. Finalize the list of items to discuss and place them in priority order.	10	_____	_____	_____

Steps	Possible Points	Attempt 1	Attempt 2	Attempt 3
*6. Delegate any tasks that others can accomplish and follow up to be sure they fulfill their duties before the meeting.	10	_____	_____	_____
*7. Assign a staff member the task of taking notes and keeping time during the meeting.	10	_____	_____	_____
*8. Make a list of all items to take to the meeting (e.g., microphones, projectors, screens, computers, disks containing presentations).	10	_____	_____	_____
*9. Compile the final agenda for the meeting.	10	_____	_____	_____
*10. On the meeting day, transport all items needed to the meeting room. Begin and end the meeting on time. Stay on track and follow the agenda.	10	_____	_____	_____

Comments:

Points earned _____ **÷ 100 possible points = Score** _____ **% Score**

Instructor's signature _____

Name _____ Date _____ Score _____

PROCEDURE 26-1 Design a Presentation

ABHES COMPETENCIES: 7.b

TASK: To gain skill in designing presentations that can be used for a variety of projects in the medical facility.

Equipment and Supplies
- Information about presentation subject
- Software (e.g., PowerPoint), if needed
- Computer access
- Peripheral computer equipment, if needed

Standards: Complete the Procedure and all critical steps in _____ minutes with a minimum score of 85% within three attempts.

Scoring: Divide the points earned by the total possible points. Failure to perform a critical step, indicated by an asterisk (*), results in an unsatisfactory overall score.

Time began _____   Time ended _____   Total minutes: _____

Steps	Possible Points	Attempt 1	Attempt 2	Attempt 3
*1. Determine the goals of the presentation.	10	_____	_____	_____
2. Write an outline of the entire presentation.	10	_____	_____	_____
3. Build the presentation using software (e.g., PowerPoint), highlighting the major points of the presentation.	5	_____	_____	_____
*4. Evaluate the audience and adjust the presentation to appeal to that audience.	10	_____	_____	_____
5. Rehearse the presentation several times in front of a mirror.	5	_____	_____	_____
6. Make a list of all equipment and materials to take to the presentation.	10	_____	_____	_____
*7. Arrive for the presentation 15 to 30 minutes early, depending on the preparation and setup required.	10	_____	_____	_____
8. Deliver the presentation within the prescribed period.	10	_____	_____	_____
9. Ask the audience whether they have any questions about the information in the presentation.	10	_____	_____	_____
10. Thank the audience and remove all equipment and supplies when appropriate.	10	_____	_____	_____
11. Send a thank you note to the organization for allowing the presentation, if appropriate.	10	_____	_____	_____

Comments:

Points earned _____ ÷ 100 possible points = Score _____ % Score

Instructor's signature _____

Procedure **26-1 Design a Presentation**

Name _____ Date _____ Score _____

PROCEDURE 26-2 Prepare a Presentation Using PowerPoint

ABHES COMPETENCIES: 7.b

TASK: To enhance presentations using PowerPoint as a visual aid.

Equipment and Supplies
- Information about presentation subject
- Software (for this exercise, PowerPoint)
- Computer access
- Peripheral computer equipment, if needed

Standards: Complete the Procedure and all critical steps in _____ minutes with a minimum score of 85% within three attempts.

Scoring: Divide the points earned by the total possible points. Failure to perform a critical step, indicated by an asterisk (*), results in an unsatisfactory overall score.

Time began _____ Time ended _____ Total minutes: _____

Steps	Possible Points	Attempt 1	Attempt 2	Attempt 3
1. Open the PowerPoint program.	5	_____	_____	_____
2. Have the outline of the presentation available.	5	_____	_____	_____
3. Click on the NEW SLIDE icon on the program menu.	5	_____	_____	_____
4. Create the title slide using the slide layout section on the right side of the screen.	5	_____	_____	_____
5. Create additional slides using the slide layout section or design the slides manually.	5	_____	_____	_____
*6. Limit the number of words on the slides so that a concise message results.	5	_____	_____	_____
7. Make sure the font is as large as possible on the slide, beginning with a size 18 font and increasing from there.	5	_____	_____	_____
*8. Do not use more than three fonts per slide.	5	_____	_____	_____
*9. Do not use more than three text-only slides in a row.	5	_____	_____	_____
10. Insert photographs or clip art into the presentation: click on INSERT and then on PICTURE; then choose CLIP ART or FROM FILE.	5	_____	_____	_____
11. Format the background of each slide or of all slides: click on FORMAT, and then BACKGROUND; then choose a color or fill effect.	5	_____	_____	_____

Steps	Possible Points	Attempt 1	Attempt 2	Attempt 3
12. Click on SLIDE SHOW and adjust the slide transitions so that the slides appear and disappear as desired and are timed correctly.	5	_____	_____	_____
13. Click on CUSTOM ANIMATION to change the entrance and exit of the slides to achieve the desired effect.	5	_____	_____	_____
*14. Save the presentation frequently while working on it.	5	_____	_____	_____
15. Click on VIEW in the task bar and then on SLIDE SORTER to be able to move the slides around in the presentation.	5	_____	_____	_____
16. To run the show continuously, click on SLIDE SHOW and then on SET UP SHOW; in the Show Options box, click in the box labeled Loop Continuously Until Escape.	5	_____	_____	_____
17. Make sure the presentation has been saved.	5	_____	_____	_____
*18. Practice the presentation several times to smooth all transitions and to become thoroughly familiar with the content.	5	_____	_____	_____
*19. Anticipate questions the audience may ask and have answers prepared.	5	_____	_____	_____
20. Offer other visual aids (e.g., handouts), if appropriate, when giving the presentation.	5	_____	_____	_____

Documentation in the Medical Record:

Comments:

Points earned _____ ÷ 100 possible points = Score _____ % Score

Instructor's signature _____

Name _____ Date _____ Score _____

PROCEDURE 27-1 Train in and Practice Standard Precautions: Use Standard Precautions to Remove Contaminated Gloves and Discard Biohazardous Material

CAAHEP COMPETENCIES: III.PIII.1, III.PIII.2, III.PIII.3
ABHES COMPETENCIES: 9.a, 10.c

TASK: To minimize exposure to pathogens by aseptically removing and discarding contaminated gloves.

Equipment and Supplies
- Latex or alternative disposable examination gloves
- Biohazard waste container with labeled red biohazard bag

Standards: Complete the Procedure and all critical steps in _____ minutes with a minimum score of 85% within three attempts.

Scoring: Divide the points earned by the total possible points. Failure to perform a critical step, indicated by an asterisk (*), results in an unsatisfactory overall score.

Time began _____ Time ended _____ Total minutes: _____

Steps	Possible Points	Attempt 1	Attempt 2	Attempt 3
1. With the dominant hand, grasp the glove of the opposite hand near the palm and begin removing the first glove. The arms should be extended from the body with the hands pointed down.	20	_____	_____	_____
2. Pull the glove inside out until you reach the fingers, holding the contaminated glove in the dominant gloved hand.	20	_____	_____	_____
3. Insert the thumb of the nongloved hand inside the cuff of the remaining contaminated glove. Pull the glove down the hand inside out over the contaminated glove being held, leaving the contaminated side of both gloves on the inside.	20	_____	_____	_____
4. Properly dispose of the inside-out contaminated gloves in a biohazardous waste container.	10	_____	_____	_____
5. Perform a medical aseptic hand wash as described in Procedure 27-4.	10	_____	_____	_____

Comments:

Points earned _____ ÷ 100 possible points = Score _____ % Score

Instructor's signature _____

Name _____ Date _____ Score _____

PROCEDURE 27-2 Demonstrate the Proper Use of Eye Wash Equipment: Perform an Emergency Eye Wash

CAAHEP COMPETENCIES: X.PXI.5.a
ABHES COMPETENCIES: 9.a

TASK: To minimize the risk of occupational exposure to pathogens if body fluids come in contact with the eyes.

Equipment and Supplies
- Plumbed or self-contained eyewash unit
- Disposable gloves

Standards: Complete the Procedure and all critical steps in _____ minutes with a minimum score of 85% within three attempts.

Scoring: Divide the points earned by the total possible points. Failure to perform a critical step, indicated by an asterisk (*), results in an unsatisfactory overall score.

Time began _____   Time ended _____   Total minutes: _____

Steps	Possible Points	Attempt 1	Attempt 2	Attempt 3
1. Put on gloves and remove contact lenses or glasses.	10	_____	_____	_____
2. Following the manufacturer's directions, turn on the eyewash unit. If it is a plumbed unit, the control valve should remain on until manually shut off.	20	_____	_____	_____
3. Hold the eyelids open with the thumb and index finger to ensure adequate rinsing of the entire eye and eyelid surface.	20	_____	_____	_____
4. Do not aim the water stream directly onto the eyeball.	10	_____	_____	_____
5. Flush the eyes and eyelids for a minimum of 15 minutes, rolling the eyes periodically to ensure complete removal of the foreign material.	20	_____	_____	_____
6. Sanitize your hands.	10	_____	_____	_____
7. After completing the eyewash, follow postexposure follow-up procedures.	10	_____	_____	_____

Comments:

Points earned _____ ÷ 100 possible points = Score _____ % Score

Instructor's signature _____

Procedure **27-2 Demonstrate the Proper Use of Eye Wash Equipment**

Name _____ Date _____ Score _____

PROCEDURE 27-3 Participate in a Mock Environmental Exposure Event with Documentation of Steps: Implement the Facility's Environmental Safety Plan

CAAHEP COMPETENCIES: X.PXI.4, X.PXI.6
ABHES COMPETENCIES: 9.a, 9.g

TASK: To manage an exposure incident according to OSHA standards.

SCENARIO: As Rosa administers a hepatitis B injection, the patient jumps back. The needle becomes dislodged, and Rosa is accidentally jabbed by the contaminated needle. What procedural steps must Rosa take to comply with OSHA standards?

Equipment and Supplies
- Antibacterial soap and warm running water
- Exposure incident report form

Standards: Complete the Procedure and all critical steps in _____ minutes with a minimum score of 85% within three attempts.

Scoring: Divide the points earned by the total possible points. Failure to perform a critical step, indicated by an asterisk (*), results in an unsatisfactory overall score.

Time began _____ **Time ended** _____ **Total minutes:** _____

Steps	Possible Points	Attempt 1	Attempt 2	Attempt 3
1. Immediately wash the exposed site with antibacterial soap and warm running water.	10	_____	_____	_____
2. Immediately report the exposure incident to the site supervisor.	10	_____	_____	_____
3. Complete an exposure incident report that details the type of injury, the events of the incident, the equipment involved, and any other pertinent information.	20	_____	_____	_____
4. After the incident report has been completed, the employee immediately is sent for a confidential medical evaluation. This may be done in a related employee health office, local emergency department, or private physician's office. The employer must cover the costs of all related healthcare.	20	_____	_____	_____
5. A blood sample is taken from the employee to test for HBV, HCV, and HIV. If the employee refuses testing, a blood sample is taken and stored for 90 days; if the employee still refuses testing after 90 days, the sample is destroyed.	20	_____	_____	_____
6. If the patient's blood tests negative for HBV, HCV, and HIV, the employer must provide free education and counseling. If the patient's blood tests positive for these pathogens, the employee is offered free care and counseling.	10	_____	_____	_____

Comments:

Points earned _____ ÷ 100 possible points = Score _____ % Score

Instructor's signature _____

Procedure **27-3 Implement the Facility's Environmental Safety Plan**

Name _____ Date _____ Score _____

PROCEDURE 27-4 Train in and Practice Standard Precautions: Perform Medical Aseptic Hand Washing

CAAHEP COMPETENCIES: III.PIII.1, III.PIII.2, III.PIII.4
ABHES COMPETENCIES: 9.a

TASK: To minimize the number of pathogens on the hands, thus reducing the risk of transmission of pathogens.

Equipment and Supplies
- Sink with running water
- Antimicrobial liquid soap in a dispenser (bar soap is not acceptable)
- Nail brush or orange stick
- Paper towels in a dispenser
- Water-based antimicrobial lotion
- Biohazardous waste container with labeled red biohazard bag

Standards: Complete the Procedure and all critical steps in _____ minutes with a minimum score of 85% within three attempts.

Scoring: Divide the points earned by the total possible points. Failure to perform a critical step, indicated by an asterisk (*), results in an unsatisfactory overall score.

Time began _____   Time ended _____   Total minutes: _____

Steps	Possible Points	Attempt 1	Attempt 2	Attempt 3
1. Remove all jewelry except your wristwatch, which should be pulled up above your wrist or removed, and a plain gold wedding ring.	10	_____	_____	_____
2. Turn on the faucet with a paper towel and regulate the water temperature to lukewarm	10	_____	_____	_____
3. Allow your hands to become wet, apply soap, and lather using a circular motion with friction while keeping your fingertips pointed downward. Rub well between your fingers. If this is the first hand washing of the day, thoroughly inspect the area under each fingernail and clean with a nail brush or an orange stick.	10	_____	_____	_____
4. Rinse well, holding your hands so that the water flows from your wrists downward to your fingertips.	10	_____	_____	_____
5. Wet your hands again and repeat the scrubbing procedure using a vigorous, circular motion over the wrists and hands for at least 1 to 2 minutes.	10	_____	_____	_____
6. Rinse your hands a second time, keeping your fingers lower than your wrists.	10	_____	_____	_____
7. Dry your hands with paper towels. Do not touch the paper towel dispenser as you get the towels.	10	_____	_____	_____

251

Copyright © 2014 Elsevier, Inc. All rights reserved.

Procedure **27-4 Train in and Practice Standard Precautions**

Steps	Possible Points	Attempt 1	Attempt 2	Attempt 3
*8. If the faucets are not foot operated, turn off the water faucet with the paper towel.	**10**	_____	_____	_____
9. After you finish drying your hands and turning off the faucets, discard the used towels in a biohazardous waste container.	**10**	_____	_____	_____
10. Apply a water-based antibacterial hand lotion to prevent chapped or dry skin.	**10**	_____	_____	_____

Comments:

Points earned _____ ÷ 100 possible points = Score _____ % Score

Instructor's signature _____

Procedure **27-4 Train in and Practice Standard Precautions**

Name _____ Date _____ Score _____

PROCEDURE 27-5 Train in and Practice Standard Precautions: Use Standard Precautions for Sanitizing Instruments and Discarding Biohazardous Material

CAAHEP COMPETENCIES: III.PIII.1, III.PIII.2, III.PIII.3, III.PIII.4
ABHES COMPETENCIES: 9.a, 10.c

TASK: Following Standard Precautions, remove all contaminated matter from instruments in preparation for disinfection or sterilization.

Equipment and Supplies
- Sink with hot running water
- Sanitizing agent or low-sudsing soap with enzymatic action
- Utility gloves that are decontaminated and show no signs of deterioration
- Chin-length face shield or goggles and face mask if contamination with droplets of blood-borne pathogens is possible
- Disposable brush
- Disposable paper towels
- Disposable gloves
- Disinfectant cleaner prepared according to manufacturer directions
- Biohazardous waste container with labeled red biohazard bag

Standards: Complete the Procedure and all critical steps in _____ minutes with a minimum score of 85% within three attempts.

Scoring: Divide the points earned by the total possible points. Failure to perform a critical step, indicated by an asterisk (*), results in an unsatisfactory overall score.

Time began _____   Time ended _____   Total minutes: _____

Steps	Possible Points	Attempt 1	Attempt 2	Attempt 3
1. Put on utility gloves.	5	_____	_____	_____
2. Put on a face shield or goggles and mask if the possibility exists of splashing of infectious material.	5	_____	_____	_____
3. Separate sharp instruments from other instruments to be sanitized.	10	_____	_____	_____
4. Rinse the instruments under cold running water.	10	_____	_____	_____
5. Open hinged instruments and scrub all grooves, crevices, and serrations with a disposable brush.	10	_____	_____	_____
6. Rinse well with hot water.	10	_____	_____	_____
7. Towel dry all instruments thoroughly and dispose of the contaminated towels and disposable brush in a biohazardous waste container. Do not touch the paper towel dispenser as you get the towels.	10	_____	_____	_____

253

Steps	Possible Points	Attempt 1	Attempt 2	Attempt 3
8. Remove the utility gloves and wash your hands according to Procedure 27-4.	10	_____	_____	_____
9. Towel dry your hands and put on disposable gloves. Decontaminate the utility gloves and work surfaces using a disinfectant cleaner. Dispose of the contaminated towels in a biohazardous waste container.	10	_____	_____	_____
10. Remove the disposable gloves according to Procedure 27-1. Dispose of the gloves in a biohazardous waste container. Sanitize your hands.	10	_____	_____	_____
11. Towel dry your hands and place the sanitized instruments in the designated area for disinfection or sterilization.	10	_____	_____	_____

Comments:

Points earned _____ ÷ 100 possible points = Score _____ % Score

Instructor's signature _____

Name _____ Date _____ Score _____

PROCEDURE 28-1 Obtain and Record a Patient History

CAAHEP COMPETENCIES: I.AI.2, I.AI.3, IV.PIV.1, IV.PIV.8, IV.PIV.11, IV.AIV.1, IV.AIV.10
ABHES COMPETENCIES: 9.b

NOTE: Complete this procedure with another student role-playing the patient. To make the experience more realistic, choose a student about whom you know very little. To maintain the privacy of your student partner, he or she does not have to share any confidential information while participating in the role-play.

TASK: To obtain an acceptable written background from a patient to help the physician determine the cause and effects of the present illness. This includes the chief complaint (CC), present illness (PI), past history (PH), family history (FH), and social history (SH).

Equipment and Supplies

- History form
- Two pens—a red pen for recording patient allergies and a black pen to meet legal documentation guidelines
- Quiet, private area

Standards: Complete the Procedure and all critical steps in _____ minutes with a minimum score of 85% within three attempts.

Scoring: Divide the points earned by the total possible points. Failure to perform a critical step, indicated by an asterisk (*), results in an unsatisfactory overall score.

Time began _____   Time ended _____   Total minutes: _____

Steps	Possible Points	Attempt 1	Attempt 2	Attempt 3
1. Greet and identify the patient in a pleasant manner. Introduce yourself and explain your role.	10	_____	_____	_____
2. Take the patient to a quiet, private area for the interview and explain why the information is needed.	10	_____	_____	_____
3. Complete the history form by using therapeutic communication techniques. Make sure all medical terminology is adequately explained. A self-history may have been mailed to the patient before the visit. If so, review the self-history for completeness.	10	_____	_____	_____
4. Speak in a pleasant, distinct voice, remembering to maintain eye contact with the patient. Be sensitive to your patient's diverse needs throughout the interview.	10	_____	_____	_____
5. Remain sensitive to the diverse needs of your patient throughout the interview process.				

Steps	Possible Points	Attempt 1	Attempt 2	Attempt 3
6. Record the following statistical information on the patient information form:	10			
a. Patient's full name, including middle initial		_____	_____	_____
b. Address, including apartment number and ZIP code		_____	_____	_____
c. Marital status		_____	_____	_____
d. Sex (gender)		_____	_____	_____
e. Age and date of birth		_____	_____	_____
f. Telephone number for home and work		_____	_____	_____
g. Insurance information, if not already available		_____	_____	_____
h. Employer's name, address, and telephone number		_____	_____	_____
7. Record the following medical history on the patient history (PH) form:	10			
a. Chief complaint (CC)		_____	_____	_____
b. Present illness		_____	_____	_____
c. Past history		_____	_____	_____
d. Family history		_____	_____	_____
e. Social history		_____	_____	_____
8. Ask about allergies to drugs and any other substances and record any allergies in red ink on every page of the history form, on the front of the chart, and on each progress note page. Some practices apply allergy alert labels to the front of each patient record or mark the record accordingly if using an EHR system.	10	_____	_____	_____
9. Record all information legibly and neatly and spell words correctly. Print rather than writing in longhand. Do not erase, scribble, or use whiteout. If you make an error, draw a single line through the error, write "error" above it, add the correction, and initial and date the entry.	10	_____	_____	_____
10. Thank the patient for cooperating and direct the person back to the reception area.	10	_____	_____	_____
11. Review the record for errors before you pass it to the physician. Use the information on the record to complete the patient's medical record.	10	_____	_____	_____
12. Keep the information confidential.				

Documentation in the Medical Record:

Mr. Borski is a new patient being seen today for the first time. His CC is dizziness for 2 weeks. He denies having headaches and has no previous Hx of ear infections or hypertension. He does not take any prescribed medications but uses Tylenol as needed for a headache. His vital signs are: T, 97.6; P, 88; R, 22; BP, 172/94. Document the pertinent patient findings using the SOAPE method.

S _____

   _____

   _____

O _____

   _____

   _____

Comments:

Points earned _____ ÷ 100 possible points = Score _____ % Score

Instructor's signature _____

PROCEDURE 30-1 Teach the Patient to Understand Food Labels

CAAHEP COMPETENCIES: I.AI.1, I.AI.2, III.AIII.2, IV.PIV.5, IV.PIV.9, IV.PIV.11, IV.AIV.1, IV.AIV.3
ABHES COMPETENCIES: 9.h

TASK: To explain the nutritional labeling of food products accurately to the patient.

Equipment and Supplies
- One each of three bars: Snickers candy bar, granola bar, fat-free fruit bar
- Pencil and paper
- Patient's record

Standards: Complete the Procedure and all critical steps in _____ minutes with a minimum score of 85% within three attempts.

Scoring: Divide the points earned by the total possible points. Failure to perform a critical step, indicated by an asterisk (*), results in an unsatisfactory overall score.

Time began _____   **Time ended** _____   **Total minutes:** _____

Steps	Possible Points	Attempt 1	Attempt 2	Attempt 3
1. Asses the patient using the patient health and family histories to determine cultural influences that may affect dietary choices.	5	____	____	____
2. Introduce yourself and explain to the patient that you are going to teach him or her how to read a food label. Be sure to include reasons food labels are a valuable source of nutritional information in diet planning.	10	____	____	____
3. Using the labels on each bar, point out the nutritional information according to the guidelines in the text.	10	____	____	____
4. Give the patient the pencil and paper to write down the serving size of each type of bar.	10	____	____	____
5. Compare similarities and differences.	10	____	____	____
6. Have the patient write down the total calories for each product serving.	10	____	____	____
7. Compare similarities and differences.	10	____	____	____
8. Have the patient write down the percentage of total, saturated, trans, and unsaturated fats.	10	____	____	____
9. Compare similarities and differences.	10	____	____	____
10. Together, analyze the nutritional level of each.	5	____	____	____
11. Discuss any new information the patient learned.	5	____	____	____
12. Ask the patient whether he or she will use this information when shopping and how it will be implemented in nutritional planning.	5	____	____	____

259

Comments:

Points earned _____ ÷ 100 possible points = Score _____ % Score

Instructor's signature _____

Procedure 30-1 Teach the Patient to Read Food Labels

PROCEDURE 31-1 Obtain Vital Signs: Obtain an Oral Temperature Using a Digital Thermometer

CAAHEP COMPETENCIES: I.PI.1, I.AI.2, III.PIII.2, IV.PIV.2, IV.PIV.8
ABHES COMPETENCIES: 9.b

TASK: To determine and record a patient's temperature accurately using a digital thermometer.

Equipment and Supplies
- Digital thermometer
- Probe covers
- Biohazardous waste container
- Disposable gloves as appropriate
- Patient's record

Standards: Complete the Procedure and all critical steps in _____ minutes with a minimum score of 85% within three attempts.

Scoring: Divide the points earned by the total possible points. Failure to perform a critical step, indicated by an asterisk (*), results in an unsatisfactory overall score.

Time began _____   Time ended _____   Total minutes: _____

Steps	Possible Points	Attempt 1	Attempt 2	Attempt 3
1. Sanitize your hands.	5	____	____	____
2. Assemble the needed equipment and supplies.				
*3. Identify your patient and explain the procedure. Make sure the patient has not eaten, consumed any hot or cold fluids, smoked, or exercised during the 30 minutes before the procedure.	20	____	____	____
4. Prepare the probe according to the package's directions. Make sure always to use probe covers.	10	____	____	____
5. Place the probe under the patient's tongue and instruct the patient to close the mouth tightly without biting down on the thermometer. Assist the patient by holding the probe's end.	10	____	____	____
*6. When the "beep" sounds, remove the probe from the patient's mouth and immediately eject the probe cover into the appropriate waste container.	20	____	____	____
7. Note the reading in the LED window of the processing unit.	10	____	____	____
*8. Record the reading on the patient's medical record (e.g., T = 97.7°).	10	____	____	____
9. Sanitize your hands and disinfect the equipment as indicated.	10	____	____	____

Documentation in the Medical Record:

A 55-year-old patient arrives today complaining of cough and congestion for 5 days. She states that she has had a fever of 100.7° F for 2 days at home. She is not taking any medication currently and is allergic to Amoxil. Obtain an oral temperature and document the case below using SOAPE format.

S _____

   _____

   _____

O _____

   _____

   _____

Comments:

Points earned _____ ÷ **100 possible points = Score** _____ **% Score**

Instructor's signature _____

Name _____ Date _____ Score _____

PROCEDURE 31-2 Obtain Vital Signs: Obtain an Aural Temperature Using the Tympanic Thermometer

CAAHEP COMPETENCIES: I.PI.1, I.AI.2, III.PIII.2, IV.PIV.2, IV.PIV.8
ABHES COMPETENCIES: 9.b

TASK: To measure and record a patient's temperature accurately using a tympanic thermometer.

Equipment and Supplies
- Tympanic thermometer
- Disposable probe covers
- Biohazardous waste container
- Disposable gloves as appropriate
- Patient's record

Standards: Complete the Procedure and all critical steps in _____ minutes with a minimum score of 85% within three attempts.

Scoring: Divide the points earned by the total possible points. Failure to perform a critical step, indicated by an asterisk (*), results in an unsatisfactory overall score.

Time began _____ Time ended _____ Total minutes: _____

Steps	Possible Points	Attempt 1	Attempt 2	Attempt 3
1. Sanitize your hands.	5	_____	_____	_____
2. Gather the necessary equipment and supplies.	10	_____	_____	_____
3. Identify your patient and explain the procedure.	10	_____	_____	_____
4. Place a disposable cover on the probe.	10	_____	_____	_____
5. Follow the package's directions to start the thermometer.	10	_____	_____	_____
6. Insert the probe into the ear canal far enough to seal the opening. Do not apply pressure. For children under age 3, gently pull the earlobe down and back; for patients over age 3, gently pull the top of the ear up and back.	10	_____	_____	_____
7. Press the button on the probe as directed. The temperature will appear on the display screen in 1 to 2 seconds.	10	_____	_____	_____
8. Remove the probe, note the reading, and discard the probe cover without touching it.				
9. Sanitize your hands and disinfect the equipment if indicated.	10	_____	_____	_____
*10. Record the temperature (e.g., T = 98.6° [T]) in the patient's medical record.	10	_____	_____	_____

Documentation in the Medical Record:

The mother of a 3-year-old patient brings her toddler to the physician's office because the child has had a rash on the left forearm for 3 days. The patient is not allergic to any medication and does not take any medications daily. Obtain an aural temperature and document the case using the SOAPE format.

S   _____

    _____

    _____

O   _____

    _____

    _____

Comments:

Points earned _____ ÷ 100 possible points = Score _____ % Score

Instructor's signature _____

Name _____ Date _____ Score _____

PROCEDURE 31-3 Obtain Vital Signs: Obtain a Temporal Artery Temperature

CAAHEP COMPETENCIES: I.PI.1, I.AI.2, III.PIII.2, IV.PIV.2, IV.PIV.8
ABHES COMPETENCIES: 9.b

TASK: To determine and record a patient's temperature accurately using a temporal artery scanner.

Equipment and Supplies
- Temporal artery thermometer
- Alcohol swab
- Patient's record

Standards: Complete the Procedure and all critical steps in _____ minutes with a minimum score of 85% within three attempts.

Scoring: Divide the points earned by the total possible points. Failure to perform a critical step, indicated by an asterisk (*), results in an unsatisfactory overall score.

Time began _____ Time ended _____ Total minutes: _____

Steps	Possible Points	Attempt 1	Attempt 2	Attempt 3
1. Sanitize your hands.	5	_____	_____	_____
2. Gather the necessary equipment and supplies.	10	_____	_____	_____
3. Introduce yourself, identify your patient, and explain the procedure.	10	_____	_____	_____
4. Remove the protective cap on the probe. The probe can be cleaned by lightly wiping the surface with an alcohol swab.	10	_____	_____	_____
5. Push the patient's hair up off the forehead to expose the site. Gently place the probe on the patient's forehead, halfway between the eyebrows and the hairline.	10	_____	_____	_____
6. Depress and hold the SCAN button and lightly glide the probe sideways across the patient's forehead to the hairline just above the ear. As the sensor is moved across the forehead, a beep sounds and a red light flashes.	10	_____	_____	_____
7. Keep the button depressed, lift the thermometer, and place the probe on the upper neck behind the earlobe. The thermometer may continue to beep, indicating that the temperature is rising.	10	_____	_____	_____
8. When scanning is complete, release the button and lift the probe. Note the temperature recorded on the digital display. The scanner automatically turns off 15 to 30 seconds after the button is released.	10	_____	_____	_____
9. Disinfect the thermometer if indicated and replace the protective cap.	10	_____	_____	_____
10. Sanitize your hands.	5	_____	_____	_____
11. Record the temperature results (e.g., T = 101.6° [TA]) in the patient's medical record.	10	_____	_____	_____

265

Comments:

Points earned _____ ÷ 100 possible points = Score _____ % Score

Instructor's signature _____

Procedure **31-3 Obtain Vital Signs**

PROCEDURE 31-4 Obtain Vital Signs: Obtain an Axillary Temperature

CAAHEP COMPETENCIES: I.PI.1, I.AI.2, III.PIII.2, IV.PIV.2, IV.PIV.8
ABHES COMPETENCIES: 9.b

TASK: To determine and record a patient's temperature accurately using the axillary method.

Equipment and Supplies

- Digital unit
- Thermometer sheath or probe cover
- Supply of tissues
- Biohazardous waste container
- Disposable gloves as appropriate
- Patient gown as needed
- Patient's record

Standards: Complete the Procedure and all critical steps in _____ minutes with a minimum score of 85% within three attempts.

Scoring: Divide the points earned by the total possible points. Failure to perform a critical step, indicated by an asterisk (*), results in an unsatisfactory overall score.

Time began _____ Time ended _____ Total minutes: _____

Steps	Possible Points	Attempt 1	Attempt 2	Attempt 3
1. Sanitize your hands.	5	_____	_____	_____
2. Gather the needed equipment and supplies.	10	_____	_____	_____
*3. Introduce yourself, identify your patient, and explain the procedure.	10	_____	_____	_____
4. Prepare the thermometer or digital unit in same manner as for oral use.	10	_____	_____	_____
5. Remove the patient's clothing, and gown the patient as needed to access the axillary region. Pat the axillary area dry with tissues if necessary.	10	_____	_____	_____
*6. Cover the thermometer or probe and place the tip in the center of the armpit, pointing the stem toward the upper chest and making sure the thermometer touches only skin, not clothing.	10	_____	_____	_____
7. Instruct the patient to hold the arm snugly across the chest or abdomen until the thermometer beeps.	10	_____	_____	_____
8. Remove the thermometer, note the digital reading, and dispose of the cover in the biohazardous waste container.	10	_____	_____	_____
9. Disinfect the thermometer if indicated.	10	_____	_____	_____
10. Sanitize your hands.	5	_____	_____	_____
*11. Record the axillary temperature in the patient's medical record (e.g., T 5 97.6° [A]).	10	_____	_____	_____

Documentation in the Medical Record:

A 7-month-old patient is brought to the office today. The child's mother states that the baby has been pulling at the left ear for 2 days. She also states that the baby has had no appetite. The mother says she doesn't have a thermometer at home, so she's not sure whether the child has had a fever. Obtain an axillary temperature and document your finding using the SOAPE format.

S   _____

     _____

     _____

O   _____

     _____

     _____

     _____

Comments:

Points earned _____ ÷ 100 possible points = **Score** _____ **% Score**

             Instructor's signature _____

Name _____ Date _____ Score _____

PROCEDURE 31-5 Obtain Vital Signs: Obtain an Apical Pulse

CAAHEP COMPETENCIES: I.PI.1, I.AI.2, III.PIII.2, IV.PIV.2, IV.PIV.8
ABHES COMPETENCIES: 9.b

TASK: To determine and record accurately a patient's apical heart rate.

Equipment and Supplies
- Watch with a second hand
- Patient gown as needed
- Stethoscope
- Alcohol wipes
- Patient's record

Standards: Complete the Procedure and all critical steps in _____ minutes with a minimum score of 85% within three attempts.

Scoring: Divide the points earned by the total possible points. Failure to perform a critical step, indicated by an asterisk (*), results in an unsatisfactory overall score.

Time began _____   Time ended _____   Total minutes: _____

Steps	Possible Points	Attempt 1	Attempt 2	Attempt 3
1. Sanitize your hands and clean the stethoscope's earpieces and diaphragm with alcohol swabs.	5	_____	_____	_____
*2. Introduce yourself, identify your patient, and explain the procedure.	20	_____	_____	_____
3. If necessary, help the patient disrobe from the waist up and provide a gown that opens in the front.	10	_____	_____	_____
4. Assist the patient into the sitting or supine position.	10	_____	_____	_____
5. Hold the stethoscope's diaphragm against the palm of your hand for a few seconds.	10	_____	_____	_____
6. Place the stethoscope just below the left nipple in the intercostal space between the fifth and sixth ribs, over the apex of the heart.	10	_____	_____	_____
*7. Listen carefully for the heartbeat. Count the pulse for 1 full minute. Note any irregularities in rhythm and volume.	10	_____	_____	_____
8. Help the patient sit up and dress.	5	_____	_____	_____
9. Sanitize your hands.	5	_____	_____	_____
*10. Record the pulse in the patient's chart (e.g., AP = 96), as well as any arrhythmias.	10	_____	_____	_____

Documentation in the Medical Record:

A patient comes to the office today complaining that he has had pain in the left lower abdominal quadrant for 3 weeks. The patient also complains of nausea after eating. The patient denies any constipation or diarrhea. Obtain an apical pulse and document the case using the SOAPE format.

S _____

   _____

   _____

O _____

   _____

   _____

Comments:

Points earned _____ ÷ 100 possible points = Score _____ % Score

           Instructor's signature _____

PROCEDURE 31-6 Obtain Vital Signs: Assess the Patient's Radial Pulse

CAAHEP COMPETENCIES: I.PI.1, I.AI.2, III.PIII.2, IV.PIV.2, IV.PIV.8
ABHES COMPETENCIES: 9.b

TASK: To determine and record accurately a patient's radial pulse rate, rhythm, and volume.

Equipment and Supplies
- Watch with a second hand
- Patient's record

Standards: Complete the Procedure and all critical steps in _____ minutes with a minimum score of 85% within three attempts.

Scoring: Divide the points earned by the total possible points. Failure to perform a critical step, indicated by an asterisk (*), results in an unsatisfactory overall score.

Time began _____ **Time ended** _____ **Total minutes:** _____

Steps	Possible Points	Attempt 1	Attempt 2	Attempt 3
1. Sanitize your hands.	5	_____	_____	_____
*2. Introduce yourself, identify your patient, and explain the procedure.	10	_____	_____	_____
3. Place the patient's arm in a relaxed position, palm downward, at or below the level of the heart.	10	_____	_____	_____
4. Gently grasp the palm side of the patient's wrist with your first three fingertips approximately 1 inch below the base of the thumb.	20	_____	_____	_____
*5. Using a watch with a second hand, count the beats for 1 full minute.	20	_____	_____	_____
6. Sanitize your hands.	5	_____	_____	_____
*7. Record the count and any irregularities in the patient's medical record (e.g., P = 72).	20	_____	_____	_____

Documentation in the Medical Record:

A 32-year-old patient arrives today to follow up on her diabetes medication. She has no other complaints. Obtain a pulse and document the finding using the SOAPE format.

S   _____

     _____

     _____

O   _____

     _____

     _____

Comments:

Points earned _____ ÷ 100 possible points = **Score** _____ **% Score**

Instructor's signature _____

Procedure **31-6 Obtain Vital Signs**

Name _____ Date _____ Score _____

PROCEDURE 31-7 Obtain Vital Signs: Determine the Respiratory Rate

CAAHEP COMPETENCIES: I.PI.1, I.AI.2, III.PIII.2, IV.PIV.2, IV.PIV.8
ABHES COMPETENCIES: 9.b

TASK: To determine and record a patient's respirations accurately. Remember that the respiratory count may be altered if the patient is aware that you are counting his or her breaths. Respirations are typically are counted immediately after taking the pulse has been taken while the fingers are still at the radial site.

Equipment and Supplies
- Watch with a second hand
- Patient's record

Standards: Complete the Procedure and all critical steps in _____ minutes with a minimum score of 85% within three attempts.

Scoring: Divide the points earned by the total possible points. Failure to perform a critical step, indicated by an asterisk (*), results in an unsatisfactory overall score.

Time began _____   Time ended _____   Total minutes: _____

Steps	Possible Points	Attempt 1	Attempt 2	Attempt 3
1. Sanitize your hands.	5	_____	_____	_____
2. Identify your patient.	10	_____	_____	_____
3. Place the patient's arm in the same position as for counting the pulse. If you are having difficulty noticing breathing, place the arm across the chest to pick up movement.	10	_____	_____	_____
*4. Note the rise and fall of the patient's chest.	20	_____	_____	_____
5. Using a watch with a second hand, count the respirations for 30 seconds and multiply by 2.	20	_____	_____	_____
6. Release the patient's wrist.	10	_____	_____	_____
7. Sanitize your hands.	5	_____	_____	_____
*8. Record the respirations in the patient's medical record after the pulse recording (e.g., R = 18).	10	_____	_____	_____

Documentation in the Medical Record:

A 32-year-old patient arrives today to follow up on her blood pressure medication. She has no other complaints. Measure the respirations and document the finding using the SOAPE format.

S _____

_____

_____

O _____

_____

_____

Comments:

Points earned _____ ÷ 100 possible points = Score _____ % Score

Instructor's signature _____

PROCEDURE 31-8 Obtain Vital Signs: Determine a Patient's Blood Pressure

CAAHEP COMPETENCIES: I.PI.1, I.AI.2, III.PIII.2, IV.PIV.2, IV.PIV.8
ABHES COMPETENCIES: 9.b

TASK: To perform a blood pressure measurement that is correct in technique, accurate, and comfortable for the patient.

Equipment and Supplies
- Sphygmomanometer
- Stethoscope
- Antiseptic wipes/alcohol swabs
- Patient's record

Standards: Complete the Procedure and all critical steps in _____ minutes with a minimum score of 85% within three attempts.

Scoring: Divide the points earned by the total possible points. Failure to perform a critical step, indicated by an asterisk (*), results in an unsatisfactory overall score.

Time began _____   **Time ended** _____   **Total minutes:** _____

Steps	Possible Points	Attempt 1	Attempt 2	Attempt 3
1. Sanitize your hands.	5	_____	_____	_____
2. Assemble the needed equipment and supplies. Clean the stethoscope's earpieces and diaphragm with alcohol swabs.	5	_____	_____	_____
*3. Introduce yourself, identify the patient, and explain the procedure.	5	_____	_____	_____
4. Select the appropriate arm for the cuff (e.g., no mastectomy on that side, no injury or disease).	5	_____	_____	_____
5. Seat the patient in a comfortable position with the legs uncrossed and the arm resting on the lap or a table, palm up, at heart level.	5	_____	_____	_____
6. Roll up the sleeve to about 5 inches above the elbow or have the patient remove the arm from the sleeve.	5	_____	_____	_____
*7. Determine the correct cuff size.	5	_____	_____	_____
8. Palpate the brachial artery at the antecubital space in both arms. If one arm has a stronger pulse, use that arm. If the pulses are equal, select the right arm.	5	_____	_____	_____
9. Center the cuff bladder over the brachial artery; the connecting tube is away from the patient's body and the tube to the bulb is close to the body.	5	_____	_____	_____

275

Steps	Possible Points	Attempt 1	Attempt 2	Attempt 3
*10. Place the lower edge of the cuff about 1 inch above the palpable brachial pulse (normally located in the natural crease of the inner elbow) and wrap the cuff snugly and smoothly.	5	_____	_____	_____
11. Position the gauge of the sphygmomanometer so that it is easily seen.	5	_____	_____	_____
12. Palpate the brachial pulse, tighten the screw valve on the air pump, and inflate the cuff until the pulse can no longer be felt. Make a note at the point on the gauge where the pulse could no longer be felt. Mentally add 30 mm Hg to the reading. Deflate the cuff and wait for 15 seconds.	10	_____	_____	_____
13. Insert the earpieces of the stethoscope turned forward into the ear canals.	5	_____	_____	_____
14. Place the stethoscope bell or diaphragm over the palpated brachial artery firmly enough to obtain a seal but not so tightly as to constrict the artery.	5	_____	_____	_____
15. Close the valve and squeeze the bulb to inflate the cuff rapidly but smoothly to 30 mm above the previously palpated pulse level.	5	_____	_____	_____
*16. Open the valve slightly and deflate the cuff at a constant rate of 2 to 3 mm Hg per heartbeat.	5	_____	_____	_____
17. Listen throughout the entire deflation; note the point on the gauge where you hear the first sound (systolic) and the last sound (diastolic) until the sounds have stopped for at least 10 mm Hg. Read the pressure to the closest even number.	10	_____	_____	_____
18. Do not reinflate the cuff once the air has been released. Wait 30 to 60 seconds to repeat the procedure if needed.	10	_____	_____	_____
19. Remove the stethoscope from your ears and record the systolic and diastolic readings as BP systolic/diastolic (e.g., BP 120/80).	10	_____	_____	_____
20. Remove the cuff from the patient's arm and return it to its proper storage area. Clean the earpieces of the stethoscope with alcohol and return it to storage. Sanitize your hands.	10	_____	_____	_____
21. Sanitize your hands.	5	_____	_____	_____

Documentation in the Medical Record:
A 32-year-old patient arrives today to follow up on her blood pressure medication. She has no other complaints. She states that she has stopped taking her Diovan 80 mg because of lack of prescription coverage. Measure her blood pressure and document the finding using the SOAPE format.

S _____

_____

_____

O _____

_____

_____

Comments:

Points earned _____ ÷ **100 possible points = Score** _____ **% Score**

Instructor's signature _____

PROCEDURE 31-9 Obtain Vital Signs: Measure a Patient's Weight and Height

CAAHEP COMPETENCIES: I.PI.1, I.AI.2, III.PIII.2, IV.PIV.2, IV.PIV.8
ABHES COMPETENCIES: 9.b

TASK: To weigh a patient and measure the height accurately as part of the physical assessment procedure.

Note: Make sure the scale is located in an area away from traffic to maintain patient privacy.

Equipment and Supplies
- Balance scale with a measuring bar
- Paper towel
- Patient's record

Standards: Complete the Procedure and all critical steps in _____ minutes with a minimum score of 85% within three attempts.

Scoring: Divide the points earned by the total possible points. Failure to perform a critical step, indicated by an asterisk (*), results in an unsatisfactory overall score.

Time began _____   **Time ended** _____   **Total minutes:** _____

Steps	Possible Points	Attempt 1	Attempt 2	Attempt 3
1. Sanitize your hands.	5	_____	_____	_____
*2. Introduce yourself, identify your patient, and explain the procedure.	5	_____	_____	_____
3. If the patient is to remove the shoes for weighing, place a paper towel on the scale platform, or the patient may be given disposable slippers to wear.	5	_____	_____	_____
4. Check to see that the balance bar pointer floats in the middle of the balance frame when all weights are at zero.	10	_____	_____	_____
5. Help the patient onto the scale. Make sure the patient has removed any heavy objects from the pockets and that a female patient is not holding a purse.	10	_____	_____	_____
*6. Move the large weight into the groove closest to the patient's estimated weight.	10	_____	_____	_____
7. While the patient is standing still, slide the small upper weight to the right along the pound markers until the pointer balances in the middle of the balance frame.				
8. Leave the weights in place.	5	_____	_____	_____
9. Ask the patient to stand up straight and look straight ahead. On some scales the patient may need to turn with the back to the scale.	5	_____	_____	_____
*10. Adjust the height bar so that it just touches the top of the patient's head.	10	_____	_____	_____

Steps	Possible Points	Attempt 1	Attempt 2	Attempt 3
11. Leave the elevation bar set but fold down the horizontal bar.				
12. Assist the patient off the scale. Make sure all items removed for weighing are given back to the patient.	5	_____	_____	_____
13. Read the weight scale. Add the numbers at the markers of the large and the small weights and record the total to the nearest ¼ pound in the patient's medical record (e.g., Wt: 136½).	10	_____	_____	_____
14. Record the height. Read the marker at the movable point of the ruler and record the measurement to the nearest ¼ inch in the patient's medical record (e.g., Ht: 64¼).	10	_____	_____	_____
15. Use the patient's weight and height to record the BMI if this is part of office procedure.	5	_____	_____	_____
16. Return the weights and the measuring bar to zero.	5	_____	_____	_____
17. Sanitize your hands.	5	_____	_____	_____
*18. Record the results in the patient's medical record.	5	_____	_____	_____

Documentation in the Medical Record:

A patient arrives today for a general physical. Measure and record the patient's weight and height using the SOAPE format.

S   _____

      _____

      _____

O   _____

      _____

      _____

Comments:

Points earned _____ ÷ 100 possible points = Score _____ % Score

Instructor's signature _____

Name _____ Date _____ Score _____

PROCEDURE 32-1 Prepare and Maintain the Examination and Treatment Areas

CAAHEP COMPETENCIES: I.PI.10, III.PIII.2
ABHES COMPETENCIES: 9.c

TASK: To prepare an examination room for a patient procedure, maintain equipment and supplies needed for the physical examination, and demonstrate maintenance of the room after a patient visit.

Equipment and Supplies

- Examination table
- Patient gown
- Drape
- Stethoscope
- Ophthalmoscope
- Disposable gloves
- Scale with height measurement bar
- Tongue depressor
- Cotton balls
- Examination light
- Percussion hammer
- Lubricating gel
- Examination gloves
- Sphygmomanometer
- Otoscope with disposable speculum
- Tape measure
- Gauze sponges
- Pen light
- Nasal speculum
- Tuning fork
- Biohazardous waste container
- Laboratory request forms
- Specimen bottles/lab requisitions
- Thermometer
- Cotton-tipped applicators
- Hemoccult supplies
- Table paper
- Spray disinfectant

Standards: Complete the procedure and all critical steps in _____ minutes with a minimum score of 85% in three attempts.

Scoring: Divide the points earned by the total possible points. Failure to perform a critical step, indicated by an asterisk (*), results in an unsatisfactory overall score.

Time began _____ **Time ended** _____ **Total minutes:** _____

Steps	Possible Points	Attempt 1	Attempt 2	Attempt 3
1. Check the area at the start of each day and between patients to make sure it is completely stocked with equipment and supplies and that the equipment is functioning properly.	10	_____	_____	_____
2. Check all equipment and instruments to make sure they are operational; refer to the manual supplied by the manufacturer as needed.	10	_____	_____	_____
*3. Check expiration dates on all packages and supplies regularly; discard expired materials as needed.	20	_____	_____	_____
4. Check to make sure the room is private, well lit, and a comfortable temperature for the patient.	10	_____	_____	_____
*5. Prepare the examination room before and between patients according to the rules of acceptable medical asepsis.	10	_____	_____	_____
6. After each patient use, put on disposable examination gloves, spray the table and any other contaminated surface with a disinfectant, clean the area with disposable towels, dispose of waste and the gloves in an appropriate biohazardous waste container, and put clean paper on the table.	20	_____	_____	_____
7. Sanitize your hands.	10	_____	_____	_____
8. Inventory the supplies needed after each patient visit and restock as needed.	10	_____	_____	_____

Comments:

Points earned _____ ÷ 100 possible points = Score _____ % Score

Instructor's signature _____

PROCEDURE 32-2 Prepare the Patient for and Assist with Routine and Specialty Examinations: The Fowler's and Semi-Fowler's Positions

CAAHEP COMPETENCIES: I.PI.10, I.AI.2
ABHES COMPETENCIES: 9.d

TASK: To position and drape the patient for examinations of the head, neck, and chest or for patients who have difficulty breathing when lying flat.

Equipment and Supplies
- Examination table
- Table paper
- Patient gown
- Drape
- Spray disinfectant
- Examination gloves

Standards: Complete the procedure and all critical steps in _____ minutes with a minimum score of 85% in three attempts.

Scoring: Divide the points earned by the total possible points. Failure to perform a critical step, indicated by an asterisk (*), results in an unsatisfactory overall score.

Time began _____   Time ended _____   Total minutes: _____

Steps	Possible Points	Attempt 1	Attempt 2	Attempt 3
1. Prepare the examination room according to the rules of medical asepsis.	10	_____	_____	_____
2. Sanitize your hands.	10	_____	_____	_____
3. Greet and identify the patient and determine whether the person understands the procedure. If not, explain what to expect.	10	_____	_____	_____
*4. Give the patient a gown and explain the clothing that must be removed for this particular examination. Also explain whether the gown should open in the front or the back. Provide assistance as needed. Give the patient privacy while changing. Knock on the examination room door before re-entering to make sure the patient has finished undressing and gowning.	10	_____	_____	_____
5. Either elevate the head of the table 90 degrees or instruct the patient to sit at the end of the table. Extend the foot rest for the patient's comfort. The patient may be more comfortable in a semi-Fowler's position. In this modification of the Fowler's position, the head of the table is elevated 45 degrees. This position may be used for postsurgical follow-up or for patients with a fever, head injuries, or pain. It also is a comfortable, supported position for patients with breathing disorders.	10	_____	_____	_____

Steps	Possible Points	Attempt 1	Attempt 2	Attempt 3
6. Drape the patient according to the type of examination and the patient exposure required.	10	_____	_____	_____
7. After the examination, assist the patient as needed to get off the table and get dressed.	10	_____	_____	_____
8. Clean and disinfect the examination room according to Standard Precautions. Roll clean paper over the table.	10	_____	_____	_____
9. Sanitize your hands.	10	_____	_____	_____
10. Follow up with the physician's orders regarding scheduling of diagnostic studies, collection of specimens, and/or scheduling of future appointments.	10	_____	_____	_____

Comments:

Points earned _____ ÷ 100 possible points = Score _____ % Score

Instructor's signature _____

Procedure **32-2 Fowler's and Semi-Fowler's Positions**

PROCEDURE 32-3 Prepare the Patient for and Assist with Routine and Specialty Examinations: The Horizontal Recumbent and Dorsal Recumbent Positions

CAAHEP COMPETENCIES: I.PI.10, I.AI.2
ABHES COMPETENCIES: 9.c, 9.d

TASK: To position and drape the patient for examinations of the abdomen, heart, and breasts in the horizontal recumbent (supine) position and for examinations of the rectal, vaginal, and perineal areas in the dorsal recumbent position.

Equipment and Supplies
- Examination table
- Table paper
- Patient gown
- Drape
- Spray disinfectant
- Examination gloves

Standards: Complete the procedure and all critical steps in _____ minutes with a minimum score of 85% in three attempts.

Scoring: Divide the points earned by the total possible points. Failure to perform a critical step, indicated by an asterisk (*), results in an unsatisfactory overall score.

Time began _____ **Time ended** _____ **Total minutes:** _____

Steps	Possible Points	Attempt 1	Attempt 2	Attempt 3
1. Prepare the examination room according to the rules of medical asepsis.	10	_____	_____	_____
2. Sanitize your hands.	10	_____	_____	_____
3. Greet and identify the patient and determine whether the person understands the procedure. If not, explain what to expect.	10	_____	_____	_____
*4. Give the patient a gown and explain the clothing that must be removed for this examination; also explain whether the gown should open in the front or the back. Provide assistance as needed. For the horizontal recumbent position, the gown should open in the front. Give the patient privacy while changing. Knock on the examination room door before re-entering to make sure the patient has finished undressing and gowning.	10	_____	_____	_____
5. Do not place the patient in these positions until the physician is ready for that part of the examination.	5	_____	_____	_____
6. Pull out the table extension that supports the patient's legs. For the horizontal recumbent (supine) position, help the patient lie flat on the table, face up. For the dorsal recumbent position, have the patient lie flat on the back and flex the knees so that the feet are flat on the table. If needed, help the patient move down toward the foot of the table for the examination.	10	_____	_____	_____

285

Steps	Possible Points	Attempt 1	Attempt 2	Attempt 3
7. For the supine position, drape the patient from the nipple line to the feet. For the dorsal recumbent position, position the drape diagonally with the point of the drape between the feet.	10	_____	_____	_____
8. After the examination, assist the patient as needed to get off the table and get dressed.	5	_____	_____	_____
9. Clean and disinfect the examination room according to Standard Precautions. Roll clean paper over the table.	10	_____	_____	_____
10. Sanitize your hands.	10	_____	_____	_____
11. Follow up with the physician's orders regarding scheduling of diagnostic studies, collection of specimens, and/or scheduling of future appointments.	10	_____	_____	_____

Comments:

Points earned _____ ÷ 100 possible points = Score _____ % Score

Instructor's signature _____

Name _____ Date _____ Score _____

PROCEDURE 32-4 Prepare the Patient for and Assist with Routine and Specialty Examinations: The Lithotomy Position

CAAHEP COMPETENCIES: I.PI.10, I.AI.2
ABHES COMPETENCIES: 9.c, 9.d

TASK: To position and drape the patient primarily for vaginal and pelvic examinations and Pap smears.

Equipment and Supplies
- Examination table
- Table paper
- Patient gown
- Drape
- Spray disinfectant
- Examination gloves

Standards: Complete the procedure and all critical steps in _____ minutes with a minimum score of 85% in three attempts.

Scoring: Divide the points earned by the total possible points. Failure to perform a critical step, indicated by an asterisk (*), results in an unsatisfactory overall score.

Time began _____   Time ended _____   Total minutes: _____

Steps	Possible Points	Attempt 1	Attempt 2	Attempt 3
1. Prepare the examination room according to the rules of medical asepsis.	10	_____	_____	_____
2. Sanitize your hands.	10	_____	_____	_____
3. Greet and identify the patient and determine whether the person understands the procedure. If not, explain what to expect.	10	_____	_____	_____
*4. Give the patient a gown and instruct the patient to undress from the waist down with the gown open in the back. If the physician will also be doing a breast examination, the gown should open in the front. Provide assistance as needed. Give the patient privacy while changing. Knock on the examination room door before re-entering to make sure the patient has finished undressing and gowning. Do not place the patient in this position until the physician is ready for that part of the examination.	10	_____	_____	_____
5. Pull out the table extension that supports the patient's legs and help the patient lie face up on the table. Pull out the stirrups, adjust their extension length for the patient's comfort, and lock them in place.	10	_____	_____	_____
6. Reinsert the table extension and have the patient move toward the foot of the table with her buttocks on the bottom table edge. Gently place the patient's legs in the stirrups, checking for comfort. Some offices stock cloth or paper stirrup covers to protect the patient and make the position more comfortable. The patient's arms can be placed alongside the body or across the chest.	10	_____	_____	_____

287

Steps	Possible Points	Attempt 1	Attempt 2	Attempt 3
7. Drape the patient diagonally with the point of the drape between the feet. The drape should be large enough to cover the patient from the nipple line to the ankles and wide enough to prevent exposure of the patient's thighs.	**10**	_____	_____	_____
8. After the examination, assist the patient as needed to get off the table and get dressed.	**10**	_____	_____	_____
9. Clean and disinfect the examination room according to Standard Precautions. Roll clean paper over the table.	**10**	_____	_____	_____
10. Sanitize your hands.	**10**	_____	_____	_____
11. Follow up with the physician's orders regarding scheduling of diagnostic studies, collection of specimens, and/or scheduling of future appointments.	**10**	_____	_____	_____

Comments:

Points earned _____ ÷ 100 possible points = Score _____ % Score

Instructor's signature _____

Name _____ Date _____ Score _____

PROCEDURE 32-5 Prepare the Patient for and Assist with Routine and Specialty Examinations: The Sims' Position

CAAHEP COMPETENCIES: I.P.I.10, I.A.I.2
ABHES COMPETENCIES: 9.c, 9.d

TASK: To position and drape the patient for examinations of the rectum, rectal thermometer readings, instillation of rectal medications, perineal examinations, and some pelvic examinations.

Equipment and Supplies
- Examination table
- Table paper
- Patient gown
- Drape
- Spray disinfectant
- Examination gloves

Standards: Complete the procedure and all critical steps in _____ minutes with a minimum score of 85% in three attempts.

Scoring: Divide the points earned by the total possible points. Failure to perform a critical step, indicated by an asterisk (*), results in an unsatisfactory overall score.

Time began _____ Time ended _____ Total minutes: _____

Steps	Possible Points	Attempt 1	Attempt 2	Attempt 3
1. Prepare the examination room according to the rules of medical asepsis.	10	_____	_____	_____
2. Sanitize your hands.	10	_____	_____	_____
3. Greet and identify the patient and determine whether the person understands the procedure. If not, explain what to expect.	10	_____	_____	_____
*4. Give the patient a gown and explain the clothing that must be removed for this examination; also explain that the gown should open in the back. Provide assistance as needed. Give the patient privacy while changing. Knock on the examination room door before re-entering to make sure the patient has finished undressing and gowning. Do not place the patient in the Sims' position until the physician is ready for that part of the examination.	10	_____	_____	_____
5. Help the patient turn onto the left side; the left arm and shoulder should be drawn back behind the body so that the patient is tilted onto the chest. Flex the right arm upward for support, slightly flex the left leg, and sharply flex the right leg upward. Help the patient move the buttocks to the side edge of the table.	10	_____	_____	_____

289

Steps	Possible Points	Attempt 1	Attempt 2	Attempt 3
6. Drape the patient diagonally in a diamond shape, with the point of the diamond dropping below the buttocks. Make sure the drape is large enough to prevent unnecessary exposure of the patient.	10	_____	_____	_____
7. After the examination, assist the patient as needed to get off the table and get dressed.	10	_____	_____	_____
8. Clean and disinfect the examination room according to Standard Precautions. Roll clean paper over the table.	10	_____	_____	_____
9. Sanitize your hands.	10	_____	_____	_____
10. Follow up with the physician's orders regarding scheduling of diagnostic studies, collection of specimens, and/or scheduling of future appointments.	10	_____	_____	_____

Comments:

Points earned _____ ÷ 100 possible points = Score _____ % Score

Instructor's signature _____

Procedure **32-5** **The Sims' Position**

Name _____ Date _____ Score _____

PROCEDURE 32-6 Prepare the Patient for and Assist with Routine and Specialty Examinations: The Prone Position

CAAHEP COMPETENCIES: I.PI.10, I.AI.2
ABHES COMPETENCIES: 9.c, 9.d

TASK: To position and drape the patient for examinations of the back and for certain surgical procedures.

Equipment and Supplies
- Examination table
- Table paper
- Patient gown
- Drape
- Spray disinfectant
- Examination gloves

Standards: Complete the procedure and all critical steps in _____ minutes with a minimum score of 85% in three attempts.

Scoring: Divide the points earned by the total possible points. Failure to perform a critical step, indicated by an asterisk (*), results in an unsatisfactory overall score.

Time began _____ Time ended _____ Total minutes: _____

Steps	Possible Points	Attempt 1	Attempt 2	Attempt 3
1. Prepare the examination room according to the rules of medical asepsis.	10	_____	_____	_____
2. Sanitize your hands.	10	_____	_____	_____
3. Greet and identify the patient and determine whether the person understands the procedure. If not, explain what to expect.	10	_____	_____	_____
*4. Give the patient a gown and explain the clothing that must be removed for this examination; also explain that the gown should open in the back. Provide assistance as needed. Give the patient privacy while changing. Knock on the examination room door before re-entering to make sure the patient has finished undressing and gowning. Do not place the patient in the prone position until the physician is ready for that part of the examination.	10	_____	_____	_____
5. Pull out the table extension if necessary and help the patient lie down flat on the back.	5	_____	_____	_____
6. Drape the patient over any exposed area that is not included in the examination. For female patients, the drape should be large enough to cover from the breasts to the feet, so if the patient is asked to roll over, she will not be exposed accidentally.	10	_____	_____	_____

Steps	Possible Points	Attempt 1	Attempt 2	Attempt 3
7. After the examination, assist the patient as needed to get off the table and get dressed.	5	_____	_____	_____
8. Clean and disinfect the examination room according to Standard Precautions. Roll clean paper over the table.	10	_____	_____	_____
9. Sanitize your hands.	10	_____	_____	_____
10. Follow up with the physician's orders regarding scheduling of diagnostic studies, collection of specimens, and/or scheduling of future appointments.	10	_____	_____	_____

Comments:

Points earned _____ ÷ 100 possible points = Score _____ % Score

Instructor's signature _____

292

Name _____ Date _____ Score _____

PROCEDURE 32-7 Prepare the Patient for and Assist with Routine and Specialty Examinations: The Knee-Chest Position

CAAHEP COMPETENCIES: I.PI.10, I.AI.2
ABHES COMPETENCIES: 9.c, 9.d

TASK: To position and drape the patient for examinations of the back and for certain surgical procedures.

Equipment and Supplies
- Examination table
- Table paper
- Patient gown
- Drape
- Spray disinfectant
- Examination gloves

Standards: Complete the procedure and all critical steps in _____ minutes with a minimum score of 85% in three attempts.

Scoring: Divide the points earned by the total possible points. Failure to perform a critical step, indicated by an asterisk (*), results in an unsatisfactory overall score.

Time began _____ Time ended _____ Total minutes: _____

Steps	Possible Points	Attempt 1	Attempt 2	Attempt 3
1. Prepare the examination room according to the rules of medical asepsis.	10	_____	_____	_____
2. Sanitize your hands.	10	_____	_____	_____
3. Greet and identify the patient and determine whether the person understands the procedure. If not, explain what to expect.	10	_____	_____	_____
*4. Give the patient a gown and explain the clothing that must be removed for this examination; also explain that the gown should open in the back. Provide assistance as needed. Give the patient privacy while changing. Knock on the examination room door before re-entering to make sure the patient has finished undressing and gowning. Do not place the patient in the knee-chest position until the physician is ready for that part of the examination.	10	_____	_____	_____
5. Pull out the table extension if necessary. Help the patient to lie flat on the back and then turn over to the prone position. Ask the patient to move up onto the knees, spread the knees apart, and lean forward onto the head so that the buttocks are raised. Tell the patient to keep the back straight and turn the face to either side. The patient should rest his or her weight on the chest and shoulders. If the patient has difficulty maintaining this position, weight can be placed on the bent elbows with the head off the table.	10	_____	_____	_____

293

Steps	Possible Points	Attempt 1	Attempt 2	Attempt 3
6. Drape the patient diagonally so that the point of the drape is on the table between the legs.	10	_____	_____	_____
7. After the examination, assist the patient as needed to get off the table and get dressed.	10	_____	_____	_____
8. Clean and disinfect the examination room according to Standard Precautions. Roll clean paper over the table.	10	_____	_____	_____
9. Sanitize your hands.	10	_____	_____	_____
10. Follow up with the physician's orders regarding scheduling of diagnostic studies, collection of specimens, and/or scheduling of future appointments.	10	_____	_____	_____

Comments:

Points earned _____ ÷ 100 possible points = Score _____ % Score

Instructor's signature _____

Procedure **32-7 The Knee-Chest Position**

PROCEDURE 32-8 Prepare the Patient for and Assist with Routine and Specialty Examinations: the Physical Examination

CAAHEP COMPETENCIES: I.AI.1, I.AI.2, III.PIII.2, IV.PIV.2, IV.PIV.8, I.PI.10, I.AI.2
ABHES COMPETENCIES: 9.c, 9.d

TASK: To help the physician examine patients by preparing the patient and the necessary equipment and ensuring the patient's safety and comfort during the examination.

Equipment and Supplies

- Stethoscope
- Gauze sponges
- Ophthalmoscope
- Pen light
- Scale with height measurement bar
- Nasal speculum
- Tuning fork
- Tongue depressor
- Biohazardous waste container
- Cotton balls
- Examination light
- Laboratory request forms
- Percussion hammer
- Specimen bottles and laboratory requisitions
- Lubricating gel
- Examination gloves
- Patient gown
- Sphygmomanometer
- Drapes
- Otoscope with disposable speculum
- Thermometer
- Cotton-tipped applicators
- Tape measure
- Hemoccult supplies
- Spray disinfectant
- Table paper

Standards: Complete the procedure and all critical steps in _____ minutes with a minimum score of 85% in three attempts.

Scoring: Divide the points earned by the total possible points. Failure to perform a critical step, indicated by an asterisk (*), results in an unsatisfactory overall score.

Time began _____   **Time ended** _____   **Total minutes:** _____

Steps	Possible Points	Attempt 1	Attempt 2	Attempt 3
1. Prepare the examining room according to the rules of medical asepsis.	5	_____	_____	_____
2. Sanitize your hands.	5	_____	_____	_____
3. Locate the instruments for the procedure. Set them out in order of use, in the physician's reach, and cover them until the physician enters the examination room.	5	_____	_____	_____
4. Identify the patient and determine whether the person understands the procedure. If not, explain what to expect.	5	_____	_____	_____
*5. Review the medical history with the patient and investigate the purpose of the visit. Record the interview results.	10	_____	_____	_____
6. Measure and record the patient's vital signs, height, weight, and BMI.	5	_____	_____	_____
7. Instruct the patient in the collection of a urine specimen, if ordered, and give the patient the properly labeled specimen container. Obtain blood samples for any tests ordered. Obtain a resting ECG if ordered.	10	_____	_____	_____
*8. Hand the patient a gown and explain what clothing should be removed for this examination; also explain whether the gown should open in the front or back. Help the patient with undressing as needed; however, most patients prefer to undress in private. Knock on the door before re-entering to protect the patient's privacy.	10	_____	_____	_____
9. Help the patient into sitting position at the foot of the examination table. Place the drape over the patient's lap and legs. If the patient is elderly, confused, or feeling faint or dizzy, do not leave the person alone.	10	_____	_____	_____
*10. Place the patient's medical record in the designated area or inform the physician that the patient is ready. Be careful to keep the patient's identity information out of sight to protect the patient's privacy.	5	_____	_____	_____
11. Assist during the examination by handing the physician each instrument as it is needed and by positioning and draping the patient.	10	_____	_____	_____
12. After the examination, allow the patient to rest for a moment and then help the person from the table. Help the patient to dress, if necessary. Use proper body mechanics if assistance in transfer is needed.	5	_____	_____	_____
13. When the patient has finished dressing, return to the room and ask whether he or she has any questions. Give the patient any final instructions and schedule tests as ordered by the physician.	5	_____	_____	_____
14. Put on gloves and dispose of used supplies and linens in designated biohazardous waste containers. Clean surfaces with a disinfectant, and disinfect all equipment. Remove your gloves, discard them in the biohazardous waste container, and sanitize your hands. Replace used supplies and prepare the room for the next patient.	10	_____	_____	_____

Comments:

Points earned _____ ÷ 100 possible points = Score _____ % Score

Instructor's signature _____

Name _____ Date _____ Score _____

PROCEDURE 33-1 Maintain Medication and Immunization Records: Prepare a Prescription for the Physician's Signature

CAAHEP COMPETENCIES: I.PI.10
ABHES COMPETENCIES: 4.a, 6.c.3

TASK: To prepare a prescription for the physician's signature accurately using appropriate abbreviations and the prescription format.

Equipment and Supplies

- Prescription pad
- Drug reference materials if needed
- Black pen
- Patient's chart

Standards: Complete the procedure and all critical steps in _____ minutes with a minimum score of 85% in three attempts.

Scoring: Divide the points earned by the total possible points. Failure to perform a critical step, indicated by an asterisk (*), results in an unsatisfactory overall score.

Time began _____   Time ended _____   Total minutes: _____

Steps	Possible Points	Attempt 1	Attempt 2	Attempt 3
1. Refer to the physician's written order for the prescription. If the physician gives a verbal order to write a prescription, write down the order and review it with the physician for accuracy.	10	_____	_____	_____
*2. If unfamiliar with the medication, look up the drug in a drug reference book (e.g., the PDR).	5	_____	_____	_____
*3. Ask the patient whether he or she is allergic to any drugs.	10	_____	_____	_____
4. Using a prescription pad that has the physician's name, address, telephone number, and DEA registration number preprinted on each slip, begin to transcribe the physician's order.	10	_____	_____	_____
5. Record the patient's name and address and the date on which the prescription is being written.	10	_____	_____	_____
6. Next to the Rx, write in legible handwriting the name of the drug (correctly spelled), the dosage form (e.g., tablet, capsule, and so forth, using correct abbreviations), and the strength ordered.	10	_____	_____	_____
7. On the next line write Disp. This is the subscription, which includes directions to the pharmacist on the amount to be dispensed and the form of the drug.	10	_____	_____	_____
8. Next comes the signature. This includes directions for the patient, such as how and when to take the medicine; it usually is preceded by the symbol Sig.	10	_____	_____	_____

299

Steps	Possible Points	Attempt 1	Attempt 2	Attempt 3
9. The physician has told you the patient can get three refills of the prescription; therefore, this information should be added at the bottom of the prescription on the designated line.	10	_____	_____	_____
10. The physician must review and sign the prescription before it is given to the patient.	5	_____	_____	_____
11. In the following Documentation in the Medical Record section, document the medication order and any pertinent details as you would in the patient's record. Include patient education and refill information.	10	_____	_____	_____

Documentation in the Medical Record:

Comments:

Points earned _____ ÷ 100 possible points = Score _____ % Score

Instructor's signature _____

WORK PRODUCT 33-1

Name: _____

Prepare a Prescription for the Physician's Signature

Corresponds to Procedure 33-1

<u>CAAHEP COMPETENCIES:</u> I.PI.10

<u>ABHES COMPETENCIES:</u> 4.a, 6.c.3

Telephoning a Prescription into the Pharmacy

Using the steps outlined above, complete the prescription including the patient's full name and address; the practitioner's full name and address; the DEA number if the prescription is for a controlled substance (Schedule II drugs must be filled with a written prescription and/or an EHR program that is authorized to fill scheduled drugs); and the drug name, strength, dosage form, quantity prescribed, direction for use, and the number of refills (if any) authorized. The physician must review the prescription for accuracy before the medical assistant telephones the pharmacy. Document the telephoned pharmacy order in the patients's medical record as you would for any prescribed drug.

```
┌─────────────────────────────────────────────────────┐
│                                                         │
│   DEA#: 8543201      John Jones, M.D.   Tel: 544-8976  │
│                      108 N. Main St.                    │
│                      City, State                        │
│                                                         │
│   Patient _____  DATE _____           │
│                                                         │
│   ADDRESS _____              │
│                                                         │
│   Rx:                                                   │
│                                                         │
│   Disp:                                                 │
│                                                         │
│   Sig:                                                  │
│                                                         │
│                                                         │
│   Refill ____ Times                                     │
│   Please label ☑  _____         │
│                                                         │
└─────────────────────────────────────────────────────┘
```

Name _____ Date _____ Score _____

PROCEDURE 34-1 Prepare Proper Dosages of Medication for Administration: Apply Mathematic Computations to Solve Equations

CAAHEP COMPETENCIES: I.AI.1, II.CII.1, II.CII.2, II.CII.3, II.CII.4, II.CII.6, II.PII.1, II.AII.1
ABHES COMPETENCIES: 6.b

TASK: To calculate the correct dose amount and choose the correct equipment when the physician orders 2.4 million IU of penicillin G benzathine (Bicillin).

Equipment and Supplies
- Premixed syringes of Bicillin, available as:
  - 0.6 million IU/syringe
  - 1.2 million IU/syringe

Standards: Complete the procedure and all critical steps in _____ minutes with a minimum score of 85% in three attempts.

Scoring: Divide the points earned by the total possible points. Failure to perform a critical step, indicated by an asterisk (*), results in an unsatisfactory overall score.

Time began _____   Time ended _____   Total minutes: _____

Steps	Possible Points	Attempt 1	Attempt 2	Attempt 3
1. Read the order in quiet surroundings to make sure you fully understand it.	10	_____	_____	_____
2. Write out the order.	15	_____	_____	_____
3. Examine the drug labels to see what strengths and amounts are available.	15	_____	_____	_____
4. Write down the standard formula: $$\frac{\text{Available strength}}{\text{Ordered strength}} = \frac{\text{Available amount}}{\text{Amount to give}}$$	15	_____	_____	_____
5. Rewrite the formula, replacing the unknown values with the known quantities. The unknown, x, will be the amount of the drug to give.	15	_____	_____	_____
6. Work the proportion problem by cross-multiplying to solve for x.	15	_____	_____	_____
7. State your answer by filling in the blanks: To administer 2.4 million IU of Bicillin, I would select _____ of the premixed syringes labeled _____.	15	_____	_____	_____

Comments:

Points earned _____ ÷ 100 possible points = Score _____ % Score

Instructor's signature _____

Procedure **34-1 Prepare Proper Dosages of Medication for Administration**

Name _____ Date _____ Score _____

PROCEDURE 34-2 Prepare Proper Dosages of Medication for Administration: Convert Among Measurement Systems

CAAHEP COMPETENCIES: I.AI.1, II.CII.1, II.CII.2, II.CII.3, II.CII.4, II.CII.5, II.CII.6, II.PII.1, II.AII.1
ABHES COMPETENCIES: 6.b

TASK: To choose the correct system of measurement and calculate the correct dose amount when the physician orders 120 mg of a drug to be administered to a patient. (Label reads 1 gr each.)

Equipment and Supplies
- Tablets labeled 1 gr (grain) each
- Standard mathematical formula:

$$\frac{\text{Available strength}}{\text{Ordered strength}} = \frac{\text{Available amount}}{\text{Amount to give}}$$

Conversion equivalent: 1 gr = 60 mg

Standards: Complete the procedure and all critical steps in _____ minutes with a minimum score of 85% in three attempts.

Scoring: Divide the points earned by the total possible points. Failure to perform a critical step, indicated by an asterisk (*), results in an unsatisfactory overall score.

Time began _____ Time ended _____ Total minutes: _____

Steps	Possible Points	Attempt 1	Attempt 2	Attempt 3
1. Read the order in quiet surroundings to make sure you fully understand it.	5	_____	_____	_____
2. Write out the order.	10	_____	_____	_____
*3. Examine the drug labels to see what strengths and amounts are available.	15	_____	_____	_____
4. Convert the ordered system of measurement to the system of measurement on the label.	10	_____	_____	_____
5. Place the amount ordered on the left side of the equation and the conversion factor on the right side so that similar units can be cancelled when cross-multiplied.	10	_____	_____	_____

$$120 \text{ mg} \times \frac{1 \text{ gr}}{60 \text{ mg}} = 120 \text{ gr} \div 60 = 2 \text{ gr}$$

6. Write down the standard formula.	10	_____	_____	_____

$$\frac{\text{Available strength}}{\text{Ordered strength}} = \frac{\text{Available amount}}{\text{Amount to give}}$$

Steps	Possible Points	Attempt 1	Attempt 2	Attempt 3
7. Rewrite the formula, replacing the unknown values with the known quantities and using the system of measurement on the label. The unknown, *x*, will be the amount of the drug to give (amount to give). $$\frac{1\,gr}{2\,gr} \times \frac{1\,tab}{X\,tab}$$	10	_____	_____	_____
8. Work the proportion problem by cross-multiplying to solve for *x*.	15	_____	_____	_____
9. State your answer by filling in the blank: To administer 120 mg of a drug from tablets labeled 1 gr (grain) each, give _____ tablet(s).	15	_____	_____	_____

Comments:

Points earned _____ **÷ 100 possible points = Score** _____ **% Score**

Instructor's signature _____

306

Procedure **34-2 Prepare Proper Dosages of Medication for Administration**

Name _____ Date _____ Score _____

PROCEDURE 34-3 Apply Mathematic Computations to Solve Equations: Calculate the Correct Pediatric Dosage Using the Body Surface Area

CAAHEP COMPETENCIES: I.AI.1, II.CII.1, II.CII.2, II.CII.3, II.CII.6
ABHES COMPETENCIES: 6.b

TASK: To calculate the correct dose amount using the body surface area (BSA) method for a 90-pound child who is 48 inches tall when the adult dose is 250 mg/mL.

Equipment and Supplies
- Accurate scale with length measurement
- West's nomogram
- Adult dosage 250 mg/mL

$$\text{Pediatric dose} = \frac{\text{BSA of child (m}^2)}{1.7\ \text{m}_2\ \text{(average adult BSA)}} \times \text{Adult dose}$$

Standards: Complete the procedure and all critical steps in _____ minutes with a minimum score of 85% in three attempts.

Scoring: Divide the points earned by the total possible points. Failure to perform a critical step, indicated by an asterisk (*), results in an unsatisfactory overall score.

Time began _____ **Time ended** _____ **Total minutes:** _____

Steps	Possible Points	Attempt 1	Attempt 2	Attempt 3
1. Read the order in quiet surroundings to make sure you fully understand it.	5	_____	_____	_____
2. Write out the order.	10	_____	_____	_____
*3. Examine the drug labels to see what strengths and amounts are available.	15	_____	_____	_____
4. Write down the BSA formula.	10	_____	_____	_____
5. Using the BSA method, determine the BSA in square meters (m²) by intersecting the child's height in the left column with the weight in the right column (child is overweight).	15	_____	_____	_____
6. Divide the child's BSA by 1.7 m² (the average adult BSA).	15	_____	_____	_____
7. Multiply this number by the adult dose (250 mg).	15	_____	_____	_____
8. State your answer by filling in the blank: To administer an adult medication labeled 250 mg/mL to a 90-pound child, give _____ mg.	15	_____	_____	_____

Comments:

Points earned _____ ÷ 100 possible points = Score _____ % Score

Instructor's signature _____

Procedure **34-3 Apply Mathematic Computations to Solve Equations**

Name _____ Date _____ Score _____

PROCEDURE 34-4 Apply Mathematic Computations to Solve Equations: Calculate the Correct Pediatric Dosage Using Body Weight

CAAHEP COMPETENCIES: I.AI.1, II.CII.1, II.CII.2, II.CII.3, II.CII.6
ABHES COMPETENCIES: 6.b

TASK: To calculate a pediatric dosage correctly using the body weight method.

Prescriber's order: Zithromax suspension, 5 mg/kg bid × 5 days for a patient diagnosed with otitis media. The patient weighs 22 pounds. The suspension is labeled 100 mg/5mL.

Weight conversion: 2.2 lb = 1 kg

Equipment and Supplies

- Suspension labeled 100 mg/5 mL
- Balance scale
- Formula for conversion of pounds to kilograms
- Paper and pencil
- Standard math formula:

Standards: Complete the procedure and all critical steps in _____ minutes with a minimum score of 85% in three attempts.

Scoring: Divide the points earned by the total possible points. Failure to perform a critical step, indicated by an asterisk (*), results in an unsatisfactory overall score.

Time began _____ **Time ended** _____ **Total minutes:** _____

Steps	Possible Points	Attempt 1	Attempt 2	Attempt 3
1. Read the order in quiet surroundings to make sure you fully understand it.	5	_____	_____	_____
2. Write out the order.	10	_____	_____	_____
*3. Examine the drug label to check the strength and amount.	10	_____	_____	_____
4. Convert the patient's weight from pounds to kilograms.	10	_____	_____	_____
5. Calculate the total daily amount of medication by multiplying the weight in kilograms by the mg/kg factor.	10	_____	_____	_____
6. Calculate the individual dose of Zithromax; divide the daily dose by 2 (bid means twice a day).	10	_____	_____	_____
7. Compare the ordered daily dose with the dose information on the medication label (100 mg = 5 mL).	10	_____	_____	_____
8. Write down the standard formula.	10	_____	_____	_____
9. Rewrite the formula, replacing the unknown values with the known quantities. The unknown, x, will be the amount of the drug to give. Work the problem by cross-multiplying to solve for x.	10	_____	_____	_____
10. State your answer by filling in the blank: To administer 5 mg/kg of body weight of Zithromax from capsules labeled 100 mg/5 mL, give _____ mL.	15	_____	_____	_____

309

Comments:

Points earned _____ $\div$ 100 possible points = **Score** _____ **% Score**

Instructor's signature _____

PROCEDURE 35-1 Administer Medications and Document Patient Care: Safety Measures in Preparing, Administering, and Documenting Medications

CAAHEP COMPETENCIES: I.PI.10, I.AI.1, II.AII.1, III.PIII.2, IV.PIV.2, IV.PIV.8
ABHES COMPETENCIES: 4.a, 6.b, 9.f

TASK: To safely prepare, administer, and document completion of a medication order.

SCENARIO: Dr. Thau writes this order: Administer Recombivax 10 mcg IM to Chris MacCarthy.

Equipment and Supplies

- Physician's written order, including the drug name, strength, dose, and route of administration
- PDR reference
- Container of ordered medication
- Correct equipment for dispensing the drug
- Patient's medical record

Standards: Complete the procedure and all critical steps in _____ minutes with a minimum score of 85% in three attempts.

Scoring: Divide the points earned by the total possible points. Failure to perform a critical step, indicated by an asterisk (*), results in an unsatisfactory overall score.

Time began _____ Time ended _____ Total minutes: _____

Steps	Possible Points	Attempt 1	Attempt 2	Attempt 3
1. Read the order and clarify any questions with the physician.	5	_____	_____	_____
2. If you are unfamiliar with the drug, refer to the PDR or the package insert to determine the purpose of the drug, common side effects, the typical dose, and any pertinent precautions or contraindications. Recombivax is a hepatitis B immunization. Use the "seven rights" to prevent errors.	5	_____	_____	_____
3. Take the written order with you to the medication room and compare the drug label with the physician's order. Based on the information printed on the medication label, perform the calculations needed to match the physician's order. Confirm the answer with the physician if you have any questions.	5	_____	_____	_____
4. Dispense the medication in a well-lit, quiet area.	5	_____	_____	_____
5. Sanitize your hands.	5	_____	_____	_____
6. Compare the written order with the label on the multidose vial when you remove the vial from storage. Check the expiration date on the container (if it was used previously, the date of the first use) and dispose of the medication if it has expired.	5	_____	_____	_____

311

Steps	Possible Points	Attempt 1	Attempt 2	Attempt 3
7. Compare the order with the label on the multidose vial just before drawing it up into the appropriate syringe unit. Make sure the strength on the label matches the order or that you dispense the correctly calculated dose.	10	_____	_____	_____
8. Compare the label and the physician's order before returning the vial to storage.	5	_____	_____	_____
9. Identify and greet the patient by name and inform him you are going to administer a hepatitis B immunization.	5	_____	_____	_____
10. Mention the name of the drug and the reason it is being given. Ask the patient whether he has any allergies to the medication.	5	_____	_____	_____
11. If necessary, help the patient into a sitting position.	5	_____	_____	_____
12. Give the injection in the left deltoid muscle using correct administration techniques and observing OSHA precautions.	10	_____	_____	_____
13. Provide patient education on typical side effects of the drug. Consult the physician to clarify information if needed.	10	_____	_____	_____
14. The patient must remain in the office for 20 to 30 minutes after administration of the drug as a precaution against untoward effects.	5	_____	_____	_____
15. If the patient experiences any discomfort after receiving a drug, the physician should be notified immediately and the incident documented completely and accurately.	5	_____	_____	_____
16. Sanitize your hands.	5	_____	_____	_____
17. In the following Documentation in the Medical Record section, document the administration of the drug as you would in the patient's record. Include the date and time; the drug's name, dose, and strength and the route of administration; any side effects that occur; and the patient education provided about the drug.	5	_____	_____	_____

Documentation in the Medical Record:

Comments:

Points earned _____ ÷ 100 possible points = Score _____ % Score

Instructor's signature _____

Name _____ Date _____ Score _____

PROCEDURE 35-2 Document Patient Care and Patient Education: Maintain Medication Records

CAAHEP COMPETENCIES: IV.PIV.2, IV.PIV.8, IV.PIV.9
ABHES COMPETENCIES: 4.a, 6.e, 9.h

TASK: To document completion of medication orders.

SCENARIO: Dr. Thau writes these orders for Mrs. Lange's hypertension:
  Lasix 20 mg PO qd
  Potassium chloride 20 mEq PO qd to Alice Lange

You review the orders for clarification, complete the three label checks, confirm the identity of the patient, ask the patient about drug allergies, administer the medications as ordered, and answer the patient's questions about the continuation of drug therapy at home. Now, you must document this process in the patient's medical record.

Equipment and Supplies
- Physician's written orders, including the name, strength, dose, and route of administration
- PDR reference
- Patient's medical record

Standards: Complete the procedure and all critical steps in _____ minutes with a minimum score of 85% in three attempts.

Scoring: Divide the points earned by the total possible points. Failure to perform a critical step, indicated by an asterisk (*), results in an unsatisfactory overall score.

Time began _____   Time ended _____   Total minutes: _____

Steps	Possible Points	Attempt 1	Attempt 2	Attempt 3
1. Identify Mrs. Lange, greet her by name, and inform her you are going to administer a diuretic and a potassium supplement.	10	_____	_____	_____
*2. Mention the names of the drugs and the reason they are being given. Ask her whether she is allergic to those medications.	20	_____	_____	_____
3. Sanitize your hands and administer the medications orally as ordered, making sure Mrs. Lange swallows the pills without difficulty.	10	_____	_____	_____
4. Provide patient education about the purpose of the drugs, typical side effects, and dosage and storage recommendations. Consult the physician to clarify information if needed.	10	_____	_____	_____
5. The patient must remain in the office for 20 to 30 minutes after administration of the drugs as a precaution against untoward effects.	10	_____	_____	_____
6. If the patient experiences any discomfort after taking a medication, the physician should be notified immediately and the incident documented completely and accurately.	10	_____	_____	_____
7. Sanitize your hands.	10	_____	_____	_____
*8. In the following Documentation in the Medical Record section, document the administration of the medications as you would in the patient's record. Include the date and time; the drugs' names, doses, strengths, and route of administration; any side effects noted; and the patient education provided about the drugs.	20	_____	_____	_____

Documentation in the Medical Record:

Additional Documentation in the Medical Record:

Practice documenting the following orders:

- Tylenol elixir 120 mg PO to Anthony Baker, 8 years old, for a fever
- Gantrisin Pediatric 500 mg PO to Samantha Carpassi, 3 years old, for a urinary tract infection
- Dilaudid cough syrup 2 mg PO to Roberto Alphonse, 43 years old, for bronchitis
- Diflucan 400 mg PO loading dose to Anastasia Smith, 19 years old, for a vaginal yeast infection

Comments:

Points earned _____ ÷ 100 possible points = Score _____ % Score

Instructor's signature _____

PROCEDURE 35-3 Administer Oral Medications

CAAHEP COMPETENCIES: I.PI.8, I.PI.9, I.PI.10, I.AI.1, II.AII.1, III.PIII.2, IV.PIV.2, IV.PIV.8, IV.PIV.9
ABHES COMPETENCIES: 6.b, 9.f, 9.h

TASK: To safely dispense, administer to a patient, and document the administration of an oral medication.

Prescriber's Order: Administer hydrochlorothiazide (HydroDiuril) 100 mg PO tab stat for hypertension

Equipment and Supplies
- Prescriber's written order, including the drug name, strength, dose, and route
- Container of ordered medication
- Calibrated medication cup
- Water, if appropriate
- Patient's medical record

Standards: Complete the procedure and all critical steps in _____ minutes with a minimum score of 85% in three attempts.

Scoring: Divide the points earned by the total possible points. Failure to perform a critical step, indicated by an asterisk (*), results in an unsatisfactory overall score.

Time began _____   Time ended _____   Total minutes: _____

Steps	Possible Points	Attempt 1	Attempt 2	Attempt 3
1. Read the order and clarify any questions with the prescriber.	10	_____	_____	_____
2. If you are unfamiliar with HydroDiuril, refer to the PDR or the package insert to determine the purpose of the drug, common side effects, typical dose, and any pertinent precautions or contraindications. Be prepared to answer the patient's questions about the medication. Use the "seven rights" to prevent errors.	10	_____	_____	_____
3. Perform the calculations needed to match the prescriber's order. Confirm the answer with the prescriber if you have any questions.	10	_____	_____	_____
4. Dispense the medication in a well-lit, quiet area.	10	_____	_____	_____
5. Sanitize your hands.	10	_____	_____	_____
6. Compare the order with the label on the medicine container when you remove the container from storage.	10	_____	_____	_____
7. Compare the order with the label on the medicine container just before dispensing the ordered dose. Make sure the strength on the label matches the order or that you dispense the correctly calculated dose.	10	_____	_____	_____

Steps	Possible Points	Attempt 1	Attempt 2	Attempt 3
To Dispense Solid Oral Medications (HydroDiuril Tablet)				
8. Gently tap the prescribed dose into the lid of the medication container. Do not touch the inside of the lid or the medication.	10	_____	_____	_____
9. Empty the medication in the container lid into a medicine cup.	10	_____	_____	_____
To Dispense Liquid Oral Preparations (HydroDiuril Solution)				
10. Shake the medication well if required.	5	_____	_____	_____
*11. When liquid medications are poured, the label should be held in the palm of the hand.	10	_____	_____	_____
12. Place the medicine cup on a flat surface and, at eye level, pour the medication to the prescribed dose mark on the medicine cup.	20	_____	_____	_____
For Both Solid and Liquid Oral Medications				
13. Recap the container and compare the label and the prescriber's order before replacing the container in storage.	10	_____	_____	_____
14. Take the medication to the patient.	10	_____	_____	_____
15. Identify the patient and greet the person by name.	10	_____	_____	_____
*16. Mention the name of the drug and why it is being given, and ask the patient whether he or she is allergic to the medication.	10	_____	_____	_____
17. If necessary, help the patient into a sitting position.	5	_____	_____	_____
18. Administer the tablets, capsules, or caplets with water. If the patient is receiving liquid medication, offer water after the person takes the medication if appropriate. Make sure the patient swallows the entire dose.	10	_____	_____	_____
*19. Provide patient education on the purpose of the drug, typical side effects, and dosage and storage recommendations. Consult the prescriber to clarify information if needed.	10	_____	_____	_____
20. The patient must remain in the office for 20 to 30 minutes after administration of the drug as a precaution against untoward effects.	5	_____	_____	_____
21. If the patient experiences any discomfort after taking the medication, the prescriber should be notified immediately and the incident documented completely and accurately.	10	_____	_____	_____
22. Sanitize your hands.	10	_____	_____	_____
23. In the following Documentation in the Medical Record section, document the administration of the drug as you would in the patient's record. Include the date and time; the drug name, dose, and strength and the route of administration; any side effects noted; and patient education provided about the drug.	10	_____	_____	_____

Documentation in the Medical Record:

Comments:

Points earned _____ ÷ 100 possible points = Score _____ % Score

Instructor's signature _____

Name _____ Date _____ Score _____

PROCEDURE 35-4 Administer Parenteral (Excluding IV) Medications: Fill a Syringe from an Ampule

CAAHEP COMPETENCIES: I.PI.9, I.PI.10, I.AI.1, II.AII.1, III.PIII.2
ABHES COMPETENCIES: 6.b, 9.f

TASK: To remove medication for administration correctly and safely from a glass ampule.

Equipment and Supplies
- Prescriber's written order
- Syringe/needle unit
- Medication ampule
- Filter needle
- Sterile gauze squares
- Alcohol squares
- Sharps container
- Disposable gloves
- Biohazardous waste container
- Patient's medical record

Standards: Complete the procedure and all critical steps in _____ minutes with a minimum score of 85% in three attempts.

Scoring: Divide the points earned by the total possible points. Failure to perform a critical step, indicated by an asterisk (*), results in an unsatisfactory overall score.

Time began _____   Time ended _____   Total minutes: _____

Steps	Possible Points	Attempt 1	Attempt 2	Attempt 3
1. Review the prescriber's medication order for clarity. If you are unfamiliar with the drug, look it up in a reference book.	5	_____	_____	_____
2. Sanitize your hands and assemble the necessary equipment.	5	_____	_____	_____
3. Perform the medication label and prescriber's order checks when removing the ampule from storage. Check the expiration date on the ampule.	5	_____	_____	_____
4. Gently tap the top of the ampule with your fingers to settle all the medication to the bottom portion of the flask.	5	_____	_____	_____
5. Thoroughly disinfect the neck of the ampule with alcohol squares. Check the label against the order a second time.	5	_____	_____	_____
6. Wrap the top of the ampule with a gauze square to protect yourself from the glass. Hold the covered ampule between your thumb and finger, in front of you and above waist level.	10	_____	_____	_____
7. Push the top of the ampule away from your body to break the neck. You will hear a pop because the ampule is vacuum sealed. The glass is designed not to shatter, and the medication will not spill out. Dispose of the gauze square and glass top in the sharps container.	10	_____	_____	_____

319

Steps	Possible Points	Attempt 1	Attempt 2	Attempt 3
*8. Open the sterile syringe and needle unit. Touching the needle covers only, unscrew the needle from the syringe, place it on the counter, and attach the sterile filter needle.	10	_____	_____	_____
9. Without touching the sides of the opened ampule, insert the syringe unit with the filter needle attached into the ampule and withdraw the ordered dose. Then recover the needle.	10	_____	_____	_____
10. Before discarding the ampule in the sharps container, check the prescriber's order against the label one more time to complete the three label checks. If you are drawing the medication up for the prescriber to administer, take the ampule and the syringe unit to the prescriber for the final safety check.	5	_____	_____	_____
11. Exchange the filter needle, safeguarding the sterility of the injection unit, for a needle of the appropriate length and gauge based on the ordered route of administration and patient characteristics. Discard the used filter needle into the sharps container.	5	_____	_____	_____
12. Dispose of used alcohol and gauze squares.	5	_____	_____	_____
13. Take the ordered medication in the injection unit to the patient. Verify that you have the correct patient. Put on gloves and administer the medication as ordered. Discard the used syringe unit into a sharps container in the patient's room. Remove your gloves, discard them in a biohazardous waste container, and sanitize your hands.	10	_____	_____	_____
14. Answer any questions the patient may have and document the procedure in the medical record.	10	_____	_____	_____

Comments:

Points earned _____ ÷ 100 possible points = Score _____ % Score

Instructor's signature _____

Name _____ Date _____ Score _____

PROCEDURE 35-5 Administer Parenteral (Excluding IV) Medications: Fill a Syringe from a Vial

CAAHEP COMPETENCIES: I.PI.9, I.PI.10, I.AI.1, II.AII.1, III.PIII.2
ABHES COMPETENCIES: 6.b, 9.f

TASK: To fill a syringe from a multidose vial using sterile technique.

Equipment and Supplies
- Prescriber's written order, including the drug name, strength, and route of administration
- Multidose vial containing the medication ordered
- Alcohol wipes
- Sterile needle and syringe unit

Standards: Complete the procedure and all critical steps in _____ minutes with a minimum score of 85% in three attempts.

Scoring: Divide the points earned by the total possible points. Failure to perform a critical step, indicated by an asterisk (*), results in an unsatisfactory overall score.

Time began _____ Time ended _____ Total minutes: _____

Steps	Possible Points	Attempt 1	Attempt 2	Attempt 3
1. Sanitize your hands.	5	_____	_____	_____
2. Read the order and choose the correct vial of medication.	5	_____	_____	_____
3. Choose the correct syringe and needle size, depending on the site, patient characteristics, and the quantity of medication to be injected.	5	_____	_____	_____
4. Compare the order both with the name of the drug on the medication vial and the amount to be withdrawn in the syringe.	5	_____	_____	_____
5. Gently agitate the medication by rolling the vial between your palms.	5	_____	_____	_____
6. Check the quality of the medication and the expiration date.	5	_____	_____	_____
7. Cleanse the rubber stopper of the vial with an alcohol wipe, using a circular motion. Place the vial on a secure flat surface, leaving the alcohol swab over the rubber stopper.	5	_____	_____	_____
8. With the needle cover in place, grasp the syringe plunger and draw up an amount of air equal to the amount of medication ordered.	5	_____	_____	_____
9. Remove the needle cover and insert the needle into the center of the rubber stopper. Hold the vial firmly against a flat surface and take care that the needle touches only the cleaned rubber area.	10	_____	_____	_____
10. Inject the aspirated air in the syringe into the vial.	10	_____	_____	_____

321

Steps	Possible Points	Attempt 1	Attempt 2	Attempt 3
11. Keeping the syringe unit in the vial, pick them up and invert them. Slowly pull back on the plunger with the unit at eye level until the proper amount of medication has been withdrawn.	10	_____	_____	_____
12. With the needle still in the vial, check that the syringe has no air bubbles.	5	_____	_____	_____
13. If air bubbles are present, slip the fingers holding the vial down to grasp the vial and syringe as a single unit.	5	_____	_____	_____
14. With your free hand, tap the syringe until the air bubbles dislodge and float into the tip of the syringe.	5	_____	_____	_____
15. Gently expel these tiny air bubbles through the needle and then continue withdrawing until the accurate amount of medication has been withdrawn.	5	_____	_____	_____
16. Withdraw the needle from the vial and carefully replace the needle cover without letting the needle touch the outside of the cover.	5	_____	_____	_____
17. Return the medication to the shelf or the refrigerator and check that you have the correct drug and dosage.	5	_____	_____	_____

Comments:

Points earned _____ ÷ 100 possible points = Score _____ % Score

Instructor's signature _____

Procedure **35-5 Administer Parenteral (Excluding IV) Medications**

PROCEDURE 35-6 Administer Parenteral (Excluding IV) Medications: Reconstitute a Powdered Drug for Administration

CAAHEP COMPETENCIES: I.PI.9, I.PI.10, I.AI.1, II.AII.1, III.PIII.2
ABHES COMPETENCIES: 6.b, 9.f

TASK: To reconstitute a powdered drug for intramuscular injection as ordered by the physician.

Equipment and Supplies

- Physician's written order, including the patient's name, when to give the drug, the route of administration, and the name and strength of the drug
- Vial containing the ordered powdered medication
- Diluent—sterile saline
- Alcohol wipes
- Cotton ball
- Two sterile needle and syringe units
- Disposable gloves
- Sharps container

Standards: Complete the procedure and all critical steps in _____ minutes with a minimum score of 85% in three attempts.

Scoring: Divide the points earned by the total possible points. Failure to perform a critical step, indicated by an asterisk (*), results in an unsatisfactory overall score.

Time began _____ Time ended _____ Total minutes: _____

Steps	Possible Points	Attempt 1	Attempt 2	Attempt 3
1. Sanitize your hands; observe Standard Precautions.	5	____	____	____
*2. Select the correct vial of powdered medication from the shelf and the recommended diluent for reconstitution. Perform the three drug label and physician's order checks during preparation and verify the "seven rights" throughout the procedure.	10	____	____	____
3. Read the label to determine the correct amount of diluent to add to create the dose ordered by the physician. Calculate the correct dose, if necessary, and continue with the three label checks.	10	____	____	____
4. Remove the tops from each vial and clean the rubber stopper of each vial with an alcohol wipe. Leave the wipes in place on top the vials.	5	____	____	____
5. Using one of the syringe units with the needle cover in place, grasp the syringe plunger and draw up an amount of air equal to the amount of diluent needed to reconstitute the drug.	10	____	____	____

323

Steps	Possible Points	Attempt 1	Attempt 2	Attempt 3
6. Remove the needle cover and insert the needle into the center of the rubber stopper of the diluent. Hold the vial firmly against a flat surface and take care that the needle touches only the cleaned rubber area.	10	_____	_____	_____
7. Inject the aspirated air into the diluent vial.	5	_____	_____	_____
*8. Invert the diluent vial and aspirate the calculated or recommended amount of diluent.	10	_____	_____	_____
9. Remove the needle from the diluent vial and inject the diluent into the drug vial. Remove the needle and discard the syringe unit into the sharps container.	10	_____	_____	_____
10. Roll the vial with the drug and diluent mixture between the palms of your hands to mix it thoroughly. Do not shake the vial unless directed to do so on the drug label. No residue or crystals are seen on the bottom of the vial when the medication has been completely mixed.	10	_____	_____	_____
11. Using the second syringe unit, aspirate an amount of air equal to the calculated amount of medication to be administered.	10	_____	_____	_____
12. Inject the air into the mixed drug vial, invert the vial, and withdraw the ordered amount of medication.	10	_____	_____	_____
13. Proceed as outlined in steps 6-22 in Procedure 35-10 to administer the medication.	10	_____	_____	_____

Comments:

Points earned _____ ÷ 100 possible points = Score _____ % Score

Instructor's signature _____

Name _____ Date _____ Score _____

PROCEDURE 35-7 Administer Parenteral (Excluding IV) Medications: Give an Intradermal Injection

CAAHEP COMPETENCIES: I.PI.9, I.PI.10, I.AI.1, II.AII.1, III.PIII.2
ABHES COMPETENCIES: 6.b, 9.f

TASK: To inject 0.1 mL of purified protein derivative (PPD) to perform a Mantoux test as ordered by the physician.

Physician's Order: Administer 0.1 mL PPD ID for a Mantoux test for TB screening.

Equipment and Supplies
- Physician's order, including the patient's name, when to give the drug, the route of administration, and the name and strength of the drug
- Vial of tuberculin PPD
- Alcohol wipes
- 27-gauge, ⅜-inch sterile needle and syringe unit with safety needle cover device
- Disposable gloves
- Gauze squares
- Sharps container
- Written patient instructions for follow-up
- Patient's medical record

Standards: Complete the procedure and all critical steps in _____ minutes with a minimum score of 85% in three attempts.

Scoring: Divide the points earned by the total possible points. Failure to perform a critical step, indicated by an asterisk (*), results in an unsatisfactory overall score.

Time began _____ Time ended _____ Total minutes: _____

Steps	Possible Points	Attempt 1	Attempt 2	Attempt 3
1. Sanitize your hands; observe Standard Precautions.	2	_____	_____	_____
2. Select the correct medication from the shelf or the refrigerator.	2	_____	_____	_____
*3. Read the label to make sure you have the right drug (PPD) and the right strength. Perform the three label and order checks as the medication is dispensed.	2	_____	_____	_____
4. Warm refrigerated medications by gently rolling the container between your palms.	2	_____	_____	_____
5. Prepare the syringe as described in PROCEDURE 35-5 in the text, withdrawing the correct dose in milliliters (mL).	2	_____	_____	_____
6. Take the medication to the patient.	2	_____	_____	_____
7. Greet the patient by name and verify that you have the correct patient.	2	_____	_____	_____

Steps	Possible Points	Attempt 1	Attempt 2	Attempt 3
8. Ask the patient whether he or she has ever had a positive reaction to a PPD injection (TB test). If so, report this information to the physician before administering the test. (A person who has had a positive PPD test result will always have a positive result because of antibody action.)	2	_____	_____	_____
9. Put on gloves and position the patient comfortably.	2	_____	_____	_____
10. Locate the antecubital space and then find a site several fingerwidths down the midanterior aspect of the forearm. Avoid any scarred, discolored, or pigmented areas.	5	_____	_____	_____
11. Loosen the needle cover so that the needle can be picked up with one hand after the site is cleansed.				
12. Wrap the thumb and first two fingers of your nondominant hand around the patient's forearm, pulling downward and apart to stretch the skin of the forearm taut at the location of the injection.	5	_____	_____	_____
13. Cleanse the patient's skin with an alcohol wipe using a circular motion and moving from the center outward.	5	_____	_____	_____
14. Allow the antiseptic to dry.	2	_____	_____	_____
15. Remove the cap from the needle.	2	_____	_____	_____
16. Wrap the thumb and first two fingers of your nondominant hand around the patient's forearm, pulling downward and apart to stretch the skin of the forearm taut at the location of the injection.	5	_____	_____	_____
17. Grasp the syringe between the thumb and first two fingers of your dominant hand, palm down, with the needle bevel upward. Hold the syringe close to the plunger end.	5	_____	_____	_____
18. At a 15-degree angle, with the syringe unit parallel to the surface of the skin, carefully insert the needle just until the bevel point is under the skin's surface.	5	_____	_____	_____
*19. Slowly and steadily inject the medication by depressing the plunger with your little finger. Do not aspirate. A wheal should appear.	10	_____	_____	_____
20. After administering all of the medication (0.1 mL), withdraw the needle.	2	_____	_____	_____
21. Immediately cover the contaminated needle with the safety device and dispose of the syringe unit in a sharps container.	5	_____	_____	_____
22. Do not massage the area; however, you may blot it with a cotton ball or gauze square. Do not cover the site with a bandage.	5	_____	_____	_____
23. Make sure the patient is comfortable and safe.	2	_____	_____	_____
24. Observe the patient for any adverse reaction.	2	_____	_____	_____
25. Dispose of the gloves in the biohazardous waste container and sanitize your hands.	2	_____	_____	_____

326

Steps	Possible Points	Attempt 1	Attempt 2	Attempt 3
26. In the patient's medical record, document the procedure and any reactions that occurred at the site of the injection. Include the exact site of the injection.	5	_____	_____	_____
*27. Tell the patient when to return to the office to have the site checked for a reaction or give the patient a postcard to be completed and returned.	5	_____	_____	_____

Reading the Mantoux Test

Steps	Possible Points	Attempt 1	Attempt 2	Attempt 3
*28. Put on latex gloves. Using good lighting and with the patient's arm slightly flexed, measure the induration at the site of the injection. Measure only the raised area; do not include any areas of inflammation.	5	_____	_____	_____
29. Discard the gloves in the biohazardous waste container and sanitize your hands.	5	_____	_____	_____
30. In the following Documentation in the Medical Record section, document the results of the Mantoux test as you would in the patient's record. Include a complete description of the size of the induration, if any, and the appearance of the test site. Notify the physician.	5	_____	_____	_____

Documentation in the Medical Record:

Comments:

Points earned _____ ÷ 100 possible points = Score _____ % Score

Instructor's signature _____

Name _____ Date _____ Score _____

PROCEDURE 35-8 Select the Proper Sites for Administering a Parenteral Medication: Give a Subcutaneous Injection

CAAHEP COMPETENCIES: I.PI.7, I.PI.9, I.PI.10, I.AI.1, II.AII.1, III.PIII.2, IV.PIV.2
ABHES COMPETENCIES: 4.a, 6.b, 9.f

TASK: To inject 0.5 mL of medication into the subcutaneous tissue using a 25-gauge, ⅝-inch needle and syringe of the correct size and type, as directed by the physician.

Physician's Order: Administer 0.5 mL varicella vaccine SC stat to Mandy Leno, age 11.

Equipment and Supplies
- Physician's written order, including the patient's name, when to give the drug, the route of administration, and the name and strength of the drug
- Vial of ordered medication
- Alcohol wipes
- Gauze squares or cotton balls
- A sterile needle and syringe unit with safety cover device
- Disposable gloves
- Sharps container
- Patient's medical record

Standards: Complete the procedure and all critical steps in _____ minutes with a minimum score of 85% in three attempts.

Scoring: Divide the points earned by the total possible points. Failure to perform a critical step, indicated by an asterisk (*), results in an unsatisfactory overall score.

Time began _____ Time ended _____ Total minutes: _____

Steps	Possible Points	Attempt 1	Attempt 2	Attempt 3
1. Sanitize your hands; observe Standard Precautions.	2	____	____	____
2. Select the correct medication from the shelf or the refrigerator.	5	____	____	____
*3. Read the label to make sure you have the right drug and the right strength. Perform the three label and order checks while dispensing the medication, and verify the "seven rights." Perform any necessary dose calculations.	5	____	____	____
4. Warm refrigerated medications by gently rolling the container between your palms.	2	____	____	____
5. Prepare the syringe, withdrawing the correct dose.	5	____	____	____
6. Document the vaccine dose on the vaccination log. Each physician's office has a policy for documenting vaccinations.	10	____	____	____
7. Take the medication to the patient.	2	____	____	____
*8. Greet the patient by name and verify that you have the correct patient. Explain the purpose of the immunization.	5	____	____	____

329

Steps	Possible Points	Attempt 1	Attempt 2	Attempt 3
9. Ask the patient to sit upright and help position the person comfortably if necessary.	2	___	___	___
10. Expose the upper posterior arm.	2	___	___	___
11. Put on gloves. With the thumb and fingers of your non-dominant hand, grasp the tissue of the posterior upper arm. Cleanse the patient's skin with the antiseptic sponge, using a circular motion and moving outward from the center.	10	___	___	___
12. Remove the cap from the needle.	2	___	___	___
13. Hold the syringe between the thumb and the first two fingers of your dominant hand and with one swift movement, insert the entire needle up to the hub at a 45-degree angle.	10	___	___	___
14. Aspirate (except when administering heparin or insulin) by withdrawing the plunger slightly to make sure no blood enters the syringe.	10	___	___	___
15. If blood appears, immediately withdraw the unit without injecting the medication and dispose of it in the sharps container. Compress the injection site with an alcohol swab or gauze bandage.	10	___	___	___
16. Begin again with step 1.	5	___	___	___
17. If no blood appears in the syringe, push in the plunger slowly and steadily until all the medication has been administered.	10	___	___	___
18. Place the gauze square next to the needle and withdraw it at the same angle of insertion. Immediately cover the contaminated needle with the syringe unit safety device and discard the unit in the sharps container.	10	___	___	___
19. Gently massage the site with the gauze square (do not massage insulin or heparin injections).	2	___	___	___
20. Make sure the patient is comfortable and safe.	2	___	___	___
21. Dispose of the gloves in the biohazardous waste container and sanitize your hands.	2	___	___	___
22. Observe the patient for any adverse reaction. You may need to keep the patient under observation for 20 to 30 minutes.	2	___	___	___
23. In the following Documentation in the Medical Record section, record the administration of the drug as you would in the patient's record, including the exact injection site. Also show the notation that would be made in the immunization record.	5	___	___	___

Procedure 35-8 Give a Subcutaneous Injection

Documentation in the Medical Record:

Comments:

Points earned _____ ÷ **100 possible points = Score** _____ **% Score**

Instructor's signature _____

Name _____ Date _____ Score _____

PROCEDURE 35-9 Administer Parenteral (Excluding IV) Medications: Mix Two Different Types of Insulin in One Syringe

CAAHEP COMPETENCIES: I.PI.9, I.PI.10, I.AI.1, II.AII.1, III.PIII.2
ABHES COMPETENCIES: 4.a, 6.b, 9.f

TASK: To mix two different types of insulin from two different multidose vials in one injection unit for administration.

Physician's Order: Administer 5 U of Lispro and 15 U NPH insulin stat to Gregor Thomas.

Equipment and Supplies
- Physician's written order, including the patient's name, when to give the drug, the route of administration, and the name and strength of the drug
- Multidose vial of Lispro insulin
- Multidose vial of NPH insulin
- Alcohol wipes
- Gauze squares or cotton balls
- Sterile needle and insulin syringe unit with safety cover device (because the total amount of insulin ordered is 20 U, use a 30-U insulin syringe)
- Disposable gloves
- Sharps container
- Patient's medical record

Standards: Complete the procedure and all critical steps in _____ minutes with a minimum score of 85% in three attempts.

Scoring: Divide the points earned by the total possible points. Failure to perform a critical step, indicated by an asterisk (*), results in an unsatisfactory overall score.

Time began _____ Time ended _____ Total minutes: _____

Steps	Possible Points	Attempt 1	Attempt 2	Attempt 3
1. Sanitize your hands; observe Standard Precautions.	5	_____	_____	_____
2. Select the correct multidose vials of insulin from the refrigerator.	5	_____	_____	_____
3. Read the label to make sure you have the right types of insulin. Perform the three label and order checks for each vial while dispensing the medication, and verify the "seven rights."	5	_____	_____	_____
4. Inspect the appearance of the medication in each vial. Lispro and Regular insulin are clear and colorless. NPH is opaque or cloudy and colorless.	5	_____	_____	_____
5. Mix the insulin vials by gently rolling the containers between your palms.	5	_____	_____	_____
6. Check to make sure the total amount of insulin is less than the insulin syringe chosen.	5	_____	_____	_____

333

Steps	Possible Points	Attempt 1	Attempt 2	Attempt 3
7. Clean the tops of each vial with individual alcohol wipes, leaving the wipe on the top of each vial.	5	_____	_____	_____
8. Remove the alcohol swab and inject 15 U of air into the NPH vial, being careful not to touch the insulin in the vial with the needle and withdraw the needle.	5	_____	_____	_____
9. Remove the alcohol swab and inject 5 U of air into the Lispro vial; keeping the needle in the vial, invert the vial and immediately withdraw the ordered dose of 5 U.	5	_____	_____	_____
10. Reinsert the needle into the NPH vial and carefully withdraw the ordered 15 U dose.	5	_____	_____	_____
11. Complete the final label check and return the two insulin vials to the refrigerator.	5	_____	_____	_____
12. Take the syringe unit to the patient.	5	_____	_____	_____
13. Administer the medication according to the steps in PROCEDURE 35-8 in the text. If a microneedle is used, you can administer insulin at a 90-degree angle.	5	_____	_____	_____
14. Do not aspirate when administering insulin.	5	_____	_____	_____
15. Immediately cover the contaminated needle with the syringe unit safety device and discard the unit in the sharps container.	5	_____	_____	_____
16. Do not massage the site after administration.	5	_____	_____	_____
17. Make sure the patient is comfortable and safe.	5	_____	_____	_____
18. Dispose of the gloves in the biohazardous waste container and sanitize your hands.	5	_____	_____	_____
19. Observe the patient for any adverse reaction. You may need to keep the patient under observation for 20 to 30 minutes.	5	_____	_____	_____
20. In the following Documentation in the Medical Record section, record the administration of the drug as you would in the patient's record, including the exact injection site.	5	_____	_____	_____

Documentation in the Medical Record:

Procedure **35-9** **Administer Parenteral (Excluding IV) Medications**

Comments:

Points earned _____ ÷ 100 possible points = Score _____ % Score

Instructor's signature _____

PROCEDURE 35-10 Administer Parenteral (Excluding IV) Medications: Give an Intramuscular Injection into the Deltoid

CAAHEP COMPETENCIES: I.PI.7, I.PI.9, I.PI.10, I.AI.1, II.AII.1, III.PIII.2, IV.PIV.2
ABHES COMPETENCIES: 4.a, 6.b, 6.e, 9.a, 9.f

TASK: To inject ordered medication into the muscle using a 22-gauge, 1½-inch needle and 3-mL syringe, as directed by the prescriber.

Prescriber's Order: Administer 300,000 U Penicillin G IM stat to Ramon Diez, age 23.

Equipment and Supplies
- Prescriber's written order, including the patient's name, when to give the drug, the route of administration, and the name and strength of the drug
- Vial containing ordered medication
- Alcohol wipes
- Cotton ball
- Sterile needle and syringe unit with safety needle cover
- Disposable gloves
- Sharps container
- Patient's medical record

Standards: Complete the procedure and all critical steps in _____ minutes with a minimum score of 85% in three attempts.

Scoring: Divide the points earned by the total possible points. Failure to perform a critical step, indicated by an asterisk (*), results in an unsatisfactory overall score.

Time began _____ Time ended _____ Total minutes: _____

Steps	Possible Points	Attempt 1	Attempt 2	Attempt 3
1. Sanitize your hands; observe Standard Precautions.	2	_____	_____	_____
2. Select the correct medication from storage.	5	_____	_____	_____
*3. Read the label to make sure you have the right drug and the right strength.	2	_____	_____	_____
4. Warm refrigerated medications by gently rolling the container between your palms.	2	_____	_____	_____
5. Calculate the correct dose, if necessary, and continue with the three label checks while drawing the medication into the syringe.	5	_____	_____	_____
6. Take the medication to the patient.	2	_____	_____	_____
7. Greet the patient by name and verify that you have the correct patient.	2	_____	_____	_____
*8. Ask the patient whether he is allergic to penicillin or any other antibiotics.	10	_____	_____	_____
9. Help the patient into an upright sitting position.	2	_____	_____	_____

337

Steps	Possible Points	Attempt 1	Attempt 2	Attempt 3
10. Put on gloves and expose the deltoid site. The mid-deltoid site is approximately 2 to 3 fingerwidths below the acromial process.	5	_____	_____	_____
11. Cleanse the patient's skin with the alcohol wipe, using a circular motion and moving outward from the center.	5	_____	_____	_____
12. Remove the needle cover. Place your nondominant hand on the patient's shoulder, and with the thumb and first two fingers, spread the skin tightly and grasp the muscle deeply on each side.	5	_____	_____	_____
13. Grasp the syringe as you would a dart and with one swift movement, insert the entire needle up to the hub, at a 90-degree angle, into the muscle.	10	_____	_____	_____
*14. Aspirate; withdraw the plunger slightly to be make sure no blood enters the syringe.	5	_____	_____	_____
15. If blood appears, immediately withdraw the syringe, discard it in the sharps container, and compress the injection site with the cotton ball.	5	_____	_____	_____
16. Begin again with step 1.	2	_____	_____	_____
17. If no blood appears in the syringe, push in the plunger slowly and steadily until all the medication has been administered.	5	_____	_____	_____
18. Place the cotton ball next to the needle and apply counterpressure to the area while you withdraw the needle at the same angle used for insertion. Immediately cover the contaminated needle with the syringe unit safety device and discard the syringe unit in the sharps container.	10	_____	_____	_____
19. Gently massage the site with the cotton ball.	5	_____	_____	_____
20. Make sure the patient is comfortable and safe.	2	_____	_____	_____
21. Observe the patient for any adverse reaction. You may need to keep the patient under observation for 20 to 30 minutes.	2	_____	_____	_____
22. Dispose of the gloves in the biohazardous waste container and sanitize your hands.	2	_____	_____	_____
23. In the following Documentation in the Medical Record section, record the administration of the drug as you would in the patient's record. Also show the required DEA entry if the medication is a controlled substance.	5	_____	_____	_____

Documentation in the Medical Record:

Comments:

Points earned _____ ÷ 100 possible points = Score _____ % Score

Instructor's signature _____

Name _____ Date _____ Score _____

PROCEDURE 35-11 Select the Proper Sites for Administering a Parenteral Medication: Administer a Pediatric Intramuscular Vastus Lateralis Injection

CAAHEP COMPETENCIES: I.PI.7, I.PI.9, I.PI.10, I.AI.1, II.AII.1, III.PIII.2, IV.PIV.2
ABHES COMPETENCIES: 4.a, 6.b, 6.e, 9.a, 9.f

TASK: To inject 0.5 mL of vaccine into the vastus lateralis muscle, using a 22-gauge, ⅝-inch needle.

Prescriber's Order: Administer 0.5 mL of Haemophilus influenzae (Hib) vaccine IM stat to Lizzy Dearborne, age 4 months.

Equipment and Supplies
- Prescriber's written order, including the patient's name, when to give the drug, the route of administration, and the name and strength of the drug
- Vial containing Hib vaccine
- Alcohol wipes
- Cotton ball or 2 × 2 gauze square
- Sterile needle and syringe unit with safety device
- Disposable gloves
- Sharps container
- Patient's medical record

Standards: Complete the procedure and all critical steps in _____ minutes with a minimum score of 85% in three attempts.

Scoring: Divide the points earned by the total possible points. Failure to perform a critical step, indicated by an asterisk (*), results in an unsatisfactory overall score.

Time began _____ Time ended _____ Total minutes: _____

Steps	Possible Points	Attempt 1	Attempt 2	Attempt 3
1. Check the patient's medical record for a previous allergic reaction to the Hib vaccine. Check the baby's temperature and ask the caregiver about recent illnesses, because infants with moderate to severe illness should not be vaccinated.	5	____	____	____
2. Sanitize your hands; observe Standard Precautions.	2	____	____	____
3. Select the correct medication from storage.	5	____	____	____
*4. Read the label to make sure you have the right drug and the right strength; also check the expiration date.	2	____	____	____
5. Warm refrigerated medications by gently rolling the container between your palms.	2	____	____	____
6. Calculate the correct dose, if necessary, and continue with the three label checks while drawing the medication into the syringe. Follow the steps in PROCEDURE 35-5 in the text to draw up the vaccine correctly.	5	____	____	____

Steps	Possible Points	Attempt 1	Attempt 2	Attempt 3
7. Complete the vaccination log according to office procedure.	2	_____	_____	_____
8. Take the medication to the patient.	2	_____	_____	_____
9. Greet the patient's caregiver by name and verify that you have the correct patient.	2	_____	_____	_____
*10. Explain the procedure to the caregiver.	2	_____	_____	_____
11. Position the infant on her back. Ask the caregiver to remove any clothing necessary to expose the infant's thighs. Choose either the right or the left thigh for the injection.	5	_____	_____	_____
12. Put on gloves. Cleanse the patient's skin with the alcohol wipe, using a circular motion and moving outward from the center.	5	_____	_____	_____
13. If necessary, ask for the caregiver's assistance in holding the child still.	2	_____	_____	_____
14. Remove the needle cover and with the thumb and first two fingers of your nondominant hand, spread the skin at the site tightly.	5	_____	_____	_____
15. Grasp the syringe as you would a dart and with one swift movement, insert the needle at a 45-degree angle into the muscle, with the needle pointing toward the feet.	10	_____	_____	_____
*16. Aspirate; withdraw the plunger slightly to make sure no blood enters the syringe.	5	_____	_____	_____
17. If blood appears, immediately withdraw the syringe, discard it in the sharps container, and compress the injection site with the cotton ball. Begin again with step 2.	5	_____	_____	_____
18. If no blood appears in the syringe, push in the plunger slowly and steadily until all the medication has been injected.	5	_____	_____	_____
19. Place the cotton ball next to the needle and apply counterpressure to the area while you withdraw the needle at the same angle used for insertion. Immediately place the safety cover over the contaminated needle and discard the syringe unit in the sharps container.	10	_____	_____	_____
20. Gently massage the site with the cotton ball.	2	_____	_____	_____
21. Make sure the infant is safely held by the caregiver.	2	_____	_____	_____
22. Dispose of your gloves in the biohazardous waste container and sanitize your hands.	5	_____	_____	_____
23. Observe the patient for 20 to 30 minutes for any adverse reaction.	5	_____	_____	_____
*24. In the following Documentation in the Medical Record section, record the administration of the drug as you would in the patient's record. Also show the notation that would appear in the vaccination log.	5	_____	_____	_____

Documentation in the Medical Record:

Comments:

Points earned _____ ÷ 100 possible points = Score _____ % Score

Instructor's signature _____

Name _____ Date _____ Score _____

PROCEDURE 35-12 Administer Parenteral (Excluding IV) Medications: Give a Z Track Intramuscular Injection into the Dorsogluteal Site

CAAHEP COMPETENCIES: I.PI.7, I.PI.9, I.PI.10, I.AI.1, II.AII.1, III.PIII.2, IV.PIV.2
ABHES COMPETENCIES: 4.a, 6.b, 6.e, 9.a, 9.f

TASK: To inject 1 mL of medication into the muscle using a 23-gauge, 2-inch needle and 3-mL syringe and the Z-track method, as directed by the physician.

Equipment and Supplies
- Physician's written order, including the patient's name, when to give the drug, the route of administration, and the name and strength of the drug
- Vial containing the ordered medication
- Alcohol wipes
- Cotton ball
- Disposable gloves
- Sharps container
- Sterile needle and syringe unit with safety needle cover
- Additional sterile needle
- Patient's medical record

Standards: Complete the procedure and all critical steps in _____ minutes with a minimum score of 85% in three attempts.

Scoring: Divide the points earned by the total possible points. Failure to perform a critical step, indicated by an asterisk (*), results in an unsatisfactory overall score.

Time began _____ Time ended _____ Total minutes: _____

Steps	Possible Points	Attempt 1	Attempt 2	Attempt 3
1. Sanitize your hands; observe Standard Precautions.	2	___	___	___
2. Select the correct medication from the shelf or the refrigerator.	5	___	___	___
*3. Perform the three order and label checks and verify the "seven rights."	2	___	___	___
4. Warm refrigerated medications by gently rolling the container between your palms.	2	___	___	___
5. Draw up the ordered amount of medication into the syringe unit.	5	___	___	___
6. Replace the needle cover and give a slight turn to loosen the needle. Secure a new needle, still in its sheath, to the tip of the syringe, taking care not to contaminate the needle or the hub of the syringe. Discard the contaminated needle.	5	___	___	___
7. Take the medication to the patient.	2	___	___	___

345

Copyright © 2014 Elsevier, Inc. All rights reserved.

Procedure **35-12 Administer Parenteral (Excluding IV) Medications**

Steps	Possible Points	Attempt 1	Attempt 2	Attempt 3
8. Greet the patient by name and verify that you have the correct patient.	2	_____	_____	_____
9. Position the patient comfortably in Sims' position.	2	_____	_____	_____
*10. Expose the site and put on gloves. The dorsogluteal site is found by placing the palm of the nondominant hand on the greater trochanter of the femur, pointing your fingers toward the posterior iliac spine, and the index finger toward the anterior iliac spine. The injection site is in the upper outer area of the gluteus medius. This area needs to be seen for a Z-track injection.	10	_____	_____	_____
11. Cleanse the patient's skin with the alcohol wipe, using a circular motion and moving outward from the center. Make sure to clean the actual area of injection.	5	_____	_____	_____
12. Remove the needle cover.	2	_____	_____	_____
13. Push the skin to one side and hold it firmly in place. If the skin is slippery, use a dry gauze sponge to hold the skin in place.	5	_____	_____	_____
14. Grasp the syringe as you would a dart and with one swift movement, insert the entire needle up to the hub, at a 90-degree angle, into the upper outer area of the gluteus medius muscle.	5	_____	_____	_____
*15. Aspirate; withdraw the plunger slightly to make sure no blood enters the syringe.	5	_____	_____	_____
16. If blood appears, immediately withdraw the syringe, dispose of the syringe unit in the sharps container, and compress the injection site with a gauze square or cotton ball.	5	_____	_____	_____
17. Begin again with step 1.	2	_____	_____	_____
18. If no blood appears in the syringe, push in the plunger slowly and steadily until all the medication has been administered.	5	_____	_____	_____
*19. Wait 10 seconds for the medication to disperse and then withdraw the needle at the same angle used for insertion. As the needle is withdrawn, release the displaced skin to prevent the tracking of medication to the surface.	5	_____	_____	_____
20. Immediately cover the contaminated needle with the syringe unit safety device and dispose of the needle and syringe unit in the sharps container.	5	_____	_____	_____
21. If the drug manufacturer recommends it, gently massage the site with the gauze square or cotton ball. (Many medications that require Z-track administration should not be massaged.)	5	_____	_____	_____
22. Make sure the patient is comfortable and safe.	2	_____	_____	_____

Steps	Possible Points	Attempt 1	Attempt 2	Attempt 3
23. Dispose of the gloves in the biohazardous waste container and wash your hands.	5	_____	_____	_____
24. Observe the patient for any adverse reaction. You may need to keep the patient under observation for 20 to 30 minutes.	2	_____	_____	_____
25. In the following Documentation in the Medical Record section, record the administration of the drug as you would in the patient's record, including the exact site of the injection.	5	_____	_____	_____

Documentation in the Medical Record:

Comments:

Points earned _____ ÷ 100 possible points = Score _____ % Score

Instructor's signature _____

Name _____ Date _____ Score _____

PROCEDURE 36-1 Develop a Patient Safety Plan: Order the Correct Medication from the Pharmacy

CAAHEP COMPETENCIES: X.PXI.3
ABHES COMPETENCIES: 4.a, 6.c.2, 6.d, 6.e

TASK: To telephone the correct medication prescription order into the pharmacy.

SCENARIO: The physician writes an order to be phoned into the pharmacy for a new patient diagnosed with depression. You think the order reads "Avinza, 30mg PO bid." The pharmacist asks you for the physician's DEA number, because Avinza is a narcotic analgesic. You ask the physician for clarification and are told the order was for Avanza, an antidepressant. Look up both medications in a drug reference. What could have happened if a powerful narcotic had been ordered rather than the antidepressant the physician intended?

Equipment and Supplies
- Notepad with pen
- PDR or other drug reference
- Patient's record

Standards: Complete the procedure and all critical steps in _____ minutes with a minimum score of 85% in three attempts.

Scoring: Divide the points earned by the total possible points. Failure to perform a critical step, indicated by an asterisk (*), results in an unsatisfactory overall score.

Time began _____ Time ended _____ Total minutes: _____

Steps	Possible Points	Attempt 1	Attempt 2	Attempt 3
1. Review the physician's written order for a prescription or repeat the order back to the physician if it is a verbal order. For a verbal order, write down the order and have the physician review it to make sure you have the correct medication before calling the pharmacy.	20	____	____	____
2. If you are unfamiliar with the medication, look up the drug in a reference book.	20	____	____	____
3. Once you are familiar with a medication, if the order does not match the patient's diagnosis, ask the physician for clarification.	20	____	____	____
4. Refer to the office's policy and procedures manual to review the procedure for calling in a prescription order to the pharmacy.	20	____	____	____
5. Clarify any questions with the office manager to prevent any future errors.	20	____	____	____

Comments:

Points earned _____ ÷ 100 possible points = Score _____ % Score

Instructor's signature _____

Procedure **36-1 Develop a Patient Safety Plan**

Name _____ Date _____ Score _____

PROCEDURE 36-2 Evaluate the Work Environment to Identify Safe and Unsafe Working Conditions: Develop an Environmental Safety Plan

CAAHEP COMPETENCIES: X.PXI.2, X.PXI.4
ABHES COMPETENCIES: 9.g

TASK: To assess the healthcare facility for possible safety issues and develop a safety plan.

SCENARIO: Work with a partner to evaluate environmental safety in the laboratory at your school. Record your results and discuss with the class. After the class members share their observations, develop a safety plan for your lab.

Equipment and Supplies
- Pen and paper
- Policy and procedure for environmental safety issues in the facility

Standards: Complete the procedure and all critical steps in _____ minutes with a minimum score of 85% in three attempts.

Scoring: Divide the points earned by the total possible points. Failure to perform a critical step, indicated by an asterisk (*), results in an unsatisfactory overall score.

Time began _____   Time ended _____   Total minutes: _____

Steps	Possible Points	Attempt 1	Attempt 2	Attempt 3
1. Check the floors and hallways for obstructions and possible tripping hazards, including torn carpets, possible spills, protruding electrical cords, and so on.	10	____	____	____
2. Check storage areas to make sure the tops of cabinets are clear and heavier items are stored closer to the floor.	10	____	____	____
3. Assess the location and security of handrails placed around the facility. They should be placed with all stairs, in bathrooms, and in any other areas staff members or patients may need assistance.	10	____	____	____
4. Examine all electrical plugs and outlets to prevent electrical overload.	10	____	____	____
5. Check all equipment to make sure it is in safe working condition.	10	____	____	____
6. Make sure all lights are working (both inside and outside the facility). Also make sure there is adequate lighting and that light fixtures are in good condition.	10	____	____	____
7. Check the working condition of smoke alarms and examine all fire extinguishers.	10	____	____	____
8. Make sure evacuation routes are posted throughout the facility, with clearly marked exit routes and floor plans with exits marked.	10	____	____	____
9. Record your observations and share them with the class.	10	____	____	____
10. Based on group discussion, develop a plan of action for improving the safety of the laboratory.	10	____	____	____

351

Comments:

Points earned _____ ÷ 100 possible points = Score _____ % Score

Instructor's signature _____

Procedure **36-2 Develop an Environmental Safety Plan**

Name _____ Date _____ Score _____

PROCEDURE 36-3 Develop an Employee Safety Plan: Manage a Difficult Patient

CAAHEP COMPETENCIES: X.PXI.3
ABHES COMPETENCIES: 5.a, 9.g

TASK: To communicate with an angry patient in a safe, therapeutic manner. The following procedure is part of an overall employee safety plan.

SCENARIO: You are working at the admissions desk when an extremely angry patient comes storming into the office, yelling about a mistake on his bill. Although the facility uses an outside billing center, you recognize that you should try to help the patient and attempt to defuse the situation. Remember: Call 911 immediately and alert any available security if you or one of your co-workers is threatened with violence.

Equipment and Supplies
- Telephone
- Policy and procedures manual
- Patient's record

Standards: Complete the procedure and all critical steps in _____ minutes with a minimum score of 85% in three attempts.

Scoring: Divide the points earned by the total possible points. Failure to perform a critical step, indicated by an asterisk (*), results in an unsatisfactory overall score.

Time began _____   Time ended _____   Total minutes: _____

Steps	Possible Points	Attempt 1	Attempt 2	Attempt 3
1. Although it is important to safeguard a patient's privacy, do not ask an angry patient into an isolated room; do not close the door.	10	____	____	____
2. Alert other staff members about the situation if possible.	10	____	____	____
3. If you do not feel physically threatened, allow the patient to blow off steam.	10	____	____	____
4. When the patient begins to slow down, offer supportive statements, such as, "I understand it is frustrating to receive a bill you think is unfair." Continue to make supportive statements until the patient is calmer (think of it as the patient screaming his way up a mountain; sooner or later he is going to run out of steam; when he begins to slow down, you can then start offering supportive statements).	10	____	____	____
5. Once you can discuss the situation, ask the patient for the details of the problem. Gather as much information as possible so you can work together on a possible solution.	20	____	____	____
6. After determining the problem, suggest a possible solution. For example, you will contact the billing office with the information and make sure they get back to the patient as soon as possible.	10	____	____	____

353

Steps	Possible Points	Attempt 1	Attempt 2	Attempt 3
7. Report the incident to your supervisor. In the following Documentation in the Medical Record section, document the problem and the agreed-upon action as you would in the patient's record, being careful not to use judgmental statements.	20	_____	_____	_____
8. Discuss your approach to managing the difficult patient at the next staff meeting. With your supervisor's permission, summarize your approach and include it as part of the facility's employee safety plan.	10	_____	_____	_____

Documentation in the Medical Record:

Comments:

Points earned _____ ÷ 100 possible points = Score _____ % Score

Instructor's signature _____

Name _____ Date _____ Score _____

PROCEDURE 36-4 Demonstrate the Proper Use of a Fire Extinguisher

CAAHEP COMPETENCIES: X.PXI.5
ABHES COMPETENCIES: 9.g

TASK: To role-play the safe and proper use of a fire extinguisher.

Equipment and Supplies
• Portable, office-size ABC fire extinguisher that has been discharged

Standards: Complete the procedure and all critical steps in _____ minutes with a minimum score of 85% in three attempts.

Scoring: Divide the points earned by the total possible points. Failure to perform a critical step, indicated by an asterisk (*), results in an unsatisfactory overall score.

Time began _____ **Time ended** _____ **Total minutes:** _____

Steps	Possible Points	Attempt 1	Attempt 2	Attempt 3
1. Pull the pin from the handle of the extinguisher.	20	_____	_____	_____
2. Aim the discharge from the extinguisher toward the bottom of the flames.	20	_____	_____	_____
3. Squeeze the handle of the extinguisher so that it begins to discharge.	20	_____	_____	_____
4. Sweep the extinguisher from side to side toward the base of the fire until it is out or until fire officials arrive.	20	_____	_____	_____
5. Check on the safety of all patients and other personnel.	20	_____	_____	_____

Comments:

Points earned _____ ÷ 100 possible points = Score _____ % Score

Instructor's signature _____

356

PROCEDURE 36-5 Participate in a Mock Environmental Exposure Event: Evacuate a Physician's Office

CAAHEP COMPETENCIES: XI.PXI.6, XI.PXI.7
ABHES COMPETENCIES: 9.g

TASK: To role-play an environmental disaster and implement an evacuation plan.

SCENARIO: Role-play this scenario with your lab group: The building next door to the physician's office where you work is on fire. One member of the group is the designated emergency action coordinator, two individuals are responsible for helping patients with special needs out of the facility, and one person is designated to be the last to leave after the building has been cleared. In a community emergency situation, certain staff members may be designated to provide immediate assistance to survivors. Two medical assistants are sent to help with fire victims. How could medical assistants help in this situation? After the evacuation is complete, meet in a designated spot to discuss the process and determine whether the evacuation plan could be improved in any areas. Document the steps taken throughout the mock environmental event.

Equipment and Supplies
- Pen and paper
- Policy and procedure for evacuation of the facility and response to an environmental disaster

Standards: Complete the procedure and all critical steps in _____ minutes with a minimum score of 85% in three attempts.

Scoring: Divide the points earned by the total possible points. Failure to perform a critical step, indicated by an asterisk (*), results in an unsatisfactory overall score.

Time began _____ Time ended _____ Total minutes: _____

Steps	Possible Points	Attempt 1	Attempt 2	Attempt 3
1. An emergency action coordinator is put in charge.	5	____	____	____
2. The coordinator takes action to manage the emergency at the facility and notifies and works with community emergency services.	5	____	____	____
3. Victims of the fire are being cared for across the street, where a triage and treatment center has been set up by the city's police, fire, and emergency responder units. Two medical assistant staff members are sent to help. They do the following:	10			
a. Use therapeutic communication techniques to calm and care for victims.		____	____	____
b. Implement appropriate Standard Precautions.		____	____	____
c. Monitor and record vital signs.		____	____	____
d. Gather pertinent health histories.		____	____	____
e. Observe victims for possible complications (e.g., breathing problems, shock, angina).		____	____	____
f. Immediately report any life-threatening changes in a patient's status to emergency responders.		____	____	____
g. Use first aid skills as needed.		____	____	____

357

Steps	Possible Points	Attempt 1	Attempt 2	Attempt 3
4. The coordinator designates an employee to immediately shut down any combustibles (e.g., oxygen tanks).	10	_____	_____	_____
5. Using the posted evacuation routes, staff members follow floor plan diagrams to the closest safe exit. They also identify any hazardous areas in the facility to avoid during the emergency evacuation.	10	_____	_____	_____
6. Staff members provide assistance for employees and patients with special needs who may require extra help during the evacuation.	10	_____	_____	_____
7. One staff member checks to make sure everyone has left the facility and that fire doors have been closed before leaving the building.	10	_____	_____	_____
8. All evacuated personnel and patients meet in a designated area to count heads and make sure everyone exited the facility safely.	10	_____	_____	_____
9. After everyone has been accounted for and the office's patients are safe, staff members who are not needed report to the triage area to provide assistance to rescue workers and victims.	10	_____	_____	_____
10. Discuss the evacuation exercise and response to a community disaster with the class.	10	_____	_____	_____
11. Document your role in the exercise. What were the strengths and weaknesses of the group's response to an environmental emergency?	10	_____	_____	_____

Comments:

Points earned _____ ÷ 100 possible points = Score _____ % Score

Instructor's signature _____

358

Name _____ Date _____ Score _____

PROCEDURE 36-6 Maintain an Up-to-Date List of Community Resources for Emergency Preparedness

CAAHEP COMPETENCIES: X.PXI.12
ABHES COMPETENCIES: 9.g, 9.i

TASK: To develop and maintain a list of community agencies that would respond to a natural disaster or other emergency.

SCENARIO: You are asked by your employer to develop a list of groups in your community that are part of the community-wide emergency preparedness plan mandated by the state and federal government. Using multiple resources, develop a comprehensive list of emergency services for your area.

Equipment and Supplies

- Telephone
- Internet access
- Pen and paper
- Electronic record

Standards: Complete the procedure and all critical steps in _____ minutes with a minimum score of 85% in three attempts.

Scoring: Divide the points earned by the total possible points. Failure to perform a critical step, indicated by an asterisk (*), results in an unsatisfactory overall score.

Time began _____   Time ended _____   Total minutes: _____

Steps	Possible Points	Attempt 1	Attempt 2	Attempt 3
1. Start with an online search for the area LEMA office sponsored by the Department of Homeland Security. If the office has a Web site, check it for information about the emergency preparedness plan in your community. You can begin the search at www.ready.gov/america.	25	_____	_____	_____
2. Gather contact information for local police, fire, and EMS services that can be posted next to all telephones in the facility.	25	_____	_____	_____
3. Investigate services provided by your local Public Health office and the American Red Cross.	25	_____	_____	_____
4. Organize the information you gathered about community resources for emergency preparedness. With your supervisor's approval, post a copy of this information in all appropriate locations in the facility. Prepare a data base in the computer that can be updated as the information changes.	25	_____	_____	_____

Comments:

Points earned _____ ÷ 100 possible points = Score _____ % Score

Instructor's signature _____

Name _____ Date _____ Score _____

PROCEDURE 36-7 Maintain Provider/Professional-Level CPR Certification: Use an Automated External Defibrillator

CAAHEP COMPETENCIES: X.PXI.9
ABHES COMPETENCIES: 9.e, 9.g

TASK: To defibrillate adult victims with cardiac arrest. Most adult victims in sudden cardiac arrest are in ventricular fibrillation. The survival rate for victims with ventricular fibrillation is as high as 90% when defibrillation occurs within the first minute of collapse; however, the survival rate for these patients declines 7% to 10% with every minute defibrillation does not occur.

Equipment and Supplies
- Practice automated external defibrillator (AED)
- Approved mannequin

Standards: Complete the procedure and all critical steps in _____ minutes with a minimum score of 85% in three attempts.

Scoring: Divide the points earned by the total possible points. Failure to perform a critical step, indicated by an asterisk (*), results in an unsatisfactory overall score.

Time began _____ **Time ended** _____ **Total minutes:** _____

These steps are to be performed only on an approved mannequin

If the healthcare worker witnesses a cardiac arrest, an AED should be used as soon as possible. If CPR has already been started, continue performing CPR until the AED machine is turned on, pads are applied, and the machine is ready.

Steps	Possible Points	Attempt 1	Attempt 2	Attempt 3
1. Place the AED near the victim's left ear and then turn on the machine.	10	_____	_____	_____
2. Attach electrode pads to the victim's bare dry chest as pictured on the AED. Place the electrodes at the sternum and apex of the heart. Make sure the pads are in complete contact with the victim's chest and that they do not overlap (see Figure 36-3).	20	_____	_____	_____
3. All rescuers must clear away from the victim. Press the Analyze button; the AED analyzes the victim's coronary status, announces whether the victim is going to be shocked, and automatically charges the electrodes.	20	_____	_____	_____
*4. All rescuers must clear away from the victim. If the machine is not automated, press the Shock button. Three analyze-shock cycles may be performed.	20	_____	_____	_____
5. Deliver one shock; leave the AED attached and immediately perform CPR, starting with chest compressions.	10	_____	_____	_____
6. After five cycles of CPR (about 2 minutes), repeat the AED analysis and deliver another shock if indicated. If a nonshockable rhythm is detected, the AED should instruct the rescuer to resume CPR immediately, beginning with chest compressions.	10	_____	_____	_____
7. If the machine gives the "no shock indicated" signal, assess the victim. Check the carotid pulse and the person's breathing status and keep the AED attached until emergency medical services arrive.	10	_____	_____	_____

361

Comments:

Points earned _____ ÷ 100 possible points = Score _____ % Score

Instructor's signature _____

362

Procedure **36-7** **Maintain Provider/Professional-Level CPR Certification**

PROCEDURE 36-8 Perform Patient Screening Using Established Protocols: Telephone Screening and Appropriate Documentation

CAAHEP COMPETENCIES: I.P.I.6
ABHES COMPETENCIES: 8.f, 9.b

TASK: To assess the direction of emergency care and document information appropriately in the patient's record.

SCENARIO: Cheryl is working with the telephone screening staff when they receive a call from the mother of a 5-year-old patient. The mother reports that her son fell and cut his arm. What type of information should Cheryl gather about the injury? What action should be taken? How should the incident be documented?

Equipment and Supplies

- Notepad with pen or pencil
- Facility's emergency procedures manual
- Appointment book or computer program
- Area emergency numbers
- Patient's medical record

Standards: Complete the procedure and all critical steps in _____ minutes with a minimum score of 85% in three attempts.

Scoring: Divide the points earned by the total possible points. Failure to perform a critical step, indicated by an asterisk (*), results in an unsatisfactory overall score.

Time began _____   Time ended _____   Total minutes: _____

Steps	Possible Points	Attempt 1	Attempt 2	Attempt 3
1. Stay calm and reassure the caller.	10	_____	_____	_____
2. Verify the identity of the caller and the injured patient.	10	_____	_____	_____
3. Immediately record the names of the caller and the patient, their location, and the phone number.	10	_____	_____	_____
4. Determine whether the patient's condition is life-threatening. Quantify the amount of blood loss and determine whether the patient is alert and responsive and breathing is normal. Notify EMS if necessary.	10	_____	_____	_____
5. If EMS is notified, stay on the line with the caller until EMS personnel arrive at the scene.	10	_____	_____	_____

Steps	Possible Points	Attempt 1	Attempt 2	Attempt 3
6. If emergency services are not needed, gather details about the injury to determine whether the patient can be seen in the office or should be referred to an emergency department (ED). Consider the following questions:	10			
a. Is there a suspected head or neck injury?		_____	_____	_____
b. Has the patient been moved?		_____	_____	_____
c. Is there a possible fracture? If so, where?		_____	_____	_____
d. Are there any other symptoms?		_____	_____	_____
e. Is there anything pertinent in the patient's health history that would complicate the situation?		_____	_____	_____
f. Has the caller administered any first aid? If so, what type?		_____	_____	_____
7. Based on the information gathered, determine when the patient should be seen in the office if the person is not referred to an ED.	10	_____	_____	_____
8. At any point in this process, do not hesitate to consult the physician or experienced staff members or refer to the facility's emergency procedures manual to determine how to manage the patient's problem.	10	_____	_____	_____
9. Always allow the caller to hang up first, just in case more information or assistance is needed.	10	_____	_____	_____
10. In the following Documentation in the Medical Record section, document as you would in the patient's record the information gathered, the actions taken or recommended, any home care recommendations, and whether the physician was notified.	10	_____	_____	_____

Documentation in the Medical Record:

Comments:

Points earned _____ ÷ 100 possible points = Score _____ % Score

Instructor's signature _____

Procedure 36-8 **Perform Patient Screening Using Established Protocols**

PROCEDURE 36-9 Maintain Provider/Professional-Level CPR Certification: Perform Adult Rescue Breathing and One-Rescuer CPR; Perform Pediatric and Infant CPR

CAAHEP COMPETENCIES: X.PXI.9
ABHES COMPETENCIES: 9.e, 9.g

TASK: To restore a victim's breathing and circulation when respiration or pulse or both stop.

Equipment and Supplies
- Disposable gloves
- CPR ventilator mask for the adult, child, and infant
- Approved mannequins

Standards: Complete the procedure and all critical steps in _____ minutes with a minimum score of 85% in three attempts.

Scoring: Divide the points earned by the total possible points. Failure to perform a critical step, indicated by an asterisk (*), results in an unsatisfactory overall score.

Time began _____   Time ended _____   Total minutes: _____

Steps	Possible Points	Attempt 1	Attempt 2	Attempt 3
1. Establish unresponsiveness. Tap the victim and ask, "Are you OK?" Wait a moment for a response.	10	_____	_____	_____
2. Activate the emergency response system. Put on gloves and get the ventilator mask.	5	_____	_____	_____
3. Tilt the victim's head by placing one hand on the forehead and applying enough pressure to push the head back; with the fingers of the other hand under the chin, lift up and pull the jaw forward. Look, listen, and feel for signs of breathing. Place your ear over the mouth and listen for breathing. Watch the rising and falling of the chest for evidence of breathing. If breathing is absent or inadequate, open the airway and place the ventilator mask over the victim's mouth and nose.	10	_____	_____	_____
4. Give 2 slow breaths (1½ to 2 seconds per breath for an adult; 1 to 2 seconds per breath for an infant or child), holding the ventilator mask tightly against the face while tilting the victim's chin up to keep the airway open. Remove your mouth from the mouthpiece between breaths to allow time for the patient to exhale between breaths.	10	_____	_____	_____

Steps	Possible Points	Attempt 1	Attempt 2	Attempt 3
*5. Check the patient's pulse (at the carotid artery for an adult or older child; at the brachial artery for an infant). If a pulse is present, continue rescue breathing (1 breath every 4 to 5 seconds—about 10 to 12 breaths per minute for an adult; 1 breath every 3 seconds—about 12 to 20 breaths per minute for an infant or child). If no signs of circulation are present, begin cycles of 30 chest compressions (at a rate of about 100 compressions per minute for an adult) followed by 2 slow breaths.	10	_____	_____	_____
6. To deliver chest compressions, kneel at the victim's side a couple of inches from the chest. Move your fingers up the ribs to the point where the sternum and the ribs join in the center of the lower part of the sternum but above the xiphoid process.	10	_____	_____	_____
*7. Place the heel of your hand on the chest over the lower part of the sternum.	5	_____	_____	_____
*8. Place your other hand on top of the first and either interlace or lift your fingers upward off of the chest.	5	_____	_____	_____
9. Bring your shoulders directly over the victim's sternum as you compress downward, keeping your elbows locked.	5	_____	_____	_____
10. Depress the sternum at least 2 inches in an adult victim. Relax the pressure on the sternum after each compression but do not remove your hands from the sternum.	10	_____	_____	_____
11. After performing 30 compressions (at a rate of about 100 compressions per minute), perform the head tilt–chin lift maneuver to open the airway and give 2 slow rescue breaths.	5	_____	_____	_____
12. After 5 cycles of compressions and breaths (30:2 ratio, about 2 minute) recheck the breathing and carotid pulse. If a pulse is present but breathing is not, continue rescue breathing (1 breath every 5 seconds, about 10 to 12 breaths per minute) and re-evaluate the victim's breathing and pulse every few minutes. If no signs of circulation are present, continue 30:2 cycles of compressions and ventilations, starting with chest compressions. Continue giving CPR until an AED is available or EMS relieves you.	5	_____	_____	_____

Performing CPR on a child: The procedure for performing CPR on a child ages 1 through 8 years is essentially the same as that for an adult. The differences are as follows:

a. Perform 5 cycles of compressions and breaths on the child (30:2 ratio, about 2 minutes) before calling 911 or the local emergency number or using an AED. If another person is available, have that person activate EMS while you care for the child.		_____	_____	_____
b. Use only one hand to perform chest compressions.		_____	_____	_____
c. Breathe more gently.		_____	_____	_____
d. Use the same compression-to-breath ratio as used for adults, 30 compressions followed by 2 breaths per cycle; after 2 breaths, immediately begin the next cycle of compressions and breaths.		_____	_____	_____
e. After 5 cycles (about 2 minutes) of CPR without response, use a pediatric AED if available.		_____	_____	_____
f. Continue until the child responds or help arrives.		_____	_____	_____

Steps	Possible Points	Attempt 1	Attempt 2	Attempt 3
Performing CPR on an infant: Infant cardiac arrest typically is caused by a lack of oxygen from drowning or choking. If you know the infant has an airway obstruction, clear the obstruction; if you do not know why the infant is unresponsive, perform CPR for 2 minutes (about 5 cycles) before calling 911 or the local emergency number. If another person is available, have that person call for help immediately while you attend to the baby.				
a. Draw an imaginary line between the infant's nipples. Place two fingers on the sternum just below this intermammary line.		———	———	———
b. Gently compress the chest.		———	———	———
c. Compression rate should be 100 to 120 per minute.		———	———	———
d. Administer 2 slow breaths after every 30 compressions.		———	———	———
e. After about five 30:2 cycles, activate EMS.		———	———	———
f. Continue CPR until the infant responds or help arrives.		———	———	———
Rescue breathing for an infant: Use an infant ventilator mask or cover the baby's mouth and nose with your mouth.				
a. Give 2 rescue breaths by gently puffing out the cheeks and slowly breathing into the infant's mouth, taking about 1 second for each breath.		———	———	———
13. Remove your gloves and the ventilator mask valve and discard them in the biohazard container. Disinfect the ventilator mask per the manufacturer's recommendations. Sanitize your hands.	5	———	———	———
14. In the following Documentation in the Medical Record section, document the procedure and the patient's condition as you would in the patient's medical record.	5	———	———	———

Documentation in the Medical Record:

Comments:

Points earned _____ ÷ 100 possible points = Score _____ % Score

Instructor's signature _____

367

Name _____ Date _____ Score _____

PROCEDURE 36-10 Perform First Aid Procedures: Administer Oxygen

CAAHEP COMPETENCIES: X.PXI.10
ABHES COMPETENCIES: 9.e

TASK: To provide oxygen for a patient in respiratory distress.

Equipment and Supplies
- Physician's order
- Portable oxygen tank
- Pressure regulator
- Flow meter
- Nasal cannula with connecting tubing
- Patient's medical record

Standards: Complete the procedure and all critical steps in _____ minutes with a minimum score of 85% in three attempts.

Scoring: Divide the points earned by the total possible points. Failure to perform a critical step, indicated by an asterisk (*), results in an unsatisfactory overall score.

Time began _____ Time ended _____ Total minutes: _____

Steps	Possible Points	Attempt 1	Attempt 2	Attempt 3
1. Gather the necessary equipment and sanitize your hands.	10	_____	_____	_____
2. Identify the patient and explain the procedure.	10	_____	_____	_____
3. Check the pressure gauge on the tank to determine the amount of oxygen in the tank.	10	_____	_____	_____
4. If necessary, open the cylinder on the tank one full counterclockwise turn; then attach the cannula tubing to the flow meter.	10	_____	_____	_____
*5. Adjust the flow of oxygen according to the physician's order. Usually the flow meter is set at 12 to 15 liters per minute (LPM). Check to make sure oxygen is flowing through the cannula.	20	_____	_____	_____
6. Insert the cannula tips into the patient's nostrils and adjust the tubing around the back of the ears.	10	_____	_____	_____
7. Make sure the patient is comfortable and answer any questions the patient may have. Continue to monitor the patient throughout the procedure and document any changes in the person's condition.	10	_____	_____	_____
8. Sanitize your hands.	10	_____	_____	_____
9. In the following Documentation in the Medical Record section, document the procedure as you would in the patient's record. Include the number of liters of oxygen being administered and the patient's condition.	10	_____	_____	_____

Documentation in the Medical Record:

Comments:

Points earned _____ ÷ 100 possible points = Score _____ % Score

Instructor's signature _____

370

Name _____ Date _____ Score _____

PROCEDURE 36-11 Perform First Aid Procedures: Respond to an Airway Obstruction in an Adult

CAAHEP COMPETENCIES: X.PXI.10
ABHES COMPETENCIES: 9.e

TASK: To remove an airway obstruction and restore ventilation.

Equipment and Supplies
- Disposable gloves
- Ventilation mask (for unconscious victim)
- Approved mannequin for practicing removal of a foreign body airway obstruction (FBAO)

Standards: Complete the procedure and all critical steps in _____ minutes with a minimum score of 85% in three attempts.

Scoring: Divide the points earned by the total possible points. Failure to perform a critical step, indicated by an asterisk (*), results in an unsatisfactory overall score.

Time began _____ **Time ended** _____ **Total minutes:** _____

Steps	Possible Points	Attempt 1	Attempt 2	Attempt 3
1. Ask the victim, "Are you choking?" If the victim indicates yes, ask, "Can you speak?" If the victim is unable to speak, tell the person you are going to help.	10	____	____	____
2. Stand behind the victim with your feet slightly apart.	5	____	____	____
3. Reach around the victim's abdomen and place an index finger into the victim's navel or at the level of the belt buckle. Make a fist of the opposite hand (do not tuck the thumb into the fist) and place the thumb side of the fist against the victim's abdomen above the navel. If the victim is pregnant, place the fist above the enlarged uterus. If the victim is obese, you may need to place the fist higher in the abdomen. (Chest thrusts may need to be performed on a pregnant or obese victim.)	10	____	____	____
*4. Place the opposite hand over the fist and give abdominal thrusts in a quick inward and upward movement.	10	____	____	____
5. Repeat the abdominal thrusts until the object is expelled or the victim becomes unresponsive.	5	____	____	____
Unresponsive Victim				
1. Carefully lower the patient to the ground, activate the emergency response system, and put on disposable gloves.	10	____	____	____
2. Immediately begin CPR with 30 compressions and 2 breath cycles using the ventilator mask.	10	____	____	____

Steps	Possible Points	Attempt 1	Attempt 2	Attempt 3
3. Each time the airway is opened to deliver a rescue breath during CPR, look for an object in the victim's mouth and remove it if visible. If no object is found, immediately return to the cycle of 30 chest compressions.	10	_____	_____	_____
4. A finger sweep should be used only if the obstruction is visible.	5	_____	_____	_____
5. Continue cycles of 30 compressions to 2 rescue breaths until either the obstruction is removed or EMS arrives.	5	_____	_____	_____
6. If the obstruction is removed, assess the victim for breathing and circulation. If a pulse is present but the patient is not breathing, begin rescue breathing.	10	_____	_____	_____
7. Once either the patient's condition has stabilized or EMS has taken over, remove your gloves and the ventilator mask valve and discard them in the biohazardous waste container. Disinfect the ventilator mask according to the manufacturer's recommendations. Sanitize your hands.	5	_____	_____	_____
8. In the following Documentation in the Medical Record section, document the procedure and the patient's condition as you would in the patient's record.	5	_____	_____	_____

Documentation in the Medical Record:

Comments:

Points earned _____ ÷ 100 possible points = Score _____ % Score

Instructor's signature _____

372

Name _____ Date _____ Score _____

PROCEDURE 36-12 Perform First Aid Procedures: Care for a Patient Who Has Fainted

CAAHEP COMPETENCIES: X.PXI.10
ABHES COMPETENCIES: 9.e, 9.g

TASK: To provide emergency care for and assessment of a patient who has fainted.

Equipment and Supplies
- Sphygmomanometer
- Stethoscope
- Watch with second hand
- Blanket
- Foot stool or box
- Pillows
- Oxygen equipment, if ordered by the physician:
  - Portable oxygen tank
  - Pressure regulator
  - Flow meter
  - Nasal cannula with connecting tubing
- Patient's record

Standards: Complete the procedure and all critical steps in _____ minutes with a minimum score of 85% in three attempts.

Scoring: Divide the points earned by the total possible points. Failure to perform a critical step, indicated by an asterisk (*), results in an unsatisfactory overall score.

Time began _____ Time ended _____ Total minutes: _____

Steps	Possible Points	Attempt 1	Attempt 2	Attempt 3
*1. If a warning is given that the patient feels faint, have the patient lower the head to the knees to increase the blood supply to the brain. If this does not stop the episode, either have the patient lie down on the examination table or lower the patient to the floor. If the patient collapses to the floor when fainting, treat with caution because of possible head or neck injuries.	10	_____	_____	_____
2. Immediately notify the physician of the patient's condition and assess the patient for life-threatening emergencies, such as respiratory or cardiac arrest. If the patient is breathing and has a pulse, monitor the vital signs.	10	_____	_____	_____
3. Loosen any tight clothing and keep the patient warm. Cover the person with a blanket if needed.	10	_____	_____	_____
*4. If a head or neck injury is not a concern, elevate the patient's legs above the level of the heart, using a footstool with pillow if available.	20	_____	_____	_____
5. Continue to monitor the vital signs. Provide oxygen via nasal cannula if ordered by the physician.	10	_____	_____	_____

Steps	Possible Points	Attempt 1	Attempt 2	Attempt 3
6. If the vital signs are unstable or the patient does not respond quickly, activate emergency medical services.	10	_____	_____	_____
7. If the patient vomits, roll the person onto his or her side to prevent aspiration of vomitus into the lungs.	10	_____	_____	_____
8. Once the patient has recovered completely, help the person into a sitting position. Do not leave the patient unattended on the examination table.	10	_____	_____	_____
9. In the following Documentation in the Medical Record section, document the incident as you would in the patient's record; include a description of the episode, the patient's symptoms and vital signs, the duration of the faint, and any complaints. If oxygen was administered, document the number of liters and how long it was administered.	10	_____	_____	_____

Documentation in the Medical Record:

Comments:

Points earned _____ ÷ 100 possible points = Score _____ % Score

Instructor's signature _____

374

Name _____ Date _____ Score _____

PROCEDURE 36-13 Perform First Aid Procedures: Control Bleeding

CAAHEP COMPETENCIES: III.PIII.2, III.PIII.3, X.PXI.10
ABHES COMPETENCIES: 9.a, 9.e

TASK: To stop hemorrhaging from an open wound.

Equipment and Supplies

- Gloves (sterile if available)
- Appropriate personal protective equipment (PPE) according to OSHA guidelines, including:
- Impermeable gown
- Goggles or face shield
- Impermeable mask
- Impermeable foot covers if indicated
- Sterile dressings
- Bandaging material
- Biohazardous waste container
- Patient's record

Standards: Complete the procedure and all critical steps in _____ minutes with a minimum score of 85% in three attempts.

Scoring: Divide the points earned by the total possible points. Failure to perform a critical step, indicated by an asterisk (*), results in an unsatisfactory overall score.

Time began _____   Time ended _____   Total minutes: _____

Steps	Possible Points	Attempt 1	Attempt 2	Attempt 3
1. Sanitize your hands and put on the appropriate PPE.	10	_____	_____	_____
2. Assemble the necessary equipment and supplies.	10	_____	_____	_____
3. Apply several layers of sterile dressing material directly to the wound and exert pressure.	10	_____	_____	_____
4. Wrap the wound with bandage material. Add more dressing and bandaging material if the bleeding continues.	10	_____	_____	_____
5. If the bleeding persists and the wound is on an extremity, elevate the extremity above the level of the heart. Notify the physician immediately if the bleeding cannot be controlled.	10	_____	_____	_____
6. If the bleeding still continues, maintain direct pressure and elevation; also apply pressure to the appropriate artery. If the wound is in the arm, apply pressure to the brachial artery by squeezing the inner aspect of the upper middle arm. If the wound is in the leg, apply pressure to the femoral artery on the affected side by pushing with the heel of the hand into the femoral crease at the groin. If the bleeding cannot be controlled, activate emergency medical services.	10	_____	_____	_____

Steps	Possible Points	Attempt 1	Attempt 2	Attempt 3
7. Once the bleeding has been controlled and the patient's condition has been stabilized, dispose of contaminated materials in the biohazardous waste container.	10	_____	_____	_____
8. Disinfect the area, remove your gloves, and discard them in the biohazardous waste container.	10	_____	_____	_____
9. Sanitize your hands.	10	_____	_____	_____
10. In the following Documentation in the Medical Record section, document the incident as you would in the patient's record; include the details of the wound, when and how it occurred, the patient's symptoms and vital signs, the treatment provided by the physician, and the patient's current condition.	10	_____	_____	_____

Documentation in the Medical Record:

Comments:

Points earned _____ ÷ 100 possible points = Score _____ % Score

Instructor's signature _____

PROCEDURE 37-1 Perform Patient Screening Using Established Protocols: Measure Distance Visual Acuity with the Snellen Chart

CAAHEP COMPETENCIES: I.PI.6, I.PI.10
ABHES COMPETENCIES: 9.d

TASK: To determine the patient's degree of visual clarity at a measured distance of 20 feet using the Snellen chart.

Equipment and Supplies
- Snellen eye chart
- Eye occluder
- Pen or pencil and paper
- Patient's record

Standards: Complete the procedure and all critical steps in _____ minutes with a minimum score of 85% in three attempts.

Scoring: Divide the points earned by the total possible points. Failure to perform a critical step, indicated by an asterisk (*), results in an unsatisfactory overall score.

Time began _____ Time ended _____ Total minutes: _____

Steps	Possible Points	Attempt 1	Attempt 2	Attempt 3
1. Sanitize your hands.	10	_____	_____	_____
2. Prepare the examination room. Make sure (a) the room is well lit, (b) a distance marker has been placed 20 feet from the chart, and (c) the chart is at the eye level for the patient.	10	_____	_____	_____
3. Identify the patient and explain the procedure. Instruct the patient not to squint during the test, because this temporarily improves vision. The patient should not have an opportunity to study the chart before the test is given. If the patient wears corrective lenses, they should be worn during the test.	10	_____	_____	_____
*4. Position the patient in a standing or sitting position at the 20-foot marker.	10	_____	_____	_____
5. Check to make sure the Snellen chart is at the patient's eye level.	5	_____	_____	_____
*6. Instruct the patient to cover the left eye with the occluder and to keep both eyes open throughout the test (this prevents squinting).	10	_____	_____	_____
*7. Stand beside the chart and point to each row as the patient reads aloud down the chart, starting with the 20/70 row.	10	_____	_____	_____
8. Proceed down the rows of the chart until the smallest row the patient can read with a maximum of two errors is reached. If one or two letters are missed, the outcome is recorded with a minus sign and the number of errors. If more than two errors are made, the previous line should be documented.	10	_____	_____	_____

377

Steps	Possible Points	Attempt 1	Attempt 2	Attempt 3
9. Record any reactions noted while the patient is reading the chart.	10	_____	_____	_____
10. Repeat the procedure with the left eye and then with both eyes.	5	_____	_____	_____
11. In the following Documentation in the Medical Record section, document the date and time, the procedure, the visual acuity results, and any patient reactions as you would in the patient's record. Also record whether corrective lenses were worn.	10	_____	_____	_____

Documentation in the Medical Record:

Comments:

Points earned _____ ÷ 100 possible points = Score _____ % Score

Instructor's signature _____

PROCEDURE 37-2 Perform Patient Screening Using Established Protocols: Assess Color Acuity Using the Ishihara Test

CAAHEP COMPETENCIES: I.PI.6, I.PI.10
ABHES COMPETENCIES: 9.d

TASK: To assess a patient's color acuity and record the results correctly.

Equipment and Supplies

- Room area with natural light
- Ishihara color plate book
- Pen, pencil, and paper
- Watch with a second hand
- Patient's record

Standards: Complete the procedure and all critical steps in _____ minutes with a minimum score of 85% in three attempts.

Scoring: Divide the points earned by the total possible points. Failure to perform a critical step, indicated by an asterisk (*), results in an unsatisfactory overall score.

Time began _____   **Time ended** _____   **Total minutes:** _____

Steps	Possible Points	Attempt 1	Attempt 2	Attempt 3
1. Assemble the necessary equipment and prepare the room for testing. The room should be quiet and illuminated with natural light.	10	_____	_____	_____
2. Identify the patient and explain the procedure. Use a practice card during the explanation and make sure the patient understands that he or she has 3 seconds to identify each plate.	10	_____	_____	_____
*3. Hold up the first plate at a right angle to the patient's line of vision and 30 inches from the patient. Make sure both of the patient's eyes are kept open during the test.	20	_____	_____	_____
*4. Ask the patient to tell you the number on the plate. Record the plate number and the patient's answer.	10	_____	_____	_____
5. Continue this sequence until all 11 plates have been read. If the patient cannot identify the number on the plate, place an X in the record for that plate number.	10	_____	_____	_____
6. Record any unusual signs, such as eye rubbing, squinting, or excessive blinking.	10	_____	_____	_____
7. Place the book back in its cardboard sleeve and return the book to its storage space.	10	_____	_____	_____
*8. In the following Documentation in the Medical Record section, record the procedure as you would in the patient's record, including the date and time, the testing results, and any signs the patient showed during the test.	20	_____	_____	_____

Documentation in the Medical Record:

Comments:

Points earned _____ ÷ 100 possible points = Score _____ % Score

Instructor's signature _____

Procedure **37-2** **Perform Patient Screening Using Established Protocols**

PROCEDURE 37-3 Assist the Physician with Patient Care: Irrigate a Patient's Eyes

CAAHEP COMPETENCIES: I.PI.10
ABHES COMPETENCIES: 9.d

TASK: To cleanse one or both eyes as ordered by the physician.

Equipment and Supplies
- Prescribed sterile irrigation solution
- Sterile irrigating bulb syringe and sterile basin or prepackaged solution with dispenser
- Basin for drainage
- Sterile gauze squares
- Disposable drape
- Towel
- Nonsterile disposable gloves
- Biohazardous waste container
- Patient's record

Standards: Complete the procedure and all critical steps in _____ minutes with a minimum score of 85% in three attempts.

Scoring: Divide the points earned by the total possible points. Failure to perform a critical step, indicated by an asterisk (*), results in an unsatisfactory overall score.

Time began _____   Time ended _____   Total minutes: _____

Steps	Possible Points	Attempt 1	Attempt 2	Attempt 3
1. Sanitize your hands.	5	_____	_____	_____
2. Check the physician's orders to determine which eye requires irrigation (or whether both eyes require it) and the type of solution to be used.	5	_____	_____	_____
3. Assemble the necessary materials.	5	_____	_____	_____
*4. Check the expiration date of the solution and read the label three times.	5	_____	_____	_____
*5. Identify the patient and explain the procedure.	5	_____	_____	_____
6. Assist the patient into a sitting or supine position, making sure the head is turned toward the side of the affected eye. Place the disposable drape over the patient's neck and shoulder.	5	_____	_____	_____
7. Put on gloves and then rinse your gloved hands under warm water to remove all powder.	5	_____	_____	_____
8. Place or have the patient hold a drainage basin next to the affected eye to receive the solution from the eye. Place a polylined drape under the basin to prevent the solution from getting on the patient.	5	_____	_____	_____

381

Steps	Possible Points	Attempt 1	Attempt 2	Attempt 3
*9. Moisten a gauze square with solution and cleanse the eyelid and lashes. Start at the inner canthus (near the nose) and work toward the outer canthus (farthest from the nose). Dispose of the gauze square in the biohazardous waste container after each wipe.	10	_____	_____	_____
10. If using a bulb syringe, pour the required volume of body-temperature irrigating solution into the basin and withdraw solution into the bulb syringe. If using an irrigating solution in a prepackaged dispenser, remove the lid.	5	_____	_____	_____
11. Separate and hold the eyelids with the index finger and thumb of one hand. With the other hand, place the syringe or dispenser on the bridge of the nose parallel to the eye.	5	_____	_____	_____
12. Squeeze the bulb or dispenser, directing the solution toward the lower conjunctiva of the inner canthus. Allow the solution to flow steadily and slowly from the inner canthus to the outer canthus. Do not touch the eye or eyelids with the applicator.	10	_____	_____	_____
13. Refill the syringe or continue to gently squeeze the prepackaged bottle. Continue the procedure until the amount of solution ordered by the physician has been administered or until drainage from the eye is clear.	5	_____	_____	_____
14. Dry the eyelid from the inner to the outer canthus with sterile gauze. Do not use cotton balls, because fibers might remain in the eye.	5	_____	_____	_____
15. Dispose of the irrigation results and clean the work area.	5	_____	_____	_____
16. Remove your gloves and sanitize your hands.	5	_____	_____	_____
*17. In the following Documentation in the Medical Record section, document the procedure as you would in the patient's record, using appropriate abbreviations. Include the date and time, the type and amount of solution used, which eye was irrigated, any significant patient reactions, and the results in the patient's record.	10	_____	_____	_____

Documentation in the Medical Record:

Comments:

Points earned _____ ÷ 100 possible points = Score _____ % Score

Instructor's signature _____

382

PROCEDURE 37-4 Assist the Physician with Patient Care: Instill an Eye Medication

CAAHEP COMPETENCIES: I.PI.10
ABHES COMPETENCIES: 9.a, 9.e

TASK: To apply medication to one or both eyes as ordered by the physician.

Equipment and Supplies
- Sterile medication with sterile eye dropper or ophthalmic ointment
- Disposable drape
- Sterile gauze squares
- Disposable nonsterile gloves
- Patient's record

Standards: Complete the procedure and all critical steps in _____ minutes with a minimum score of 85% in three attempts.

Scoring: Divide the points earned by the total possible points. Failure to perform a critical step, indicated by an asterisk (*), results in an unsatisfactory overall score.

Time began _____ **Time ended** _____ **Total minutes:** _____

Steps	Possible Points	Attempt 1	Attempt 2	Attempt 3
1. Sanitize your hands.	5	_____	_____	_____
2. Check the physician's order to determine which eye requires medication (or whether medication has been ordered for both eyes) and also the name and strength of the medication to be used.	10	_____	_____	_____
3. Assemble the necessary equipment and supplies.	5	_____	_____	_____
4. Read the label of the medication three times.	5	_____	_____	_____
*5. Identify the patient and explain the procedure.	10	_____	_____	_____
6. Put on nonsterile gloves and rinse your gloved hands under warm water to remove all powder.	5	_____	_____	_____
7. Assist the patient into a sitting or supine position. Ask the patient to tilt the head backward and look up.	5	_____	_____	_____
*8. Pull the lower conjunctival sac downward.	5	_____	_____	_____
9. Apply the prescribed number of drops or amount of ointment into the eye. For eye drops, place the drops in the center of the lower conjunctival sac; hold the tip of the dropper parallel to the eye and ½ inch above the eye sac. For eye ointment (ung), squeeze a thin ribbon along the lower conjunctival sac from the inner to the outer canthus, making sure not to touch the eye with the applicator.	10	_____	_____	_____

383

Steps	Possible Points	Attempt 1	Attempt 2	Attempt 3
10. Instruct the patient to close the eye gently and rotate the eyeball.	10	_____	_____	_____
11. Dry any excess drainage from the inner to the outer canthus and explain that the medication may temporarily blur vision.	10	_____	_____	_____
12. Discard the unused medication and clean the procedure area.	5	_____	_____	_____
13. Remove your gloves and sanitize your hands.	5	_____	_____	_____
*14. In the following Documentation in the Medical Record section, record the procedure as you would in the patient's chart; include the date and time; the name and strength of the medication; the amount of the dose administered; which eye was treated; the patient education provided if the treatment is to continue at home; and any observations.	10	_____	_____	_____

Documentation in the Medical Record:

Comments:

Points earned _____ ÷ 100 possible points = Score _____ % Score

Instructor's signature _____

PROCEDURE 37-5 Perform Patient Screening Using Established Protocols: Measure Hearing Acuity with an Audiometer

CAAHEP COMPETENCIES: I.PI.6, I.PI.10
ABHES COMPETENCIES: 9.e

TASK: To perform audiometric testing of hearing acuity.

NOTE: Medical assistants must have specialized training to conduct this test.

Equipment and Supplies
- Audiometer with adjustable headphones
- Quiet area
- Patient's record

Standards: Complete the procedure and all critical steps in _____ minutes with a minimum score of 85% in three attempts.

Scoring: Divide the points earned by the total possible points. Failure to perform a critical step, indicated by an asterisk (*), results in an unsatisfactory overall score.

Time began _____ **Time ended** _____ **Total minutes:** _____

Steps	Possible Points	Attempt 1	Attempt 2	Attempt 3
1. Sanitize your hands, assemble the necessary equipment, and bring the patient to a quiet area.	10	_____	_____	_____
*2. Explain that the audiometer measures whether the patient can hear various sound wave frequencies through the headphones. Each ear is tested separately. When the patient hears a frequency, he or she should raise a hand.	10	_____	_____	_____
3. Place the headphones over the patient's ears, making sure to adjust them for comfort.	10	_____	_____	_____
4. Start the testing in one ear, beginning at a low frequency. If the machine does not record the results automatically, document the patient's response to the frequencies on a graph or audiogram. (The results for the left ear are marked with an X; those for the right ear are marked with an O.)	20	_____	_____	_____
5. Gradually increase the frequencies to test the patient's ability to hear. Document each response by the patient.	10	_____	_____	_____
6. Test the other ear and document the testing results using the appropriate abbreviations: AU (both ears), AD (right ear), and AS (left ear).	10	_____	_____	_____
7. Give the test results to the physician for interpretation.	10	_____	_____	_____
8. Disinfect the equipment according to the manufacturer's guidelines.	10	_____	_____	_____
9. Sanitize your hands.	10	_____	_____	_____

385

Comments:

Points earned _____ ÷ 100 possible points = Score _____ % Score

Instructor's signature _____

PROCEDURE 37-6 Assist the Physician with Patient Care: Irrigate a Patient's Ear

CAAHEP COMPETENCIES: I.PI.10
ABHES COMPETENCIES: 9.e

TASK: To remove excessive or impacted cerumen from one or both of a patient's ears.

Equipment and Supplies
- Irrigating solution
- Basin for irrigating solution
- Bulb syringe or an approved otic irrigation device
- Gauze squares
- Otoscope
- Drainage basin
- Disposable drape with polylined barrier
- Cotton-tipped applicators
- Disposable gloves
- Patient's record

Standards: Complete the procedure and all critical steps in _____ minutes with a minimum score of 85% in three attempts.

Scoring: Divide the points earned by the total possible points. Failure to perform a critical step, indicated by an asterisk (*), results in an unsatisfactory overall score.

Time began _____   Time ended _____   Total minutes: _____

Steps	Possible Points	Attempt 1	Attempt 2	Attempt 3
1. Sanitize your hands.	5	____	____	____
2. Check the physician's order and assemble the necessary materials.	5	____	____	____
3. Check the label of the solution three times: (a) when you remove it from the shelf, (b) when you pour it, and (c) when you return it to the shelf.	5	____	____	____
4. Prepare the solution as ordered. It should be body temperature to help loosen the cerumen.	10	____	____	____
*5. Identify the patient and explain the procedure.	5	____	____	____
6. View the affected ear with an otoscope to locate the cerumen impaction.	5	____	____	____
*7. Place the patient in a sitting position with the head tilted toward the affected ear. A water-absorbent towel is placed over a polylined barrier on the patient's shoulder, and the collecting basin is placed on the towel at the base of the ear. The patient can assist you by holding the collecting basin in place.	5	____	____	____

387

Steps	Possible Points	Attempt 1	Attempt 2	Attempt 3
8. Put on gloves and wipe any particles from the outside of the ear with gauze squares.	5	_____	_____	_____
9. Test the solution to make sure it is warm, fill the syringe, and expel air.	5	_____	_____	_____
10. Straighten the external ear canal. For adults and children over age 3, gently pull the pinna of the ear up and back; for children under age 3, pull the earlobe down and back.	10	_____	_____	_____
11. Place the tip of the syringe into the meatus of the ear.	5	_____	_____	_____
12. Gently direct the flow of the solution toward the roof of the canal.	5	_____	_____	_____
13. Refill the syringe with warm solution and continue irrigating until all the material has been removed. Note the particles in the collecting basin to evaluate when the material has been completely removed.	5	_____	_____	_____
14. Dry the external ear with gauze squares; gently dry the visible ear canal with cotton-tipped applicators.	5	_____	_____	_____
15. Inspect the ear with an otoscope to assess the results.	5	_____	_____	_____
16. Place a clean, absorbent towel on the examination table and allow the patient to rest quietly with the head turned to the irrigated side while you wait for the physician to check the affected ear.	5	_____	_____	_____
17. Clean the work area. Properly disinfect all equipment and return it to storage. Then sanitize your hands.	5	_____	_____	_____
18. In the following Documentation in the Medical Record section, record the procedure as you would in the patient's record. Include the date and time; which ear was irrigated, using the appropriate abbreviations (AU [both ears], AD [right ear], AS [left ear]); the type and amount of irrigating solution used; the characteristics of the material returned from the irrigation; the visibility of the tympanic membrane after irrigation; and any patient reactions.	5	_____	_____	_____

Documentation in the Medical Record:

Additional Documentation Exercise:

You are ordered to perform an irrigation of both ears on Mrs. Ophelia Black because of impacted cerumen. An otoscopic examination before the irrigation revealed a large amount of dark brown ear wax in both ears. After irrigation, both tympanic membranes were visible, and Mrs. Black had no complaints of discomfort. Document the procedure and all findings in this space as you would in the patient's record.

Comments:

Points earned _____ ÷ 100 possible points = Score _____ % Score

Instructor's signature _____

Procedure **37-6 Assist the Physician with Patient Care**

Name _____ Date _____ Score _____

PROCEDURE 37-7 Assist the Physician with Patient Care: Instill Medicated Ear Drops

CAAHEP COMPETENCIES: I.PI.10
ABHES COMPETENCIES: 4.a, 6.e, 9.e

TASK: To instill the correct medication in the accurate dose directly into the external auditory canal.

Equipment and Supplies
- Prescribed otic drops in dispenser bottle
- Cotton balls
- Disposable gloves
- Patient's record

Standards: Complete the procedure and all critical steps in _____ minutes with a minimum score of 85% in three attempts.

Scoring: Divide the points earned by the total possible points. Failure to perform a critical step, indicated by an asterisk (*), results in an unsatisfactory overall score.

Time began _____ **Time ended** _____ **Total minutes:** _____

Steps	Possible Points	Attempt 1	Attempt 2	Attempt 3
1. Sanitize your hands and gather the needed equipment and supplies.	10	_____	_____	_____
2. Check the medication label three times: (a) when you remove it from the shelf, (b) when you prepare it, and (c) when you return it to the shelf.	10	_____	_____	_____
*3. Identify the patient and explain the procedure.	10	_____	_____	_____
4. Have the patient sit up and tilt the head away from the affected ear or lie down on the side with the affected ear upward.	10	_____	_____	_____
5. Check the temperature of the medication bottle. If it feels cold, gently roll the bottle back and forth between your hands to warm the drops.	10	_____	_____	_____
6. Hold the dropper firmly in your dominant hand. With the other hand, gently pull the pinna up and back if the patient is older than 3; or, pull the earlobe down and back if the patient is under age 3.	10	_____	_____	_____
*7. Place the tip of the dropper in the ear canal meatus and instill the drops along the side of the canal.	10	_____	_____	_____
8. Instruct the patient to rest on the opposite side of the affected ear and to remain in this position for approximately 3 minutes.	5	_____	_____	_____
9. If instructed to do so by the physician, place a moistened cotton ball in the ear canal.	5	_____	_____	_____

Steps	Possible Points	Attempt 1	Attempt 2	Attempt 3
10. Clean the work area and sanitize your hands.	10	_____	_____	_____
*11. In the following Documentation in the Medical Record section, record the procedure as you would in the patient's record, using the appropriate abbreviations. Include the date and time; name, dose, and strength of the medication; which ear was treated; and patient reactions on the chart.	10	_____	_____	_____

Documentation in the Medical Record:

Comments:

Points earned _____ ÷ 100 possible points = Score _____ % Score

Instructor's signature _____

392

PROCEDURE 37-8 Perform Patient Screening Using Established Protocols: Collect a Specimen for a Throat Culture

CAAHEP COMPETENCY: I.PI.6, I.PI.10
ABHES COMPETENCIES: 9.e, 10.d.4

TASK: To collect a throat culture, using sterile technique, for immediate testing or for transportation to the laboratory.

Equipment and Supplies

- Nonsterile gloves
- Face protection barrier if the patient is coughing or if there is danger of splattering of body fluids
- Sterile swab
- Sterile tongue depressor
- Transport medium
- Biohazardous waste container
- Laboratory requisition if sample is being sent out for examination
- Patient's record

Standards: Complete the procedure and all critical steps in _____ minutes with a minimum score of 85% in three attempts.

Scoring: Divide the points earned by the total possible points. Failure to perform a critical step, indicated by an asterisk (*), results in an unsatisfactory overall score.

Time began _____   **Time ended** _____   **Total minutes:** _____

Steps	Possible Points	Attempt 1	Attempt 2	Attempt 3
1. Sanitize your hands.	5	____	____	____
2. Gather the materials needed.	5	____	____	____
3. Put on gloves and face protection if needed.	10	____	____	____
4. Position the patient so that the light will shine into the mouth.	10	____	____	____
5. Remove the sterile swab from the sterile wrap with your dominant hand and grasp the sterile tongue depressor with your nondominant hand.	10	____	____	____
6. Ask the patient to open the mouth and say "ah." Depress the tongue with the depressor.	10	____	____	____
*7. Swab the back of the throat between the tonsillar pillars, especially any reddened, patchy areas of the throat, white pus pockets, purulent areas, and the tonsils.	10	____	____	____
8. Place the swab in the transport medium, label it, and send it to the laboratory. If direct slide testing is requested, send the labeled swab to the laboratory.	10	____	____	____
9. Dispose of contaminated supplies in the biohazardous waste container.	5	____	____	____
10. Disinfect the work area.	5	____	____	____

393

Steps	Possible Points	Attempt 1	Attempt 2	Attempt 3
11. Remove your gloves and discard them in the biohazardous waste container.	5	_____	_____	_____
12. Sanitize your hands.	5	_____	_____	_____
*13. In the following Documentation in the Medical Record section, record the procedure as you would in the patient's record.	10	_____	_____	_____

Documentation in the Medical Record:

Comments:

Points earned _____ **÷ 100 possible points = Score** _____ **% Score**

Instructor's signature _____

PROCEDURE 38-1 Obtain Specimens for Microbiologic Testing: Collect a Wound Specimen for Testing and/or Culture

MAERB/CAAHEP COMPETENCIES: I.PI.6, I.PI.10, III.PIII.7
ABHES COMPETENCIES: 9.e, 10.d.3

TASK: To obtain an adequate sample for culture without contaminating the specimen.

Equipment and Supplies

- Sterile culture kit containing tube, swabs, and transport media (for swabbing)
- Sterile culture kit containing syringe and transport media (for aspirating)
- Laboratory requisition
- Sterile gauze squares
- Recommended wound-cleansing solution
- Sterile dressing
- Gloves
- Biohazardous waste container
- Face guard
- Patient's record

Standards: Complete the procedure and all critical steps in _____ minutes with a minimum score of 85% in three attempts.

Scoring: Divide the points earned by the total possible points. Failure to perform a critical step, indicated by an asterisk (*), results in an unsatisfactory overall score.

Time began _____   Time ended _____   Total minutes: _____

Steps	Possible Points	Attempt 1	Attempt 2	Attempt 3
1. Sanitize your hands, gather the necessary supplies, and put on gloves and face protection.	10	_____	_____	_____
2. Remove the dressing from the wound and discard it in the biohazardous waste container.	10	_____	_____	_____
3. Observe the wound and make note of the color, odor, and amount of exudate present.	10	_____	_____	_____
4. *Aspiring.* Remove the syringe from the kit, insert the tip into the wound exudate, and draw back the plunger, drawing the exudate up into the syringe. Remove the needle and dispose of it in a sharps container. Place the labeled syringe in a biohazard bag for transport to the clinical laboratory with the appropriate physician order.	10	_____	_____	_____
5. *Swabbing.* Remove the swab from the culture kit, insert it into the wound, and saturate it with the exudate. If necessary, use more than one swab, properly labeling each container, to obtain exudates from the entire wound. If preparing an anaerobic culture, place the specimen in the culture tube as quickly as possible to prevent oxygen exposure and possible destruction of microbes.	10	_____	_____	_____

395

Steps	Possible Points	Attempt 1	Attempt 2	Attempt 3
6. Place the swab in the culture tube. Crush the transport medium ampule, which is in the transport tube, by squeezing the walls of the transport tube slightly, or place the exudate-filled syringe directly in the transport tube.	10	_____	_____	_____
7. Label the culture tube accurately. Include on the laboratory slip the patient's recent antibiotic therapy and the wound site.	10	_____	_____	_____
8. Clean the wound as ordered by the physician and apply a sterile dressing. (See Chapter 57 for the sterile dressing procedure.)	10	_____	_____	_____
9. Clean the area and dispose of all waste materials in the biohazardous waste container. Remove your gloves and sanitize your hands.	5	_____	_____	_____
10. Place the culture tube in the laboratory collection area.	5	_____	_____	_____
11. In the following Documentation in the Medical Record section, document the procedure and all wound data as you would in the patient's record.	10	_____	_____	_____

Documentation in the Medical Record:

Comments:

Points earned _____ ÷ 100 possible points = Score _____ % Score

Instructor's signature _____

PROCEDURE 39-1 Perform Patient Screening Using Established Protocols: Telephone Screening of a Patient with a Gastrointestinal Complaint

MAERB/CAAHEP COMPETENCIES: I.AI.1, I.PI.6, IV.PIV.2
ABHES COMPETENCIES: 8.f, 9.b

TASK: To answer the telephone professionally and manage patient phone calls according to the physician's guidelines.

SCENARIO: A 22-year-old woman reports acute abdominal pain.

Equipment and Supplies
- Telephone
- Message pad
- Pen
- Access to appointment schedule
- Access to patient's records
- Policy and procedures manual for managing patient phone calls

Standards: Complete the procedure and all critical steps in _____ minutes with a minimum score of 85% in three attempts.

Scoring: Divide the points earned by the total possible points. Failure to perform a critical step, indicated by an asterisk (*), results in an unsatisfactory overall score.

Time began _____ Time ended _____ Total minutes: _____

Steps	Possible Points	Attempt 1	Attempt 2	Attempt 3
1. Answer the telephone by the third ring, speaking directly into the mouthpiece.	10	_____	_____	_____
2. Speak distinctly in a pleasant tone, at a moderate rate, and with sufficient volume.	10	_____	_____	_____
3. Greet the caller, identify the office and/or the physician and yourself, and offer to help the caller.	10	_____	_____	_____
4. Verify the caller's identity and access the patient's record.	10	_____	_____	_____
5. Determine the caller's needs using therapeutic communication skills.	10	_____	_____	_____

Steps	Possible Points	Attempt 1	Attempt 2	Attempt 3
6. Considering the patient's complaint, formulate questions designed to gather the information needed for a decision on when the patient should be seen and the physician notified. For example, a patient may complain of acute abdominal pain. Consider the patient's gender, age, and the complaint in asking questions such as:	20			
a. What were the onset, frequency, and duration of the abdominal pain?		_____	_____	_____
b. What is the exact anatomic location of the discomfort?		_____	_____	_____
c. What is the quality of the pain? Is it sharp, dull, stabbing (and so on)?		_____	_____	_____
d. On a scale of 1 to 10, with 10 being the worst pain possible, what is the patient's level of pain?		_____	_____	_____
e. Does the patient have a history of this occurrence? If the patient is a female, does she have a history of gynecologic or pelvic disorders?		_____	_____	_____
f. Has the patient taken any medication for the discomfort? If so, has it been effective?		_____	_____	_____
7. Refer to the physician's policy regarding patient phone calls as needed.	10	_____	_____	_____
8. Depending on the patient's answers to your questions and the physician's policies regarding the management of abdominal discomfort, refer to the appointment schedule and make an appointment for the patient or take a message for the physician to return the call.	10	_____	_____	_____
9. In the following Documentation in the Medical Record section, document the details of the interaction and the results as you would in the patient's chart.	10	_____	_____	_____

Documentation in the Medical Record:

Comments:

Points earned _____ ÷ 100 possible points = Score _____ % Score

Instructor's signature _____

398

PROCEDURE 39-2 Prepare a Patient for Procedures and/or Treatments: Assist with an Endoscopic Examination of the Colon

MAERB/CAAHEP CAAHEP COMPETENCIES: I.PI.6, I.PI.10, III.PIII.7, IV.PIV.2, IV.PIV.6
ABHES COMPETENCIES: 9.d

TASK: To assist the physician with the examination, to prepare collected specimens as requested, and to ensure the patient's comfort and safety.

Equipment and Supplies

- Nonsterile gloves (for the medical assistant and the physician)
- Appropriate instrument: sigmoidoscope or proctoscope
- Water-soluble lubricant
- Drape and patient gown
- Long cotton-tipped swabs
- Suction source
- Sterile biopsy forceps
- Rectal speculum
- Specimen containers with appropriate preservative added
- Laboratory requisition forms
- Tissue wipes
- Biohazardous waste container
- Patient's record

Standards: Complete the procedure and all critical steps in _____ minutes with a minimum score of 85% in three attempts.

Scoring: Divide the points earned by the total possible points. Failure to perform a critical step, indicated by an asterisk (*), results in an unsatisfactory overall score.

Time began _____ Time ended _____ Total minutes: _____

Steps	Possible Points	Attempt 1	Attempt 2	Attempt 3
1. Sanitize your hands and assemble the necessary equipment and supplies.	5	_____	_____	_____
*2. Identify the patient and explain the procedure. Be sure the patient has completed the proper preparation procedures.	5	_____	_____	_____
3. Ask the patient to empty his or her bladder.	5	_____	_____	_____
4. Give the patient an examination gown. Instruct the patient to remove all clothing below the waist and to put on the gown so that it opens in the back. Provide a drape for additional privacy.	5	_____	_____	_____
5. Obtain and record the patient's vital signs.	10	_____	_____	_____
6. Assist the patient onto the table. When the physician is ready, place the patient in Sims' position.	5	_____	_____	_____
7. Drape the patient so that only the anus is exposed. A fenestrated drape (a drape with a circular opening that is placed over the anus) may be used in place of the rectangular drape.	10	_____	_____	_____

399

Steps	Possible Points	Attempt 1	Attempt 2	Attempt 3
8. Put gloves and assist the physician as requested during the examination. This includes:	20			
a. Lubricating the physician's gloved index finger for the digital examination		____	____	____
b. Lubricating the obturator tip of the instrument before insertion		____	____	____
c. Plugging in the scope's light source when the physician is ready		____	____	____
d. Handing the physician needed supplies		____	____	____
e. Collecting specimens by holding the container to accept the sample		____	____	____
f. Immediately labeling specimens, because several specimens may be taken from different areas		____	____	____
g. Disposing of contaminated supplies as the physician gives them to you		____	____	____
9. Throughout the examination, observe the patient for any undue reactions. Encourage the patient to breathe slowly through pursed lips to facilitate relaxation.	5	____	____	____
10. When the examination is finished, provide the patient with tissues to cleanse the anal area. Remove your gloves, sanitize your hands, and assist the patient into a resting position. Allow the patient time to recover from the procedure. Monitor the blood pressure if indicated.	5	____	____	____
11. When the patient's condition has stabilized, assist the patient off the table and instruct the person to get dressed. Show the patient where the sink, towels, and tissues are and provide assistance if needed.	5	____	____	____
12. Complete all laboratory request forms and specimen container labels and place specimens in the appropriate location for laboratory pickup.	5	____	____	____
13. Put on gloves and clean the work area and all the equipment used. The endoscope is first sanitized and then sterilized according to the manufacturer's recommendations. Dispose of your gloves in biohazardous waste container and wash your hands.	5	____	____	____
14. In the following Documentation in the Medical Record section, record the procedure and any pertinent information as you would in the patient's record.	10	____	____	____

Documentation in the Medical Record:

Comments:

Points earned _____ ÷ 100 possible points = Score _____ % Score

Instructor's signature _____

Procedure **39-2 Prepare a Patient for Procedures and/or Treatments**

PROCEDURE 39-3 Instruct Patients According to Their Needs to Promote Health Maintenance and Disease Prevention: Instruct Patients in the Collection of a Fecal Specimen

MAERB/CAAHEP CAAHEP COMPETENCIES: I.PI.6, I.PI.10, III.PIII.7, IV.PIV.2, IV.PIV.5, IV.PIV.6
ABHES COMPETENCIES: 9.h, 10.e.2

TASK: To assist the physician with collection of a fecal sample and processing of the sample for Hemoccult screening; also, to instruct the patient in Hemoccult screening at home.

Equipment and Supplies
- Hemoccult slides
- Hemoccult developer
- Applicator sticks
- Disposable examination gloves
- Biohazardous waste container
- Patient's record

Standards: Complete the procedure and all critical steps in _____ minutes with a minimum score of 85% in three attempts.

Scoring: Divide the points earned by the total possible points. Failure to perform a critical step, indicated by an asterisk (*), results in an unsatisfactory overall score.

Time began _____   Time ended _____   Total minutes: _____

Steps	Possible Points	Attempt 1	Attempt 2	Attempt 3
1. Sanitize your hands and assemble all necessary equipment and supplies.	2	_____	_____	_____
2. Identify the patient and explain the procedure.	2	_____	_____	_____
3. Give the patient an examination gown. Instruct the person to remove all clothing below the waist and to put on the gown so that it opens in the back. Provide a drape for additional privacy.	2	_____	_____	_____
4. Assist the patient onto the table. When the physician is ready, place the patient in the appropriate position for the type of examination ordered.	5	_____	_____	_____
5. Drape the patient so that only the anus is exposed. A fenestrated drape (a drape with a circular opening that is placed over the anus) may be used in place of the rectangular drape.	5	_____	_____	_____

Steps	Possible Points	Attempt 1	Attempt 2	Attempt 3
6. Put on gloves and assist the physician as requested during the examination. This includes:	10			
a. Handing the physician needed supplies		_____	_____	_____
b. Collecting specimens by holding the Hemoccult card to accept the sample		_____	_____	_____
c. Placing a thin smear of fecal material inside Box A		_____	_____	_____
d. Applying a second sample from a different part of the stool inside Box B		_____	_____	_____
e. Closing the cover		_____	_____	_____
f. Disposing of contaminated supplies as the physician gives them to you		_____	_____	_____
7. When the examination is finished, remove your gloves, sanitize your hands, and assist the patient into a sitting position.	5	_____	_____	_____
8. Wait 3 to 5 minutes before developing the sample.	2	_____	_____	_____
9. Put on gloves and open the flap in the back of the card. Apply 2 drops of Hemoccult developer directly over the smear.	5	_____	_____	_____
10. Interpret the results in 60 seconds.	2	_____	_____	_____
11. The Hemoccult test result is negative if no trace of color can be seen on or at the edge of the smear; it is positive if any trace of blue is seen on or at the edge of the smear.	5	_____	_____	_____
12. Put on gloves and clean the work area and all the equipment used. Then dispose of the gloves in the biohazardous waste container and sanitize your hands.	5	_____	_____	_____
13. In the following Documentation in the Medical Record section, record the procedure and any pertinent information as you would in the patient's record.	5	_____	_____	_____

Home Collection of a Fecal Sample

1. Give the patient a kit for collecting stool samples as ordered by the physician. Typically the physician orders a sample from three different bowel movements. The patient must follow the recommended medication restrictions and dietary guidelines throughout the testing period, including:	10			
a. No aspirin or nonsteroidal antiinflammatory drugs (NSAIDs) for 7 days before the test		_____	_____	_____
b. No more than 250 mg of vitamin C per day		_____	_____	_____
c. No red meat, including processed meats or cold cuts		_____	_____	_____
d. No raw fruits and vegetables, especially melons, radishes, turnips, and horseradish, for 72 hours before the stool collections		_____	_____	_____
2. Instruct the patient to store the kit in the bathroom at home or to carry it with him while away from home until the three different stool samples have been collected.	5	_____	_____	_____

Steps	Possible Points	Attempt 1	Attempt 2	Attempt 3
3. Instruct the patient to write his or her name and other required information on the front of the collection cards.	5	_____	_____	_____
4. Tell the patient to flush the toilet twice before a bowel movement or to cover the toilet with plastic wrap to collect the stool specimen.	5	_____	_____	_____
5. Instruct the patient to use one of the applicator sticks to collect a small fecal sample. A smear of stool is placed in the designated area on the first card.	5	_____	_____	_____
6. Tell the patient to close the cards and store it away from heat, light, and strong chemicals, such as bleach. It should not be placed in a plastic bag.	5	_____	_____	_____
7. Tell the patient to repeat this procedure for 2 more days or two more bowel movements as ordered by the physician, using a different card for each sample.	5	_____	_____	_____
8. Explain that, after all samples have been collected as ordered, the patient should seal the test envelope and return the kit to the physician's office. Instruct the patient not to send stool samples in the mail unless the patient has a special envelope from the physician.	5	_____	_____	_____

Documentation in the Medical Record:

Comments:

Points earned _____ ÷ 100 possible points = Score _____ % Score

Instructor's signature _____

PROCEDURE 40-1 Instruct Patients According to Their Needs to Promote Health Maintenance and Disease Prevention: Teach Testicular Self-Examination

MAERB/CAAHEP COMPETENCIES: I.PI.10, IV.PIV.5
ABHES COMPETENCIES: 9.d, 9.h

TASK: To instruct the patient in the steps of testicular self-examination.

Equipment and Supplies
- Self-examination pamphlet and shower card
- Demonstration model
- Nonsterile gloves
- Patient's record

Standards: Complete the procedure and all critical steps in _____ minutes with a minimum score of 85% in three attempts.

Scoring: Divide the points earned by the total possible points. Failure to perform a critical step, indicated by an asterisk (*), results in an unsatisfactory overall score.

Time began _____   Time ended _____   Total minutes: _____

Steps	Possible Points	Attempt 1	Attempt 2	Attempt 3
1. Sanitize your hands and assemble the necessary supplies.	10	_____	_____	_____
2. Identify the patient. Explain the procedure and that you will use a demonstration model for it.	10	_____	_____	_____
*3. Begin by explaining to the patient that testicular cancer may have no symptoms in the early stages, so it is important to examine the testes once a month for abnormal changes and to detect the disease early. This should begin at puberty or approximately 15 years of age. The examination is best done in the shower or a warm bath, and the total examination takes about 3 minutes.	10	_____	_____	_____
4. To start the examination, hold the scrotum in the palms of the hands. Then feel one testicle. Apply a small amount of pressure. Slowly roll the testicle between the thumb and fingers and feel for any hard, painless lumps.	10	_____	_____	_____
5. Next, examine the epididymis, a comma-shaped cord found behind the testis that stores and transports sperm. It is tender when touched, and it is the location of most noncancerous problems. Check for hard spots and lumps.	10	_____	_____	_____
6. Continue by examining the vas deferens, the sperm-carrying tube that runs up the epididymis. Normally, the vas feels like a firm, movable, smooth tube.	10	_____	_____	_____
7. Now repeat the entire examination on the other side, beginning with the opposite testis.	10	_____	_____	_____

Steps	Possible Points	Attempt 1	Attempt 2	Attempt 3
*8. After completing the examination on the model, ask the patient to do a return-examination using the model. A male assistant can have the patient do a self-testicular examination.	10	_____	_____	_____
9. Give the patient the pamphlet and the shower card. Instruct him to hang the card in the shower as a monthly reminder and guide.	10	_____	_____	_____
10. In the following Documentation in the Medical Record section, record the instructional interaction as you would in the patient's record.	10	_____	_____	_____

Documentation in the Medical Record:

Comments:

Points earned _____ ÷ 100 possible points = Score _____ % Score

Instructor's signature _____

Procedure **40-1** **Teach Testicular Self-Examination**

PROCEDURE 41-1 Prepare a Patient for Procedures and/or Treatments: Assist with the Examination of a Female Patient and Obtain a Pap Smear

MAERB/CAAHEP COMPETENCIES: I.PI.10, IV.PIV.5, IV.PIV.6
ABHES COMPETENCIES: 9.d

TASK: To assist the physician in the examination of a female patient and in obtaining a diagnostic Pap smear.

Equipment and Supplies
- Patient gown
- Lubricant
- 4 × 4-inch gauze squares
- Laboratory requisition slips
- Drape sheet
- Examination light
- Cervical spatula and Cytobrush
- ThinPrep container
- Vaginal speculum
- Uterine sponge forceps
- Disposable examination gloves
- Urine specimen container if needed
- Stool for occult blood test, if needed
- Biohazardous waste container
- Appropriate patient education materials
- Patient's record

Standards: Complete the procedure and all critical steps in _____ minutes with a minimum score of 85% in three attempts.

Scoring: Divide the points earned by the total possible points. Failure to perform a critical step, indicated by an asterisk (*), results in an unsatisfactory overall score.

Time began _____   **Time ended** _____   **Total minutes:** _____

Steps	Possible Points	Attempt 1	Attempt 2	Attempt 3
1. Assemble the necessary materials and prepare the examination room. Prepare the equipment and supplies needed for the Pap smear.	5	_____	_____	_____
2. Sanitize your hands; observe Standard Precautions.	2	_____	_____	_____
3. Identify the patient and briefly explain the procedure.	2	_____	_____	_____
4. Instruct the patient to empty the bladder and collect a urine specimen if needed.	2	_____	_____	_____
5. Instruct the patient to disrobe completely and to put on a gown with the opening in the front.	2	_____	_____	_____

Steps	Possible Points	Attempt 1	Attempt 2	Attempt 3
6. Assist the physician with the breast examination. So start, the patient should sit at the end of the examination table. Drape the patient and assist the physician with the examination. Reassure the patient as needed.	5	_____	_____	_____
7. When the physician is ready to examine the breasts and the abdomen with the patient in the supine position, assist the patient into the supine position and drape as needed.	5	_____	_____	_____
8. When the physician is ready to begin the vaginal examination, assist the patient into the lithotomy position. Have her slide down to the end of the table; then, adjust the stirrups as needed so that the knees are relaxed and rotated outward. Remember always to position the patient underneath the drape.	5	_____	_____	_____
9. Direct the light source onto the perineum.	5	_____	_____	_____
*10. Put on gloves. Warm the stainless steel vaginal speculum in warm water (the physician may prefer a disposable plastic speculum). Pass the proper instruments to the physician in the proper sequence. The Cytobrush is needed to obtain cervical cells and the spatula for the cervical sample.	10	_____	_____	_____
*11. Assist the physician with the ThinPrep preparation, if asked, by swirling the cervical specimen in the preservative solution at least 10 times to ensure that the specimen has been mixed with the preservative solution.	5	_____	_____	_____
12. Label the specimen container and place it in a biohazard bag.	5	_____	_____	_____
13. Apply water-soluble lubricant to the physician's gloved fingers for the rectal examination.	2	_____	_____	_____
14. The physician may want to prepare a stool specimen for occult blood testing after the rectal examination. Have the materials ready.	5	_____	_____	_____
15. For the rectal exam, instruct the patient to breathe deeply through the mouth with the hands crossed over the chest.	5	_____	_____	_____
16. Place the soiled instruments in a basin.	5	_____	_____	_____
17. Assist the patient off the table and help her dress if necessary.	5	_____	_____	_____
18. While the patient is in the dressing room, clean the examination room and remove used equipment.	5	_____	_____	_____
*19. Sanitize and sterilize stainless steel equipment. Remove your gloves, discard them in the biohazardous waste container, and sanitize your hands.	5	_____	_____	_____
20. Prepare the Pap smear and other samples for transportation to the laboratory. Complete the requisitions, noting the patient's LMP date and whether she is on hormone therapy.	10	_____	_____	_____
21. In the following Documentation in the Medical Record section, record all procedures as you would in the patient's record.	5	_____	_____	_____

410

Documentation in the Medical Record:

Comments:

Points earned _____ ÷ 100 possible points = Score _____ % Score

Instructor's signature _____

PROCEDURE 41-2 Prepare a Patient for Procedures and/or Treatments: Prepare the Patient for Cryosurgery

MAERB/CAAHEP COMPETENCIES: I.PI.10, IV.PIV.5, IV.PIV.6
ABHES COMPETENCIES: 9.a, 9.e

TASK: To prepare the patient and assist the physician in cryosurgery.

Equipment and Supplies

- Cryosurgery machine equipped with liquid nitrogen canister
- Cryoprobe
- Cervical tenaculum
- Cervical ring forceps or disposable cervical swabs
- Vaginal speculum
- 4 × 4-inch gauze squares
- Disposable examination gloves
- Gowns and face protection
- Specimen containers
- Biohazardous waste container
- Cytology request forms
- Patient's record

Standards: Complete the procedure and all critical steps in _____ minutes with a minimum score of 85% in three attempts.

Scoring: Divide the points earned by the total possible points. Failure to perform a critical step, indicated by an asterisk (*), results in an unsatisfactory overall score.

Time began _____   Time ended _____   Total minutes: _____

Steps	Possible Points	Attempt 1	Attempt 2	Attempt 3
1. Assemble the necessary equipment.	10	_____	_____	_____
2. Sanitize your hands.	10	_____	_____	_____
*3. Take the patient's temperature and blood pressure and record them in the patient's record.	10	_____	_____	_____
4. Drape the patient and assist her into the lithotomy position. Put on gloves.	10	_____	_____	_____
5. Assist with the procedure by handing the physician the equipment as needed.	5	_____	_____	_____
6. Encourage the patient to take deep breaths to promote relaxation of the pelvic muscles during the procedure. Observe the patient for any signs of distress.	5	_____	_____	_____
*7. When the procedure is finished, place the patient in a supine position and allow her to rest while you tidy the room and remove the used supplies. Retake the patient's temperature and blood pressure.	10	_____	_____	_____

413

Steps	Possible Points	Attempt 1	Attempt 2	Attempt 3
8. Assist the patient with sitting up and dressing as needed.	5	_____	_____	_____
9. Remove your gloves and sanitize your hands.	10	_____	_____	_____
10. Disinfect and sterilize the equipment used per manufacturer's directions and return it to the proper storage area.	10	_____	_____	_____
11. Provide patient instruction on follow-up care as ordered by the physician.	5	_____	_____	_____
12. In the following Documentation in the Medical Record section, record the procedure and the final vital sign measurements as you would in the patient's record.	10	_____	_____	_____

Documentation in the Medical Record:

Comments:

Points earned _____ ÷ 100 possible points = Score _____ % Score

Instructor's signature _____

Name _____ Date _____ Score _____

PROCEDURE 41-3 Instruct Patients According to Their Needs to Promote Health Maintenance and Disease Prevention: Teach the Patient Breast Self-Examination

MAERB/CAAHEP COMPETENCIES: IV.PIV.5
ABHES COMPETENCIES: 9.h

TASK: To teach the patient how to palpate her breasts for abnormalities.

Equipment and Supplies
- Instruction pamphlet/shower card
- Teaching model (to use to demonstrate the technique before a return demonstration by the patient)
- Patient's record

Standards: Complete the procedure and all critical steps in _____ minutes with a minimum score of 85% in three attempts.

Scoring: Divide the points earned by the total possible points. Failure to perform a critical step, indicated by an asterisk (*), results in an unsatisfactory overall score.

Time began _____ Time ended _____ Total minutes: _____

Steps	Possible Points	Attempt 1	Attempt 2	Attempt 3
1. Assemble the necessary equipment.	10	_____	_____	_____
2. Inform the patient that she should examine her breasts while bathing or showering in warm water. The best time to perform this examination is immediately after the end of the menstrual period, because breast engorgement is minimal. Nonmenstruating women should examine their breasts on the first of the month.	10	_____	_____	_____
*3. Have the patient raise one arm. With her fingers flat, she should press gently in small circles, starting at the outermost top edge of the breast and spiraling in toward the nipple. She should touch every part of each breast, including the axillary region, gently feeling for a lump or thickening. The right hand is used to examine the left breast, and the left hand is used for the right breast.	10	_____	_____	_____
*4. After the bath or shower, the patient should continue the examination in front of a mirror with the arms at the sides. Then, with the arms raised above the head, she should check carefully for changes in the size, shape, and contour of each breast. She should look for puckering, dimpling, or changes in skin texture.	20	_____	_____	_____
5. Each nipple is gently squeezed to check for discharge.	10	_____	_____	_____

415

Steps	Possible Points	Attempt 1	Attempt 2	Attempt 3
6. Before dressing, the patient should lie on the bed. She should put a towel or pillow under her right shoulder and her right hand behind her head. She then should examine the right breast using the left hand. She should press gently in small circles, starting at the outermost top edge, including the axillary region, and spiraling in toward the nipple. The process is repeated with the left breast.	10	_____	_____	_____
7. Have the patient return the breast examination demonstration to confirm understanding.	10	_____	_____	_____
*8. Give the patient the instruction pamphlet to use at home. If a shower card is provided, instruct her to hang the card inside the shower on a faucet or the shower nozzle as a quick reference guide.	10	_____	_____	_____
9. In the following Documentation in the Medical Record section, record all procedures as you would in the patient's record.	10	_____	_____	_____

Documentation in the Medical Record:

Comments:

Points earned _____ ÷ 100 possible points = Score _____ % Score

Instructor's signature _____

PROCEDURE 41-4 Prepare a Patient for Procedures and/or Treatments: Assist with a Prenatal Examination

MAERB/CAAHEP COMPETENCIES: I.PI.10, IV.PIV.5, IV.PIV.6
ABHES COMPETENCIES: 9.d

TASK: To promote a healthy pregnancy for the mother and fetus and to screen for potential problems.

Equipment and Supplies

- Scale with height measure
- Sphygmomanometer
- Stethoscope
- Tape measure
- Doppler fetoscope
- Ultrasound gel
- Urine specimen container
- Disposable examination gloves, vaginal speculum, and lubricant if vaginal examination conducted
- STI test setups
- Laboratory requisition slips
- Biohazardous waste container
- Biohazard bags for specimen transport
- Patient education materials
- Patient's medical record

Standards: Complete the procedure and all critical steps in _____ minutes with a minimum score of 85% in three attempts.

Scoring: Divide the points earned by the total possible points. Failure to perform a critical step, indicated by an asterisk (*), results in an unsatisfactory overall score.

Time began _____ **Time ended** _____ **Total minutes:** _____

Steps	Possible Points	Attempt 1	Attempt 2	Attempt 3
1. Sanitize your hands, assemble the necessary equipment, and identify the patient.	10	_____	_____	_____
2. Weigh the patient and record the weight.	5	_____	_____	_____
3. Collect a urine specimen, perform urinalysis, and record the results to determine whether protein, glucose, or ketones are present in the urine.	10	_____	_____	_____
4. Take the patient's blood pressure and record it.	5	_____	_____	_____
5. Instruct the patient to disrobe from the waist down. Have her put on a gown so that it opens in the front to allow measurement of the uterine fundal height.	10	_____	_____	_____
6. Assist the patient onto the examination table, if needed, and provide a drape for privacy.	10	_____	_____	_____

417

Steps	Possible Points	Attempt 1	Attempt 2	Attempt 3
7. Assist the physician as needed throughout the examination. If a Doppler fetoscope is to be used to listen to the fetal heart tones, apply a liberal amount of ultrasound gel to the patient's abdomen and hand the fetoscope to the physician. After the procedure, clean the Doppler head with a paper towel and offer the patient tissues to wipe the gel off her abdomen.	10	_____	_____	_____
8. When the examination is finished, assist the patient off the examination table; make sure to observe for signs of dizziness or problems with balance.	5	_____	_____	_____
*9. Answer any questions the patient may have and provide patient education materials as needed.	10	_____	_____	_____
10. Collect and package all specimens for transport. Complete labels as needed.	5	_____	_____	_____
11. Put on gloves. Discard the used supplies and disinfect the equipment according to the manufacturer's guidelines. Follow OSHA guidelines for handling any contaminated items.	5	_____	_____	_____
12. Sanitize your hands.	5	_____	_____	_____
13. In the following Documentation in the Medical Record section, document pertinent information as you would in the patient's medical record.	10	_____	_____	_____

Documentation in the Medical Record:

Comments:

Points earned _____ ÷ 100 possible points = Score _____ % Score

Instructor's signature _____

Name _____ Date _____ Score _____

PROCEDURE 42-1 Maintain Medication and Immunization Records: Document Immunizations

MAERB/CAAHEP COMPETENCIES: I.PI.10, IV.PIV.5, IV.PIV.6, IV.PIV8
ABHES COMPETENCIES: 4.a, 9.h

TASK: To document the administration of a pediatric immunization accurately.

SCENARIO: Samantha Anderson, a 5-week-old infant, has just received her second dose of the hepatitis B (HBV) vaccine. Document the administration of the vaccine.

Equipment and Supplies

- Vaccine immunization administration record.
- Parent's immunization booklet
- VIS form for hepatitis B
- Patient's medical record

Standards: Complete the procedure and all critical steps in _____ minutes with a minimum score of 85% in three attempts.

Scoring: Divide the points earned by the total possible points. Failure to perform a critical step, indicated by an asterisk (*), results in an unsatisfactory overall score.

Time began _____ **Time ended** _____ **Total minutes:** _____

Steps	Possible Points	Attempt 1	Attempt 2	Attempt 3
1. Assemble the necessary forms.	10	_____	_____	_____
2. Make sure the physician has obtained informed consent from the parent, that the hepatitis B VIS form was given, and that any questions the parents had were answered.	20	_____	_____	_____
3. After dispensing the vaccine dose but before administering it, complete the information required on the vaccine administration record, including the name of the vaccine, the date given, the route of administration and site, the vaccine lot number and manufacturer, the date on the VIS form, the date the form was given to the parent, and your signature or initials.	20	_____	_____	_____
4. Administer the vaccine intramuscularly as (see Chapter 35 in the text).	20	_____	_____	_____
5. In the parent's immunization booklet, record the date of administration, the name and address of the physician's practice, and the type of vaccine given.	10	_____	_____	_____

419

Steps	Possible Points	Attempt 1	Attempt 2	Attempt 3
6. After administering the vaccine, record the following details in the child's medical record:	20			
a. Date the vaccine was administered		_____	_____	_____
b. Vaccine's manufacturer, batch and lot numbers, and the expiration date		_____	_____	_____
c. Type of vaccine administered and dose		_____	_____	_____
d. Route of administration and exact site if an injection was given		_____	_____	_____
e. Any reported or observed side effects		_____	_____	_____
f. Publication date of the VIS form given to the parent (found on the bottom of the form)		_____	_____	_____
g. Parent education provided regarding possible side effects of the vaccination		_____	_____	_____
h. Name and title of the person who administered the vaccine		_____	_____	_____

Comments:

Points earned _____ ÷ 100 possible points = Score _____ % Score

Instructor's signature _____

PROCEDURE 42-2 Maintain Growth Charts: Measure the Circumference of an Infant's Head

MAERB/CAAHEP COMPETENCIES: I.PI.10, II.CII.7, II.PII.3, IV.PIV.6
ABHES COMPETENCIES: 9.d

TASK: To obtain an accurate measurement of the circumference of an infant's head and plot the result on the patient's growth chart.

Equipment and Supplies
- Flexible disposable tape measure
- Age- and gender-specific growth chart
- Pen
- Patient's record with appropriate growth chart

Standards: Complete the procedure and all critical steps in _____ minutes with a minimum score of 85% in three attempts.

Scoring: Divide the points earned by the total possible points. Failure to perform a critical step, indicated by an asterisk (*), results in an unsatisfactory overall score.

Time began _____ **Time ended** _____ **Total minutes:** _____

Steps	Possible Points	Attempt 1	Attempt 2	Attempt 3
1. Sanitize your hands.	10	_____	_____	_____
2. Identify the patient. If the child is old enough, gain his or her cooperation through conversation.	10	_____	_____	_____
3. Place an infant in the supine position or have a parent hold the baby; an older child may sit on the examination table.	5	_____	_____	_____
*4. Hold the tape measure with the zero mark against the infant's forehead, slightly above the eyebrows and the top of the ears. Ask the parent for assistance if necessary.	20	_____	_____	_____
*5. Bring the tape measure around the head, just above the ears, until it meets. Read to the nearest 0.01 cm or ¼ inch.	20	_____	_____	_____
6. In the following Documentation in the Medical Record section, record the measurement as you would in the patient's medical record.	20	_____	_____	_____
7. Dispose of the tape measure.	5	_____	_____	_____
8. Sanitize your hands.	10	_____	_____	_____

Documentation in the Medical Record:

Comments:

Points earned _____ ÷ 100 possible points = Score _____ % Score

Instructor's signature _____

PROCEDURE 42-3 Maintain Growth Charts: Measure an Infant's Length and Weight

MAERB/CAAHEP COMPETENCIES: I.PI.10, II.CII.7, II.PII.3, IV.PIV.6
ABHES COMPETENCIES: 9.d

TASK: To measure an infant's length and weight accurately so that growth patterns can be recorded and monitored.

Equipment and Supplies
- Infant scale with paper cover
- Flexible measuring tape
- Examination table paper
- Pen
- Pediatric length board if available
- Gender-specific infant growth chart
- Biohazardous waste container
- Patient's medical record

Standards: Complete the procedure and all critical steps in _____ minutes with a minimum score of 85% in three attempts.

Scoring: Divide the points earned by the total possible points. Failure to perform a critical step, indicated by an asterisk (*), results in an unsatisfactory overall score.

Time began _____   Time ended _____   Total minutes: _____

Steps	Possible Points	Attempt 1	Attempt 2	Attempt 3
Measuring an Infant's Length				
1. Sanitize your hands, assemble the necessary equipment, and explain the procedure to the infant's caregiver.	5	_____	_____	_____
2. Undress the infant in preparation for length measurement and weighing. The diaper may be left on while the length is measured, but it must be removed before the infant is weighed.	5	_____	_____	_____
*3. Ask the caregiver to place the infant on his or her back on the examination table, which is covered with paper. If it is a pediatric table with a headboard, ask the caregiver to gently hold the infant's head against the board while you straighten the infant's leg and note the location of the heel on the measurement area. If there is no headboard, ask the caregiver to gently hold the infant's head still while you draw a line on the paper at the back of the baby's head and at the heel after extending the leg.	10	_____	_____	_____
4. Measure the infant's length with the tape measure and record it.	10	_____	_____	_____
5. Document the results in either inches or centimeters, depending on office policy, on the infant's growth chart, in the progress notes, and in the caregiver's record if requested. Complete the growth chart graph by connecting the dot from the last visit.	10	_____	_____	_____

423

Steps	Possible Points	Attempt 1	Attempt 2	Attempt 3
Weighing an Infant				
6. Sanitize your hands, assemble the necessary equipment, and explain the procedure to the infant's caregiver.	5	____	____	____
7. Prepare the scale by sliding the weights to the left and covering it with disposable paper to reduce the risk of pathogen transmission.	10	____	____	____
8. Undress the infant completely, including the diaper.	5	____	____	____
9. Place the infant gently on the center of the scale, keeping your hand directly above the infant's trunk for safety.	10	____	____	____
*10. Slide the weights across the scale until balance is achieved. Attempt to read the infant's weight while he or she is still.	10	____	____	____
*11. Return the weights to the far left of the scale and remove the baby. The caregiver can rediaper the infant while you discard the paper covering the scale. If it has become contaminated during the procedure, follow OSHA guidelines for gloves and disposal of contaminated waste. Disinfect the equipment according to the manufacturer's guidelines.	5	____	____	____
12. Sanitize your hands.	5	____	____	____
13. Document the results in either pounds or kilograms, depending on office policy, on the infant's growth chart, in the progress notes, and in the caregiver's record if requested. Complete the growth chart graph by connecting the dot from the last visit.	10	____	____	____

Comments:

Points earned _____ ÷ 100 possible points = Score _____ % Score

Instructor's signature _____

Procedure **42-3** Maintain Growth Charts

Name _____ Date _____ Score _____

PROCEDURE 42-4 Assist the Physician with Patient Care: Obtain Pediatric Vital Signs and Perform Vision Screening

MAERB/CAAHEP COMPETENCIES: I.PI.1, I.PI.10, IV.PIV.5, IV.PIV.6, IV.PIV8
ABHES COMPETENCIES: 9.b, 9.d

TASK: To obtain vital signs and assess the vision of a pediatric patient accurately.

Equipment and Supplies
- Digital, tympanic, or temporal thermometer
- Pediatric blood pressure cuff
- Wristwatch with sweep second hand
- Weight scale with height bar
- Stethoscope
- Snellen E eye chart and oculator
- Pen
- Patient's medical record

Standards: Complete the procedure and all critical steps in _____ minutes with a minimum score of 85% in three attempts.

Scoring: Divide the points earned by the total possible points. Failure to perform a critical step, indicated by an asterisk (*), results in an unsatisfactory overall score.

Time began _____   Time ended _____   Total minutes: _____

Steps	Possible Points	Attempt 1	Attempt 2	Attempt 3
1. Gather the necessary equipment.	5	_____	_____	_____
2. Sanitize your hands.	5	_____	_____	_____
*3. Explain the procedure to the parent. If you want the parent to help by holding the child, explain the technique to use for this purpose.	5	_____	_____	_____
4. Help the child stand in the center of the scale and then weigh the child. Ask the child to turn around and then obtain the child's height. Record your findings.	5	_____	_____	_____
5. Obtain the tympanic or axillary temperature using the procedure explained in Chapter 31 in the text.	5	_____	_____	_____
6. Record the temperature. Indicate the method used: A = axillary, T = tympanic.	5	_____	_____	_____
*7. Place the stethoscope on the child's chest at the midpoint between the sternum and the left nipple. Listen for the apical beat.	5	_____	_____	_____
*8. Count the apical beat for 1 full minute.	10	_____	_____	_____
9. Record the apical pulse. Be sure to place an Ap before the rate to indicate that this is an apical pulse reading.	5	_____	_____	_____

Steps	Possible Points	Attempt 1	Attempt 2	Attempt 3
10. Observe the child's chest, or place the palm of your hand on the child's chest, and count the respirations for 1 full minute.	5	_____	_____	_____
11. Record the respiratory rate.	5	_____	_____	_____
12. Check to make sure you have the correct size blood pressure cuff and then take the child's blood pressure.	10	_____	_____	_____
13. Record the blood pressure.	5	_____	_____	_____
*14. For vision screening, first familiarize the child with the E chart. Make an E with your middle three fingers and ask the child to make an E that points the same way as your E. Then position the child in front of the pediatric E Snellen chart and have him or her match the E sign (using the fingers) with the E on the chart to which you are pointing.	5	_____	_____	_____
15. Record the vision results: OD = right eye; OS = left eye; OU = both eyes.	5	_____	_____	_____
16. Compliment the child on his or her performance; if the parent is present, share the praise with the parent.	5	_____	_____	_____
17. Sanitize your hands.	5	_____	_____	_____
18. Perform the appropriate disinfection procedures and return all equipment to the proper storage area.	5	_____	_____	_____

Documentation in the Medical Record:

Comments:

Points earned _____ ÷ 100 possible points = Score _____ % Score

Instructor's signature _____

Name _____ Date _____ Score _____

PROCEDURE 42-5 Assist the Physician with Patient Care: Apply a Urinary Collection Device

MAERB/CAAHEP COMPETENCIES: I.PI.10, IV.PIV.5, IV.PIV.6, IV.PIV8
ABHES COMPETENCIES: 9.d

TASK: To apply a pediatric urinary collection device properly.

Equipment and Supplies
- Pediatric urine collection bag
- Labeled laboratory urinary container
- Laboratory test request form
- Antiseptic wipes
- Biohazardous waste container
- Disposable examination gloves
- Patient's record

Standards: Complete the procedure and all critical steps in _____ minutes with a minimum score of 85% in three attempts.

Scoring: Divide the points earned by the total possible points. Failure to perform a critical step, indicated by an asterisk (*), results in an unsatisfactory overall score.

Time began _____   **Time ended** _____   **Total minutes:** _____

Steps	Possible Points	Attempt 1	Attempt 2	Attempt 3
1. Assemble all necessary supplies.	10	_____	_____	_____
2. Sanitize your hands and put on gloves.	5	_____	_____	_____
3. Ask the parent to remove the child's diaper or place the child in a supine position on the examination table and remove the diaper.	5	_____	_____	_____
4. Cleanse the genitalia with antiseptic wipes.	10			
a. Male: Cleanse the urinary meatus in a circular motion, starting directly on the meatus and working in an outward pattern. Repeat with a clean wipe. If the child has not been circumcised, retract the foreskin to expose the meatus. When you are finished cleansing, return the foreskin to its natural position.		_____	_____	_____
b. Female: Hold the labia open with your nondominant hand and with your dominant hand cleanse the inner labia, from the clitoris to the vaginal meatus, in a superior to inferior pattern.		_____	_____	_____
*5. Discard the first wipe and repeat with a clean wipe.	5	_____	_____	_____

427

Steps	Possible Points	Attempt 1	Attempt 2	Attempt 3
6. Make sure the area is dry. Unfold the collection device, remove the paper from the upper portion, place this portion over the mons pubis, and press it securely into place. Continue by removing the lower portion of the paper and securing this portion against the perineum. Make sure the device is attached smoothly and that you have not taped it to part of the infant's thigh.	10	_____	_____	_____
7. Rediaper the infant or, if the parent is helping, the parent may rediaper the infant. The diaper helps hold the bag in place.	5	_____	_____	_____
8. Suggest that the parent give the child liquids, if allowed, and check the bag for urine at frequent intervals.	5	_____	_____	_____
9. When the bag has a noticeable amount of urine, remove the device, cleanse the skin where the device was attached, and rediaper the child.	10	_____	_____	_____
10. Pour the urine carefully into the laboratory urine container and handle the sample in a routine manner.	5	_____	_____	_____
11. Dispose of all used supplies in the biohazardous waste container.	10	_____	_____	_____
12. Remove your gloves, dispose of them in the biohazardous waste container, and sanitize your hands.	10	_____	_____	_____
13. In the following Documentation in the Medical Record section, record the procedure as you would in the patient's record.	10	_____	_____	_____

Documentation in the Medical Record:

Comments:

Points earned _____ ÷ 100 possible points = Score _____ % Score

Instructor's signature _____

WORK PRODUCT 42-1

Name: _____

Maintain Growth Charts: Measure Infant Length and Weight

Corresponds to PROCEDURE 42-3

<u>CAAHEP COMPETENCIES:</u> I.PI.10., II.CII.7., II.PII.3., IV.PIV.6

<u>ABHES COMPETENCIES:</u> 9.d

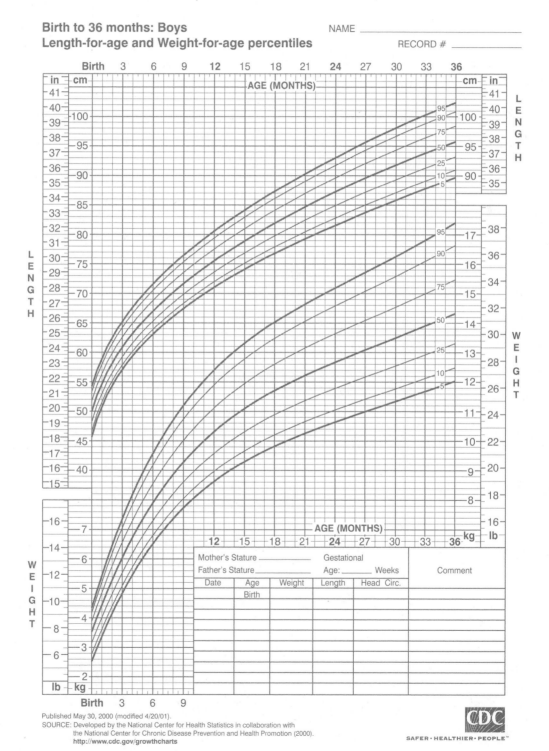

Birth to 36 months: Boys
Length-for-age and Weight-for-age percentiles

NAME _____

RECORD # _____

Published May 30, 2000 (modified 4/20/01).
SOURCE: Developed by the National Center for Health Statistics in collaboration with
the National Center for Chronic Disease Prevention and Health Promotion (2000).
http://www.cdc.gov/growthcharts

CDC
SAFER · HEALTHIER · PEOPLE™

429

WORK PRODUCT 42-2

Name: _____

Maintaining Immunization Records

Corresponds to PROCEDURE 42-1

CAAHEP COMPETENCIES: I.PI.10., IV.PIV.5., IV.PIV.6., IV.PIV.8

ABHES COMPETENCIES: 4.a, 9.h

Using the CDC-recommended immunization schedule in Figure 42-6 of the text, answer the following questions.

1. A mother brings her 15-month-old child to the office today for a checkup. The mother has brought a copy of the child's immunization record (listed in the table below). Using the CDC's recommended immunization schedule, which immunizations should the mother expect her child to receive today?

_____

_____

_____

2. After the physician has finished the examination, she orders the following immunizations. Gather the necessary VIS from the CDC Web site *(www.cdc.gov/).* Document the patient education and administration of the vaccines in the chart. Record the immunizations in the patient's immunization record, which follows.

   Physician's orders

   1. DTaP: Lot# 23155

      Expiration Date: October 2015

      Dose 0.5 mL administered IM

      Manufacturer: Overtus Pharmaceuticals

      Site: right proximal vastus lateralis

   2. Poliovirus: Lot# 54633

      Expiration Date: May 2015

      Dose: 0.5 mL IM

      Manufacturer: Parker

      Site: right distal vastus lateralis

   3. MMR: Lot# 99332

      Expiration Date: Dec. 2015

      Dose: 0.5 mL SQ

      Manufacturer: Parker

      Site: left vastus lateralis

4. Document in the chart record: Patient had chickenpox in August, 2005.

Corresponds to PROCEDURE 42-1

CAAHEP COMPETENCIES: I.PI.10., IV.PIV.5., IV.PIV.6., IV.PIV.8

ABHES COMPETENCIES: 4.a, 9.h

Vaccine Administration Record for Children and Teens

Patient name: _____

Birthdate: _____

Chart number: _____

Before administering any vaccines, give the parent/guardian all appropriate copies of Vaccine Information Statements (VISs) and make sure they understand the risks and benefits of the vaccine(s). Update the patient's personal record card or provide a new one whenever you administer vaccine.

Vaccine	Type of Vaccine[1] (generic abbreviation)	Date given (mo/day/yr)	Route	Site given (RA, LA, RT, LT)	Vaccine		Vaccine Information Statement		Signature/ initials of vaccinator
					Lot #	Mfr.	Date on VIS[2]	Date given[2]	
Hepatitis B[3] e.g., HepB, Hib-HepB, DTaP-HepB-IPV			IM						
			IM						
			IM						
			IM						
Diphtheria, Tetanus, Pertussis[3] e.g., DTaP, DT, Tdap, DTaP-Hib, DTaP-HepB-IPV, Td			IM						
			IM						
			IM						
			IM						
			IM						
			IM						
			IM						
Haemophilus influenzae **type b**[3] e.g., Hib, Hib-HepB, DTaP-Hib			IM						
			IM						
			IM						
			IM						
Polio[3] e.g., IPV, DTaP-HepB-IPV			IM•SC						
			IM•SC						
			IM•SC						
			IM•SC						
Pneumococcal PCV (conjugate) PPV (polysaccharide)			IM						
			IM						
			IM						
			IM						
Measles, Mumps, Rubella[3] e.g., MMR, MMRV			SC						
			SC						
Varicella[3] e.g., Var, MMRV			SC						
			SC						
Hepatitis A HepA			IM						
			IM						
Meningococcal[4] MCV4 (conjugate) MPSV4 (polysaccharide)									
Influenza[5] TIV (inactivated) LAIV (live, attenuated)									
Other									

1. Record the generic abbreviation for the type of vaccine given (e.g., DTaP-Hib, PCV), *not* the trade name.
2. Record the publication date of each VIS as well as the date it is given to the patient. According to federal law, VISs must be given to patients (or parent/guardian of a minor child) before administering each dose of DTaP, Td, Hib, polio, MMR, varicella, PCV, or HepB vaccine, or combinations thereof. Use of the VISs for hepatitis A, influenza, and meningococcal vaccines will become mandatory in later 2005.
3. For combination vaccines, fill in a row for each separate antigen in the combination.
4. Give MCV4 via the IM route and MPSV4 via the SC route.
5. Give TIV via the IM route and LAIV intranasally (IN).

www.immunize.org/catg.d/p2022b.pdf • Item #P2022 (10/05)

Immunization Action Coalition • 1573 Selby Ave. • St. Paul, MN 55104 • (651) 647-9009 • www.immunize.org • www.vaccineinformation.org

Name _____ Date _____ Score _____

PROCEDURE 43-1 Assist the Physician with Patient Care: Assist with Cold Application

MAERB/CAAHEP COMPETENCIES: I.PI.1, I.PI.10, IV.PIV.5, IV.PIV.6, IV.PIV8
ABHES COMPETENCIES: 9.d

TASK: To apply a cold compress to a body area to decrease pain, prevent further swelling, and/or decrease inflammation.

Equipment and Supplies
- Small ice cubes or ice chips
- Ice bag or closable disposable plastic kitchen food bag
- Towel
- Patient's record

Standards: Complete the procedure and all critical steps in _____ minutes with a minimum score of 85% within three attempts.

Scoring: Divide the points earned by the total possible points. Failure to perform a critical step, indicated by an asterisk (*), results in an unsatisfactory overall score.

Time began _____ **Time ended** _____ **Total minutes:** _____

Steps	Possible Points	Attempt 1	Attempt 2	Attempt 3
1. Sanitize your hands.	10	_____	_____	_____
*2. Explain the procedure to the patient and answer any questions.	10	_____	_____	_____
3. Check the bag for possible leaks.	10	_____	_____	_____
4. Fill the bag with small cubes or chips of ice until it is about two thirds full.	10	_____	_____	_____
5. Push down on the top of the bag to expel excess air and put on the cap.	10	_____	_____	_____
6. Dry the outside of the bag and cover it with one or two towel layers.	10	_____	_____	_____
7. Help the patient position the ice bag on the injured area.	10	_____	_____	_____
*8. Advise the patient to leave the ice bag in place for about 20 to 30 minutes or until the area feels numb, whichever is first.	10	_____	_____	_____
9. Check the skin for color, feeling, and pain.	10	_____	_____	_____
10. In the following Documentation in the Medical Record section, record the procedure as you would in the patient's medical record.	10	_____	_____	_____

Documentation in the Medical Record:

Comments:

Points earned _____ ÷ 100 possible points = Score _____ % Score

Instructor's signature _____

Name _____ Date _____ Score _____

PROCEDURE 43-2 Assist the Physician with Patient Care: Assist with Moist Heat Application

MAERB/CAAHEP COMPETENCIES: I.PI.1, I.PI.10, IV.PIV.5, IV.PIV.6, IV.PIV8
ABHES COMPETENCIES: 9.d

TASK: To apply moist heat to a body area to increase circulation, increase metabolism, and relax muscles.

Equipment and Supplies
- Commercial hot moist heat packs
- Towel
- Patient's record

Standards: Complete the procedure and all critical steps in _____ minutes with a minimum score of 85% within three attempts.

Scoring: Divide the points earned by the total possible points. Failure to perform a critical step, indicated by an asterisk (*), results in an unsatisfactory overall score.

Time began _____   Time ended _____   Total minutes: _____

Steps	Possible Points	Attempt 1	Attempt 2	Attempt 3
1. Sanitize your hands.	20	_____	_____	_____
*2. Explain the procedure to the patient and answer any questions.	20	_____	_____	_____
3. Ask the patient to remove all jewelry from the area to be treated.	10	_____	_____	_____
4. Place one or two towel layers over the area to be treated.	10	_____	_____	_____
5. Apply the commercial moist heat packs.	10	_____	_____	_____
6. Cover them with the remaining part of the towel.	10	_____	_____	_____
*7. Advise the patient to leave the heat pack in place no longer than 20 to 30 minutes, off for the same amount of time, and repeat if needed.	20	_____	_____	_____
8. Record the procedure in the patient's medical record.	10	_____	_____	_____

Documentation in the Medical Record:

Comments:

Points earned _____ ÷ 100 possible points = Score _____ % Score

Instructor's signature _____

Procedure **43-2 Assist the Physician with Patient Care**

Name _____ Date _____ Score _____

PROCEDURE 43-3 Assist the Physician with Patient Care: Assist with Therapeutic Ultrasonography

MAERB/CAAHEP COMPETENCIES: I.PI.1, I.PI.10, IV.PIV.5, IV.PIV.6, IV.PIV.8
ABHES COMPETENCIES: 9.d

TASK: To apply ultra-high-frequency sound waves to a patient's deep tissues for therapy.

NOTE: The medical assistant should perform ultrasound therapy only under the supervision of the physician or a physical therapist.

Equipment and Supplies
- Ultrasound machine
- Ultrasound gel or lotion
- Paper towels
- Patient's record

Standards: Complete the procedure and all critical steps in _____ minutes with a minimum score of 85% within three attempts.

Scoring: Divide the points earned by the total possible points. Failure to perform a critical step, indicated by an asterisk (*), results in an unsatisfactory overall score.

Time began _____   Time ended _____   Total minutes: _____

Steps	Possible Points	Attempt 1	Attempt 2	Attempt 3
1. Prepare your equipment and sanitize your hands.	5	_____	_____	_____
2. Confirm the patient's identity.	5	_____	_____	_____
*3. Explain the procedure and instruct the patient to tell you of any discomfort that occurs during the procedure.	5	_____	_____	_____
4. Ask the patient about any internal or external metal objects.	5	_____	_____	_____
5. Position the patient comfortably, with the area to be treated exposed.	5	_____	_____	_____
6. Apply a warmed ultrasound gel liberally over the area to be treated and to the applicator head.	5	_____	_____	_____
7. Begin the treatment with the intensity control at the lowest setting.	5	_____	_____	_____
8. Set the timer on the machine to the ordered time.	5	_____	_____	_____
9. Slowly increase the intensity control to the ordered amount.	5	_____	_____	_____
*10. Hold the applicator with the head firmly and completely against the patient's skin over the ultrasound gel in the treatment area.	5	_____	_____	_____

Steps	Possible Points	Attempt 1	Attempt 2	Attempt 3
*11. Work the applicator over the area to be treated by moving it continuously in a circular fashion at a speed of 2 inches per second or as directed by the physician.	5	_____	_____	_____
*12. Keep the applicator head in contact with the patient's skin at all times while the machine is on and keep it moving continuously during the treatment time.	5	_____	_____	_____
13. When the timer sounds, the machine shuts off automatically. The applicator head then may be safely lifted away from the patient.	5	_____	_____	_____
14. Return the intensity control to zero.	5	_____	_____	_____
15. Use a tissue or paper wipe to remove the ultrasound gel from the patient's skin and the applicator head.	5	_____	_____	_____
16. Help the patient to dress if necessary.	5	_____	_____	_____
17. In the following Documentation in the Medical Record section, record the procedure in the patient's medical record, including the date, area treated, intensity setting, duration of treatment, and any unusual reactions during treatment. If none occurred, indicate that also.	20	_____	_____	_____

Documentation in the Medical Record:

Comments:

Points earned _____ ÷ 100 possible points = Score _____ % Score

Instructor's signature _____

438

Name _____ Date _____ Score _____

PROCEDURE 43-4 Assist the Physician with Patient Care: Teach the Patient Crutch Walking and the Swing-Through Gait

CAAHEP COMPETENCIES: I.PI.1., I.PI.10., IV.PIV.5., IV.PIV.6., IV.PIV8
ABHES COMPETENCIES: 9.d, 9.h

TASK: To fit crutches properly and to teach the patient how to use the crutches in three-point walking.

Equipment and Supplies
- Crutches with arm pads and foam handgrips
- Patient's record

Standards: Complete the procedure and all critical steps in _____ minutes with a minimum score of 85% within three attempts.

Scoring: Divide the points earned by the total possible points. Failure to perform a critical step, indicated by an asterisk (*), results in an unsatisfactory overall score.

Time began _____ Time ended _____ Total minutes: _____

Steps	Possible Points	Attempt 1	Attempt 2	Attempt 3
1. Fit the crutches to the patient so that they are 1 to 1½ inches (2 fingerwidths) below the armpits when the person is standing up straight. The handgrips should be even with the top of the hip line.	10	_____	_____	_____
2. Make sure all the wing nuts are tight.	5	_____	_____	_____
3. Make sure the foam pads at the armpits and around the handgrips are comfortable.	5	_____	_____	_____
4. Instruct the patient to keep the injured leg as relaxed as possible and slightly bent at the knee.	10	_____	_____	_____
*5. The patient's elbow should be bent approximately 30 degrees when holding the handgrip.				
*6. Place the crutch tips about 2 inches in front of each foot and approximately 6 inches to the side of each foot before having the patient begin crutch walking.	10	_____	_____	_____
7. Ask the patient to push down on the crutches and lift the body slightly, nearly straightening the arms. The patient should hold the tops of the crutches tightly to the sides and use the hands to absorb the weight. The tops of the crutches should not be allowed to press into the armpits.	10	_____	_____	_____
8. Have the patient swing the body forward about 12 inches.	10	_____	_____	_____
9. Instruct the patient to stand on the good leg, move the crutches just ahead of the good foot, and then repeat.	10	_____	_____	_____

Steps	Possible Points	Attempt 1	Attempt 2	Attempt 3
*10. Additional crutch gait patterns:	10			
a. Two-point crutch gait: Left crutch and right foot together, then the right crutch and left foot together. Repeat. Used if both legs are weak; can be a challenge for the patient to learn the pattern.		_____	_____	_____
b. Three-point crutch gait: Move both crutches and the affected leg forward, then bear weight down through the crutches and move the unaffected leg forward. Repeat. Use if unable to bear weight on one leg.		_____	_____	_____
c. Four-point crutch gait: Move right crutch forward, then left foot, followed by left crutch and then right foot; provides the best stability but is slow; helpful if both legs are weak.		_____	_____	_____
11. Instruct the patient as follows for using crutches on stairs: To walk up and down stairs with crutches, face the steps, hold the handrail with one hand, and tuck both crutches under the armpit on the other side. To go up the steps, start with the uninjured side, keeping the injured side raised behind. When going down, hold the injured foot up in front, and hop down each stair on the good foot. If the stairway does not have handrails, use the crutches under both arms and hop up or down each step on the uninjured leg. If necessary, the patient can sit on the stairs and move up or down each step.	10	_____	_____	_____
*12. In the following Documentation in the Medical Record section, document the patient education intervention as you would in the patient's record.	10	_____	_____	_____

Documentation in the Medical Record:

Comments:

Points earned _____ ÷ 100 possible points = Score _____ % Score

        Instructor's signature _____

PROCEDURE 43-5 Assist the Physician with Patient Care: Assist with Application of a Cast

MAERB/CAAHEP COMPETENCIES: I.PI.1, I.PI.10, IV.PIV.5, IV.PIV.6, IV.PIV8
ABHES COMPETENCIES: 9.d

TASK: To assist the physician in applying a fiberglass cast.

Equipment and Supplies

- Rolls of fiberglass
- Basin casting material
- Bandage
- Stockinette
- Gloves for physician and medical assistant
- Sheet wadding and/or spongy padding
- Stand to support foot (lower extremity)
- Tape
- Scissors
- Water
- Patient's record

Standards: Complete the procedure and all critical steps in _____ minutes with a minimum score of 85% within three attempts.

Scoring: Divide the points earned by the total possible points. Failure to perform a critical step, indicated by an asterisk (*), results in an unsatisfactory overall score.

Time began _____   Time ended _____   Total minutes: _____

Steps	Possible Points	Attempt 1	Attempt 2	Attempt 3
1. Sanitize your hands.	5	_____	_____	_____
2. Identify the patient.	5	_____	_____	_____
*3. Explain the procedure for applying a cast and answer questions.	5	_____	_____	_____
4. Assemble the necessary equipment.	5	_____	_____	_____
5. Seat the patient comfortably, as directed by the physician. If the cast will be applied to the lower extremity, the toes must be supported by a stand.	5	_____	_____	_____
6. Clean the area the cast will cover. Note any objective signs and ask about subjective symptoms (chart them at the end of the procedure).	5	_____	_____	_____
7. Cut stockinette to fit the area the cast will cover.	5	_____	_____	_____
*8. Apply stockinette smoothly to the area the cast will cover. Leave 1 or 2 inches of stockinette above and below the cast area to finish the cast.	10	_____	_____	_____

441

Steps	Possible Points	Attempt 1	Attempt 2	Attempt 3
9. Excess stockinette may be cut away where wrinkles form (e.g., at the front of the ankle).	5	_____	_____	_____
*10. Apply sheet wadding along the length of the cast using a spiral bandage turn. Extra padding may be used over bony prominences, such as the bones of the elbow or ankle.	5	_____	_____	_____
11. Put on gloves.	5	_____	_____	_____
12. With lukewarm water in the basin, wet the fiberglass tape as directed by the physician.	5	_____	_____	_____
*13. Assist as directed as the physician applies the inner layer of fiberglass tape. A length of 1 to 2 inches of stockinette is rolled over the inner layer of the cast to form a smooth edge when the outer layer is applied.	10	_____	_____	_____
14. Assist as directed by the physician to open and apply an outer layer of fiberglass tape.	5	_____	_____	_____
15. Assist in shaping the cast as directed. All contours must be smooth.	5	_____	_____	_____
16. Discard the water and excess materials. Remove your gloves and wash your hands.	5	_____	_____	_____
*17. Reassure the patient, review cast care verbally, and provide written instructions.	5	_____	_____	_____
18. In the following Documentation in the Medical Record section, document your observations and the procedure as you would in the patient's record.	5	_____	_____	_____

Documentation in the Medical Record:

Comments:

Points earned _____ ÷ 100 possible points = Score _____ % Score

Instructor's signature _____

Name _____ Date _____ Score _____

PROCEDURE 43-6 Assist the Physician with Patient Care: Assist with Cast Removal

MAERB/CAAHEP COMPETENCIES: I.PI.1, I.PI.10, IV.PIV.5, IV.PIV.6, IV.PIV8
ABHES COMPETENCIES: 9.d

TASK: To remove a cast.

Equipment and Supplies
- Cast cutter
- Cast spreader
- Large bandage scissors
- Basin of warm water
- Mild soap
- Towel
- Skin lotion
- Patient's record

Standards: Complete the procedure and all critical steps in _____ minutes with a minimum score of 85% within three attempts.

Scoring: Divide the points earned by the total possible points. Failure to perform a critical step, indicated by an asterisk (*), results in an unsatisfactory overall score.

Time began _____   Time ended _____   Total minutes: _____

Steps	Possible Points	Attempt 1	Attempt 2	Attempt 3
*1. Explain the procedure to the patient.	10	_____	_____	_____
2. Provide adequate support for the limb throughout the entire procedure.	10	_____	_____	_____
3. Make a cut on the medial side and the lateral side of the long axis of the cast.	10	_____	_____	_____
4. Pry the two halves apart using the cast spreader.	10	_____	_____	_____
5. Carefully remove the two parts of the cast.	10	_____	_____	_____
6. Use the large bandage scissors to cut away the stockinette and padding remaining.	10	_____	_____	_____
*7. Gently wash the area that had been casted with mild soap and warm water.	10	_____	_____	_____
8. Dry the area and apply a gentle skin lotion.	10	_____	_____	_____
9. Give the patient appropriate instructions for exercising and using the limb, as directed by the physician.	10	_____	_____	_____
10. In the following Documentation in the Medical Record section, record the procedure as you would in the patient's medical record.	10	_____	_____	_____

443

Documentation in the Medical Record:

Comments:

Points earned _____ ÷ 100 possible points = Score _____ % Score

Instructor's signature _____

PROCEDURE 44-1 Assist the Physician with Patient Care: Assist with the Neurologic Examination

CAAHEP COMPETENCIES: I.PI.1., I.PI.10., IV.PIV.5., IV.PIV.6., IV.PIV8.
ABHES COMPETENCIES: 9.d

TASK: To assist the physician in performing a neurologic examination of the patient.

Equipment and Supplies

- Patient gown
- Drape
- Otoscope
- Ophthalmoscope
- Percussion hammer
- Disposable pinwheel
- Penlight
- Tuning fork
- Cotton ball
- Small vials of warm and cold liquids prepared according to the physician's instructions
- Small vials of sweet and salty liquids prepared according to the physician's instructions
- Small vials containing substances with distinct odors (e.g., instant coffee, cinnamon, vanilla) prepared according to the physician's instructions
- Patient's record

Standards: Complete the procedure and all critical steps in _____ minutes with a minimum score of 85% within three attempts.

Scoring: Divide the points earned by the total possible points. Failure to perform a critical step, indicated by an asterisk (*), results in an unsatisfactory overall score.

Time began _____ **Time ended** _____ **Total minutes:** _____

Steps	Possible Points	Attempt 1	Attempt 2	Attempt 3
1. Assemble and prepare the equipment and supplies needed for the neurologic examination; also prepare the exam room.	10	_____	_____	_____
2. Sanitize your hands; observe Standard Precautions.	10	_____	_____	_____
3. Identify the patient and briefly explain the procedure.	10	_____	_____	_____
4. Instruct the patient to disrobe as needed for the examination and to put on a gown so that it opens in the back.	10	_____	_____	_____
5. During the examination, be prepared to help the patient change positions as necessary. Have the necessary examination instruments ready for the physician at the appropriate time during the examination. Record all results from the examination as indicated by the physician.	20	_____	_____	_____

445

Steps	Possible Points	Attempt 1	Attempt 2	Attempt 3
*6. A neurologic examination proceeds as follows (although it can be modified according to the physician's preference):	20			
a. Mental status examination		_____	_____	_____
b. Proprioception and cerebellar function		_____	_____	_____
c. Cranial nerve assessment		_____	_____	_____
d. Sensory nerve function		_____	_____	_____
e. Reflexes		_____	_____	_____
7. In the following Documentation in the Medical Record section, record all procedures performed as you would in the patient's medical record.	20	_____	_____	_____

Documentation in the Medical Record:

Comments:

Points earned _____ ÷ 100 possible points = Score _____ % Score

Instructor's signature _____

PROCEDURE 44-2 Assist the Physician with Patient Care: Prepare the Patient for an Electroencephalogram

CAAHEP COMPETENCIES: I.PI.1., I.PI.10., IV.PIV.5., IV.PIV.6., IV.PIV8.
ABHES COMPETENCIES: 9.d

TASK: To prepare a patient properly, both physically and psychologically, so that an accurate and useful EEG recording can be obtained.

Equipment and Supplies

- Patient's record

Standards: Complete the procedure and all critical steps in _____ minutes with a minimum score of 85% within three attempts.

Scoring: Divide the points earned by the total possible points. Failure to perform a critical step, indicated by an asterisk (*), results in an unsatisfactory overall score.

Time began _____   Time ended _____   Total minutes: _____

Steps	Possible Points	Attempt 1	Attempt 2	Attempt 3
*1. Greet the patient and introduce yourself. Explain that you will go over what happens during a EEG, step by step, to ensure the best results.	10	____	____	____
2. Explain the purpose of the EEG, how the procedure will be carried out, and what will be expected of the patient during the test.	10	____	____	____
3. Inform the patient that the electrodes pick up tiny electrical signals from the body and that there is no danger of electrical shock.	10	____	____	____
4. Explain that the test is painless, because the electrodes are attached to the scalp with paste.	10	____	____	____
5. If the patient is to have a sleep EEG, suggest that he or she stay up later than usual the night so as to fall asleep more easily for the test.	10	____	____	____
6. Go over the physical preparation, including the diet to be followed for the 48 hours before the test. This usually includes no stimulants (e.g., coffee, chocolate, and soda) and no skipping meals.	10	____	____	____
7. Tell the patient that a baseline EEG will be taken at the beginning of the test, and during this time the patient will be asked to keep absolutely still, avoiding even eye and tongue movement.	10	____	____	____
8. If a stimulation examination is to be performed, explain that the patient will be asked to view flickering lights that are intended to stimulate the brain. The EEG will measure the brain's response to this stimulation.	10	____	____	____

Steps	Possible Points	Attempt 1	Attempt 2	Attempt 3
*9. Ask the patient whether he or she has any questions. If so, answer the questions so that the patient understands the procedure clearly.	10	_____	_____	_____
10. In the following Documentation in the Medical Record section, document the patient education intervention as you would in the patient's record.	10	_____	_____	_____

Documentation in the Medical Record:

Comments:

Points earned _____ ÷ 100 possible points = Score _____ % Score

Instructor's signature _____

Procedure **44-2 Assist the Physician with Patient Care**

Name _____ Date _____ Score _____

PROCEDURE 44-3 Assist the Physician with Patient Care: Prepare the Patient for and Assist with a Lumbar Puncture

CAAHEP COMPETENCIES: I.PI.1., I.PI.10., IV.PIV.5., IV.PIV.6., IV.PIV8.
ABHES COMPETENCIES: 9.d

TASK: To prepare a patient physically and mentally for a lumbar puncture so that a specimen of CSF can be obtained for testing.

Equipment and Supplies

- Patient gown
- Drape
- Local anesthetic
- Sterile, disposable lumbar puncture kit
- Instrument stand
- Sterile gloves
- Permanent marker to label tubes
- Laboratory requisitions as needed
- Biohazard laboratory transport bag
- Patient's record

Standards: Complete the procedure and all critical steps in _____ minutes with a minimum score of 85% within three attempts.

Scoring: Divide the points earned by the total possible points. Failure to perform a critical step, indicated by an asterisk (*), results in an unsatisfactory overall score.

Time began _____ Time ended _____ Total minutes: _____

Steps	Possible Points	Attempt 1	Attempt 2	Attempt 3
1. Assemble the necessary materials and prepare the room. Prepare the equipment and supplies needed for the lumbar puncture.	5	_____	_____	_____
2. Sanitize your hands; observe Standard Precautions.	5	_____	_____	_____
*3. Identify the patient and introduce yourself. Explain that you will go over what will happen, step by step, to ensure the best results.	5	_____	_____	_____
4. Have the patient void just before the procedure.	5	_____	_____	_____
5. Give the patient a hospital gown and instruct him or her to put it on so that it opens in the back.	5	_____	_____	_____
6. Place the patient in a left side-lying fetal position for the lumbar puncture.	5	_____	_____	_____
7. Support the patient's head with a pillow, as necessary, and provide a pillow for between the knees if needed.	5	_____	_____	_____
8. Perform a sterile skin preparation of the lumbar region in the usual manner.	5	_____	_____	_____

449

Steps	Possible Points	Attempt 1	Attempt 2	Attempt 3
9. Place the sterile disposable lumbar puncture kit on an instrument stand and open it, establishing a sterile field. Drape a sterile, fenestrated drape over the lumbar region so that only the L3-L4 region of the lower spine is exposed.	10	____	____	____
10. When the physician is ready to do the lumbar puncture, hold the vial of local anesthetic for the physician.	5	____	____	____
*11. Reassure the patient and help him or her hold still during injection of the local anesthetic and insertion of the spinal needle.	5	____	____	____
*12. Using the permanent marker, label the specimens #1, #2, and #3 in the order in which they were collected. This is a crucial step in the procedure.	10	____	____	____
13. Complete the laboratory requisition form and prepare the CSF specimens for transport to the laboratory.	10	____	____	____
14. Clean the area by disposing of sharps, biohazardous materials, and regular waste in the normal manner.	5	____	____	____
15. Monitor the patient and give the person liquids as directed by the physician.	5	____	____	____
16. In the following Documentation in the Medical Record section, document the procedure as you would in the patient's medical record.	10	____	____	____

Documentation in the Medical Record:

Comments:

Points earned _____ ÷ 100 possible points = Score _____ % Score

Instructor's signature _____

PROCEDURE 45-1 Assist the Physician with Patient Care: Perform a Blood Glucose Accu-Chek Test

CAAHEP COMPETENCIES: I.PI.1, I.PI.10, IV.PIV.5, IV.PIV.6, IV.PIV8
ABHES COMPETENCIES: 9.d, 10.b.2

TASK: To perform a blood test for diabetes mellitus accurately and to educate the patient on maintaining a glucose flow sheet.

Equipment and Supplies
- Accu-Chek glucose monitor or similar glucose monitoring device
- Accu-Chek glucose testing strip
- Lancet and autoloading finger-puncturing device
- Alcohol preps
- Gauze squares
- Sharps container
- Disposable gloves
- Patient's glucose log
- Patient's record

Standards: Complete the procedure and all critical steps in _____ minutes with a minimum score of 85% within three attempts.

Scoring: Divide the points earned by the total possible points. Failure to perform a critical step, indicated by an asterisk (*), results in an unsatisfactory overall score.

Time began _____ Time ended _____ Total minutes: _____

Steps	Possible Points	Attempt 1	Attempt 2	Attempt 3
1. Check the physician's order. Assemble the equipment and supplies needed to perform the testing procedure. Perform quality-control measures according to the manufacturer's guidelines and office policy.	5	_____	_____	_____
2. Sanitize your hands and put on gloves.	5	_____	_____	_____
3. Ask the patient to wash his or her hands in warm, soapy water, rinse them in warm water, and dry them completely.	5	_____	_____	_____
4. Check the patient's index and ring fingers and select the site for puncture.	5	_____	_____	_____
5. Turn on the Accu-Chek monitor by pressing the ON button.	5	_____	_____	_____
*6. Make sure the code number on the LED display matches the code number on the container of test strips.	5	_____	_____	_____
7. Remove a test strip from the vial and immediately replace the vial cover.	5	_____	_____	_____
8. Check the strip for discoloration by comparing the color of the round window on the back of the test strip with the designated "unused" color chart provided on label of the test strip vial.	5	_____	_____	_____

451

Steps	Possible Points	Attempt 1	Attempt 2	Attempt 3
9. Do not touch the yellow test pad or the round window on the back of the strip when handling the strip.	5	_____	_____	_____
10. When the test strip symbol begins flashing in the lower right corner of the display screen, insert the test strip into the designated testing slot until it locks into place. If the test strip has been inserted correctly, the arrows on the strip face up and point toward the monitor.	5	_____	_____	_____
*11. Cleanse the selected site on the patient's fingertip with the alcohol wipe and allow the finger to air dry.	5	_____	_____	_____
12. Perform the finger puncture and wipe away the first drop of blood.	5	_____	_____	_____
13. Apply a large hanging drop of blood to the center of the yellow testing pad.	5			
a. Do not touch the patient's finger to the pad.		_____	_____	_____
b. Do not apply a second drop of blood.		_____	_____	_____
c. Do not smear the blood with your finger.		_____	_____	_____
d. Make sure the yellow test pad is saturated with blood.		_____	_____	_____
14. Give the patient a gauze square to hold securely over the puncture site.	5	_____	_____	_____
15. The monitor automatically begins the measurement process as soon as it senses the drop of blood. Read the test result when it is displayed in the display window in milligrams per deciliter (mg/dL). Turn off the monitor by pressing the "O" button.	5	_____	_____	_____
16. Discard all biohazardous waste in the proper waste containers.	5	_____	_____	_____
17. Clean the glucometer according to the manufacturer's guidelines. Disinfect the work area, remove your gloves, and dispose of them properly. Sanitize your hands.	5	_____	_____	_____
18. In the following Documentation in the Medical Record section, record the testing results as you would in the patient's medical record.	5	_____	_____	_____
19. Teach the patient the importance of recording daily blood glucose levels:	10			
a. Write down the glucose levels in the space provided.		_____	_____	_____
b. Record the medication dose.		_____	_____	_____
c. Record changes in food, activity, illness, stress, or insulin reactions in the Notes or Comments section.		_____	_____	_____
d. Bring the log book to all appointments with the physician		_____	_____	_____

The first entry in the Sample Glucose Log, below, is an example of how patients can use the log sheet.

Documentation in the Medical Record:

Sample Glucose Log

Date	Breakfast Blood	Glucose Level	Lunch Blood Glucose Level	Supper Blood Glucose Level	Bedtime Blood Glucose Level	Medications	Comments
3/2/XX	172	135	144	210	500 mg Metfor-min	Family birth-day party at dinner	
3/3/XX							

Comments:

Points earned _____ ÷ 100 possible points = Score _____ % Score

Instructor's signature _____

Procedure **45-1 Assist the Physician with Patient Care**

PROCEDURE 46-1 Instruct Patients According to Their Needs: Teach a Patient How to Use a Peak Flow Meter

CAAHEP COMPETENCIES: I.PI.1, I.PI.10, IV.PIV.5, IV.PIV.6, IV.PIV8, IV.PIV9
ABHES COMPETENCIES: 9.e, 9.h

TASK: To instruct the patient in the proper method of performing a peak flow meter test.

Equipment and Supplies
- Peak flow meter
- Disposable mouthpiece
- Notebook with pen
- Biohazardous waste container
- Patient's record

Standards: Complete the procedure and all critical steps in _____ minutes with a minimum score of 85% within three attempts.

Scoring: Divide the points earned by the total possible points. Failure to perform a critical step, indicated by an asterisk (*), results in an unsatisfactory overall score.

Time began _____ **Time ended** _____ **Total minutes:** _____

Steps	Possible Points	Attempt 1	Attempt 2	Attempt 3
1. Sanitize your hands.	5	_____	_____	_____
*2. Place the mouthpiece on the peak flow meter and slide the marker to the bottom of the scale.	5	_____	_____	_____
3. Introduce yourself and confirm that you have the correct patient.	5	_____	_____	_____
4. Explain the purpose of the test.	5	_____	_____	_____
5. Explain the actual maneuver of forced expiration.	5	_____	_____	_____
6. Make sure the patient is comfortable and in a proper position, either sitting upright or standing (standing is preferred).	5	_____	_____	_____
7. Loosen any tight clothing, such as a necktie, bra, or belt.	5	_____	_____	_____
8. Hold the meter upright, taking care not to block the opening with your fingers.	5	_____	_____	_____
9. Instruct the patient to inhale as deeply as possible, insert the mouthpiece into mouth beyond the teeth, and form a tight seal with the lips. Caution the patient not to put the tongue in the mouthpiece when exhaling.	5	_____	_____	_____
10. Instruct the patient to exhale as strongly and quickly as possible into the peak flow meter.	5	_____	_____	_____

Steps	Possible Points	Attempt 1	Attempt 2	Attempt 3
11. The forced exhalation moves the marker up the scale and stops at the point of the peak expiratory flow. Record this number and return the marker to the bottom of the scale.	10	_____	_____	_____
*12. Repeat the procedure two more times, sliding the indicator to the bottom of the scale before each reading, and record each result.	5	_____	_____	_____
13. Encourage the patient to inhale as deeply as possible and to exhale as forcefully and quickly as possible with each effort.	5	_____	_____	_____
14. Place the test results in the patient's chart for the physician to review; note the time and date of the highest reading.	10	_____	_____	_____
15. Clean and disinfect the equipment, discarding waste in a biohazardous waste container, or give the patient the meter for continued use at home with instructions to follow the manufacturer's cleaning recommendations.	5	_____	_____	_____
16. Sanitize your hands.	5	_____	_____	_____
17. In the following Documentation in the Medical Record section, record the testing information as you would in the patient's chart.	10	_____	_____	_____

Documentation in the Medical Record:

Comments:

Points earned _____ ÷ 100 possible points = Score _____ % Score

Instructor's signature _____

Name _____ Date _____ Score _____

PROCEDURE 46-2 Assist the Physician with Patient Care: Administer a Nebulizer Treatment

CAAHEP COMPETENCIES: I.PI.1, I.PI.10, IV.PIV.5, IV.PIV.6, IV.PIV8
ABHES COMPETENCIES: 9.e

TASK: To perform a nebulizer treatment.

Equipment and Supplies
- Nebulizer machine
- Disposable connector tubing with medication dispenser
- Disposable mouthpiece or mask as ordered
- Medication as ordered
- Biohazardous waste container
- Patient's record and pen

Standards: Complete the procedure and all critical steps in _____ minutes with a minimum score of 85% within three attempts.

Scoring: Divide the points earned by the total possible points. Failure to perform a critical step, indicated by an asterisk (*), results in an unsatisfactory overall score.

Time began _____ Time ended _____ Total minutes: _____

Steps	Possible Points	Attempt 1	Attempt 2	Attempt 3
1. Plug the nebulizer into a properly grounded electrical outlet.	5	_____	_____	_____
*2. Introduce yourself and confirm that you have the correct patient.	5	_____	_____	_____
3. Explain the purpose of the treatment.	5	_____	_____	_____
4. Sanitize your hands.	5	_____	_____	_____
5. Measure the prescribed dose of drug into the nebulizer's medication cup.	5	_____	_____	_____
6. Replace the top of the medication cup and connect it to the mouthpiece or face mask.	5	_____	_____	_____
7. Connect the disposable tubing to both the nebulizer and the medication cup.	5	_____	_____	_____
8. Have the patient sit upright to allow total lung expansion.	5	_____	_____	_____
9. Turn on the nebulizer; mist should be visible coming from the back of the tube opposite the mouthpiece or into the face mask.	5	_____	_____	_____
10. If a mask is used, position it comfortably but securely over the patient's mouth and nose.	5	_____	_____	_____
11. If a mouthpiece is used, instruct the patient to hold it between the teeth with the lips pursed around the mouthpiece.	5	_____	_____	_____

457

Steps	Possible Points	Attempt 1	Attempt 2	Attempt 3
*12. Encourage the patient to take slow, deep breath through the mouth and to hold each breath 2 to 3 seconds to allow the medication to disperse through the lungs.	5	_____	_____	_____
13. Continue the treatment until aerosol is no longer produced (about 10 minutes).	5	_____	_____	_____
14. Turn off the nebulizer.	5	_____	_____	_____
*15. Encourage the patient to take several deep breaths and to cough loosened secretions into disposable tissues.	10	_____	_____	_____
16. Dispose of the mouthpiece or mask, tubing, and contaminated tissues in a biohazardous waste container.	5	_____	_____	_____
17. Sanitize your hands.	5	_____	_____	_____
18. In the following Documentation in the Medical Record section, record the nebulizer treatment and the patient's response as you would in the patient's record. Include the amount of coughing, whether coughing was productive or nonproductive, and any side effects of the medication.	5	_____	_____	_____
19. If the patient is to continue home nebulizer treatments, provide patient education for both the patient and caregivers as appropriate. Make sure to confirm understanding by having them demonstrate the treatment steps.	5	_____	_____	_____

Documentation in the Medical Record:

Comments:

Points earned _____ **÷ 100 possible points = Score** _____ **% Score**

Instructor's signature _____

Name _____ Date _____ Score _____

PROCEDURE 46-3 Assist the Physician with Patient Care: Perform Volume Capacity Spirometry Testing

CAAHEP COMPETENCIES: I.PI.1, I.PI.10, IV.PIV.5, IV.PIV.6, IV.PIV8
ABHES COMPETENCIES: 9.e

TASK: To perform volume capacity testing.

Equipment and Supplies
- Scale with height measuring device
- Sphygmomanometer and stethoscope
- Spirometer with recording paper in place
- External spirometric tubing
- Disposable mouthpiece
- Nasal clip if needed
- Biohazardous waste container
- Patient's record

Standards: Complete the procedure and all critical steps in _____ minutes with a minimum score of 85% within three attempts.

Scoring: Divide the points earned by the total possible points. Failure to perform a critical step, indicated by an asterisk (*), results in an unsatisfactory overall score.

Time began _____   Time ended _____   Total minutes: _____

Steps	Possible Points	Attempt 1	Attempt 2	Attempt 3
1. Sanitize your hands and assemble the spirometer.	5	_____	_____	_____
2. Introduce yourself and confirm that you have the correct patient. Determine whether the patient required any special preparation and whether it was done.	5	_____	_____	_____
3. Explain the purpose of the test.	5	_____	_____	_____
*4. Measure and record the patient's vital signs, height, and weight.	5	_____	_____	_____
5. Explain the maneuver required by the test.	5	_____	_____	_____
6. Make sure the patient is comfortable; he or she should be standing or sitting with the legs uncrossed and the feet on floor.	5	_____	_____	_____
7. Loosen any tight clothing, such as a necktie, bra, or belt.	5	_____	_____	_____
8. Show the patient the proper chin and neck position; the chin should be slightly elevated and the neck slightly extended.	5	_____	_____	_____
9. Practice the maneuver with the patient before you begin.	5	_____	_____	_____
*10. If the facility's procedure requires it, place a soft nose clip on the patient's nose.	5	_____	_____	_____

Steps	Possible Points	Attempt 1	Attempt 2	Attempt 3
11. Place the mouthpiece in the mouth and instruct the patient to seal the lips around the piece.	5	_____	_____	_____
12. Have the patient inhale according to instructions.	5	_____	_____	_____
*13. Use active, forceful coaching during exhalation.	5	_____	_____	_____
14. Provide the patient with feedback after the maneuver is finished.	5	_____	_____	_____
15. Carefully observe the patient for indications of vertigo or dyspnea or any other signs of difficulty. If complications occur, stop the test and inform the physician.	5	_____	_____	_____
16. Continue the testing until three acceptable maneuvers have been performed.	5	_____	_____	_____
17. Place the test results in the patient's medical record for the physician to review.	5	_____	_____	_____
18. Clean and disinfect the equipment. Discard waste in a biohazardous waste container.	5	_____	_____	_____
19. Sanitize your hands.	5	_____	_____	_____
20. In the following Documentation in the Medical Record section, record the testing information as you would in the patient's medical record	5	_____	_____	_____

Documentation in the Medical Record:

Comments:

Points earned _____ ÷ 100 possible points = **Score** _____ **% Score**

Instructor's signature _____

Name _____ Date _____ Score _____

PROCEDURE 46-4 Obtain Specimens for Microbiologic Testing: Obtain a Sputum Sample for Culture

CAAHEP COMPETENCIES: I.PI.1, I.PI.10, III.PIII 2, III.PIII 3, III.PIII.7, IV.PIV.5, IV.PIV.6, IV.PIV8
ABHES COMPETENCIES: 9.a, 10.e.3

TASK: To collect a sputum sample while observing Standard Precautions.

Equipment and Supplies
- Sterile laboratory specimen cup, accurately labeled
- Biohazard laboratory specimen bag with laboratory requisition
- Disposable examination gloves
- Face shield with goggles
- Impervious gown
- Biohazardous waste container
- Cup of water
- Ginger ale or juice
- Patient's record

Standards: Complete the procedure and all critical steps in _____ minutes with a minimum score of 85% within three attempts.

Scoring: Divide the points earned by the total possible points. Failure to perform a critical step, indicated by an asterisk (*), results in an unsatisfactory overall score.

Time began _____ **Time ended** _____ **Total minutes:** _____

Steps	Possible Points	Attempt 1	Attempt 2	Attempt 3
1. Assemble the equipment and label the specimen cup.	5	_____	_____	_____
2. Identify the patient and explain the procedure.	5	_____	_____	_____
3. Sanitize your hands and put on gloves, a face shield with goggles, and an impervious gown.	5	_____	_____	_____
4. Have the patient rinse his or her mouth with water.	5	_____	_____	_____
5. Carefully remove the specimen cup lid, taking care not to touch the inside of the lid or the inside of the container, and place it upside down on a side table.	10	_____	_____	_____
*6. Instruct the patient to take three deep breaths and then cough deeply to bring up secretions from the lower respiratory tract.	10	_____	_____	_____
7. Tell the patient to spit directly into the specimen container and to avoid getting any sputum on the exterior of the container. Do not touch the inside of the container during the procedure.	5	_____	_____	_____

461

Steps	Possible Points	Attempt 1	Attempt 2	Attempt 3
*8. Place the lid on the container securely, taking care not to touch the inside of the lid, and then put the container in the plastic specimen bag.	10	_____	_____	_____
9. Offer the patient a glass of juice or ginger ale.	5	_____	_____	_____
*10. If another test has been ordered for the next morning, instruct the patient when to come to the office or explain how to complete the procedure at home. Remind the patient to follow the same instructions for preparation. Stress the importance of maintaining the sterility of the container and of collecting the specimen first thing in the morning.	10	_____	_____	_____
11. Clean the work area and properly dispose of all supplies.	5	_____	_____	_____
12. Sanitize your hands.	5	_____	_____	_____
13. Process the specimen immediately to ensure optimum test results or refrigerate the specimen until it is sent to the laboratory for analysis.	10	_____	_____	_____
14. In the following Documentation in the Medical Record section, record the procedure as you would in the patient's record.	10	_____	_____	_____

Documentation in the Medical Record:

Comments:

Points earned _____ ÷ 100 possible points = Score _____ % Score

Instructor's signature _____

Procedure **46-4 Obtain Specimens for Microbiologic Testing**

PROCEDURE 48-1 Instruct Individuals According to Their Needs: Understand the Sensorimotor Changes of Aging

CAAHEP COMPETENCIES: IV.PIV.5
ABHES COMPETENCIES: 9.j

TASK: Role-play with a partner to better understand the needs of aging individuals.

Equipment and Supplies
- Yellow-tinted glasses, ski goggles, or laboratory goggles
- Pink, white, yellow "pills" (various colors of Tic Tacs work)
- Vaseline
- Cotton balls
- Eye patches
- Tape
- Thick gloves
- Utility glove
- Tongue depressors
- Ace bandages
- Medical forms in small print
- Pennies
- Button shirts
- Walker

Standards: Complete the procedure and all critical steps in _____ minutes with a minimum score of 85% within three attempts.

Scoring: Divide the points earned by the total possible points. Failure to perform a critical step, indicated by an asterisk (*), results in an unsatisfactory overall score.

Time began _____ **Time ended** _____ **Total minutes:** _____

Steps	Possible Points	Attempt 1	Attempt 2	Attempt 3
1. Role-play vision and hearing loss:	10			
a. Put two cotton balls in each ear and an eye patch over one eye. Follow your partner's instructions.		_____	_____	_____
b. Partner: Stand out of your partner's line of vision (to prevent lip-reading). Without using gestures or changing the volume of your voice, tell your partner to cross the room and pick up a book.		_____	_____	_____
2. Role-play yellowing of the lens of the eye:	10			
a. Line up "pills" of different pastel colors.		_____	_____	_____
b. Partner: Pick out the different colors while wearing the yellow tinted glasses.		_____	_____	_____

463

Steps	Possible Points	Attempt 1	Attempt 2	Attempt 3
3. Role-play difficulty with focusing:	10			
a. Put on goggles smeared with Vaseline and follow your partner's directions.		_____	_____	_____
b. Partner: Stand at least 3 feet in front of your partner and motion for him or her to come to you (your partner is deaf, so talking will not help).		_____	_____	_____
4. Role-play loss of peripheral vision:	10			
a. Put on goggles with black paper taped to the sides.		_____	_____	_____
b. Partner: Stand to the side, out of your partner's field of vision, and motion for your partner to follow you.		_____	_____	_____
5. Role-play aphasia and partial paralysis:	10			
a. You are unable to use your right arm or leg. Place tape over your mouth. Let your partner know you need to go to the bathroom.		_____	_____	_____
b. Partner: Stand at least 3 feet away with your back to your partner and wait for instructions.		_____	_____	_____
6. Role-play problems with dexterity:	10			
a. Put thick gloves on your hands and try to sign your name, button a shirt, tie your shoes, and pick up pennies.		_____	_____	_____
7. Role-play problems with mobility:	10			
a. Use the walker to cross the room.		_____	_____	_____
b. Partner: After your partner starts walking with the walker, hand him or her a book to carry.		_____	_____	_____
8. Role-play changes in sensation:	10			
a. Put on a rubber utility glove; turn on hot water and notice the difference in temperature between the gloved hand and the ungloved hand.		_____	_____	_____
*9. In the following Documentation in the Medical Record section, summarize your impressions of the effect of age-related sensorimotor changes.	20	_____	_____	_____

Documentation in the Medical Record:

Comments:

Points earned _____ ÷ 100 possible points = Score _____ % Score

Instructor's signature _____

Name _____ Date _____ Score _____

PROCEDURE 49-1 Perform Electrocardiography: Obtain a 12-Lead ECG

CAAHEP COMPETENCIES: I.PI.5, I.PI.10, I.AI.1, IV.PIV.5, IV.PIV.6
ABHES COMPETENCIES: 9.e

TASK: To obtain an accurate, artifact-free recording of the electrical activity of the heart.

Equipment and Supplies
- ECG machine with patient lead cable and labeled lead wires
- 10 disposable, self-adhesive electrodes
- Patient gown and drape
- Patient's record

Standards: Complete the procedure and all critical steps in _____ minutes with a minimum score of 85% within three attempts.

Scoring: Divide the points earned by the total possible points. Failure to perform a critical step, indicated by an asterisk (*), results in an unsatisfactory overall score.

Time began _____   **Time ended** _____   **Total minutes:** _____

Steps	Possible Points	Attempt 1	Attempt 2	Attempt 3
1. Sanitize your hands.	5	_____	_____	_____
*2. Explain the procedure to the patient.	5	_____	_____	_____
3. Ask the patient to disrobe to the waist (female patients should also remove their bra) and to remove belts, jewelry, socks, stockings, or pantyhose as necessary.	5	_____	_____	_____
4. Position the patient on the examination table and drape appropriately.	5	_____	_____	_____
5. Turn on the machine to allow the stylus to warm up (this may not be necessary with newer machines).	5	_____	_____	_____
6. Label the beginning of the tracing paper with the patient's name, the date and time, and the patient's current cardiovascular medications; or, input the information into the machine.	5	_____	_____	_____
7. Clean the skin with an alcohol wipe at each site where an electrode will be placed.	5	_____	_____	_____
*8. Apply the self-adhesive electrodes to clean, dry, fleshy areas of the extremities. Extremely hairy areas may need to be shaved to achieve adequate electrode attachment; as alternatively, place a piece of tape over the electrode to make sure it is secure.	10	_____	_____	_____

467

Steps	Possible Points	Attempt 1	Attempt 2	Attempt 3
*9. Apply the self-adhesive electrodes to clean areas on the chest.	10	_____	_____	_____
10. Carefully connect the lead wires to the correct electrode with the alligator clips on the end of each lead. Make sure the lead wires are not crossed.	10	_____	_____	_____
11. Press the AUTO button on the machine and run the ECG tracing. The machine automatically places the standardization at the beginning and the 12 leads then follow in the three-channel matrix with a lead II rhythm strip across the bottom of the page.	5	_____	_____	_____
*12. Watch for artifacts during the recording. If artifacts are present, make appropriate corrections and repeat the recording to obtain a clean reading.	5	_____	_____	_____
13. Remove the lead wires from the electrodes and then remove the electrodes from the patient.	5	_____	_____	_____
14. Assist the patient with getting dressed as needed. Clean and return the ECG machine to its storage area.	5	_____	_____	_____
15. Place the ECG recording in the patient's medical record for physician review.	5	_____	_____	_____
16. Sanitize your hands.	5	_____	_____	_____
17. In the following Documentation in the Medical Record section, document the procedure as you would in the patient's medical record.	5	_____	_____	_____

Documentation in the Medical Record:

Comments:

Points earned _____ ÷ 100 possible points = Score _____ % Score

Instructor's signature _____

PROCEDURE 49-2 Assist the Physician with Patient Care: Fit a Patient with a Holter Monitor

CAAHEP COMPETENCIES: I.PI.10, I.AI.1, IV.PIV.5, IV.PIV.6, IV.PIV.8, IV.PIV9
ABHES COMPETENCIES: 9.d, 9.h

TASK: To establish a possible correlation between coronary disorders and the patient's 24-hour daily activities.

Equipment and Supplies
- Holter monitor with new batteries
- Disposable electrodes
- Razor
- Gauze pads or abrasive tool as needed
- Activity diary
- Carrying case with belt or shoulder strap
- Alcohol swabs
- Cloth tape (nonallergenic)
- Patient's record

Standards: Complete the procedure and all critical steps in _____ minutes with a minimum score of 85% within three attempts.

Scoring: Divide the points earned by the total possible points. Failure to perform a critical step, indicated by an asterisk (*), results in an unsatisfactory overall score.

Time began _____   Time ended _____   Total minutes: _____

Steps	Possible Points	Attempt 1	Attempt 2	Attempt 3
1. Sanitize your hands.	5	_____	_____	_____
2. Assemble the necessary equipment.	5	_____	_____	_____
3. Install batteries in the monitor.	5	_____	_____	_____
*4. Greet the patient and explain the procedure.	5	_____	_____	_____
5. Ask the patient to disrobe to the waist and to sit at the end of the examination table or lie down.	5	_____	_____	_____
6. Clean each electrode application site with the alcohol swab and allow the sites to air dry.	5	_____	_____	_____
7. If the patient has a hairy chest, dry shave the area at each of the electrode sites.	5	_____	_____	_____
8. Fold a gauze pad over your index finger and briskly rub the sites or use an abrasive tool as indicated.	5	_____	_____	_____
*9. Apply the electrodes to the sites recommended by the manufacturer; use enough pressure to ensure that they adhere to the skin completely. Rub the edges of each electrode a second time to make sure the electrode will stay in place.	5	_____	_____	_____

469

Steps	Possible Points	Attempt 1	Attempt 2	Attempt 3
10. Attach the lead wires to the electrodes and connect the end terminal to the patient cable.	5	_____	_____	_____
11. Place a strip of cloth tape over each electrode.	5	_____	_____	_____
12. Attach the test cable to the monitor and plug it into the electrocardiograph. Run a baseline test tracing as directed by the manufacturer.	5	_____	_____	_____
13. Help the patient get dressed without disturbing the connected electrodes. Make sure the cable extends through the buttoned front or out the bottom of the shirt or blouse.	5	_____	_____	_____
14. Place the monitor in the carrying case and attach it to the patient's belt or place it over the patient's shoulder. Make sure the wires are not being pulled or bent in half.	5	_____	_____	_____
15. Plug the electrode cable into the monitor.	5	_____	_____	_____
16. Record the patient's name and date of birth, as well as the starting date and time, in the patient's activity diary.	5	_____	_____	_____
*17. Give the patient the activity diary and advise him or her to begin by writing in the present activity. Include patient education information on the importance of continually recording activities in the diary; using the event marker on the monitor if the patient experiences any symptoms; and correlating the event with a recording in the diary, including the time and details of the related activity before or during the event.	5	_____	_____	_____
18. Schedule the patient for a return appointment in 24 hours.	5	_____	_____	_____
19. Sanitize your hands.	5	_____	_____	_____
20. In the following Documentation in the Medical Record section, record the procedure as you would in the patient's medical record.	5	_____	_____	_____

Documentation in the Medical Record:

Comments:

Points earned _____ ÷ 100 possible points = Score _____ % Score

Instructor's signature _____

WORK PRODUCT 49-1

Name: _____

Performing Electrocardiography

Corresponds to Procedure 49-1

<u>CAAHEP COMPETENCIES:</u> I.PI.5., I.PI.10., I.AI.1., IV.PIV.5., IV.PIV.6

<u>ABHES COMPETENCIES:</u> 9.e

A 46-year-old woman comes into the office today complaining of episodes of chest pain over the past 2 months. The doctor has ordered electrocardiography. Role-play this case with a classmate and then document it below.

1. Position and drape the patient in preparation for the procedure.

2. Provide patient education and instruction related to electrocardiographic testing.

3. Perform the procedure. Attach a copy of the Work Product to your Procedure Checklist.

4. Include the patient's vital signs and a current list of medications.

Name _____ Date _____ Score _____

PROCEDURE 51-1 Use the Microscope

CAAHEP COMPETENCIES: III.AIII.2
ABHES COMPETENCIES: 9.d

TASK: To focus the microscope properly, using a prepared slide, under low power, high power, and oil immersion.

Equipment and Supplies
- Microscope
- Lens cleaner
- Lens tissue
- Biohazardous waste container
- Slide containing specimen
- Immersion oil

Standards: Complete the procedure and all critical steps in _____ minutes with a minimum score of 85% within three attempts.

Scoring: Divide the points earned by the total possible points. Failure to perform a critical step, indicated by an asterisk (*), results in an unsatisfactory overall score.

Time began _____ Time ended _____ Total minutes: _____

Steps	Possible Points	Attempt 1	Attempt 2	Attempt 3
1. Sanitize your hands.	2	_____	_____	_____
2. Gather the necessary materials.	2	_____	_____	_____
*3. Clean the lenses with lens tissue and lens cleaner.	2	_____	_____	_____
4. Adjust the seating to a comfortable height.	2	_____	_____	_____
5. Plug the microscope into an electrical outlet and turn on the light switch.	2	_____	_____	_____
6. Place the slide specimen on the stage and secure it.	5	_____	_____	_____
7. Turn the revolving nosepiece to engage the 4× or 10× lens.	5	_____	_____	_____
8. Carefully raise the stage while observing with the naked eye from the side.	5	_____	_____	_____
9. Focus the specimen using the coarse adjustment knob.	5	_____	_____	_____
10. Adjust the amount of light by closing the iris diaphragm or adjusting the light from the source.	5	_____	_____	_____
11. Switch to the 40× lens. Use the fine adjustment knob to focus the specimen in detail.	5	_____	_____	_____
12. Turn the revolving nosepiece to the area between the high-power objective and oil immersion.	5	_____	_____	_____
13. Place a small drop of oil on the slide.	5	_____	_____	_____
14. Carefully rotate the oil immersion objective into place. The objective will be immersed in the oil.	10	_____	_____	_____

475

Steps	Possible Points	Attempt 1	Attempt 2	Attempt 3
15. Adjust the focus with the fine adjustment knob.	5	_____	_____	_____
16. Increase the light by opening the iris diaphragm and raising the condenser.	5	_____	_____	_____
17. Identify the specimen.	2	_____	_____	_____
18. Return to low power but do not drag the 40× lens through the oil.	10	_____	_____	_____
19. Remove the slide and dispose of it in a biohazardous waste container.	2	_____	_____	_____
20. Lower the stage.	2	_____	_____	_____
21. Center the stage.	2	_____	_____	_____
22. Switch off the light and unplug the microscope.	2	_____	_____	_____
23. Clean the lenses with lens tissue and remove oil with lens cleaner.	2	_____	_____	_____
24. Wipe the microscope with a cloth.	2	_____	_____	_____
25. Cover the microscope.	2	_____	_____	_____
26. Sanitize the work area.	2	_____	_____	_____
27. Sanitize your hands.	2	_____	_____	_____

Comments:

Points earned _____ ÷ 100 possible points = Score _____ % Score

Instructor's signature _____

Name _____ Date _____ Score _____

PROCEDURE 52-1 Explain the Rationale for Performance of a Procedure: Instruct a Patient in the Collection of a 24-Hour Urine Specimen

CAAHEP COMPETENCIES: III.A.III.2
ABHES COMPETENCIES: 9.h, 10.d, 10.e.1

TASK: To collect a 24-hour urine sample for creatinine clearance.

Equipment and Supplies
- 3-L Urine collection container
- Printed patient instructions
- Laboratory requisition form
- Patient's medical record

Standards: Complete the procedure and all critical steps in _____ minutes with a minimum score of 85% in three attempts.

Scoring: Divide the points earned by the total possible points. Failure to perform a critical step, indicated by an asterisk (*), results in an unsatisfactory overall score.

Time began _____ Time ended _____ Total minutes: _____

Steps	Possible Points	Attempt 1	Attempt 2	Attempt 3
1. Greet the patient by name and confirm that you have the correct patient.	5	____	____	____
2. Label the container with the patient's name and the current date; note that the sample is a 24-hour urine specimen and then initial the label.	5	____	____	____
*3. Explain the following instructions to adult patients or to the guardians of pediatric patients.	5	____	____	____
Patient Instructions for Obtaining a 24-Hour Urine Specimen				
1. Empty your bladder into the toilet in the morning without saving any of the specimen. Record the time you first emptied your bladder.	10	____	____	____
2. For the next 24 hours, each time you empty your bladder, the urine should be voided directly into the large specimen container.	10	____	____	____
3. Replace the lid on the container after each urination. Throughout the 24 hours of the study, store the container either in the refrigerator or in an ice chest.	5	____	____	____
4. If at any time you forget to empty your bladder into the specimen container or if some urine is accidentally spilled, the test must be started all over again with an empty container and a newly recorded start time.	10	____	____	____

Steps	Possible Points	Attempt 1	Attempt 2	Attempt 3
*5. The last collection of urine should be done at the same time as the first specimen on the previous day so that exactly 24 hours of urine collection is completed. The collection ends with the first voided morning specimen that completes the 24-hour collection period.	10	_____	_____	_____
6. As soon as possible after completing the collection period, return the specimen container to the physician's office.	5	_____	_____	_____
7. The patient is given the specimen container and written instructions to confirm understanding.	10	_____	_____	_____
8. In the following Documentation in the Medical Record section, document the details of the patient education intervention as you would in the patient's medical record.	5	_____	_____	_____

Processing a 24-Hour Urine Specimen

1. Ask the patient whether all urine voided throughout the 24-hour period had been collected and whether any problems occurred during the collection process.	5	_____	_____	_____
2. Complete the laboratory request form and prepare the specimen for transport.	5	_____	_____	_____
3. Store the specimen in the refrigerator until it is picked up by the laboratory.	5	_____	_____	_____
4. In the following Documentation in the Medical Record section, document that the specimen was sent to the laboratory as you would in the patient's medical record. Include the type of test ordered, the date and time, and the type of specimen.	5	_____	_____	_____

Documentation in the Medical Record:

Patient Education:

Procedure **52-1 Explain the Rationale for Performance of a Procedure**

Specimen Handling:

Comments:

Points earned _____ ÷ 100 possible points = Score _____ % Score

Instructor's signature _____

Procedure **52-1** Explain the Rationale for Performance of a Procedure

Name _____ Date _____ Score _____

PROCEDURE 52-2 Instruct Patients According to Their Needs: Instruct a Patient in the Collection of a Clean-Catch Midstream Urine Specimen

CAAHEP COMPETENCIES: III.AIII.2
ABHES COMPETENCIES: 9.d, 9.h, 10.d, 10.e.1

TASK: To instruct patients in the proper way to collect a contaminant-free urine sample for culture or analysis using the clean-catch midstream specimen (CCMS) technique.

Equipment and Supplies
- Sterile container with lid and label
- Antiseptic wipes
- Patient medical record

Standards: Complete the procedure and all critical steps in _____ minutes with a minimum score of 85% in three attempts.

Scoring: Divide the points earned by the total possible points. Failure to perform a critical step, indicated by an asterisk (*), results in an unsatisfactory overall score.

Time began _____ Time ended _____ Total minutes: _____

Steps	Possible Points	Attempt 1	Attempt 2	Attempt 3
1. Label the container and give the patient the supplies.	5	_____	_____	_____
2. Explain the following instructions to adult patients or to the guardians of pediatric patients, being sensitive to privacy issues.	10	_____	_____	_____
Instructions for Obtaining a Clean-Catch Midstream Specimen (Female Patient)				
1. Wash your hands and open the antiseptic wipes package for easy access.	2	_____	_____	_____
2. Remove the lid from the specimen container, taking care not to touch the inside of the lid or the inside of the container. Put the lid, facing up, and the container on a paper towel.	5	_____	_____	_____
3. Remove your underclothing and sit on the toilet.	2	_____	_____	
4. Expose the urinary meatus by spreading apart the labia with one hand.	5	_____	_____	
*5. Cleanse each side of the urinary meatus with a front-to-back motion, from the pubis to the anus. Use a separate antiseptic wipe for each side.	5	_____	_____	_____
6. Cleanse directly across the meatus, front-to-back, using a third antiseptic wipe.	5	_____	_____	
7. Hold the labia apart throughout this procedure.	5	_____	_____	_____
*8. Void a small amount of urine into the toilet.	5	_____	_____	_____

Steps	Possible Points	Attempt 1	Attempt 2	Attempt 3
9. Move the specimen container into position and void the next portion of urine into it. Remember, this is a sterile container; do not touch the inside of the container with your fingers.	5	_____	_____	_____
10. Remove the container and void the last amount of urine into the toilet. (This means that the first part and the last part of the urinary flow have been excluded from the specimen. Only the middle portion of the flow is included.)	5	_____	_____	_____
11. Place the lid on the container taking care not to touch the interior surface of the lid. Wipe in your usual manner, redress, and return the sterile specimen to the place designated by the medical facility.	2	_____	_____	_____

Instructions for Obtaining a Clean-Catch Midstream Specimen (Male Patient)

Steps	Possible Points	Attempt 1	Attempt 2	Attempt 3
1. Wash your hands and expose the penis.	2	_____	_____	_____
2. Retract the foreskin of the penis (if not circumcised).	5	_____	_____	_____
3. Cleanse the area around the glans penis (meatus) and the urethral opening by cleaning each side of the glans with a separate antiseptic wipe.	5	_____	_____	_____
4. Cleanse directly across the urethral opening using a third antiseptic wipe.	5	_____	_____	_____
5. Void a small amount of urine into the toilet or urinal.	5	_____	_____	_____
6. Collect the next portion of the urine in the sterile container; do not touch the inside of the container with your hands or penis.	5	_____	_____	_____
7. Void the last amount of urine into the toilet or urinal.	5	_____	_____	_____
8. Wipe and redress.	2	_____	_____	_____
9. Return the specimen to the designated area.	5	_____	_____	_____

Processing a Clean-Catch Urine Specimen

1. Document the date, time, and collection type.

2. Process the specimen according to the physician's orders. Perform urinalysis in the office or prepare the specimen for transport to the laboratory. If it is to be sent to an outside laboratory, complete the following steps:
   - Make sure the label is properly completed with patient information, date, time, and test ordered.
   - Place the specimen in a biohazard specimen bag.
   - Complete a laboratory requisition and place it in the outside pocket of the specimen bag.
   - Keep the specimen refrigerated until pickup.
   - Document that the specimen was sent.

Documentation in the Medical Record:

Comments:

Points earned _____ ÷ 100 possible points = Score _____ % Score

Instructor's signature _____

Name _____ Date _____ Score _____

PROCEDURE 52-3 Perform a Urinalysis and Patient Screening Using Established Protocols: Assess Urine for Color and Turbidity—the Physical Test

CAAHEP COMPETENCIES: I.PI.6, I.PI.14
ABHES COMPETENCIES: 9.d, 10.b.1, 10.c, 10.d

TASK: To assess and record the color and clarity of a urine specimen.

Equipment and Supplies
- Urine specimen
- Centrifuge tube
- Disposable gloves
- Biohazardous waste container
- Patient's record

Standards: Complete the procedure and all critical steps in _____ minutes with a minimum score of 85% in three attempts.

Scoring: Divide the points earned by the total possible points. Failure to perform a critical step, indicated by an asterisk (*), results in an unsatisfactory overall score.

Time began _____ **Time ended** _____ **Total minutes:** _____

Steps	Possible Points	Attempt 1	Attempt 2	Attempt 3
1. Sanitize your hands and put on gloves.	10	_____	_____	_____
2. Mix the urine by swirling.	10	_____	_____	_____
3. Label a centrifuge tube if a complete urinalysis is to be done.	10	_____	_____	_____
4. Pour the specimen into a standard-size centrifuge tube.	10	_____	_____	_____
*5. Assess and record the color:	20			
a. Pale straw		_____	_____	_____
b. Yellow		_____	_____	_____
c. Amber		_____	_____	_____
*6. Assess the clarity:	20			
a. Clear—no cloudiness		_____	_____	_____
b. Slightly turbid—can see light print through tube		_____	_____	_____
c. Moderately turbid—can see only dark print through tube		_____	_____	_____
d. Very turbid—cannot see through tube		_____	_____	_____

Steps	Possible Points	Attempt 1	Attempt 2	Attempt 3
*7. Clean the work area. Remove your gloves and dispose of them and the supplies used for the procedure in the biohazardous waste container. Sanitize hands.	10	_____	_____	_____
8. In the following Documentation in the Medical Record section, record the results as you would in the patient's medical record.	10	_____	_____	_____

Documentation in the Medical Record:

Comments:

Points earned _____ ÷ 100 possible points = Score _____ % Score

Instructor's signature _____

PROCEDURE 52-4 Perform Quality Control Measures: Measure the Urine Specific Gravity with a Refractometer

CAAHEP COMPETENCIES: I.PI.11, I.PI.14
ABHES COMPETENCIES: 9.d, 10.b.1, 10.c, 10.d

TASK: To calibrate a refractometer and measure the refractive index of urine. (A refractometer is also known as a total solids [TS] meter.)

Equipment and Supplies

- Urine sample
- Urinary refractometer
- Distilled water
- Disposable pipet
- Biohazardous waste container
- Disposable gloves
- Patient's record

Standards: Complete the procedure and all critical steps in _____ minutes with a minimum score of 85% in three attempts.

Scoring: Divide the points earned by the total possible points. Failure to perform a critical step, indicated by an asterisk (*), results in an unsatisfactory overall score.

Time began _____   **Time ended** _____   **Total minutes:** _____

Steps	Possible Points	Attempt 1	Attempt 2	Attempt 3
1. Sanitize your hands and assemble the necessary equipment while the urine specimen reaches room temperature.	10	_____	_____	_____
2. Put on gloves and mix the urine specimen in the collection container.	10	_____	_____	_____
3. Using a disposable pipet, apply a drop of water to the prism of the refractometer by lifting the plastic cover. Close the cover and point the device toward a light source, such as a window or lamp. Look into the refractometer and rotate the eyepiece so that the scale can be clearly read. The scale reads from 1.000 to 1.035 in increments of 0.001.	20	_____	_____	_____
4. Calibrate the refractometer by inserting the small screwdriver provided by the manufacturer into the screw on the underside of the instrument. Turn the screw so that the line is positioned over 1.000.	10	_____	_____	_____
*5. Wipe the prism with a soft, lint-free tissue and apply a drop of mixed urine. Close the cover, point the device at a light source, and read the specific gravity on the scale. Discard the pipet in the biohazardous waste container. The value for specific gravity shown in Procedure 52-4, Figure 1, in the text is 1.020. Note that specific gravity has no units after the value.	20	_____	_____	_____

487

Steps	Possible Points	Attempt 1	Attempt 2	Attempt 3
6. Wipe the urine from the prism with a soft, lint-free, disposable tissue between samples. When finished, clean the prism with tissue moistened with alcohol or with a disposable alcohol wipe. Discard these tissues in the biohazardous waste container.	10	_____	_____	_____
7. Discard the urine sample. Remove and discard your gloves and sanitize your hands.	10	_____	_____	_____
8. In the following Documentation in the Medical Record section, document the results as you would in the patient's medical record. (The urine sample is discarded after documentation.)	10	_____	_____	_____

Documentation in the Medical Record:

Comments:

Points earned _____ ÷ 100 possible points = Score _____ % Score

Instructor's signature _____

PROCEDURE 52-5 Perform a Urinalysis and Patient Screening Using Established Protocols: Test Urine with Chemical Reagent Strips—the Chemical Urinalysis

CAAHEP COMPETENCIES: I.PI.6, I.PI.14, III.PIII.3
ABHES COMPETENCIES: 9.d, 10.b.1, 10.c, 10.d

TASK: To perform chemical testing on a urine sample.

Equipment and Supplies

- Urine specimen
- Reagent strips
- Timer
- Biohazardous waste container
- Eye protection
- Disposable gloves

Standards: Complete the procedure and all critical steps in _____ minutes with a minimum score of 85% in three attempts.

Scoring: Divide the points earned by the total possible points. Failure to perform a critical step, indicated by an asterisk (*), results in an unsatisfactory overall score.

Time began _____   **Time ended** _____   **Total minutes:** _____

Steps	Possible Points	Attempt 1	Attempt 2	Attempt 3
1. Sanitize your hands. Put on nonsterile gloves and eye protection.	5	____	____	____
2. Check the time of collection, the container, and the mode of preservation.	5	____	____	____
*3. If the specimen has been refrigerated, allow it to warm to room temperature.	5	____	____	____
4. Check the reagent strip container for the expiration date.	5	____	____	____
5. Remove the reagent strip from the container. Hold it in your hand or place it on a clean paper towel. Recap the container tightly.	5	____	____	____
6. Compare the nonreactive test pads with the negative color blocks on the container's color chart.	5	____	____	____
7. Thoroughly mix the specimen by swirling.	10	____	____	____
8. Following the manufacturer's directions, note the time, dip the strip into the urine, and then remove it.	10	____	____	____
9. Quickly remove the excess urine from the strip by touching the side of the strip to a paper towel or to the side of the urine container.	10	____	____	____

Steps	Possible Points	Attempt 1	Attempt 2	Attempt 3
*10. Hold the strip horizontally. At the exact time, compare the strip with the appropriate color chart on the reagent container. Document each result on the reagent strip flow sheet as it is read. Alternatively, the strip can be placed on a paper towel.	10	_____	_____	_____
*11. Read the concentration by comparing the strip to the color chart on the side of the bottle. Do not touch the strip to the bottle.	_____	_____	_____	_____
12. Clean the work area. Remove your gloves and sanitize your hands. If a paper towel was used, dispose of it, the reagent strip, and your gloves in the biohazardous waste container	_____	_____	_____	_____
13. In the following Documentation in the Medical Record section, document the results as you would in the patient's record.	_____	_____	_____	_____

Documentation in the Medical Record:

Comments:

Points earned _____ ÷ 100 possible points = Score _____ % Score

Instructor's signature _____

Name _____ Date _____ Score _____

PROCEDURE 52-6 Perform a Urinalysis: Prepare a Urine Specimen for Microscopic Examination

CAAHEP COMPETENCIES: I.PI.14
ABHES COMPETENCIES: 9.d, 10.b.1, 10.c, 10.d

TASK: To perform a microscopic examination of urine to determine the presence of normal and abnormal elements.

Equipment and Supplies
- Urine specimen
- Centrifuge tube
- ◇ Centrifuge
- Disposable pipet
- Microscope slide and coverslip
- Microscope
- Permanent marker
- Disposable gloves
- Face protection
- Biohazardous waste container
- Patient's record

Standards: Complete the procedure and all critical steps in _____ minutes with a minimum score of 85% in three attempts.

Scoring: Divide the points earned by the total possible points. Failure to perform a critical step, indicated by an asterisk (*), results in an unsatisfactory overall score.

Time began _____ **Time ended** _____ **Total minutes:** _____

Steps	Possible Points	Attempt 1	Attempt 2	Attempt 3
1. Sanitize your hands. Put on nonsterile gloves and face protection.	5	_____	_____	_____
2. Gently mix the urine specimen.	5	_____	_____	_____
3. Pour 10 mL of urine into a labeled centrifuge tube and cap the tube.	5	_____	_____	_____
4. Place the tube in the centrifuge.	5	_____	_____	_____
*5. Place another tube containing 10 mL of water in the opposite cup.	5	_____	_____	_____
6. Secure the lid and centrifuge the tubes for 5 minutes or for the time specified for your instrument.	5	_____	_____	_____
7. Remove the tube from the centrifuge after the instrument has come to a full stop.	5	_____	_____	_____
8. Pour off the clear supernatant from the top of the specimen by inverting the centrifuge tube over the sink drain. Do not turn the tube upright until the supernatant has been fully decanted.	5	_____	_____	_____

Steps	Possible Points	Attempt 1	Attempt 2	Attempt 3
9. Prevent the loss of sediment down the drain.	5	_____	_____	_____
*10. Thoroughly mix the sediment by grasping the tube near the top and rapidly flicking it with the fingers of the other hand until all sediment is thoroughly resuspended.	5	_____	_____	_____
*11. Transfer one drop of sediment to a clean, labeled slide using a clean, disposable transfer pipet.	5	_____	_____	_____
12. Place a clean coverslip over the drop, and place the slide on the microscope stage. Remove your face protection.	5	_____	_____	_____

The remaining steps typically are performed by a healthcare practitioner. Medical assistants should not perform the microscopic examination unless they have been specially trained to do so

Steps	Possible Points	Attempt 1	Attempt 2	Attempt 3
13. Focus under low power and reduce the light.	5	_____	_____	_____
14. First, scan the entire coverslip for abnormal findings.	5	_____	_____	_____
15. Examine five low-power fields. Count and classify each type of cast seen, if any, and note mucus if present.	5	_____	_____	_____
16. Switch to high-power magnification and adjust the light.	5	_____	_____	_____
17. In five high-power fields, count the following elements: red blood cells, white blood cells, and round, transitional, and squamous epithelial cells	5	_____	_____	_____
18. In the same five fields, report the following as few, moderate, or many: crystals (identify and report each type seen separately), bacteria (identify as rods or cocci), sperm, yeast, and parasites.	5	_____	_____	_____
19. Average the five fields. In the following Documentation in the Medical Record section, document the results as you would in the patient's medical record.	5	_____	_____	_____
20. Disinfect the work area, remove your gloves, and dispose of contaminated materials in the biohazardous waste container. Sanitize your hands.	5	_____	_____	_____

Documentation in the Medical Record:

Comments:

Points earned _____ ÷ 100 possible points = Score _____ % Score

Instructor's signature _____

Name _____ Date _____ Score _____

PROCEDURE 52-7 Perform Quality Control Measures: Determine the Reliability of Chemical Reagent Strips

CAAHEP COMPETENCIES: I.PI.11
ABHES COMPETENCIES: 9.d, 10.a, 10.b

TASK: To reconstitute a control sample and to test the reliability of the urinalysis chemical testing strip.

Equipment and Supplies
- Chek-Stix Control Strips for Urinalysis (Bayer)
- Distilled water
- Capped tube with milliliter markings
- Test tube rack
- Forceps
- Timer
- Chemical strips for urine testing
- Color chart for chemical strips
- Disposable gloves
- Biohazardous waste container

Standards: Complete the procedure and all critical steps in _____ minutes with a minimum score of 85% in three attempts.

Scoring: Divide the points earned by the total possible points. Failure to perform a critical step, indicated by an asterisk (*), results in an unsatisfactory overall score.

Time began _____   Time ended _____   Total minutes: _____

Steps	Possible Points	Attempt 1	Attempt 2	Attempt 3
1. Assemble the necessary equipment and supplies. Record the lot number and the expiration date of the Chek-Stix.	10	_____	_____	_____
2. Sanitize your hands and put on nonsterile gloves.	5	_____	_____	_____
3. Place a conical tube in the rack and remove the cap.	5	_____	_____	_____
4. Pour 15 mL of distilled water into the tube.	5	_____	_____	_____
5. Using forceps, remove one strip from the bottle. Inspect the strips for mottling or discoloration.	10	_____	_____	_____
6. Place the strip in the water and tightly cap the tube.	10	_____	_____	_____
7. Invert the tube for 2 minutes	5	_____	_____	_____
8. Allow the tube to sit in the rack for 30 minutes.	5	_____	_____	_____
9. Invert the tube one time and remove the strip with forceps.	10	_____	_____	_____
10. Discard the strip in the biohazardous waste container. Once reconstituted, the control solution is stable for 8 hours at room temperature.	5	_____	_____	_____

Steps	Possible Points	Attempt 1	Attempt 2	Attempt 3
*11. Perform quality control for the chemical reagent strip by dipping it into the control solution, as described in Procedure 52-5 in the text.	5	_____	_____	_____
12. Read the results and record them.	10	_____	_____	_____
13. Compare the results to the Chek-Stix package insert or chart on the bottle provided by the manufacturer.	5	_____	_____	_____
14. Discard the chemical reagent strip and the urine control in the biohazardous waste container.	5	_____	_____	_____
15. Sanitize the work area, remove your gloves, and sanitize your hands.	5	_____	_____	_____

Comments:

Points earned _____ ÷ 100 possible points = Score _____ % Score

Instructor's signature _____

Name _____ Date _____ Score _____

PROCEDURE 52-8 Perform a Urinalysis: Test Urine for Glucose Using the Clinitest Method

CAAHEP COMPETENCIES: I.PI.14
ABHES COMPETENCIES: 9.d, 10.b, 10.d

TASK: To perform confirmatory testing for glucose in the urine using the Clinitest procedure for reducing substances.

Equipment and Supplies
- Urine specimen
- Clinitest tablet, tube, and dropper
- Distilled water
- Test tube rack
- Color chart
- Timer
- Disposable gloves
- Eye protection
- Biohazardous waste container
- Patient's record

Standards: Complete the procedure and all critical steps in _____ minutes with a minimum score of 85% in three attempts.

Scoring: Divide the points earned by the total possible points. Failure to perform a critical step, indicated by an asterisk (*), results in an unsatisfactory overall score.

Time began _____ Time ended _____ Total minutes: _____

Steps	Possible Points	Attempt 1	Attempt 2	Attempt 3
1. Sanitize your hands and put on nonsterile gloves and eye protection.	5	_____	_____	_____
2. Holding a Clinitest dropper vertically, add 10 drops of distilled water and then 5 drops of urine to a Clinitest tube.	10	_____	_____	_____
3. Place the prepared tube in the rack.	10	_____	_____	_____
4. Make sure your hands are dry. Then remove a Clinitest tablet from the bottle by shaking a tablet into the bottle cap.	10	_____	_____	_____
5. Tap the tablet into the test tube and recap the container.	10	_____	_____	_____
6. Observe the entire reaction to detect the rapid pass-through phenomenon, which indicates that the glucose level in the urine is very high. (See step 9.)	10	_____	_____	_____
*7. When boiling stops, time exactly 15 seconds and then gently shake the tube to mix the entire contents.	10	_____	_____	_____
8. Immediately compare the color of the specimen with the 5-drop color chart and record your findings.	10	_____	_____	_____

Steps	Possible Points	Attempt 1	Attempt 2	Attempt 3
9. If an orange color briefly develops during the reaction, rapid pass-through has occurred, and the test must be repeated using the 2-drop color chart.	10	_____	_____	_____
10. Disinfect the work area and remove your gloves. Sanitize your hands.	10	_____	_____	_____
11. In the following Documentation in the Medical Record section, record the results as you would in the patient's medical record.	5	_____	_____	_____

Documentation in the Medical Record:

Comments:

Points earned _____ ÷ 100 possible points = Score _____ % Score

Instructor's signature _____

Name _____ Date _____ Score _____

PROCEDURE 52-9 Perform a Urinalysis: Perform a Pregnancy Test

CAAHEP COMPETENCIES: I.PI.6, I.PI.14
ABHES COMPETENCIES: 9.d, 10.b.6.a, 10.c, 10.d

TASK: To perform a pregnancy testing of urine using the QuickVue (Quidel) pregnancy test method.

Equipment and Supplies
- Urine specimen
- QuickVue test kit
- Disposable gloves
- Biohazardous waste container
- Patient's record

Standards: Complete the procedure and all critical steps in _____ minutes with a minimum score of 85% in three attempts.

Scoring: Divide the points earned by the total possible points. Failure to perform a critical step, indicated by an asterisk (*), results in an unsatisfactory overall score.

Time began _____ **Time ended** _____ **Total minutes:** _____

Steps	Possible Points	Attempt 1	Attempt 2	Attempt 3
1. Sanitize your hands and put on nonsterile gloves.	10	_____	_____	_____
*2. Prepare the testing equipment.	10	_____	_____	_____
3. Collect the urine specimen.	10	_____	_____	_____
4. Remove the test cassette from the foil pouch.	10	_____	_____	_____
*5. Add 3 drops of urine using the dropper that accompanies the kit. Dispose of the dropper in the biohazardous waste container.	10	_____	_____	_____
6. Wait 3 minutes to read the test results.	10	_____	_____	_____
7. Interpret the results:	10			
a. *Negative:* A blue control line is present next to the letter C. No line is present next to the letter T.		_____	_____	_____
b. *Positive:* A blue control line is present next to the letter C, and a pink line is present next to the letter T.		_____	_____	_____
8. If a blue line does not appear next to the letter C, the test is invalid and the specimen must be retested with another kit. Check the expiration date of the kit before proceeding.	10	_____	_____	_____
9. Discard the cassette in the biohazardous waste container. Remove your gloves and sanitize your hands.	10	_____	_____	_____
10. In the following Documentation in the Medical Record section, record the results as either positive or negative as you would in the patient's medical record.	10	_____	_____	_____

Documentation in the Medical Record:

Comments:

Points earned _____ ÷ 100 possible points = Score _____ % Score

Instructor's signature _____

Name _____ Date _____ Score _____

PROCEDURE 52-10 Perform a Urinalysis and Patient Screening Using Established Protocols: Perform a Multidrug Screening Test on Urine

CAAHEP COMPETENCIES: I.PI.6, I.PI.14
ABHES COMPETENCIES: 9.d, 10.b.6.c, 10.c, 10.d

TASK: To screen a urine specimen for drugs or drug metabolites at their specified cutoff levels.

Equipment and Supplies
- Instant-View Multi-Drug Screen Urine Test in a sealed pouch
- Freshly voided urine sample
- Timer
- Biohazardous waste container
- Disposable gloves
- Patient's record

Standards: Complete the procedure and all critical steps in _____ minutes with a minimum score of 85% in three attempts.

Scoring: Divide the points earned by the total possible points. Failure to perform a critical step, indicated by an asterisk (*), results in an unsatisfactory overall score.

Time began _____   Time ended _____   Total minutes: _____

Steps	Possible Points	Attempt 1	Attempt 2	Attempt 3
1. Sanitize your hands and assemble the necessary equipment and the specimen. Check the expiration date on the test kit.	10	_____	_____	_____
*2. Determine the temperature of the urine within 4 minutes of voiding. It should be between 90° and 100° F (32° and 38° C).	10	_____	_____	_____
3. Bring the specimen and the testing device to room temperature.	10	_____	_____	_____
4. Remove the device from the foil pouch and label it with the specimen identification.	10	_____	_____	_____
Dip Method				
5. Remove the cap on the specimen and dip the device into the specimen for 10 seconds. The surface of the urine must be above the sample well and below the arrowheads in the window.	10	_____	_____	_____
Alternate Method				
6. Remove the pipet from the pouch and fill it to the line on the barrel with urine. Dispense the entire volume onto the sample well on the testing device.	5	_____	_____	_____
7. Recap the urine specimen.	5	_____	_____	_____
8. Set the timer for 4 to 7 minutes. Do not read the results after 7 minutes, because they will not be valid.	5	_____	_____	_____

501

Steps	Possible Points	Attempt 1	Attempt 2	Attempt 3
*9. Interpret the results:	10			
a. *Positive:* If the C line appears and there is no T line, the test is positive for that drug.		——	——	——
b. *Negative:* If both the C and T lines appear, the level of the drug or its metabolites is below the cutoff level..		——	——	——
c. *Invalid:* If no C line appears within 5 minutes on any test strip, the assay is invalid. Make sure the urine has not been adulterated (see Procedure 52-11 in the text) and/or repeat the assay with a new testing device.		——	——	——
10. Color photocopying provides a permanent record of the results, but the copy must be made within 7 minutes of adding the urine. Make sure the photocopier does not become contaminated; wipe the glass with alcohol or another manufacturer-approved disinfectant after making the copy.	5	——	——	——
11. Discard the urine and the test device in the biohazardous waste container.	10	——	——	——
12. Remove your gloves and sanitize your hands.	5	——	——	——
13. In the following Documentation in the Medical Record section, record the results as you would in the patient's medical record.	5	——	——	——

Documentation in the Medical Record:

Comments:

Points earned _____ ÷ 100 possible points = Score _____ **% Score**

Instructor's signature _____

502

Name _____ Date _____ Score _____

PROCEDURE 52-11 Perform a Urinalysis: Assess a Urine Specimen for Adulteration Before Drug Testing

CAAHEP COMPETENCIES: I.PI.14
ABHES COMPETENCIES: 9.d, 10.b.6, 10.c, 10.d

TASK: To assess a urine specimen for additive adulteration.

Equipment and Supplies
- Quik Test Adulterant Strips (Quik Test USA, Boca Raton, Fla.)
- Urine sample (freshly voided; urine should be stored at room temperature for no longer than 2 hours or at refrigerator temperature for longer than 4 hours before testing)
- Paper towels
- Timer
- Biohazardous waste container
- Disposable gloves
- Patient's record

Standards: Complete the procedure and all critical steps in _____ minutes with a minimum score of 85% in three attempts.

Scoring: Divide the points earned by the total possible points. Failure to perform a critical step, indicated by an asterisk (*), results in an unsatisfactory overall score.

Time began _____   **Time ended** _____   **Total minutes:** _____

Steps	Possible Points	Attempt 1	Attempt 2	Attempt 3
1. Sanitize your hands and assemble the necessary equipment and the specimen. Check the expiration date on the test kit.	10	_____	_____	_____
2. Put on gloves and remove one strip from the container; immediately recap the container tightly.	10	_____	_____	_____
3. Dip the test strip briefly into the urine and remove.	10	_____	_____	_____
4. Blot the strip by touching the side of the strip to paper toweling.	10	_____	_____	_____
*5. Read the results within 1 minute by comparing each pad to the color strips on the canister.	20	_____	_____	_____
6. Dispose of the used paper towels and the test strip in the biohazardous waste container.	10	_____	_____	_____
7. Disinfect the area. Remove your gloves and dispose of them in the biohazardous waste container. Sanitize your hands.	10	_____	_____	_____
*8. In the following Documentation in the Medical Record section, record the test results as you would in the patient's medical record.	20	_____	_____	_____

Documentation in the Medical Record:

Comments:

Points earned _____ ÷ 100 possible points = Score _____ % Score

Instructor's signature _____

504

WORK PRODUCT 52-1

Name: _____

CLIA-Waived Tests: Performing Urinalysis

Corresponds to Procedures 52-3 through 52-8

<u>CAAHEP COMPETENCIES:</u> I.PI.6., I.PI.14., III.PIII.3

<u>ABHES COMPETENCIES:</u> 9.d, 10.b.6, 10.d

A 24-year-old patient comes to the office complaining of dysuria, burning on urination, and LBP for 3 days. The vital signs of the patient are as follows:

Wt: 145 lb

B/P: 112/66 mg/dL

T: 100.7° F

P: 76/minute

R: 16/minute

Obtain a urine sample from the patient and perform a urinalysis. Record the results.

Color: _____

Clarity: _____

Glucose: _____

Ketones: _____

Specific gravity: _____

pH: _____

Blood: _____

Bilirubin: _____

Leukocytes: _____

Nitrates: _____

Protein: _____

Urobilinogen: _____

Using the SOAPE format, document the case.

S _____

_____

_____

O _____

_____

_____

WORK PRODUCT 52-2

Name: _____

Screening Test Results and Follow-Up

Corresponds to Procedures 52-3 through 52-8

CAAHEP COMPETENCIES: I.PI.6., I.PI.14., III.PIII.3

ABHES COMPETENCIES: 9.d, 10.b.6, 10.d

On completion of a urinalysis, the following results were noted:

Color: Amber

Clarity: Clear

Glucose: Small

Ketones: Positive

Specific gravity: 1.005

pH: 7.5

Blood: Moderate

Bilirubin: Negative

Leukocytes: Negative

Nitrates: Negative

Protein: Small

Urobilinogen: 0.1

Using the table below, what can be noted from these test results?

Reference	Range
Color	Pale yellow to straw
Clarity	Clear to slightly turbid
Specific gravity	1.001-1.035
pH	4.6-8.0
Protein (mg/dL)	NEG
Glucose (mg/dL)	NEG
Ketone (mg/dL)	NEG
Bilirubin (mg/dL)	NEG
Blood (mg/dL)	NEG
Nitrite (mg/dL)	NEG
Urobilinogen (Ehrlich units)	0.1–1
White blood cells	NEG

Are there any questions the medical assistant should ask the patient regarding the findings?

_____

_____

_____

_____

PROCEDURE 53-1 Perform Venipuncture: Collect a Venous Blood Sample Using the Syringe Method

CAAHEP COMPETENCIES: I.AI.2, I.PI.2, I.PI.12, III.PIII.2, III.PIII.3, III.PIII7, III.AIII.1, III.AIII.2
ABHES COMPETENCIES: 9.e, 10.c, 10.d.1

TASK: To collect a venous blood specimen.

Equipment and Supplies
- Needle, syringe with 21- or 22-gauge safety needle
- Vacutainer tubes appropriate for tests ordered
- 70% isopropyl alcohol
- Sterile gauze pads
- Tourniquet
- Syringe adapter for transfer to Vacutainer tubes
- Nonallergenic tape or bandage
- Permanent marking pen
- Biohazardous waste container
- Disposable gloves
- Patient's record

Standards: Complete the procedure and all critical steps in _____ minutes with a minimum score of 85% within three attempts.

Scoring: Divide the points earned by the total possible points. Failure to perform a critical step, indicated by an asterisk (*), results in an unsatisfactory overall score.

Time began _____   Time ended _____   Total minutes: _____

Steps	Possible Points	Attempt 1	Attempt 2	Attempt 3
1. Check the requisition form to determine the tests ordered. Gather the correct tubes and supplies.	5	_____	_____	_____
2. Sanitize your hands and put on nonsterile gloves.	2	_____	_____	_____
*3. Identify the patient and explain the procedure. Obtain permission to perform the venipuncture.	10	_____	_____	_____
4. Assist the patient to sit with the arm well supported in a slightly downward position.	5	_____	_____	_____
5. Assemble the necessary equipment. The choice of syringe barrel and needle size depends on your inspection of the patient's veins and the amount of blood required for the ordered tests. Attach the needle to the syringe. Pull and depress the plunger several times to loosen it in the barrel. Keep the cover on the needle.	5	_____	_____	_____
6. Apply the tourniquet around the patient's arm 3 to 4 inches above the elbow. The tourniquet should never be tied so tightly that it restricts blood flow in the artery. The tourniquet should remain in place no longer than 1 minute.	5	_____	_____	_____

Steps	Possible Points	Attempt 1	Attempt 2	Attempt 3
7. Ask the patient to make a fist.	2	_____	_____	_____
*8. Select the venipuncture site by palpating the antecubital space; use your index finger to trace the path of the vein and to judge its depth. The vein most often used is the median cephalic vein, which lies in the middle of the elbow.	5	_____	_____	_____
9. Cleanse the site with the alcohol pad, starting in the center of the area and working outward in a circular pattern. Allow the area to dry before proceeding.	5	_____	_____	_____
10. Hold the syringe in your dominant hand. Your thumb should be on top and your fingers underneath. Remove the needle sheath.	5	_____	_____	_____
11. Grasp the patient's arm with the nondominant hand. Anchor the vein by stretching the skin downward below the collection site with the thumb of the nondominant hand.	5	_____	_____	_____
12. With the needle aligned parallel to the vein and the bevel of the needle up, insert the needle at a 15-degree angle rapidly and smoothly through the skin and into the vein. Observe for a "flash" of blood in the hub of the syringe. Ask the patient to release the fist.	5	_____	_____	_____
13. Slowly pull back the plunger of the syringe with the nondominant hand. Do not allow more than 1 mL of head space between the blood and the top of the plunger. Make sure you do not move the needle after entering the vein. Fill the barrel to the needed volume.	5	_____	_____	_____
*14. Release the tourniquet when the venipuncture is complete. It must be released before the needle is removed from the arm.	5	_____	_____	_____
15. Place sterile gauze over the puncture site as you withdraw the needle. Immediately activate the needle safety device.	5	_____	_____	_____
16. Instruct the patient to apply direct pressure on the puncture site with sterile gauze. The patient may elevate the arm, but it should not be bent.	5	_____	_____	_____
17. Transfer the blood immediately to the required tube or tubes using a syringe adapter. Do not push on the plunger during transfer. Discard the entire unit when transfer is complete. Invert the tubes after adding the blood and label them with the necessary patient information.	5	_____	_____	_____
18. Inspect the puncture site for bleeding or a hematoma.	2	_____	_____	_____
*19. Apply a hypoallergenic bandage.	2	_____	_____	_____
20. Disinfect the work area, then remove your gloves and sanitize your hands. Dispose of any blood-contaminated materials, such as gauze, in the biohazardous waste container.	5	_____	_____	_____
21. Complete the laboratory requisition form and route the specimen to the proper place. In the following Documentation in the Medical Record section, record the procedure as you would in the patient's medical record.	5	_____	_____	_____

510

Documentation in the Medical Record:

Comments:

Points earned _____ ÷ 100 possible points = Score _____ % Score

Instructor's signature _____

Name _____ Date _____ Score _____

PROCEDURE 53-2 Perform Venipuncture: Collect a Venous Blood Sample Using the Evacuated Tube Method

CAAHEP COMPETENCIES: I.AI.2, I.PI.2, I.PI.12, III.PIII.2, III.PIII.3, III.PIII7, III.AIII.1, III.AIII.2
ABHES COMPETENCIES: 9.e, 10.c, 10.d.1

TASK: To collect a venous blood specimen.

Equipment and Supplies
- Vacutainer needle and needle holder with needle safety device and proper tubes for requested tests
- 70% isopropyl alcohol
- Sterile gauze pads
- Tourniquet
- Nonallergenic tape or bandage
- Permanent marking pen or printed labels
- Biohazardous waste and Sharps containers
- Disposable gloves
- Patient's record

Standards: Complete the procedure and all critical steps in _____ minutes with a minimum score of 85% within three attempts.

Scoring: Divide the points earned by the total possible points. Failure to perform a critical step, indicated by an asterisk (*), results in an unsatisfactory overall score.

Time began _____   **Time ended** _____   **Total minutes:** _____

Steps	Possible Points	Attempt 1	Attempt 2	Attempt 3
1. Check the requisition form to determine the tests ordered. Gather the correct tubes and supplies.	5	_____	_____	_____
2. Sanitize your hands and put on nonsterile gloves.	2	_____	_____	_____
3. Identify the patient, explain the procedure, and obtain permission for the venipuncture.	5	_____	_____	_____
4. Assist the patient to sit with the arm well supported in a slightly downward position.	2	_____	_____	_____
5. Assemble the necessary equipment. The choice of needle size depends on your inspection of the patient's veins. Attach the needle firmly to the Vacutainer holder. Keep the cover on the needle.	5	_____	_____	_____
6. Apply the tourniquet around the patient's arm 3 to 4 inches above the elbow. The tourniquet should never be tied so tightly that it restricts blood flow in the artery. Tourniquets should remain in place no longer than 60 seconds.	5	_____	_____	_____
7. Ask the patient to make a fist.	2	_____	_____	_____
8. Select the venipuncture site by palpating the antecubital space; use your index finger to trace the path of the vein and to judge its depth. The vein most often used is the median cephalic vein, which lies in the middle of the elbow.	5	_____	_____	_____

513

Steps	Possible Points	Attempt 1	Attempt 2	Attempt 3
*9. Cleanse the site with the alcohol pad, starting in the center of the area and working outward in a circular pattern.	5	_____	_____	_____
10. Dry the site with a sterile gauze pad or allow the area to dry before proceeding.	2	_____	_____	_____
11. Hold the Vacutainer assembly in your dominant hand. Your thumb should be on top and your fingers underneath. You may want to position the first tube to be drawn in the needle holder, but do not push it onto the double-pointed needle past the marking on the holder. Remove the needle sheath.	5	_____	_____	_____
12. Grasp the patient's arm with your nondominant hand. Anchor the vein by stretching the skin downward below the collection site with the thumb of the nondominant hand.	5	_____	_____	_____
*13. With the needle aligned parallel to the vein ad the bevel of the needle up, insert the needle at a 15-degree angle rapidly and smoothly through the skin and into the vein. Observe for a "flash" of blood in the hub of the syringe. Ask the patient to release the fist.	5	_____	_____	_____
*14. Place two fingers on the flanges of the needle holder and use your thumb to push the tube onto the double-pointed needle. Make sure you do not change the needle's position in the vein. When blood begins to flow into the tube, ask the patient to release the fist.	5	_____	_____	_____
15. Allow the tube to fill to maximum capacity. Remove the tube by curling the fingers underneath and pushing on the needle holder with the thumb. Take care not to move the needle when removing the tube.	5	_____	_____	_____
16. Insert the second tube into the needle holder, following the instructions in the previous steps. Continue filling tubes until the order on the requisition is complete. Gently invert each tube immediately after removing it from the needle holder to mix the anticoagulants and blood. As the last tube is filling, release the tourniquet.	5	_____	_____	_____
17. Remove the last tube from the holder. Place gauze over the puncture site and quickly remove the needle, engaging the safety device. Dispose of the entire unit in the sharps container.	5	_____	_____	_____
18. Apply pressure to the gauze or instruct the patient to do so. The patient may elevate the arm but should not bend it.	5	_____	_____	_____
19. Label the tubes with the patient's name, the date, and the time.	5	_____	_____	_____
20. Check the puncture site for bleeding or a hematoma.	5	_____	_____	_____
21. Apply a hypoallergenic bandage.	2	_____	_____	_____
22. Disinfect the work area, then remove your gloves and sanitize your hands. Dispose of any blood-contaminated materials, such as gauze, in the biohazardous waste container, remove your gloves, and sanitize your hands.	5	_____	_____	_____
23. Complete the laboratory requisition and route to the proper place. In the following Documentation in the Medical Record section, record the procedure as you would in the patient's record.	5	_____	_____	_____

Documentation in the Medical Record:

Comments:

Points earned _____ ÷ 100 possible points = Score _____ % Score

Instructor's signature _____

Name _____ Date _____ Score _____

PROCEDURE 53-3 Perform Venipuncture: Obtain a Venous Sample with a Winged Infusion Set (Butterfly Needle)

CAAHEP COMPETENCIES: I.AI.2, I.PI.2, I.PI.12, III.PIII.2, III.PIII.3, III.PIII7, III.AIII.1, III.AIII.2
ABHES COMPETENCIES: 9.e, 10.c, 10.d.1

TASK: To obtain a venous sample accurately from a hand vein using a winged infusion set.

Equipment and Supplies
- Tourniquet
- Alcohol pads or other antiseptic preps
- Sterile gauze pads
- Winged infusion ("butterfly") needle set with safety needle device
- Appropriate tubes with a needle and needle adapter
- Syringe with needle
- Sharps disposal container
- Nonallergenic bandage
- Permanent marking pen or printed labels
- Biohazardous waste container
- Disposable gloves
- Patient's record

Standards: Complete the procedure and all critical steps in _____ minutes with a minimum score of 85% within three attempts.

Scoring: Divide the points earned by the total possible points. Failure to perform a critical step, indicated by an asterisk (*), results in an unsatisfactory overall score.

Time began _____   Time ended _____   Total minutes: _____

Steps	Possible Points	Attempt 1	Attempt 2	Attempt 3
1. Check the requisition and gather the appropriate tubes for the ordered tests. Assemble the balance of your supplies.	5	_____	_____	_____
2. Sanitize your hands and put on gloves.	5	_____	_____	_____
*3. Identify the patient and explain the procedure.	5	_____	_____	_____
4. Remove the butterfly device from the package and stretch the tubing slightly. Take care not to activate the needle-retracting safety device accidentally.	5	_____	_____	_____
5. Attach the butterfly device to the syringe or needle holder.	5	_____	_____	_____
6. Seat the first tube into the evacuated tube holder and put the unit carefully in a place where it will not roll away.	5	_____	_____	_____
7. Apply a tourniquet to the patient's wrist, just proximal to the wrist bone. Do not apply the tourniquet so tightly that blood flow in the arteries is impeded.	5	_____	_____	_____
8. With your nondominant hand, hold the patient's hand with the fingers lower than the wrist.	5	_____	_____	_____

517

Steps	Possible Points	Attempt 1	Attempt 2	Attempt 3
9. Select a vein and cleanse the site at the bifurcation (forking) of the veins.	5	_____	_____	_____
10. Using your thumb, pull the patient's skin taut over the knuckles.	5	_____	_____	_____
11. With the needle at a 10- to 15-degree angle, bevel up, align it with the vein.	5	_____	_____	_____
*12. Insert the needle by holding the wings or the rear of the set. After insertion the wings are never touched again. Make sure the safety device is not activated.	10	_____	_____	_____
*13. Draw blood into the syringe or push the blood-collecting tube onto the end of the holder. Note the position of the hands while drawing the blood. When drawing blood into the syringe, make sure the vacuum you create is slow and steady and that no more than 1mL of head space is seen between the blood and the plunger.	10	_____	_____	_____
14. Release the tourniquet when the blood appears in the tube or a "flash" of blood is seen in the hub of the syringe.	10	_____	_____	_____
15. Always keep the tube and the holder in a downward position so that the tube fills from the bottom up.	5	_____	_____	_____
16. Place a gauze pad over the puncture site and gently remove the needle, engaging the safety needle device. Dispose of the entire unit in the sharps container.	5	_____	_____	_____
17. Complete the procedure as you would for an antecubital draw (see Procedure 53-2 in the text, steps 19 to 23). In the following Documentation in the Medical Record section, record the procedure as you would in the patient's medical record.	5	_____	_____	_____

Documentation in the Medical Record:

Comments:

Points earned _____ ÷ **100 possible points = Score** _____ **% Score**

Instructor's signature _____

Name _____ Date _____ Score _____

PROCEDURE 53-4 Perform Capillary Puncture: Obtain a Capillary Blood Specimen by Fingertip Puncture

CAAHEP COMPETENCIES: I.AI.2, I.PI.3, I.PI.12, III.PIII.2, III.PIII.3, III.PIII7, III.AIII.1, III.AIII.2
ABHES COMPETENCIES: 9.e, 10.c, 10.d.2

TASK: To collect a capillary blood specimen suitable for testing using fingertip puncture technique.

Equipment and Supplies
- Sterile disposable safety lancet
- 70% alcohol prep pads
- Sterile gauze pads
- Nonallergenic tape
- Appropriate collection containers (e.g., capillary tubes or Microtainer devices)
- Sealing clay or caps for capillary tubes
- Permanent marking pen or printed label
- Biohazardous waste and Sharps containers
- Disposable gloves
- Patient's record

Standards: Complete the procedure and all critical steps in _____ minutes with a minimum score of 85% within three attempts.

Scoring: Divide the points earned by the total possible points. Failure to perform a critical step, indicated by an asterisk (*), results in an unsatisfactory overall score.

Time began _____ Time ended _____ Total minutes: _____

Steps	Possible Points	Attempt 1	Attempt 2	Attempt 3
1. Check the requisition and gather all needed supplies.	5	_____	_____	_____
2. Sanitize your hands and put on nonsterile gloves.	5	_____	_____	_____
*3. Identify the patient and explain the procedure.	5	_____	_____	_____
4. Select a puncture site according to the patient's age and the sample to be obtained (i.e., the side of the middle finger of the nondominant hand; the medial or lateral curved surface of the heel for an infant).	10	_____	_____	_____
5. Gently rub the finger along the sides.	5	_____	_____	_____
6. Clean the site with alcohol and dry it with sterile gauze or allow it to air dry.	5	_____	_____	_____
7. With your nondominant forefinger and thumb, grasp the patient's finger on the sides near the puncture site.	5	_____	_____	_____
8. Hold the lancet at a right angle to the patient's finger and make a rapid, deep puncture on the side of the fingertip.	5	_____	_____	_____
*9. Dispose of the lancet in the sharps container. Wipe away the first drop of blood with sterile gauze.	5	_____	_____	_____

519

Steps	Possible Points	Attempt 1	Attempt 2	Attempt 3
10. Apply gentle pressure to cause the blood to flow freely.	5	_____	_____	_____
*11. Collect the blood samples:	10			
a. Express a large drop of blood, touch the end of the tube to the drop of blood (not the finger), fill the capillary tubes, place the finger over the blood-free end of the tube, and seal the other end of the tube by inserting it into the sealing clay. The tube should be approximately three-fourths full before it is sealed.		_____	_____	_____
b. Wipe the finger with a sterile gauze pad, express another large drop of blood, and fill a Microtainer. Do not touch the container to the finger. If more blood is needed, wipe the puncture with sterile gauze and gently squeeze another drop. Cap the tube when collection is complete.		_____	_____	_____
12. Apply pressure to the site with sterile gauze when collection is complete. The patient may be able to assist with this step.	5	_____	_____	_____
13. Select an appropriate means of labeling the containers. Capillary tubes can be placed in a red-topped tube, which is subsequently labeled. Microtainers can be placed in zipper-lock bags that are subsequently labeled.	5	_____	_____	_____
14. Check the patient for bleeding, clean the site if traces of blood are visible, and apply a nonallergenic bandage if indicated.	5	_____	_____	_____
15. Dispose of used materials in the proper containers.	5	_____	_____	_____
16. Disinfect the work area. Dispose of any blood-contaminated materials, such as gauze, in the biohazardous waste container. Remove your gloves and sanitize your hands	5	_____	_____	_____
17. In the following Documentation in the Medical Record section, record the procedure as you would in the patient's medical record.	5	_____	_____	_____

Documentation in the Medical Record:

Comments:

Points earned _____ ÷ 100 possible points = Score _____ % Score

Instructor's signature _____

Name _____ Date _____ Score _____

PROCEDURE 54-1 Perform Hematology Testing: Perform a Microhematocrit Test

CAAHEP COMPETENCIES: I.PI.12, III.PIII.2, III.PIII.3
ABHES COMPETENCIES: 9.a, 10.b.2, 10.c

TASK: To perform a microhematocrit test accurately.

Equipment and Supplies
- Fresh sample of blood collected in a tube containing EDTA anticoagulant
- Capillary tubes
- Sealing clay
- Centrifuge
- Disposable gloves
- Protective eyewear
- Biohazardous waste and Sharps containers
- Patient's record

Standards: Complete the procedure and all critical steps in _____ minutes with a minimum score of 85% within three attempts.

Scoring: Divide the points earned by the total possible points. Failure to perform a critical step, indicated by an asterisk (*), results in an unsatisfactory overall score.

Time began _____ Time ended _____ Total minutes: _____

Steps	Possible Points	Attempt 1	Attempt 2	Attempt 3
1. Sanitize your hands. Put on nonsterile gloves and protective eyewear.	5	_____	_____	_____
2. Assemble the necessary materials.	5	_____	_____	_____
*3. Fill two plain (blue-tipped) capillary tubes two-thirds to three-fourths full with well-mixed blood by tipping the blood tube slightly and touching the end of the capillary tube opposite the blue band to the blood. If the capillary tube and the blood tube are held almost parallel to the table, the capillary tube fills easily by capillary action.	10	_____	_____	_____
4. Wipe the outside of the tubes with clean gauze without touching the wet, open end of the tubes.	5	_____	_____	_____
5. Tip the tube until the blood runs toward the end with the colored band.	10	_____	_____	_____
6. Seal the end with the blue band with sealing clay by holding the tube horizontally and inserting the tube into the clay. Insert the tube as many times as needed to achieve a plug up to the blue band.	10	_____	_____	_____
7. Place the tubes opposite each other in the centrifuge with the sealed ends securely against the gasket.	5	_____	_____	_____

Steps	Possible Points	Attempt 1	Attempt 2	Attempt 3
8. Record the numbers on the centrifuge slots.	5	_____	_____	_____
*9. Secure the locking top, fasten the lid down, and lock it.	5	_____	_____	_____
10. Set the timer and adjust the speed as needed.	5	_____	_____	_____
*11. Allow the centrifuge to come to a complete stop. Unlock the lids.	5	_____	_____	_____
12. Remove the tubes immediately and read the results. If this is not possible, store the tubes in an upright position.	5	_____	_____	_____
13. Determine the microhematocrit values using one of two methods.	10			
a. Centrifuge with built-in reader using calibrated capillary tubes:				
• Position the tubes according to the manufacturer's instructions.		_____	_____	_____
• Read both tubes.		_____	_____	_____
• Report the average of the two results.		_____	_____	_____
• The two values should not vary by more than 2%.		_____	_____	_____
b. Centrifuge without a built-in reader:				
• Carefully remove the tubes from the centrifuge.		_____	_____	_____
• Place a tube on the microhematocrit reader.		_____	_____	_____
• Align the clay-RBC junction with the zero line on the reader. Align the plasma meniscus with the 100% line. The value is read at the junction of the red cell layer and the buffy coat. The buffy coat is not included in the reading.		_____		
• Read both tubes.		_____	_____	_____
• Report the average of the two results.		_____	_____	_____
• The two values should not vary by more than 2%.		_____	_____	_____
14. Dispose of the capillary tubes in a sharps container.	5	_____	_____	_____
15. Disinfect the work area and properly dispose of all biohazardous materials. Remove your gloves and eyewear and sanitize your hands.	5	_____	_____	_____
16. In the following Documentation in the Medical Record section, record the results as you would in the patient's medical record.	5	_____	_____	_____

Documentation in the Medical Record:

Comments:

Points earned _____ ÷ 100 possible points = Score _____ % Score

Instructor's signature _____

523

PROCEDURE 54-2 Perform Routine Maintenance of Clinical Equipment: Perform Preventive Maintenance for the Microhematocrit Centrifuge

CAAHEP COMPETENCIES: V.pV.9
ABHES COMPETENCIES: 8.e, 10.a

TASK: To perform daily, monthly, and quarterly quality control on a microhematocrit centrifuge

Equipment and Supplies
- Microhematocrit centrifuge
- Quality control logbook
- High, normal, and low quality control samples
- Utility gloves
- Disposable gloves
- Face shield, moisture-proof gown as needed
- Disinfectant
- Biohazardous waste container
- Maintenance logbook

Standards: Complete the procedure and all critical steps in _____ minutes with a minimum score of 85% within three attempts.

Scoring: Divide the points earned by the total possible points. Failure to perform a critical step, indicated by an asterisk (*), results in an unsatisfactory overall score.

Time began _____   **Time ended** _____   **Total minutes:** _____

Steps	Possible Points	Attempt 1	Attempt 2	Attempt 3
NOTE: These are generic recommendations. Always check manufacturer's guidelines for specific instructions. Always unplug the power cord before cleaning or servicing the centrifuge. Wear protective gloves, face shield, and clothing.				
Daily Maintenance				
1. Clean the inside of the centrifuge and the gasket with a disinfectant recommended by the manufacturer. Plastic and nonmetal parts can be cleaned with a fresh solution of 5% sodium hypochlorite (bleach) mixed 1:10 with water (1 part bleach to 9 parts water).	10	_____	_____	_____
Monthly Maintenance				
1. Check the reading device. Misuse and zeroing of the reading devices can promote considerable error. Always use a second, simple reading device as a cross-check. A ruler or flat plastic card can be used; lay the spun hematocrit tube on the card and align the red cells with a line on the card to obtain the reading.	10	_____	_____	_____
2. Check the rotor for cracks or corrosion and check the interior for signs of white powder.	10	_____	_____	_____
3. Record all preventive maintenance in the laboratory logbook.	10	_____	_____	_____

525

Steps	Possible Points	Attempt 1	Attempt 2	Attempt 3
Semiannual Maintenance				
1. Check the gasket for cuts and breaks.	10	_____	_____	_____
2. Check the timer with a stopwatch.	10	_____	_____	_____
3. Perform a maximum cell pack to verify the time required for complete packing. This is done by reading a sample after centrifugation and then recentrifuging for 1 minute. The results should be the same. If they are not, perform preventive maintenance and/or call the service technician.	10	_____	_____	_____
4. Record all preventive measures in the laboratory logbook.	10	_____	_____	_____
Annual Maintenance or Maintenance Performed as Needed				
1. The centrifuge's functions and maintenance verification should be performed by qualified personnel. It includes checking the centrifuge's mechanism, rotors, timer, and speed and checking for electrical leaks.	10	_____	_____	_____
2. Record all professional service calls in the laboratory logbook.	10	_____	_____	_____

Comments:

Points earned _____ ÷ 100 possible points = Score _____ % Score

Instructor's signature _____

Name _____ Date _____ Score _____

PROCEDURE 54-3 Perform Hematology Testing: Perform a Hemoglobin Test

CAAHEP COMPETENCIES: I.PI.12, III.PIII.2, III.PIII.3, III.AIII.2
ABHES COMPETENCIES: 9.a, 10.a, 10.b.2, 10.c

TASK: To determine accurately the level of hemoglobin present in a blood sample using the HemoCue B-Hemoglobin System.

Equipment and Supplies
- Hemo-Cue (Hemo-Cue, Lake Forest, Calif.)
- Hemo-Cue cuvette
- Autolet or blood lancet
- Alcohol preps
- Gauze squares
- Disposable gloves
- Sharps container
- Biohazardous waste container
- Patient's record

Standards: Complete the procedure and all critical steps in _____ minutes with a minimum score of 85% within three attempts.

Scoring: Divide the points earned by the total possible points. Failure to perform a critical step, indicated by an asterisk (*), results in an unsatisfactory overall score.

Time began _____ Time ended _____ Total minutes: _____

Steps	Possible Points	Attempt 1	Attempt 2	Attempt 3
*1. Perform instrument quality control by inserting the control cuvette into the instrument. Make sure the reading is within acceptable limits before proceeding.	10	_____	_____	_____
2. Sanitize your hands.	5	_____	_____	_____
3. Assemble all necessary equipment and supplies.	5	_____	_____	_____
*4. Explain the procedure to the patient.	5	_____	_____	_____
5. Put on gloves.	5	_____	_____	_____
6. Examine the patient's fingers and choose the site to be used for obtaining the blood sample.	5	_____	_____	_____
7. Clean the site with alcohol or other recommended antiseptic preparation.	5	_____	_____	_____
8. Perform a capillary puncture and obtain the blood sample.	10	_____	_____	_____
*9. Wipe away the first drop of blood.	5	_____	_____	_____

Steps	Possible Points	Attempt 1	Attempt 2	Attempt 3
*10. Touch the microcuvette to the drop of blood. Do not touch the finger. The correct volume will be drawn into the cuvette by capillary action. Wipe off any excess blood on the sides of the cuvette.	10	_____	_____	_____
11. Place the cuvette in the cuvette holder and insert it into the instrument.	10	_____	_____	_____
12. Read the result. In the following Documentation in the Medical Record section, record the result as you would in the patient's medical record.	10	_____	_____	_____
13. Dispose of the biohazardous waste in the correct containers and properly disinfect the work area. Turn off the instrument and return it to the proper storage location.	10	_____	_____	_____
14. Remove your gloves and sanitize your hands.	5	_____	_____	_____

Documentation in the Medical Record:

Comments:

Points earned _____ ÷ 100 possible points = Score _____ % Score

Instructor's signature _____

PROCEDURE 54-4 Perform Hematology Testing: Determine the Erythrocyte Sedimentation Rate Using a Modified Westergren Method

CAAHEP COMPETENCIES: I.PI.12, III.PIII.2, III.PIII.3
ABHES COMPETENCIES: 9.a, 10.a, 10.b.2, 10.c

TASK: To fill a Westergren tube properly and to observe and record an erythrocyte sedimentation rate (ESR) obtained by using the Westergren method.

Equipment and Supplies
- EDTA-anticoagulated blood specimen
- Safety tube decapper
- Sediplast ESR system
- Sediplast rack
- Timer
- Disposable gloves
- Face protector/shield
- Biohazardous waste container
- Patient's record

Standards: Complete the procedure and all critical steps in _____ minutes with a minimum score of 85% within three attempts.

Scoring: Divide the points earned by the total possible points. Failure to perform a critical step, indicated by an asterisk (*), results in an unsatisfactory overall score.

Time began _____   Time ended _____   Total minutes: _____

Steps	Possible Points	Attempt 1	Attempt 2	Attempt 3
1. Sanitize your hands. Put on nonsterile gloves and face protection.	5	_____	_____	_____
2. Assemble the necessary materials.	5	_____	_____	_____
3. Check the leveling bubble of the Sediplast rack.	5	_____	_____	_____
*4. If the blood sample has been refrigerated, bring it to room temperature. Then mix the sample well by inverting the tube gently several times, making sure no bubbles are present.	10	_____	_____	_____
5. Remove the stopper on the blood sample using a tube decapper. Also remove the stopper on the prefilled Sediplast vial.	10	_____	_____	_____
6. Fill the Sediplast vial to the indicated line. Then replace the stopper on the vial and invert it several times to mix. Recap the blood collection tube.	10	_____	_____	_____
*7. Insert the Sediplast pipet through the pierceable stopper on the vial; push down until the pipet touches the bottom of the vial. The pipet automatically draws the blood up to the zero mark.	10	_____	_____	_____
8. Insert the pipet and the vial into the rack, making sure the vial is vertical.	10	_____	_____	_____

529

Steps	Possible Points	Attempt 1	Attempt 2	Attempt 3
9. Allow the vial to stand undisturbed for 60 minutes.	10	_____	_____	_____
10. Measure the distance the erythrocytes have fallen. The scale reads in millimeters, and each line is 1 mm.	10	_____	_____	_____
11. Disinfect the work area and properly dispose of all biohazardous materials. Dispose of the pipet in the biohazardous waste container. Remove your face protection and gloves and sanitize your hands.	5	_____	_____	_____
12. In the following Documentation in the Medical Record section, record the findings as you would in the patient's medical record.	10	_____	_____	_____

Documentation in the Medical Record:

Comments:

Points earned _____ ÷ 100 possible points = Score _____ % Score

Instructor's signature _____

PROCEDURE 54-5 Perform Hematology Testing: Determine the ABO Group Using a Slide Test

CAAHEP COMPETENCIES: I.PI.12, III.PIII.2, III.PIII.3, III.AIII.2
ABHES COMPETENCIES: 9.a, 10.a, 10.b.2, 10.c

TASK: To determine a patient's ABO group accurately using the slide test technique.

NOTE: Because of the serious implications of incorrect blood typing, ABO and Rh typing are not routinely performed in a physician's office laboratory. These tests are performed in a hospital or blood banking facility.

Equipment and Supplies
- Glass slides with frosted ends
- Anti-A and anti-B serum
- Applicator sticks
- Lancet and automatic finger puncture device with safety device
- Alcohol preps
- Sterile gauze squares
- Bandage strip
- Laboratory marking pen or pencil
- Disposable gloves
- Face protector/shield
- Sharps container
- Biohazardous waste container
- Patient's record

Standards: Complete the procedure and all critical steps in _____ minutes with a minimum score of 85% within three attempts.

Scoring: Divide the points earned by the total possible points. Failure to perform a critical step, indicated by an asterisk (*), results in an unsatisfactory overall score.

Time began _____   Time ended _____   Total minutes: _____

Steps	Possible Points	Attempt 1	Attempt 2	Attempt 3
1. Assemble all necessary supplies and equipment.	5	____	____	____
2. Sanitize your hands and put on face protection and gloves.	5	____	____	____
*3. Explain the procedure to the patient.	5	____	____	____
4. Label the slides in the frosted area with the patient's name.	5	____	____	____
5. Place one drop of anti-A serum on slide 1, one drop of anti-B serum on slide 2, and one drop of anti-A and anti-B serum on slide 3.	10	____	____	____
6. Select the puncture site and perform a finger puncture.	5	____	____	____
*7. Wipe away the first drop of blood.	5	____	____	____
8. Place one large drop of blood on each of the three prepared slides, close to but not touching the drop of antiserum.	10	____	____	____
9. Cover the puncture site with a sterile gauze square and instruct the patient to apply gentle pressure to the site.	5	____	____	____

531

Steps	Possible Points	Attempt 1	Attempt 2	Attempt 3
*10. Mix the antiserum and blood thoroughly, using a clean applicator stick for each slide. Rock the slide after mixing to check for agglutination. The mixture should be spread over an area approximately 20 × 40 mm.	10	_____	_____	_____
11. Read and interpret the results of the reaction for all slides.	10	_____	_____	_____
12. Make sure the patient has stopped bleeding; apply a bandage to the puncture site if needed.	5	_____	_____	_____
13. Discard all biohazardous waste in the appropriate container.	5	_____	_____	_____
14. Disinfect the testing area and sanitize your hands.	5	_____	_____	_____
15. In the following Documentation in the Medical Record section, record the test results as you would in the patient's medical record.	10	_____	_____	_____

Documentation in the Medical Record:

Comments:

Points earned _____ ÷ 100 possible points = Score _____ % Score

Instructor's signature _____

Name _____ Date _____ Score _____

PROCEDURE 54-6 Perform Hematology Testing: Determine the Rh Factor Using the Slide Method

CAAHEP COMPETENCIES: I.PI.12, III.PIII.2, III.PIII.3
ABHES COMPETENCIES: 9.a, 10.a, 10.b.2, 10.c

TASK: To determine accurately the presence or absence of anti-D agglutinations.

Equipment and Supplies
- Two glass slides with frosted ends
- Anti-D serum
- Applicator sticks
- Lancet and automatic finger puncture device with safety devices
- Alcohol preps
- Sterile gauze squares
- Laboratory marker or pencil
- Disposable gloves
- Face protector/shield
- Biohazardous waste and Sharps containers
- Patient's record

Standards: Complete the procedure and all critical steps in _____ minutes with a minimum score of 85% within three attempts.

Scoring: Divide the points earned by the total possible points. Failure to perform a critical step, indicated by an asterisk (*), results in an unsatisfactory overall score.

Time began _____ Time ended _____ Total minutes: _____

Steps	Possible Points	Attempt 1	Attempt 2	Attempt 3
1. Assemble all necessary equipment and supplies.	5	_____	_____	_____
2. Sanitize your hands and put on face protection and gloves.	5	_____	_____	_____
3. Label one slide D and the other slide C.	5	_____	_____	_____
4. Place one drop of anti-D serum on the D slide.	10	_____	_____	_____
5. Place one drop of the appropriate control reagent on the C slide.	10	_____	_____	_____
6. Perform a capillary puncture to secure a blood sample.	10	_____	_____	_____
7. To each slide add one large drop of the patient's blood, close to but not touching the antiserum.	10	_____	_____	_____
*8. Thoroughly mix the blood with the anti-D serum and the control, using a clean applicator stick for each slide. Spread the reaction mixture over an area approximately 20 × 40 mm on each slide.	10	_____	_____	_____
9. Place the slide on an Rh view box.	5	_____	_____	_____
10. Read the results immediately.	10	_____	_____	_____

Steps	Possible Points	Attempt 1	Attempt 2	Attempt 3
11. Discard all disposable equipment in the proper biohazardous waste containers.	5	_____	_____	_____
12. Disinfect the area. Remove your gloves and face protection and sanitize your hands.	5	_____	_____	_____
13. In the following Documentation in the Medical Record section, record the test results as you would in the patient's medical record.	10	_____	_____	_____

Documentation in the Medical Record:

Comments:

Points earned _____ ÷ 100 possible points = Score _____ % Score

Instructor's signature _____

PROCEDURE 54-7 Perform Chemistry Testing: Determine the Cholesterol Level Using a ProAct Testing Device

CAAHEP COMPETENCIES: I.PI.12, III.PIII.2, III.PIII.3
ABHES COMPETENCIES: 9.a, 10.a, 10.b.3, 10.c

TASK: To perform a ProAct test for the total cholesterol level and to report the results accurately.

Equipment and Supplies
- ProAct testing device
- Sterile gauze
- Lithium heparin
- Alcohol preps
- Capillary tube and capillary pipet
- Lancets and lancet device with safety device
- Disposable gloves
- Sharps container
- Biohazardous waste container
- Patient's record

Standards: Complete the procedure and all critical steps in _____ minutes with a minimum score of 85% within three attempts.

Scoring: Divide the points earned by the total possible points. Failure to perform a critical step, indicated by an asterisk (*), results in an unsatisfactory overall score.

Time began _____   Time ended _____   Total minutes: _____

Steps	Possible Points	Attempt 1	Attempt 2	Attempt 3
1. Reread the physician's order and assemble all necessary supplies and equipment.	2	_____	_____	_____
2. Sanitize your hands and put on gloves.	2	_____	_____	_____
*3. Explain the procedure to the patient.	2	_____	_____	_____
4. Load the lancet device with a sterile lancet.	2	_____	_____	_____
5. Examine the patient's index and ring fingers and pick a puncture site.	2	_____	_____	_____
6. Cleanse the chosen puncture site with alcohol and allow the site to air dry.	5	_____	_____	_____
7. Perform the puncture and wipe away the first drop of blood with a sterile gauze square.	5	_____	_____	_____
*8. Hold the capillary tube horizontally by the colored end and allow the tube to fill. Do not allow air bubbles to enter the tube; if this occurs, discard the capillary tube and continue drawing the sample with a new tube.	10	_____	_____	_____
9. Have the patient apply pressure to the puncture site with a sterile gauze square.	5	_____	_____	_____

535

Steps	Possible Points	Attempt 1	Attempt 2	Attempt 3
10. Remove a cholesterol testing strip from the container and then immediately close the container.	5	_____	_____	_____
11. Remove the foil protecting the test area of the strip and place the strip on a dry, hard, flat surface.	5	_____	_____	_____
12. Attach the capillary tube filled with blood to the pipet.	5	_____	_____	_____
13. Squeeze the plunger of the pipet completely to allow a drop of blood to form at the end of the capillary tube.	5	_____	_____	_____
14. Allow the drop of blood to fall onto the center of the red mesh application zone. Make sure the tip of the capillary tube does not touch the test strip and that all blood is dispensed.	10	_____	_____	_____
15. Allow the sample to soak into the red mesh for 3 to 15 seconds.	5	_____	_____	_____
16. Insert the cholesterol strip into the test port. The ProAct device counts down approximately 160 seconds.	5	_____	_____	_____
17. Remove the capillary tube from the pipet and discard it in the biohazardous waste container.	5	_____	_____	_____
18. When the measurement time is completed, REMOVE STRIP appears in the LED display window. Remove the test strip; the test result appears on the display.	5	_____	_____	_____
19. Examine the test area of the testing strip for uneven color development. Then discard it in the biohazardous waste container.	5	_____	_____	_____
20. Discard all biohazardous waste in the appropriate containers. Disinfect the testing area, then remove your gloves and sanitize your hands.	5	_____	_____	_____
21. In the following Documentation in the Medical Record section, record the test results as you would in the patient's medical record.	5	_____	_____	_____

Documentation in the Medical Record:

Comments:

Points earned _____ ÷ 100 possible points = Score _____ % Score

Instructor's signature _____

Name _____ Date _____ Score _____

PROCEDURE 55-1 Instruct Patients According to Their Needs: Instruct Patients in the Collection of Fecal Specimens to Be Tested for Ova and Parasites

CAAHEP COMPETENCIES: I.AI.2, III.PIII.2, III.PIII.3, III.PIII.7, III.AIII.2, IV.PIV.5
ABHES COMPETENCIES: 9.e, 10.d, 10.e.2

TASK: To instruct a patient in the proper collection of stool for an ova and parasite microscopic examination.

Equipment and Supplies
- Clean, dry container for stool collection
- Parasitology collection vials
- Plastic biohazard zipper-lock bag

Standards: Complete the procedure and all critical steps in _____ minutes with a minimum score of 85% in three attempts.

Scoring: Divide the points earned by the total possible points. Failure to perform a critical step, indicated by an asterisk (*), results in an unsatisfactory overall score.

Time began _____ Time ended _____ Total minutes: _____

Steps	Possible Points	Attempt 1	Attempt 2	Attempt 3
1. Make sure the patient has not taken any antacids, laxatives, or stool softeners before collecting the specimen.	10	_____	_____	_____
2. Instruct the patient to urinate before collecting the specimen.	10	_____	_____	_____
*3. Instruct the patient in how to collect the specimen as follows:	20			
a. *Adults:* Instruct the patient to defecate into the container. Stool cannot be retrieved from the toilet bowl.				
b. *Children:* Loosely drape the toilet rim with plastic wrap and lower the seat. Instruct the child to defecate into the toilet, onto the wrap. Remove the stool with a disposable plastic spoon.				
c. *Infants:* Fasten a "diaper" made of plastic wrap over the child using tape or diaper pins. Remove the plastic wrap immediately after a bowel movement and remove the stool using a plastic spoon. To prevent the risk of suffocation, a child should never be left unattended with the plastic wrap in place.		_____	_____	_____
4. Instruct the patient to add stool to the collection container:	20			
a. If the stool is formed, use the scoop on the lid of the container to add a large, jelly bean–sized piece of stool to the liquid in the containers.		_____	_____	_____
b. If the stool is liquid, pour it into the container until the preservative in the vial reaches the indicated level in the containers.		_____	_____	_____

539

Steps	Possible Points	Attempt 1	Attempt 2	Attempt 3
5. Instruct the patient to tighten the caps completely and wipe the outside of the vials with rubbing alcohol or to wash them carefully with soap and water.	20	_____	_____	_____
6. Instruct the patient to label the vials and transport them to the laboratory immediately if possible. The patient should not refrigerate the vials.	10	_____	_____	_____
7. Instruct the patient to wash his or her hands after the procedure.	10	_____	_____	_____

Documentation in the Medical Record:

Comments:

Points earned _____ ÷ 100 possible points = Score _____ % Score

Instructor's signature _____

Name _____ Date _____ Score _____

PROCEDURE 55-2 Inoculate a Blood Agar Plate to Culture (*Streptococcus pyogenes*)

CAAHEP COMPETENCIES: III.PIII.2, III.PIII.3, III.PIII.7
ABHES COMPETENCIES: 9.a, 9.e, 10.b.5

TASK: To inoculate a blood agar plate for the detection of the etiologic agent of "strep throat."

Equipment and Supplies

- Blood agar plate
- Bacitracin disk or strep A disk
- Incinerator
- Inoculating loop
- Permanent marker or printed label
- Swab from patient's throat (see Procedure 37-8 in the text)
- Forceps
- Bacti-Cinerator
- Disposable gloves
- Biohazardous waste container
- Face protection

Standards: Complete the procedure and all critical steps in _____ minutes with a minimum score of 85% in three attempts.

Scoring: Divide the points earned by the total possible points. Failure to perform a critical step, indicated by an asterisk (*), results in an unsatisfactory overall score.

Time began _____   **Time ended** _____   **Total minutes:** _____

Steps	Possible Points	Attempt 1	Attempt 2	Attempt 3
1. Sanitize your hands. Put on face protection and gloves.	5	_____	_____	_____
2. Remove the swab from the transport device. Grasp the plate by the bottom (media side) and lift the base from the cover; or, lift the cover while the plate is on the table.	10	_____	_____	_____
3. Roll the swab down the middle of the top half of the plate and then use the swab to streak back and forth on the same half of the plate. Dispose of the swab properly.	10	_____	_____	_____
4. Sterilize a loop in the Bacti-Cinerator and allow it to cool.	10	_____	_____	_____
5. Using the loop, streak for isolation of colonies in the second, third, and fourth quadrants. Pull the loop over the surface of the agar, pulling some of the inoculum into the uninoculated portion of the plate and then spreading it around. Flame the loop again and pull some of the inoculum from the second area into the third area.	10	_____	_____	_____
*6. Use the loop to make three slices approximately 1 cm long in the agar in the heavy inoculum–swabbed area. Sterilize the loop.	10	_____	_____	_____

Procedure **55-2 Inoculate a Blood Agar Plate**

Steps	Possible Points	Attempt 1	Attempt 2	Attempt 3
7. Sterilize the forceps and remove one disk from the bacitracin vial. Place a bacitracin differentiation disk on the agar in the first quadrant. Sterilize the forceps.	10	_____	_____	_____
8. With permanent marker, or a printed label, label the agar side of the plate with the patient's name and identification number and the date.	10	_____	_____	_____
9. Place the plate in the incubator in an inverted position.	5	_____	_____	_____
10. Incubate the plate for 24 hours and then examine it.	5	_____	_____	_____
11. Incubate negative cultures for an additional 24 hours.	5	_____	_____	_____
12. Disinfect the work area and properly dispose of all biohazardous waste.	5	_____	_____	_____
13. Remove your gloves and sanitize your hands.	5	_____	_____	_____

Documentation in the Medical Record:

Comments:

Points earned _____ ÷ 100 possible points = Score _____ % Score

Instructor's signature _____

542

Name _____ Date _____ Score _____

PROCEDURE 55-3 Perform a Urine Culture

CAAHEP COMPETENCIES: III.PIII.2, III.PIII.3, III.PIII.7
ABHES COMPETENCIES: 9.a, 9.e, 10.b.5

TASK: To inoculate three plates with 1 mL of urine in order to quantitate the number of bacteria and aid in the diagnosis of a urinary tract infection.

Equipment and Supplies
- Urine specimen, collected CCMS in a sterile container
- Bacti-Cinerator
- 1 mL calibrated inoculating loop
- Blood agar plate, MacConkey agar plate, and Columbia nutrient agar plate (or an appropriate selection of all-purpose, differential, and selective media)
- Permanent marker or printed label
- Disposable gloves
- Face protection
- Biohazard waste container

Standards: Complete the procedure and all critical steps in _____ minutes with a minimum score of 85% in three attempts.

Scoring: Divide the points earned by the total possible points. Failure to perform a critical step, indicated by an asterisk (*), results in an unsatisfactory overall score.

Time began _____   Time ended _____   Total minutes: _____

Steps	Possible Points	Attempt 1	Attempt 2	Attempt 3
1. Sanitize your hands. Put on face protection and gloves.	10	_____	_____	_____
2. With the screw-cap lid in place on the sterile container, mix the urine specimen thoroughly by swirling.	10	_____	_____	_____
3. Sterilize the calibrated loop, cool it, and dip the tip into the specimen.	10	_____	_____	_____
*4. Spread the urine on the plate by "painting" the specimen down the center of the plate and then streaking thoroughly at right angles.	10	_____	_____	_____
5. Inoculate the second and third plates in the same manner.	10	_____	_____	_____
6. Label the bottom of the plates with the patient's name and identification number and the date, using a permanent marker or printed label.	10	_____	_____	_____
7. Place the plates in the incubator with the agar sides facing up.	10	_____	_____	_____
8. Incubate the plates for 24 hours and then count the colonies on the all-purpose medium.	10	_____	_____	_____

Steps	Possible Points	Attempt 1	Attempt 2	Attempt 3
9. The results are interpreted by a physician or medical technologist as follows:	10			
a. >100 colonies = >100,000 colony-forming units per milliliter (cfu/mL) of urine indicates a urinary tract infection.		_____	_____	_____
b. 10 to 100 colonies = 10,000 to 100,000 cfu/mL of urine indicates suspicion. The urine may have been allowed to stand at room temperature, facilitating overgrowth of bacteria, or the patient may have a subclinical infection. Collection of another specimen is recommended.		_____	_____	_____
c. <10 colonies = 10,000 cfu/mL of urine indicates a normal urethral microbiota level.		_____	_____	_____
10. Disinfect the work area and dispose of all biohazardous waste appropriately. Then remove your gloves and sanitize your hands.	10	_____	_____	_____

Documentation in the Medical Record:

Comments:

Points earned _____ ÷ 100 possible points = Score _____ % Score

Instructor's signature _____

544

Name _____ Date _____ Score _____

PROCEDURE 55-4 Perform Microbiologic Testing: Perform a Screening Urine Culture Test

CAAHEP COMPETENCIES: III.PIII.2, III.PIII.3, III.PIII.7
ABHES COMPETENCIES: 9.a, 9.e, 10.b.5

TASK: To assess the level of bacteriuria using a dip and count method in order to aid the diagnosis of urinary tract infections.

Equipment and Supplies
- Clean-catch midstream urine specimen
- Uricult test kit
- Incubator
- Biohazardous waste container
- Disposable gloves
- Patient's record

Standards: Complete the procedure and all critical steps in _____ minutes with a minimum score of 85% in three attempts.

Scoring: Divide the points earned by the total possible points. Failure to perform a critical step, indicated by an asterisk (*), results in an unsatisfactory overall score.

Time began _____ Time ended _____ Total minutes: _____

Steps	Possible Points	Attempt 1	Attempt 2	Attempt 3
1. Sanitize your hands and assemble the necessary equipment and the specimen. Put on gloves. Check the expiration date on the test kit. Label the vial with the patient information.	10	____	____	____
2. Remove the slide from the test kit. Do not touch the slide or lay it down.	5	____	____	____
3. Dip the slide into the urine specimen, tipping the cup carefully if necessary. As an alternative, pour the urine over the slide and catch it in another container.	10	____	____	____
4. Allow excess urine to drain and then replace the slide in the protective vial. Screw the cap on loosely.	10	____	____	____
5. Place the vial upright in an incubator and incubate at 35° to 37° C (90° to 98.6° F) for 18 to 24 hours.	10	____	____	____
*6. After incubation, the test results are interpreted by removing the slide from its protective vial, assessing the bacterial colony density, and comparing the density on the slide with the density chart provided. No actual colony counting is necessary.	10	____	____	____

Steps	Possible Points	Attempt 1	Attempt 2	Attempt 3
7. The results are interpreted as follows:	10			
a. *Normal:* <10,000 colony-forming units per milliliter (cfu/mL) of urine: no UTI.		_____	_____	_____
b. *Borderline:* 10,000 to 100,000cfu/mL: chronic or relapsing infection may be present; the test should be repeated.		_____	_____	_____
c. *Positive:* >100,000cfu/mL: UTI is likely.		_____	_____	_____
8. Return the vial to the protective case and replace the cap.	10	_____	_____	_____
*9. Dispose of the test in the biohazardous waste container.	10	_____	_____	_____
10. Remove your gloves and sanitize your hands.	5	_____	_____	_____
11. In the following Documentation in the Medical Record section, record the results as you would in the patient's medical record.	10	_____	_____	_____

Documentation in the Medical Record:

Comments:

Points earned _____ ÷ 100 possible points = Score _____ % Score

Instructor's signature _____

546

PROCEDURE 55-5 Prepare a Direct Smear or Culture Smear for Staining

CAAHEP COMPETENCIES: III.PIII.2, III.PIII.3, III.PIII.7
ABHES COMPETENCIES: 9.a, 9.e, 10.b.5, 10.c

TASK: To prepare a smear from a clinical specimen or a culture medium for staining.

Equipment and Supplies

- Clean glass slides
- Permanent marker
- Incinerator
- Normal saline solution
- Specimen collected on a smear
- 24-hour culture on agar
- Biohazardous waste container
- Disposable gloves
- Face protection

Standards: Complete the procedure and all critical steps in _____ minutes with a minimum score of 85% in three attempts.

Scoring: Divide the points earned by the total possible points. Failure to perform a critical step, indicated by an asterisk (*), results in an unsatisfactory overall score.

Time began _____   **Time ended** _____   **Total minutes:** _____

Steps	Possible Points	Attempt 1	Attempt 2	Attempt 3
Direct Smear				
1. Sanitize your hands. Put on face protection and gloves.	5	_____	_____	_____
2. Label the slide with a permanent marking pen.	5	_____	_____	_____
3. Prepare a thin smear by rolling the swab on the slide. Make sure all areas of the swab touch the slide.	10	_____	_____	_____
*4. Allow the smear to air dry. Do not wave it or heat dry it.	10	_____	_____	_____
5. Hold the slide with the smear up. Heat fix the slide using an incinerator. Check the heating process by touching the slide to the back of the gloved hand. The slide should feel warm, not hot. Check it often by touching the back of the slide to the back of the gloved hand. Cool the slide.	10	_____	_____	_____

Steps	Possible Points	Attempt 1	Attempt 2	Attempt 3
Culture Smear				
1. Sanitize your hands. Put on face protection and gloves.	5	_____	_____	_____
2. Identify the colonies to be stained by circling them on the back of the plate and numbering them with a permanent marker. Label the slide accordingly.	10	_____	_____	_____
3. Using a loop, apply a small drop of saline solution to the slide	20	_____	_____	_____
*4. Using a sterile loop, touch only the top of the colony chosen. Transfer the material picked up to the appropriate area of the slide and spread it in a circular motion to the size of a dime. Repeat for each colony chosen using a separate slide.	10	_____	_____	_____
5. Allow the smear to air dry.	5	_____	_____	_____
6. Heat fix the smear as described for a direct smear.	10	_____	_____	_____
7. Properly dispose of all biohazardous materials and disinfect the work area.	5	_____	_____	_____
8. Remove your gloves and sanitize your hands.	5	_____	_____	_____

Comments:

Points earned _____ ÷ 100 possible points = Score _____ % Score

Instructor's signature _____

PROCEDURE 55-6 Screening Test Results: Perform a Rapid Strep Test

CAAHEP COMPETENCIES: II.AII.2, III.PIII.2, III.PIII.3, III.PIII.7
ABHES COMPETENCIES: 9.a, 9.e, 10.b.6.b, 10.c

TASK: To perform a rapid strep screening test to assist in the diagnosis of strep throat and to follow up negative results by performing a throat culture collection.

Equipment and Supplies

- Directigen Strep A test kit
- Timer or wristwatch with sweep second hand
- Throat swab specimen (see Procedure 37-8 in the text)
- Biohazardous waste container
- Disposable gloves
- Face protection
- Patient's record

Standards: Complete the procedure and all critical steps in _____ minutes with a minimum score of 85% in three attempts.

Scoring: Divide the points earned by the total possible points. Failure to perform a critical step, indicated by an asterisk (*), results in an unsatisfactory overall score.

Time began _____ **Time ended** _____ **Total minutes:** _____

Steps	Possible Points	Attempt 1	Attempt 2	Attempt 3
1. Collect all necessary supplies and equipment. Bring all reagents and reaction disks to room temperature (minimum of 30 minutes).	10	_____	_____	_____
2. Sanitize your hands. Put on gloves and face protection.	5	_____	_____	_____
3. Position all bottles vertically and dispense reagents slowly, as free-falling drops. Do not get reagent in your eyes, because it is an irritant.	5	_____	_____	_____
4. Add three drops of reagent 1 to an extraction tube. This solution should be pink.	5	_____	_____	_____
5. Add three drops of reagent 2 to the same tube. The solution should turn yellow.	5	_____	_____	_____
6. Place the specimen swab in the tube and twirl the swab to mix the contents.	5	_____	_____	_____
7. Let the mixture stand for exactly 1 minute.	5	_____	_____	_____
8. Add three drops of reagent 3 to the tube and again twirl the swab to mix the contents. This solution should be pink.	5	_____	_____	_____
*9. Express the liquid from the swab by squeezing the tube with the thumb and forefinger and rotating the swab as it is withdrawn. The liquid must be thoroughly removed from the swab. Best results are achieved when the liquid reaches or rises above the line on the tube.	10	_____	_____	_____

549

Steps	Possible Points	Attempt 1	Attempt 2	Attempt 3
10. Discard the swab in a biohazardous waste container.	5	_____	_____	_____
11. Remove the reaction disk from the pouch and place it on a dry, flat surface.	5	_____	_____	_____
12. Pour the entire contents of the tube into the reaction disk.	5	_____	_____	_____
13. Read the test results when the entire end of the assay window turns red (5 to 10 minutes).	5	_____	_____	_____
14. Properly dispose of all contaminated waste.	5	_____	_____	_____
15. Disinfect the work area. Then remove your gloves and sanitize your hands.	5	_____	_____	_____
16. In the following Documentation in the Medical Record section, record the test results as you would in the patient's medical record.	5	_____	_____	_____
*17. If the test results are negative, a second throat swab should be obtained and a throat culture performed. Often two swabs are used simultaneously when the sample is collected from the throat so that a repeat specimen need not be collected.	10	_____	_____	_____

Documentation in the Medical Record:

Comments:

Points earned _____ ÷ 100 possible points = Score _____ % Score

Instructor's signature _____

Name _____ Date _____ Score _____

PROCEDURE 55-7 Obtain a Specimen for Microbiologic Testing: Perform a Cellulose Tape Collection for Pinworms

CAAHEP COMPETENCIES: I.AI.2, III.PIII.2, III.PIII.3, III.PIII.7, III.AIII.2
ABHES COMPETENCIES: 9.a, 9.e, 10.b.5, 10.c, 10.d

TASK: To obtain a rectal sample using cellulose tape for the purpose of testing for pinworm eggs.

Equipment and Supplies
- Glass slide
- Clear cellulose tape
- Wooden tongue depressor
- Toluene
- Microscope
- Gauze or cotton balls
- Biohazardous waste container
- Disposable gloves
- Face protection
- Patient medical record

Standards: Complete the procedure and all critical steps in _____ minutes with a minimum score of 85% in three attempts.

Scoring: Divide the points earned by the total possible points. Failure to perform a critical step, indicated by an asterisk (*), results in an unsatisfactory overall score.

Time began _____   Time ended _____   Total minutes: _____

Steps	Possible Points	Attempt 1	Attempt 2	Attempt 3
1. Ask the patient to assist you with this procedure.	5	_____	_____	_____
2. Gather and prepare the supplies and equipment for obtaining the specimen.	5	_____	_____	_____
3. Place a strip of cellulose tape on a glass slide starting ½ inch from one end and running toward the same end. Continue around this end lengthwise. Tear off the strip so that it is even with the other end. *Note:* Use regular, clear cellulose tape, not "magic" transparent tape.	10	_____	_____	_____
4. Place a strip of paper measuring ½ × 1 inch between the slide and the tape at the end where the tape is torn flush; this is the specimen-labeling area. As soon as the child arrives, place the child and parent in the prepared examination room.	10	_____	_____	_____
5. Sanitize your hands and put on gloves and face protection.	5	_____	_____	_____
6. Remove the child's clothing (and diaper, if applicable). Lay the child in a prone position over the parent's lap with the buttocks in a superior plane.	10	_____	_____	_____

551

Steps	Possible Points	Attempt 1	Attempt 2	Attempt 3
*7. To obtain the perianal sample, first peel back the tape on the slide by gripping the label. With the tape looped (adhesive side outward) over a wooden tongue depressor that is held against the slide and extended about 1 inch beyond it, press the tape firmly against the right and left anal folds.	10	_____	_____	_____
8. Spread the tape back on the slide, adhesive side down.	5	_____	_____	_____
9. Smooth the tape using a cotton ball or gauze square.	5	_____	_____	_____
10. Write the patient's name and the date on the slide's label.	5	_____	_____	_____
11. Tell the parent the child can be dressed or assist with dressing the child if needed.	5	_____	_____	_____

Testing the Sample

Steps	Possible Points	Attempt 1	Attempt 2	Attempt 3
12. Lift one side of the tape and apply one drop of toluene before pressing the tape back down on the glass slide.	10	_____	_____	_____
13. Place the prepared slide under the microscope's low-power objective for examination by a physician or a medical technologist under low illumination.	10	_____	_____	_____
14. Record the procedure in the patient's medical record.				
15. Dispose of all biohazardous waste and disinfect the work area. Then remove your gloves and sanitize your hands.	5	_____	_____	_____

Comments:

Points earned _____ ÷ 100 possible points = Score _____ % Score

Instructor's signature _____

552

Procedure **55-7** Obtain a Specimen for Microbiologic Testing

Name _____ Date _____ Score _____

PROCEDURE 55-8 Perform Immunologic Testing: Perform the Mono-Test for Infectious Mononucleosis

CAAHEP COMPETENCIES: III.PIII.2, III.PIII.3, III.PIII.7
ABHES COMPETENCIES: 9.a, 9.e, 10.b.5, 10.c, 10.d.4

TASK: To perform and interpret a slide test for infectious mononucleosis.

Equipment and Supplies
- Mono-Test kit
- Blood specimen (serum or plasma)
- Timer or wristwatch with sweep second hand
- Biohazardous waste container
- Disposable gloves
- Face protection
- Patient's record

Standards: Complete the procedure and all critical steps in _____ minutes with a minimum score of 85% in three attempts.

Scoring: Divide the points earned by the total possible points. Failure to perform a critical step, indicated by an asterisk (*), results in an unsatisfactory overall score.

Time began _____ **Time ended** _____ **Total minutes:** _____

Steps	Possible Points	Attempt 1	Attempt 2	Attempt 3
1. Remove the test kit from the refrigerator and allow the reagents to come to room temperature. Check the kit's expiration date.	10	_____	_____	_____
2. Sanitize your hands. Put on face protection and gloves.	5	_____	_____	_____
*3. Fill a disposable capillary tube to the calibration mark with serum or plasma. Using the rubber bulb included in the kit, deposit the specimen in the first circle of the clean glass slide also provided in the kit.	10	_____	_____	_____
4. Place one drop of negative control in the second circle and one drop of positive control in the third circle.	10	_____	_____	_____
5. Thoroughly mix the Mono-Test reagent by rolling the bottle gently between your palms. Squeeze the enclosed dropper to mix all the contents of the bottle.	10	_____	_____	_____
6. Hold the dropper in a vertical position and add one drop of Mono-Test reagent to each area of the slide. Do not touch the dropper to the slide.	10	_____	_____	_____
7. Using separate stirrers, quickly and thoroughly mix each area, spreading each out so that it is 1 inch in diameter.	10	_____	_____	_____
8. Rock the slide gently for exactly 2 minutes and then observe immediately for agglutination. (A dark background is best for viewing.)	10	_____	_____	_____

553

Steps	Possible Points	Attempt 1	Attempt 2	Attempt 3
*9. Interpret and record the test result: agglutination is a positive result, and no agglutination is a negative result.	10	_____	_____	_____
10. Disinfect the work area. Then remove your gloves and sanitize your hands.	5	_____	_____	_____
11. In the following Documentation in the Medical Record section, record the test result as you would in the patient's medical record.	10	_____	_____	_____

Documentation in the Medical Record:

Comments:

Points earned _____ ÷ 100 possible points = Score _____ % Score

Instructor's signature _____

Procedure **55-8 Perform Immunologic Testing**

Name _____ Date _____ Score _____

PROCEDURE 56-1 Identify Surgical Instruments

CAAHEP COMPETENCIES: I.PI.10

TASK: To identify, correctly spell the names of, and determine the use or uses of standard office instruments or those selected by your instructor.

Equipment and Supplies
- Curved hemostat
- Straight hemostat
- Dressing (thumb) forceps
- Paper and pen
- Disposable scalpel and blade
- Dissecting scissors
- Towel clamp
- Vaginal speculum
- Bandage scissors
- Allis tissue forceps

Standards: Complete the procedure and all critical steps in _____ minutes with a minimum score of 85% within three attempts.

Scoring: Divide the points earned by the total possible points. Failure to perform a critical step, indicated by an asterisk (*), results in an unsatisfactory overall score.

Time began _____ Time ended _____ Total minutes: _____

Steps	Possible Points	Attempt 1	Attempt 2	Attempt 3
1. Look for the following parts that determine use: box-lock, serrations, finger rings, cutting edge, noncutting edge, thumb type, teeth ratchets, and electric attachments.	10	_____	_____	_____
2. Consider the general classification of the instrument: cutting and dissection, grasping and clamping, retracting, or probing and dilating.	10	_____	_____	_____
3. Carefully examine the teeth and serrations.	10	_____	_____	_____
*4. Look at the length of the instrument to determine the area of the body for which it is used.	10	_____	_____	_____
5. Try to remember whether the instrument was named for a famous physician, university, or clinic.	10	_____	_____	_____
6. If the instrument is a pair of scissors, look at the points and determine whether the tips are sharp-sharp, sharp-blunt, or blunt-blunt.	10	_____	_____	_____
7. Carefully compare the instrument with similar instruments that you know to determine whether it is in the same category or has the same name.	10	_____	_____	_____
8. Using the correct spelling, write the complete name of each instrument, including its category and use.	30	_____	_____	_____

555

Comments:

Points earned _____ ÷ 100 possible points = Score _____ % Score

Instructor's signature _____

Procedure **56-1 Identify Surgical Instruments**

PROCEDURE 57-1 Prepare Items for Autoclaving: Wrap Instruments and Supplies for Sterilization in an Autoclave

CAAHEP COMPETENCIES: III.PIII.2, III.PIII.5, III.PIII.6
ABHES COMPETENCIES: 9.e

TASK: To place dry, checked, sanitized, and disinfected supplies and instruments inside the appropriate wrapping materials for sterilization and storage without contamination.

Equipment and Supplies
- Dry, checked, sanitized, and disinfected items
- Autoclave paper or cloth wrapping material
- Autoclave tape
- Indicator tape
- Waterproof felt-tipped pen
- Disposable gloves (if specified by office policy)

Standards: Complete the procedure and all critical steps in _____ minutes with a minimum score of 85% in three attempts.

Scoring: Divide the points earned by the total possible points. Failure to perform a critical step, indicated by an asterisk (*), results in an unsatisfactory overall score.

Time began _____ **Time ended** _____ **Total minutes:** _____

Steps	Possible Points	Attempt 1	Attempt 2	Attempt 3
1. Sanitize your hands. Collect and assemble the already sanitized and disinfected items to be wrapped. Gloves may be worn.	5	_____	_____	_____
2. Place the wrapping material on a clean, flat surface.	5	_____	_____	_____
3. Place the item or items diagonally at the approximate center of the wrapping material. Make sure the square is large enough for the items.	10	_____	_____	_____
4. With cloth squares, use two pieces if the cloth is single layered. Follow the manufacturer's recommendation when using commercial autoclave wrapping paper.	10	_____	_____	_____
5. Open any hinged instruments. If the instrument is sharp, its teeth or tip should be shielded with cotton or gauze.	10	_____	_____	_____
6. If the package will have several items, put a commercial sterilization indicator inside the package at the approximate center.	10	_____	_____	_____
7. Bring up the bottom corner of the wrap and fold back a portion of it.	10	_____	_____	_____
8. Repeat step 7 with each corner, making sure to turn back a portion each time.	10	_____	_____	_____
9. Fold the last flap over.	10	_____	_____	_____

Steps	Possible Points	Attempt 1	Attempt 2	Attempt 3
10. Secure with autoclave tape.	10	_____	_____	_____
11. Secure with autoclave tape and label the package with the date (including the year), contents, and your initials.	10	_____	_____	_____

Comments:

Points earned _____ ÷ 100 possible points = **Score** _____ **% Score**

Instructor's signature _____

Name _____ Date _____ Score _____

PROCEDURE 57-2 Perform Sterilization Procedures: Operate the Autoclave

CAAHEP COMPETENCIES: III.PIII.2, III.PIII.5, III.PIII.6
ABHES COMPETENCIES: 9.e

TASK: To sterilize properly prepared supplies and instruments using the autoclave.

Equipment and Supplies
- Autoclave
- Wrapped items ready to be sterilized
- Heat-resistant gloves

Standards: Complete the procedure and all critical steps in _____ minutes with a minimum score of 85% in three attempts.

Scoring: Divide the points earned by the total possible points. Failure to perform a critical step, indicated by an asterisk (*), results in an unsatisfactory overall score.

Time began _____   Time ended _____   Total minutes: _____

Steps	Possible Points	Attempt 1	Attempt 2	Attempt 3
Note: The specific instructions for operating an autoclave may vary based on the model number and the manufacturer. Refer to the instructions that accompany the autoclave to be sure the appropriate steps are followed.				
1. Check the water level in the reservoir and add distilled water as necessary.	5	_____	_____	_____
2. Turn the control to "fill" to allow water to flow into the chamber. The water will flow until you turn the control to its next position. Do not let the water overflow.	5	_____	_____	_____
3. Load the chamber with wrapped items. Space the items for maximum circulation and penetration.	5	_____	_____	_____
4. Close and seal the door.	5	_____	_____	_____
5. Turn the control setting to ON or AUTOCLAVE to start the cycle.	5	_____	_____	_____
6. Watch the gauges until the temperature gauge reaches at least 121° C (250° F), and the pressure gauge reaches 15 pounds of pressure.	10	_____	_____	_____
7. Set the timer for the desired time.	5	_____	_____	_____
8. At the end of the timed cycle, turn the control setting to VENT.	10	_____	_____	_____
9. Wait for the pressure gauge to reach zero.	10	_____	_____	_____
10. Carefully open the chamber door ¼ inch.	10	_____	_____	_____

Steps	Possible Points	Attempt 1	Attempt 2	Attempt 3
11. Leave the autoclave control at VENT to continue producing heat.	10	_____	_____	_____
12. Allow complete drying of all articles.	10	_____	_____	_____
13. Using heat-resistant gloves or pads, remove the items from the chamber and place the sterilized packages on dry, covered shelves or open autoclave door and allow items to cool completely before removal and storage.	5	_____	_____	_____
14. Turn the control knob to OFF and keep the door slightly ajar.	5	_____	_____	_____

Comments:

Points earned _____ ÷ 100 possible points = Score _____ % Score

Instructor's signature _____

Name _____ Date _____ Score _____

PROCEDURE 57-3 Assist the Physician with Patient Care: Perform Skin Prep for Surgery

CAAHEP COMPETENCIES: I.AI.2, I.PI.10, III.PIII.3, III.AIII.2, III.AIII.3
ABHES COMPETENCIES: 9.e

TASK: To prepare the patient's skin and remove hair from the surgical site to reduce the risk of wound contamination.

Equipment and Supplies
- Disposal skin prep kit containing the following:
  - Gauze sponges
  - Cotton-tipped applicators
  - Antiseptic soap
  - Disposable gloves
  - Disposable razor
  - Two small bowls
  - Antiseptic or antiseptic swabs (e.g., Betadine swabs)
  - Optional: cotton balls, nail pick, scrub brush
- Sterile drape
- Biohazard sharps container and waste receptacle
- Patient's record

Standards: Complete the procedure and all critical steps in _____ minutes with a minimum score of 85% in three attempts.

Scoring: Divide the points earned by the total possible points. Failure to perform a critical step, indicated by an asterisk (*), results in an unsatisfactory overall score.

Time began _____   **Time ended** _____   **Total minutes:** _____

Steps	Possible Points	Attempt 1	Attempt 2	Attempt 3
1. Sanitize your hands.	5	_____	_____	_____
*2. Explain the skin preparation procedure to the patient; make sure the person understands the procedure and the reason for it.	5	_____	_____	_____
3. Ask the patient to remove any clothing that might interfere with exposure of the site; provide a gown if needed.	5	_____	_____	_____
*4. Assist the patient into the proper position for site exposure. Provide a drape, if necessary, to protect the patient's privacy.	5	_____	_____	_____
5. Expose the site; use a light if necessary.	5	_____	_____	_____
6. Put on gloves and open the skin prep pack.	5	_____	_____	_____
7. Add the antiseptic soap to the two bowls.	5	_____	_____	_____
8. With the antiseptic soap on a gauze sponge, start at the incision site and begin washing in a circular motion, moving from the center to the edges of the area to be scrubbed.	5	_____	_____	_____

561

Steps	Possible Points	Attempt 1	Attempt 2	Attempt 3
9. After one complete wipe, discard the sponge and begin again with a new sponge soaked in the antiseptic solution.	5	_____	_____	_____
10. When you return to the incision site for the next circular sweep, you must use clean material.	5	_____	_____	_____
11. Repeat the process, using sufficient friction, for 5 minutes (or follow office policy for the length of time required for a particular prep).	5	_____	_____	_____
12. If there is hair growth, the area may need to be shaved. Hold the skin taut and shave in the direction of growth. Take care not to injure yourself or the patient. Immediately after you finish shaving the area, dispose of the razor in the sharps container.	5	_____	_____	_____
13. After shaving, scrub the skin a second time.	5	_____	_____	_____
14. Rinse the area with a sterile solution.	5	_____	_____	_____
15. Dry the area with dry sponges, using the same circular technique. The area also may be dried by blotting with a third sterile towel.	5	_____	_____	_____
16. Paint on the antiseptic with the cotton-tipped applicators or gauze sponges, using the same circular technique and never returning to an area that has already been painted.	5	_____	_____	_____
17. Place a sterile drape or towel (or both) over the area.	5	_____	_____	_____
18. Answer any questions the patient may have to relieve the individual's anxiety about the upcoming surgery.	5	_____	_____	_____
19. In the following Documentation in the Medical Record section, document the skin prep as you would in the patient's medical record.	10	_____	_____	_____

Documentation in the Medical Record:

Comments:

Points earned _____ ÷ 100 possible points = Score _____ % Score

Instructor's signature _____

Name _____ Date _____ Score _____

PROCEDURE 57-4 Perform Hand Washing: Perform a Surgical Hand Scrub

CAAHEP COMPETENCIES: III.PIII.2, III.PIII.4
ABHES COMPETENCIES: 9.e

TASK: To scrub the hands with surgical soap, using friction, running water, and a sterile brush, to sanitize the skin before assisting with any procedure that requires surgical asepsis.

Equipment and Supplies
- Sink with foot, knee, or arm control for running water
- Surgical soap in a dispenser
- Towels (sterile towels if indicated by office policy)
- Nail file or orange stick
- Sterile brush

Standards: Complete the procedure and all critical steps in _____ minutes with a minimum score of 85% in three attempts.

Scoring: Divide the points earned by the total possible points. Failure to perform a critical step, indicated by an asterisk (*), results in an unsatisfactory overall score.

Time began _____ **Time ended** _____ **Total minutes:** _____

Steps	Possible Points	Attempt 1	Attempt 2	Attempt 3
1. Remove all jewelry.	5	_____	_____	_____
2. Roll long sleeves above the elbows.	5	_____	_____	_____
3. Inspect your fingernails for length and your hands for skin breaks.	5	_____	_____	_____
4. Turn on the faucet and regulate the water to a comfortable temperature; be careful to stand away from the sink to prevent contamination of your clothing.	5	_____	_____	_____
*5. Keep your hands upright and held at or above waist level.	10	_____	_____	_____
6. Clean your fingernails with a file, discard it (in most situations you will drop the file into the sink and discard it later to prevent contamination by lowering your hands and/or touching a waste receptacle), and rinse your hands under the faucet without touching the faucet or the inside of the sink basin.	5	_____	_____	_____
7. Allow the water to run over your hands from the fingertips to the elbows without moving your arm back and forth under the water.	5	_____	_____	_____
8. Apply surgical soap from the dispenser to the sterile brush (or use an already prepared disposable brush) and start the scrub by scrubbing the palm of your hand in a circular fashion.	5	_____	_____	_____

565

Steps	Possible Points	Attempt 1	Attempt 2	Attempt 3
9. Continue from the palm to the base of the thumb, then move on to the other fingers, scrubbing from the base, along each side, and across the nail, holding the fingertips upward and remembering to rub between the fingers. After the fingers have been completely scrubbed, clean the posterior surface of your hand in a circular fashion and then proceed to the wrist. The scrub process should take at least 5 minutes for each hand and arm.	5	_____	_____	_____
*10. Do not return to a clean area after you have moved to the next part of the hand.	10	_____	_____	_____
11. Wash your wrists and forearms in a circular fashion around the arm while holding your hands above waist level.	5	_____	_____	_____
12. Rinse your arms and forearms from the fingertips upward, holding the fingers up, without touching the faucet or the inside of the sink basin.	5	_____	_____	_____
13. Apply more solution without touching any dirty surface and repeat the scrub on the other side; remember to wash and use friction between each finger with a firm, circular motion.	5	_____	_____	_____
14. Scrub all surfaces, taking care not to abrade your skin. The second hand and arm should take at least 5 minutes.	5	_____	_____	_____
15. Rinse thoroughly, keeping your hands up and above waist level. Discard the scrub brush without lowering your arms below the waist.	5	_____	_____	_____
16. Turn off the faucet with the foot, knee or forearm lever, if available.	5	_____	_____	_____
17. Dry your hands with a sterile towel, being careful to keep your fingers pointing upward and your hands above the waist. Do not rub back and forth, dragging contaminants from the dirtier area of the upper arm down toward the hands. Use the opposite end of the towel for the other hand.	5	_____	_____	_____
18. Using a patting motion, continue to dry your forearms. Discard the towel and keep your hands up and above waist level.	5	_____	_____	_____

Comments:

Points earned _____ ÷ 100 possible points = Score _____ % Score

Instructor's signature _____

567

Name _____ Date _____ Score _____

PROCEDURE 57-5 Assist the Physician with Patient Care: Open a Sterile Pack and Create a Sterile Field

CAAHEP COMPETENCIES: I.PI.10, III.PIII.2
ABHES COMPETENCIES: 9.e

TASK: To open a sterile pack that contains a table drape using correct aseptic technique.

Equipment and Supplies
- A sterile instrument pack wrapped with either muslin or autoclave paper that will serve as a sterile table drape or field when opened
- Mayo stand or countertop

Standards: Complete the procedure and all critical steps in _____ minutes with a minimum score of 85% in three attempts.

Scoring: Divide the points earned by the total possible points. Failure to perform a critical step, indicated by an asterisk (*), results in an unsatisfactory overall score.

Time began _____   **Time ended** _____   **Total minutes:** _____

Steps	Possible Points	Attempt 1	Attempt 2	Attempt 3
1. Check that the Mayo stand or countertop is dust free and clean. If it is not, clean with 70% alcohol or another disinfectant and dry carefully.	10	_____	_____	_____
2. Sanitize your hands and make sure they are completely dry. If you will be assisting with a surgical procedure immediately after opening the sterile pack, perform the surgical hand scrub as explained in Procedure 57-4 in the text.	10	_____	_____	_____
3. Place the sterile pack on the Mayo stand or countertop and read the label.	10	_____	_____	_____
*4. Check the expiration date. If you are using an autoclaved pack, check the indicator tape for color change.	10	_____	_____	_____
5. Open the outside cover. Position the package so that the outer envelope flap is at the top and facing you.	10	_____	_____	_____
6. Open the outermost flap. Next open the first flap away from you. Do not cross over the pack.	10	_____	_____	_____
7. Open the second corner, pulling to the side.	10	_____	_____	_____
8. Be careful to lift the flaps by touching only the small, folded-back tab and without touching or crossing over the inner surface of the pack or its contents. Open the remaining two corners of the pack.	20	_____	_____	_____
9. You now have a sterile drape as a sterile field from which to work and for distribution of additional sterile supplies and instruments.	10	_____	_____	_____

569

Comments:

Points earned _____ ÷ 100 possible points = Score _____ % Score

Instructor's signature _____

PROCEDURE 57-6 Assist the Physician with Patient Care: Use Transfer Forceps

CAAHEP COMPETENCIES: I.PI.10, III.PIII.2
ABHES COMPETENCIES: 9.e

TASK: To move sterile items on a sterile field or transfer sterile items to a gloved team member.

Equipment and Supplies
- Sterile item to move or transfer
- Sterile wrapped transfer forceps
- Mayo stand setup with a sterile field and sterile instruments

Standards: Complete the procedure and all critical steps in _____ minutes with a minimum score of 85% in three attempts.

Scoring: Divide the points earned by the total possible points. Failure to perform a critical step, indicated by an asterisk (*), results in an unsatisfactory overall score.

Time began _____   **Time ended** _____   **Total minutes:** _____

Steps	Possible Points	Attempt 1	Attempt 2	Attempt 3
1. Sanitize your hands and make sure they are completely dry. If you will be assisting with a surgical procedure immediately after this procedure, perform the surgical hand scrub as explained in Procedure 57-4 in the text.	10	_____	_____	_____
2. Open a package containing a sterile transfer forceps.	10	_____	_____	_____
3. Using sterile technique, handle the sterile forceps by ring handle only. Always point the forceps' tips down.	20	_____	_____	_____
4. Grasp an item on the sterile field with sterile forceps, tips down, and move it to its proper position for the procedure, making sure not to cross the sterile field with your hand or the contaminated end of the forceps.	20	_____	_____	_____
5. An instrument also may be transferred from the autoclave to the sterile field.	20	_____	_____	_____
6. Remove the transfer forceps after one-time use.	20	_____	_____	_____

Comments:

Points earned _____ ÷ 100 possible points = Score _____ % Score

Instructor's signature _____

Procedure **57-6 Assist the Physician with Patient Care**

Name _____ Date _____ Score _____

PROCEDURE 57-7 Assist the Physician with Patient Care: Pour a Sterile Solution onto a Sterile Field

CAAHEP COMPETENCIES: I.PI.10, III.PIII.2
ABHES COMPETENCIES: 9.e

TASK: To pour a sterile solution into a sterile, stainless steel bowl or container sitting at the edge of a sterile field.

Equipment and Supplies
- Bottle of sterile solution
- Sterile bowl or container
- Sterile field
- Sink or waste receptacle

Standards: Complete the procedure and all critical steps in _____ minutes with a minimum score of 85% in three attempts.

Scoring: Divide the points earned by the total possible points. Failure to perform a critical step, indicated by an asterisk (*), results in an unsatisfactory overall score.

Time began _____   **Time ended** _____   **Total minutes:** _____

Steps	Possible Points	Attempt 1	Attempt 2	Attempt 3
1. Sanitize your hands and make sure they are completely dry. If you will be assisting with a surgical procedure immediately after this procedure, perform the surgical hand scrub as explained in Procedure 57-4 in the text.	10	_____	_____	_____
*2. Read the label of the ordered solution.	10	_____	_____	_____
3. Place your hand over the label and lift the bottle. Note: If the container has a double cap, set the outer cap on the counter inside up, then proceed.	10	_____	_____	_____
4. Lift the lid of the bottle straight up, then slightly to one side, and hold the lid in your nondominant hand facing downward.	10	_____	_____	_____
5. Pour away from the label.	10	_____	_____	_____
6. If the container does not have a double cap, before pouring the solution into the sterile container, pour off a small amount of the solution into a waste receptacle.	10	_____	_____	_____
*7. Pour away from the label, into the bowl, without allowing any part of the bottle to touch the bowl and without crossing over the sterile field.	20	_____	_____	_____
8. Tilt the bottle up to stop pouring while the bottle is still over the bowl.	10	_____	_____	_____
9. Replace the cap (or caps) off to the side, away from the sterile field, taking care not to touch (and therefore contaminate) the internal surface of the lid.	10	_____	_____	_____

Comments:

Points earned _____ ÷ 100 possible points = Score _____ % Score

Instructor's signature _____

Procedure **57-7 Assist the Physician with Patient Care**

PROCEDURE 57-8 Assist the Physician with Patient Care: Put on Sterile Gloves

CAAHEP COMPETENCIES: I.PI.10, III.PIII.2, III.PIII.6
ABHES COMPETENCIES: 9.e

TASK: To put on sterile gloves before performing sterile procedures.

Equipment and Supplies
• Pair of packaged sterile gloves in your size

Standards: Complete the procedure and all critical steps in _____ minutes with a minimum score of 85% in three attempts.

Scoring: Divide the points earned by the total possible points. Failure to perform a critical step, indicated by an asterisk (*), results in an unsatisfactory overall score.

Time began _____   Time ended _____   Total minutes: _____

Steps	Possible Points	Attempt 1	Attempt 2	Attempt 3
1. Perform the surgical hand scrub as explained in Procedure 57-4 in the text before putting on sterile gloves.	10	_____	_____	_____
2. Open the glove pack, taking care not to cross over the open area in the middle of the pack. Remember, a 1-inch area around the perimeter of the glove wrapper is considered not sterile.	10	_____	_____	_____
*3. Glove your dominant hand first.	10	_____	_____	_____
4. With your nondominant hand, pick up the glove for your dominant hand with your thumb and forefinger, grabbing the top of the folded cuff, which is the inside of the glove, being careful not to cross over the other sterile glove.	10	_____	_____	_____
5. Lift the glove up and away from the sterile package.	5	_____	_____	_____
6. Hold your hands up and away from your body and slide the dominant hand into the glove.	10	_____	_____	_____
7. Leave the cuff folded.	5	_____	_____	_____
8. With your gloved dominant hand, pick up the second glove by slipping your gloved fingers under the cuff and extending the thumb up and away from the glove so that your gloved fingers touch only the outside of the second glove.	10	_____	_____	_____
9. Slide your nondominant hand into the glove without touching the exterior of the glove or any part of the gloved hand.	10	_____	_____	_____

Steps	Possible Points	Attempt 1	Attempt 2	Attempt 3
10. Still holding your hands away from you, unroll the cuff by slipping the fingers into the cuff and gently pulling up and out. Do not touch your bare arm with any part of the sterile glove.	10	_____	_____	_____
11. Now, slip your gloved fingers up under the first cuff and unroll it, using the same technique.	10	_____	_____	_____

Comments:

Points earned _____ ÷ 100 possible points = Score _____ % Score

Instructor's signature _____

PROCEDURE 57-9 Assist the Physician with Patient Care: Assist with Minor Surgery

CAAHEP COMPETENCIES: I.PI.10, III.PIII.2, III.PIII.6, III.AIII.2, III.AIII.3
ABHES COMPETENCIES: 9.e

TASK: To maintain the sterile field and to pass instruments in a prescribed sequence during a surgical procedure that involves a surgical incision and the removal of a growth.

Equipment and Supplies

- Open patient drape pack on the side counter
- Mayo stand covered with a sterile drape
- Packaged sterile gloves (two pairs)
- Needle and syringe for anesthesia medication
- Vial of local anesthetic medication
- Sterile drape
- Disposable scalpel with No. 15 blade
- Allis tissue forceps
- Skin retractor
- Three hemostats
- Supply of sterile gauze sponges
- Biohazardous waste container
- Needle with suture material
- Specimen cup
- Laboratory requisitions
- Patient's record

Standards: Complete the procedure and all critical steps in _____ minutes with a minimum score of 85% in three attempts.

Scoring: Divide the points earned by the total possible points. Failure to perform a critical step, indicated by an asterisk (*), results in an unsatisfactory overall score.

Time began _____ **Time ended** _____ **Total minutes:** _____

Steps	Possible Points	Attempt 1	Attempt 2	Attempt 3
1. Prep the patient's skin with surgical soap and antiseptic solution as explained in Procedure 57-3 in the text. Explain the prep procedure to the patient.	2	_____	_____	_____
*2. Perform the surgical hand scrub as explained in Procedure 57-4 in the text.	2	_____	_____	_____
3. Set up the sterile field with the instruments and supplies in the sequence to be used. If you must touch sterile supplies, put on sterile gloves as explained in Procedure 57-8 in the text or use sterile transfer forceps as shown in Procedure 57-6 in the text. After the sterile field has been set up, cover it with a sterile drape.	2	_____	_____	_____

Steps	Possible Points	Attempt 1	Attempt 2	Attempt 3
4. Position the Mayo stand near the patient and the operative site, making sure the patient understands not to touch the sterile field.	2	_____	_____	_____
5. Put on sterile gloves using aseptic technique.	2	_____	_____	_____
6. Grasp the patient drape by holding one edge or corner in each hand.	2	_____	_____	_____
7. Drape the surgical site without touching any part of the patient or the operating area with your gloved hands.	2	_____	_____	_____
8. If the physician requests medication, such as a local anesthetic, a second circulating assistant holds the vial of local anesthetic so that the physician can read the label. The physician withdraws the desired amount using sterile technique.	2	_____	_____	_____
9. The surgeon injects the local anesthetic and waits a few minutes for it to take effect.	2	_____	_____	_____
10. Position yourself across from the surgeon. Arrange the sterile field. Check placement and location on the Mayo stand.	2	_____	_____	_____
11. Place two sponges on the patient, next to the wound site.	2	_____	_____	_____
12. Keep all sharp equipment conspicuously placed on the sterile field.	5	_____	_____	_____
13. Pass the scalpel, blade down and handle first, to the surgeon, or the surgeon will reach for it himself or herself. The surgeon takes the scalpel with the thumb and forefinger in the position ready for use.	5	_____	_____	_____
14. Grasp an Allis tissue forceps by the tips and pass it to the surgeon to grasp a piece of the tissue to be excised.	5	_____	_____	_____
15. Pass the handles into the surgeon's open palm with a firm, purposeful motion. A gentle "snap" is heard as the forceps comes in contact with the surgeon's gloved hand.	5	_____	_____	_____
16. Dispose of soiled sponges in the biohazardous waste receptacle; take care to keep your hands above your waist and to avoid touching any nonsterile items.	5	_____	_____	_____
17. Hold clean sponges in your hand to pat or sponge the wound as needed.	5	_____	_____	_____
18. Safely position the specimen (if any) where it will not be disturbed on the sterile field.	5	_____	_____	_____
19. If there is a bleeding vessel or if a hemostat is requested, pass the hemostat in the manner described in steps 14 and 15.	2	_____	_____	_____
20. Continue to sponge blood from the wound site.	5	_____	_____	_____
21. Retract the wound edge, as needed, with a skin retractor.	2	_____	_____	_____
22. Continue to monitor the sterile field and assist the surgeon as needed.	2	_____	_____	_____

Steps	Possible Points	Attempt 1	Attempt 2	Attempt 3
23. Pass the needle and suture material to close the wound and apply a sterile dressing as requested.	10	_____	_____	_____
24. Monitor the patient and provide assistance as needed.	2	_____	_____	_____
25. After the physician has finished the procedure, clean the area using aseptic technique.	5	_____	_____	_____
26. Collect the specimen, place it in a labeled specimen cup, and send it to the laboratory with the proper requisitions.	5	_____	_____	_____
27. In the following Documentation in the Medical Record section, document the procedure, the wound's condition, and the patient education on wound care provided as you would in the patient's medical record.	10	_____	_____	_____

Documentation in the Medical Record:

Comments:

Points earned _____ ÷ **100 possible points = Score** _____ **% Score**

Instructor's signature _____

Name _____ Date _____ Score _____

PROCEDURE 57-10 Assist the Physician with Patient Care: Assist with Suturing

CAAHEP COMPETENCIES: I.PI.10, III.PIII.2, III.PIII.6
ABHES COMPETENCIES: 9.a, 9.e

TASK: To assist the surgeon in wound closure using sterile technique.

Equipment and Supplies

- Sterile field on a Mayo stand
- Surgical scissors
- Suture material
- Sterile gloves
- Needle holder
- Sterile gauze sponges
- Sharps container
- Biohazardous waste container
- Patient's record

Standards: Complete the procedure and all critical steps in _____ minutes with a minimum score of 85% in three attempts.

Scoring: Divide the points earned by the total possible points. Failure to perform a critical step, indicated by an asterisk (*), results in an unsatisfactory overall score.

Time began _____ Time ended _____ Total minutes: _____

Steps	Possible Points	Attempt 1	Attempt 2	Attempt 3
NOTE: This procedure may be a continuation of Procedure 57-9 in the text. If done independently, you must perform the surgical scrub and gloving before beginning step 1.				
1. Hold the curved needle point in your nondominant hand, 4 to 5 inches over the sterile field.	10	_____	_____	_____
2. With the needle holder, clamp the suture needle at the upper third of its total length.	10	_____	_____	_____
3. With your dominant hand, hold the needle holder halfway down its shaft with the suture needle point up.	10	_____	_____	_____
4. With your nondominant hand, hold the suture strand and pass the needle holder into the surgeon's hand.	10	_____	_____	_____
5. Pick up the surgical scissors with your dominant hand; pick up a gauze sponge with your nondominant hand.	20	_____	_____	_____
6. After the surgeon places a closure suture, knots it, and holds the two strands taut, cut both suture strands in one motion. Cut between the knot and the surgeon, at the length requested, approximately ⅛ inch.	20	_____	_____	_____

Steps	Possible Points	Attempt 1	Attempt 2	Attempt 3
7. Gently blot the closure once with the gauze sponge in your nondominant hand.	10	_____	_____	_____
8. If additional strands of suture are needed, repeat the process.	10	_____	_____	_____

Documentation in the Medical Record:

Comments:

Points earned _____ ÷ 100 possible points = Score _____ % Score

Instructor's signature _____

Procedure **57-10 Assist the Physician with Patient Care**

PROCEDURE 57-11 Assist the Physician with Patient Care: Apply or Change a Sterile Dressing

CAAHEP COMPETENCIES: I.PI.10, III.PIII.2, III.PIII.6
ABHES COMPETENCIES: 9.d, 9.e

TASK: To apply a sterile dressing properly at the completion of a surgical procedure.

Equipment and Supplies
- Sterile dressing material or Telfa
- Sterile gloves

Standards: Complete the procedure and all critical steps in _____ minutes with a minimum score of 85% in three attempts.

Scoring: Divide the points earned by the total possible points. Failure to perform a critical step, indicated by an asterisk (*), results in an unsatisfactory overall score.

Time began _____   Time ended _____   Total minutes: _____

Steps	Possible Points	Attempt 1	Attempt 2	Attempt 3
1. When the surgery is finished, before the sterile drape is removed, use sterile gloves to pick up the dressing from the sterile field, place it on the wound, and hold it there.	25	_____	_____	_____
2. The drape then is removed while you switch hands to hold the dressing in place.	25	_____	_____	_____
3. Secure the dressing with paper tape or an appropriate bandage, or both.	25	_____	_____	_____
4. In the following Documentation in the Medical Record section, document the procedure as you would in the patient's medical record.	25	_____	_____	_____

Documentation in the Medical Record:

Comments:

Points earned _____ ÷ 100 possible points = Score _____ % Score

Instructor's signature _____

Procedure **57-11 Assist the Physician with Patient Care**

Name _____ Date _____ Score _____

PROCEDURE 57-12 Assist the Physician with Patient Care: Remove Sutures and Surgical Staples

CAAHEP COMPETENCIES: I.PI.10, III.PIII.2, III.PIII.3, III.AIII.2, III.AIII.3
ABHES COMPETENCIES: 9.d, 9.e

TASK: To remove sutures from a healed incision using sterile technique and without injuring the closed wound.

Equipment and Supplies
- Suture removal pack containing:
- Suture removal scissors
- Gauze sponges
- Thumb dressing forceps
- Steri-Strips or bandage strips
- Skin antiseptic swabs (such as Betadine swabs)
- Surgical staple remover with 4 × 4 gauze sponges
- Biohazardous waste container
- Sterile gloves
- Patient's record

Standards: Complete the procedure and all critical steps in _____ minutes with a minimum score of 85% in three attempts.

Scoring: Divide the points earned by the total possible points. Failure to perform a critical step, indicated by an asterisk (*), results in an unsatisfactory overall score.

Time began _____   Time ended _____   Total minutes: _____

Steps	Possible Points	Attempt 1	Attempt 2	Attempt 3
1. Assemble the necessary supplies.	2	_____	_____	_____
2. Sanitize your hands; observe Standard Precautions.	2	_____	_____	_____
*3. Explain the procedure to the patient and the importance of lying or sitting still during the procedure.	2	_____	_____	_____
4. Position the patient comfortably and support the sutured area.	2	_____	_____	_____
5. Place dry towels under the site.	2	_____	_____	_____
6. Check the incision line to make sure the wound edges are approximated and no signs of infection are present, such as inflammation, edema, or drainage.	5	_____	_____	_____
7. Put on disposable gloves. Using antiseptic swabs, cleanse the wound to remove exudates and destroy microorganisms around the sutures or staples. Clean the site from the inside out, starting at the top of the wound and working your way down. Use a new swab if the step needs to be repeated.	2	_____	_____	_____
8. Open the suture or staple removal pack, maintaining the sterility of the contents.	2	_____	_____	_____

Steps	Possible Points	Attempt 1	Attempt 2	Attempt 3
9. Place a sterile gauze sponge next to the wound site.	2	_____	_____	_____
10. Put on sterile gloves.	2	_____	_____	_____
11. Remove the sutures or staples.	2	_____	_____	_____
To remove sutures:				
a. Grasp the knot of the suture with the dressing forceps without pulling.	5	_____	_____	_____
b. Cut the suture at skin level.	5	_____	_____	_____
c. Lift, do not pull, the suture toward the incision and out with the dressing forceps.	5	_____	_____	_____
d. Place the suture on the gauze sponge and check that the entire suture strand has been removed.	5	_____	_____	_____
e. If any bleeding occurs, blot the area with a sterile gauze sponge before continuing.	5	_____	_____	_____
f. Continue in the same manner until all sutures have been removed.	5	_____	_____	_____
To remove staples:				
a. Gently place the bottom jaw of the staple remover under the first staple.	5	_____	_____	_____
b. Tightly squeeze the staple handles together.	5	_____	_____	_____
c. Carefully tilt the staple remover upward until the staple lifts out of the wound.	5	_____	_____	_____
d. Place the removed staple on a 4 × 4 gauze square.	5	_____	_____	_____
e. Continue the process until all staples have been removed.	5	_____	_____	_____
12. Remove the gauze sponge with the sutures on it and dispose of contaminated materials in the biohazardous waste container.	5	_____	_____	_____
13. The surgeon may apply (or ask you to apply) Steri-Strips or a bandage strip for added support, strength, and protection.	5	_____	_____	_____
14. Instruct the patient to keep the wound edges clean and dry and not to put excessive strain on the area.	5	_____	_____	_____
15. In the following Documentation in the Medical Record section, document the procedure as you would in the patient's medical record. Include the wound's condition, the number of sutures or staples removed, whether a dressing or bandage was applied, and the instructions given to the patient on wound care.	5	_____	_____	_____

Documentation in the Medical Record:

Comments:

Points earned _____ ÷ 100 possible points = Score _____ % Score

Instructor's signature _____

PROCEDURE 57-13 Assist the Physician with Patient Care: Apply an Elastic Support Bandage Using a Spiral Turn

CAAHEP COMPETENCIES: I.PI.10, III.PIII.2, III.PIII.6
ABHES COMPETENCIES: 9.d, 9.e

TASK: To apply an elastic bandage to the forearm.

Equipment and Supplies

- One 3- or 4-inch elastic bandage with clip closures

Standards: Complete the procedure and all critical steps in _____ minutes with a minimum score of 85% in three attempts.

Scoring: Divide the points earned by the total possible points. Failure to perform a critical step, indicated by an asterisk (*), results in an unsatisfactory overall score.

Time began _____ **Time ended** _____ **Total minutes:** _____

Steps	Possible Points	Attempt 1	Attempt 2	Attempt 3
1. Choose the proper-size bandage for the arm to be bandaged.	5	_____	_____	_____
2. Sanitize your hands. Perform a circular turn at the starting point, securing a corner of the bandage as you circle the site.	10	_____	_____	_____
3. Hold the roll so that the bandage can be rolled away from you.	5	_____	_____	_____
4. Keep the roll close to the patient and keep it facing upward. With each successive turn, overlap the previous bandage turn by one half.	10	_____	_____	_____
5. Maintain even tension and spacing as you continue to apply the bandage up the forearm.	10	_____	_____	_____
6. When crossing a joint, slightly flex the joint.	10	_____	_____	_____
7. Fasten the end of the bandage with clips or tape.	10	_____	_____	_____
8. Check the nail beds for cyanosis; ask the patient if the bandage is comfortable or feels too tight.	10	_____	_____	_____
*9. Check the radial pulse.	10	_____	_____	_____
10. Have the patient move his or her fingers.	10	_____	_____	_____
11. In the following Documentation in the Medical Record section, document the procedure and the patient instructions on bandage care and replacement as you would in the patient's medical record.	10	_____	_____	_____

Documentation in the Medical Record:

Comments:

Points earned _____ ÷ 100 possible points = Score _____ % Score

Instructor's signature _____

Name _____ Date _____ Score _____

PROCEDURE 58-1 Organize a Job Search

ABHES COMPETENCIES: 11.a

TASK: To devote adequate time to the job search and organize it in an efficient way to facilitate proper follow-up.

Equipment and Supplies
- Record of a job lead form
- Record of an interview form
- Copies of your resumé
- List of interview questions
- Contact information for former employers and references
- Map of geographic area (e.g., printed from an Internet mapping program)
- Internet access
- Computer
- Job search Web links
- Local newspapers
- Contact information for friends and family

Standards: Complete the procedure and all critical steps in _____ minutes with a minimum score of 85% within three attempts.

Scoring: Divide the points earned by the total possible points. Failure to perform a critical step, indicated by an asterisk (*), results in an unsatisfactory overall score.

Time began _____ Time ended _____ Total minutes: _____

Steps	Possible Points	Attempt 1	Attempt 2	Attempt 3
*1. Format the resumé as an accurate, up-to-date document.	5	_____	_____	_____
2. Make copies of the record of job lead form and the record of interview form.	5	_____	_____	_____
*3. Research job search Web sites and newspapers for job leads.	10	_____	_____	_____
*4. Network and contact employers directly to obtain job leads.	10	_____	_____	_____
*5. Gather information on job leads and complete a record of job lead form for each one.	10	_____	_____	_____
6. Prepare a targeted copy of your resumé for each job lead.	10	_____	_____	_____
7. Take the resumé to the facility and ask to complete an application, or . . .	5	_____	_____	_____
*8. E-mail the resumé to the facility according to the directions listed in the job advertisement.	5	_____	_____	_____
*9. Document all activity pertaining to each job lead.	10	_____	_____	_____
10. Schedule interviews for as many facilities as possible.	10	_____	_____	_____

Steps	Possible Points	Attempt 1	Attempt 2	Attempt 3
*11. Keep a record of job details on the record of interview form for later reference.	_____	_____	_____	_____
*12. Send thank you notes to all professionals who grant an interview when the appointment is over.	_____	_____	_____	_____
13. Compare opportunities when making a choice between offered positions.	_____	_____	_____	_____

Did the student:

	Yes	No
Show initiative in organizing the job search?	_____	_____

Comments:

Points earned _____ ÷ 100 possible points = Score _____ % Score

Instructor's signature _____

Name _____ Date _____ Score _____

PROCEDURE 58-2 Prepare a Resumé

ABHES COMPETENCIES: 11.a

TASK: To write an effective resumé for use as a tool in gaining employment

Equipment and Supplies
- Scratch paper
- Pen or pencil
- Former job descriptions, if available
- List of addresses of former employers, schools, and names of supervisors
- Computer or word processor
- Quality stationery and envelopes

Standards: Complete the procedure and all critical steps in _____ minutes with a minimum score of 85% within three attempts.

Scoring: Divide the points earned by the total possible points. Failure to perform a critical step, indicated by an asterisk (*), results in an unsatisfactory overall score.

Time began _____ **Time ended** _____ **Total minutes:** _____

Steps	Possible Points	Attempt 1	Attempt 2	Attempt 3
1. Perform a self-evaluation by making notes about your strengths as a medical assistant. Consider job skills, self-management skills, and transferable skills.	10	_____	_____	_____
2. Explore formatting and decide on a professional resumé appearance that best highlights your skills and experience. Use the templates available in word processing software or design your own.	10	_____	_____	_____
3. Put your name, address, and two telephone numbers where you can be contacted at the top of the resumé.	10	_____	_____	_____
4. Write a job objective that specifies your employment goals.	10	_____	_____	_____
5. Provide details about your educational experience. List degrees and/or certifications you have obtained.	10	_____	_____	_____
6. Provide details about your work experience. Include the names and contact information for all previous supervisors. Do not include salary expectations or reasons for leaving former jobs.	10	_____	_____	_____
7. Prepare a cover letter and a list of references. Send the references with the resumé only when requested.	10	_____	_____	_____
8. Type the resumé carefully and make sure it has no errors.	5	_____	_____	_____
9. Proofread the resumé. Allow another person to read it and check it for missed errors.	5	_____	_____	_____

Steps	Possible Points	Attempt 1	Attempt 2	Attempt 3
10. Print the resumé on high-quality paper. Review it again for errors and to make sure it looks attractive on the printed page.	5	_____	_____	_____
11. Target each resumé to a specific person or position. Do not send generic resumés to each prospective employer.	5	_____	_____	_____
12. For all resumés distributed, follow up with a phone call to arrange an interview.	10	_____	_____	_____

Did the student:

	Yes	No
Show dependability, punctuality, and a positive work ethic through his or her wording of the resumé?	_____	_____
Express a responsible attitude in his or her wording of the resumé?	_____	_____

Comments:

Points earned _____ ÷ 100 possible points = Score _____ % Score

Instructor's signature _____

PROCEDURE 58-3 Complete a Job Application

ABHES COMPETENCIES: 11.a

TASK: To complete an accurate, detailed, written job application legibly so as to secure a job offer.

Equipment and Supplies
- Record of job lead form
- Record of interview form
- Copies of your resumé
- Contact information for former employers and references
- Contact information for friends and family

Standards: Complete the procedure and all critical steps in _____ minutes with a minimum score of 85% within three attempts.

Scoring: Divide the points earned by the total possible points. Failure to perform a critical step, indicated by an asterisk (*), results in an unsatisfactory overall score.

Time began _____   **Time ended** _____   **Total minutes:** _____

Steps	Possible Points	Attempt 1	Attempt 2	Attempt 3
*1. Read the entire job application before completing any part of it.	10	_____	_____	_____
2. Gather any information that may be necessary to answer all questions on the application.	10	_____	_____	_____
*3. Begin to complete the application legibly.	10	_____	_____	_____
4. Answer each question on the document or write "not applicable."	10	_____	_____	_____
5. Do not leave any space blank.	10	_____	_____	_____
6. Do not write "See resumé" anywhere on the document.	10	_____	_____	_____
*7. Be completely honest about every fact written on the document.	10	_____	_____	_____
8. Sign the document and date it.	10	_____	_____	_____
9. Proofread the document and make sure none of the information conflicts with your resumé.	10	_____	_____	_____
10. Submit the application.	10	_____	_____	_____

Comments:

Points earned _____ ÷ 100 possible points = Score _____ % Score

Instructor's signature _____

Procedure **58-3 Complete a Job Application**

Name _____ Date _____ Score _____

PROCEDURE 58-4 Interview for a Job

MAERB/CAAHEP COMPETENCIES: IV.A.IV.6
ABHES COMPETENCIES: 11.a

TASK: To project a professional appearance during a job interview and to be able to express the reasons you, the medical assistant, are the best candidate for the position.

Equipment and Supplies
- Record of job lead form
- Record of interview form
- Job application
- Copies of your resumé
- Contact information for former employers and references
- Contact information for friends and family
- Sample interview questions

Standards: Complete the procedure and all critical steps in _____ minutes with a minimum score of 85% within three attempts.

Scoring: Divide the points earned by the total possible points. Failure to perform a critical step, indicated by an asterisk (*), results in an unsatisfactory overall score.

Time began _____ Time ended _____ Total minutes: _____

Steps	Possible Points	Attempt 1	Attempt 2	Attempt 3
*1. Prepare for the interview by studying sample interview questions and learning basic information about the facility.	10	_____	_____	_____
*2. Know all the information on your resumé so that you can discuss it confidently during the interview.	10	_____	_____	_____
*3. Prepare clothing that reflects a professional image for the facility where you hope to be employed.	10	_____	_____	_____
4. Gather all materials that might be needed during the interview, such as copies of resumés, contact information, and copies of earned certificates.	5	_____	_____	_____
*5. Arrive for the interview at least 15 minutes early.	10	_____	_____	_____
6. Stand and shake hands with the interviewer when he or she enters the room.	5	_____	_____	_____
7. Listen intently as the interviewer describes the position and be ready to explain how you fit the requirements for the position.	5	_____	_____	_____
*8. Answer all of the interviewer's questions confidently, smiling when appropriate and displaying a positive attitude.	10	_____	_____	_____
*9. When the interviewer has finished, ask intelligent questions.	10	_____	_____	_____
10. Determine a day and time when the next contact will be made.	5	_____	_____	_____

Steps	Possible Points	Attempt 1	Attempt 2	Attempt 3
11. Express interest in the position.	5	_____	_____	_____
*12. Send a thank you note or letter to the interviewer within 24 hours of the interview.	10	_____	_____	_____
*13. Follow up on the interview as appropriate.	5	_____	_____	_____

Did the student:	Yes	No
Demonstrate awareness of how an individual's personal appearance affects anticipated responses?	_____	_____
Pay attention, listen, and learn during the interview?	_____	_____
Show a positive attitude and a sense of responsibility during the interview?	_____	_____
Express an ability to adapt to change during the interview?	_____	_____

Comments:

Points earned _____ ÷ 100 possible points = Score _____ % Score

Instructor's signature _____

Name _____ Date _____ Score _____

PROCEDURE 58-5 Negotiate a Salary

ABHES COMPETENCIES: 11.a

TASK: To develop negotiation skills that will help you, as a medical assistant, obtain the salary and benefits that will sustain your family.

Equipment and Supplies
- Record of job lead form
- Record of interview form
- Information about job offers received
- Contact name at medical facility

Standards: Complete the procedure and all critical steps in _____ minutes with a minimum score of 85% within three attempts.

Scoring: Divide the points earned by the total possible points. Failure to perform a critical step, indicated by an asterisk (*), results in an unsatisfactory overall score.

Time began _____ **Time ended** _____ **Total minutes:** _____

Steps	Possible Points	Attempt 1	Attempt 2	Attempt 3
1. Study the job offer made.	5	_____	_____	_____
2. Determine whether the offer is sufficient as it stands.	5	_____	_____	_____
*3. Make a list of what additional salary and/or benefits you need, at a minimum.	10	_____	_____	_____
4. Arrive at the second or subsequent interview appointment to discuss the job with the hiring supervisor.	5	_____	_____	_____
*5. Thank the supervisor for the offer presented and express interest in the position.	5	_____	_____	_____
6. State the additional salary and/or benefits desired.	10	_____	_____	_____
7. Discuss the possibilities as to whether the facility would be willing to increase the offer to match your request.	10	_____	_____	_____
*8. Give reasons the additional benefits should be offered, based on your past performance, experience, or other valid factors.	10	_____	_____	_____
9. Discuss reasonable compromises regarding the additional salary and/or benefits.	10	_____	_____	_____
10. Ask what level of performance is expected for an increase in salary and/or benefits	5	_____	_____	_____
11. Express interest in the position and tell the supervisor you will be giving it serious consideration.	10	_____	_____	_____

Steps	Possible Points	Attempt 1	Attempt 2	Attempt 3
12. Determine the next contact time with the supervisor.	5	_____	_____	_____
13. Weigh the offer and compromises to make a good decision about the job offer.	10	_____	_____	_____

Did the student:	Yes	No
Demonstrate courteous and diplomatic behavior during salary negotiations?	_____	_____

Comments:

Points earned _____ ÷ **100 possible points = Score** _____ **% Score**

Instructor's signature _____

Procedure **58-5** **Negotiate a Salary**